ALAN AYCKBOURN

Plays Four

The Revengers' Comedies

Things We Do for Love

House & Garden

with an introduction
by the author

faber and faber

First published in 2011
by Faber and Faber Limited
74–77 Great Russell Street, London WC1B 3DA

Typeset by Country Setting, Kingsdown, Kent CT14 8ES
Printed in England by CPI Group (UK) Ltd, Croydon CR0 4YY

A CIP record for this book
is available from the British Library

ISBN 978-0-571-27461-1

2 4 6 8 10 9 7 5 3 1

Contents

Introduction

Serving as Artistic Director in Scarborough for almost forty years as I did was not without its problems. Most of these were financial, an ongoing battle year after year of vainly trying to cut the programme to accommodate a continuously shrinking budget without compromising the art. Mostly, sadly, this was achieved at the expense of the art. Productions are the most flexible element in the overall scheme of things. Where it's impractical, beyond a certain point, to lay off permanent core staff, be they box office or financial, administrators or ushers, production costs can always be reduced – one less actor here, a simplified set there. The end product logically, of course, is you find yourself in charge of a building with a full complement of permanent support staff supporting fewer and smaller plays.

Which isn't what an audience pays to enter a theatre to see. After all, there's limited appeal for playgoers in being offered guided tours round offices.

Over the years as the one responsible for choosing and scheduling the in-house play programme, I found myself juggling cost with quantity and latterly, more significantly, with quality. Alongside increasing cost considerations came the practical questions of not only how but also of *what*. What to include in the playbill year after year, winter and summer?

Personally, due to a fortunate ability to deliver speedily and regularly, I was able to provide at least one play a year, sometimes two if I was lucky. And latterly, due to my growing interest in children's plays (or family plays as I choose to call them), on occasions even three. Relying on my audience's longstanding loyalty this generally served to offset the cost of the rest of our less reliable but equally important programme of new work by other writers.

But the enemy of a permanent regional theatre, as of any business, is that it's always there and soon becomes part of the high street scenery. Once the initial blaze of the opening season is over, its novelty fades with many of the original audience dropping away until it is left with the hard-core aficionados, too few to sustain or justify its future. For many, it was never simply a question of growing disenchanted (though that might have been true for some) but simply that they'd 'forgotten to come'. While continuing to claim regular attendance, when questioned more closely it was found that it had often been eighteen months or two years since they'd last been to see anything.

It became necessary in these cases to make some sort of noise to re-attract their attention. The equivalent of waving our arms and shouting, 'We're still here!' Moreover, important not just for the audience. If we wanted to keep a contented permanent staff, those financiers and administrators, box-office staff and ushers, it was important for them too. The art of running any long-term theatre business (I'd go further and say the art of running most long-term businesses) is continually to surprise. My mentor Stephen Joseph stated the maxim, 'All new theatres should be built to self-destruct after seven years.' A trifle expensive, impractical and unpopular with funding bodies, but I know what he meant. For self-destruct read re-invent. Change the angle of approach. Give all those permanent people an uneasy sense of impermanence. In other words, every few years there needs to be 'an event'.

Which really explains the inclusion of two of the plays in this volume. The first *The Revengers' Comedies* was written in 1989 and was my response to one such period in our existence when I sensed things needed gingering up a bit. It also coincided with my fiftieth birthday, which may have had something to do with it. Maybe I needed gingering up as well. As a starting point for the plays, I used the theme of the Hitchcock film classic, *Strangers on a Train*, based on the novel by Patricia Highsmith. Two strangers meet and have reasons to want someone in their lives dead. But simple murder would in both cases be easily detectable, the motive far too obvious. So they agree to swap murders, thus creating two motiveless crimes and, with both obvious suspects with watertight alibis, virtually undetectable. On the spur of the moment, it seems such an attractively simple scheme. Only in the clear light of morning, one of the protagonists comes to his senses (as hopefully most people would) and proceeds with his half of the plan no further. But the other, the one who initially dreamt up the scheme, continues in (literally) deadly earnest.

It's a big play in two parts, which qualified it as 'an event' with an overall running time including intervals of close on five hours, allowing two parallel stories to unwind. One is the tale of the unbalanced and ambitious Karen, whom we learn is no stranger to killing, having disposed of both her parents, murderously climbing her way through big business to boardroom level; the other is the story of the mild Henry who, falling in love with Imogen, his intended victim, gets caught in Karen's vengeful and deadly comet tail. It's a play thick with narrative but I hope rich in character too. Also, unusually for me, with multiple swiftly changing sets and a sea of characters, occasionally doubling.

It played with great success during the 1989 Scarborough summer in our second home, the converted former Westwood Boys' Grammar School which we inhabited for over twenty years, overcoming the building's limitations with ever-increasing ingenuity. Along with the flooded stage of *Way Upstream*, *The Revengers' Comedies* presented the place with probably its greatest challenge. Fortunately the fickle Yorkshire weather stayed generally fine and I recall with fondness the sight of our audiences picnicking on double days in the public gardens adjoining the theatre in the intervals between Parts One and Two. Our own little Glyndebourne!

We remained in our Westwood premises for seven more years, further testing the poor building to the point of near destruction, until 1996, when we finally moved to our third converted and current home, the former Odeon Cinema building opposite the railway station.

Before that, we had been experimenting at Westwood for some years with certain smaller-scale 'fringe' activities, using the limited end-staging we'd created in the theatre's bar space. The shows were predominantly one-act lunchtime or occasionally late-night plays, largely brand new, with the occasional full-length evening show, including the first production of Robin Herford's phenomenally successful production of Susan Hill's *The Woman in Black*.

With our third home we also inherited a proper second auditorium, the McCarthy Theatre. Possessing less than half the seating capacity of our new four-hundred-seat theatre-in-the-round auditorium, this smaller end-stage space understandably began generally to be referred to as the studio theatre. I tried to discourage this, having a certain mistrust of spaces known as 'studio' theatres. The name is generally a euphemism for the small theatre where people do interesting plays they're not quite sure of – worthy pieces which the theatre suspects very few people want to see. We, on the other hand, had ever since the days of Stephen Joseph back in the fifties been a theatre which had total sink-or-swim faith in all its productions, considering them suitable for anyone to enjoy and appreciate. Perhaps we were sometimes proved wrong, but not a bad atmosphere for an aspiring writer like this one to grow up in, I feel.

Thus the McCarthy, which was to double as a cinema, became known as the other space. A year after we'd moved in, in 1997, I wrote my first play especially for 'The Mac' to underline my belief in its equal importance. Departing from my usual in-the-round venue, this became the second play in this volume, *Things We Do for Love*. It owed, like *Revengers'* before it, some of its origins to cinema. I had seen a few years previously a Clint Eastwood movie, *In the Line of Fire*, in which he plays a federal agent and includes a sequence in which he and his female partner amorously start to undress each other while attempting at the same time to make it as far as the bedroom, frenziedly scattering clothing, weaponry, walkie-talkies, bullet-proof vests and regulation FBI gear as they do so. This is wittily all shot from floor level so that all that can be seen are their feet as they pick their way through the piles of discarded equipment. It is essentially a cinematic visual joke but one I wanted to recreate on stage. Taking advantage of the end-stage format, the play, like a traditional doll's house, is set on three levels. The whole is Barbara's bijou maisonette; the ground floor, which she inhabits, we see all of; upstairs is a flat which she rents to her friend Nikki and Nikki's fiancé Hamish, and when anyone's up there we see only their feet; finally in the basement, only the top part of which is visible, is another flat, rented to Gilbert. I overcame the problem of never seeing Gilbert by having him lie on a makeshift trestle platform for sections of the play as he paints his basement ceiling.

It's a play I'm especially fond of, marking the return to my earlier domestic scale, following the recent larger-scale plays I had been producing, notably *A Small Family Business*, *Man of the Moment* and, of course, *The Revengers' Comedies*.

Barbara is a virgin of some forty-plus years who, apart from a secret yearning for her offstage married boss, has firmly resisted romantic entanglement with a man in any shape or form. But love eventually, unexpectedly without warning, catches up with her denial. Her long wait makes for a heavy fall. Barbara crashes and she does so, to her horror, passionately and with increasing violence, beginning to behave in ways she previously deplored in others, finally losing all dignity, self-respect and ruthlessly betraying friends. She is finally reduced, as she sees it, to the level of an animal. Love, says the poet, can raise you to the stars; it can also bring you to your knees. It has one of my bitter-sweet endings, where everyone is wiser about themselves if a shade sadder for knowing it.

In 1999, to coincide with my sixtieth birthday, I came up with the third play in this volume, *House & Garden*. We were by then comfortably settled in our new home and approaching our fourth year of occupancy I felt it was time, yet again, for another event. Having two theatres at my disposal was irresistible; why not a play this time that occurred simultaneously in both theatres? I had back in the seventies tentatively played around with the idea with the trilogy *The Norman Conquests*. But while these plays purported to be simultaneous, of course they aren't, and indeed were never intended to be. They merely give the impression of running in parallel times.

But with *House & Garden*, times would synchronise, minute for minute in both theatres simultaneously. Both curtains would rise at the same time and, with any luck, both curtains would come down within seconds of each other. A character would leave the stage in one theatre and seconds later would enter on the other stage.

I determined not to cheat. That is to say it would have been easy enough to achieve this if I allowed, say, thirty-minute gaps between the exit and the subsequent re-entrance, but that would make nonsense of the overall time frame besides negating the whole concept. I asked my stage manager to walk at normal pace from one space to the other, making the journey the characters in the play would make, and to time herself. She returned with the news that the journey had taken her one minute and thirty-three seconds. I decided to allow a safety margin and added another minute. Each entrance, either from the Round to the Mac or vice-versa, would be allowed that time to complete. No less, not a lot more. It was only later that I realised that it would take only a slight margin of error in the nightly running times in both theatres to throw these calculations entirely out of kilter. All it would take would be one minute to be lost in one theatre and one minute to be gained in the other for there to be a catastrophic series of non-appearances, resulting in extensive ad-libbing. To cope with such alarums we introduced the concept of 'the emergency dog'. In case of someone in danger of being late for an entrance, the onstage performers would be alerted to slow down the scene by a burst of sudden unscheduled offstage barking from Spoof, the unseen hound who prowled the estate throughout the evening. I'm delighted that Spoof was never called upon to bark, unscheduled, during the entire run. A great tribute to the actors' consistency and most especially to the two stage managers running the shows, stop watches at the ready and permanently in radio contact.

The challenges of writing it were considerable. Apart from the sheer logistics of keeping the two plays in sync – I actually prefer to think of them as one play – it was essential, as the audience would be seeing only one half of the show, that both evenings should appear complete. Indeed, it was only on the second viewing when they took in the event from the point of view of the other auditorium, that they had any sense of an offstage life carrying on elsewhere in the building.

For the actors, of course, it was all one play. A normal night's work over in two hours plus. *But* with occasional dashes from one auditorium to the other, from the set of *House* to the set of *Garden* or from *Garden* to *House*. Plus the unique experience of two quite separate audiences with often quite different responses to their character. Trish, for example, while definitely the sympathetic leading lady in *House*, on her brief visit to *Garden* is received a little more coolly, being the stand-offish rival to *Garden*'s own leading lady, Joanna.

I presumed that the play would end in Scarborough and never be seen again. I was therefore indebted to Trevor Nunn, then the National Theatre's Artistic Director, who came to see the play at its final Scarborough double Saturday matinee–evening performance, and who later brought it to the Lyttelton and Olivier auditoria. Due to the increased size of that building I had necessarily to extend the gaps between entrances but only by a minute or so.

Three plays, then, all written for live theatre – with a firm emphasis on live. Written in defiance of economic forces and driven by the need to stimulate audience interest and lastly to excite actors and all those unseen supporting troops that serve them. My love affair with live theatre continues. And at the time of writing this remains undimmed.

Alan Ayckbourn,
October 2010

THE REVENGERS' COMEDIES

The Revengers' Comedies was first performed at the Stephen Joseph Theatre in the Round, Scarborough, on 13 June 1989. The cast was as follows:

Henry Bell Jon Strickland
Karen Knightly Christine Kavanagh
Lorry Driver Jeff Shankley
Winnie Doreen Andrew
Norma Claire Skinner
Oliver Knightly Adam Godley
Lady Ganton Ursula Jones
Colonel Marcus Lipscott Donald Douglas
Percy Cutting Martin Sadler
Councillor Daphne Teale Alwyne Taylor
Anthony Staxton-Billing Rupert Vansittart
Imogen Staxton-Billing Elizabeth Bell
Lydia Lucas Frances Jeater
Tracey Willingforth Claire Skinner
Mrs Bulley Doreen Andrew
Bruce Tick Jeff Shankley
Hilary Tick Alwyne Taylor
Graham Seeds Frank Lazarus
Veronica Webb Ursula Jones
Jeremy Pride Frank Lazarus
Fireman Jeff Shankley
Eugene Chase Rupert Vansittart
Motorcyclist Jeff Shankley

Directed by Alan Ayckbourn
Designed by Roger Glossop
Lighting by Mick Hughes

The play was subsequently performed at the Strand
Theatre, London, Part One on 16 October 1991 and
Part Two on 17 October 1991. The cast was as follows:

Henry Bell Griff Rhys-Jones
Karen Knightly Lia Williams
Lorry Driver Raymond Sawyer
Winnie Doreen Andrew
Norma Rose Keegan
Oliver Knightly Adam Godley
Lady Ganton Lavinia Bertram
Colonel Marcus Lipscott Jeffry Wickham
Percy Cutting Raymond Sawyer
Councillor Daphne Teale Hazel Ellerby
Anthony Staxton-Billing Rupert Vansittart
Imogen Staxton-Billing Joanna Lumley
Lydia Lucas Lavinia Bertram
Tracey Willingforth Nina Young
Mrs Bulley Doreen Andrew
Bruce Tick Jeff Shankley
Hilary Tick Hazel Ellerby
Graham Seeds Geoffrey Whitehead
Veronica Webb Jennifer Piercey
Jeremy Pride Geoffrey Whitehead
Fireman Christopher Birch
Eugene Chase Nicholas Palliser
Motorcyclist Christopher Birch

Directed by Alan Ayckbourn
Designed by Roger Glossop
Lighting by Mick Hughes

Characters

Henry Bell
forty-two

Karen Knightly
twenty-five

Lorry Driver
forties

Winnie
a servant, sixty

Norma
a servant, sixteen

Oliver Knightly
Karen's brother, twenty-one

Lady Ganton
sixty

Colonel Marcus Lipscott
sixty

Percy Cutting
forty-five

Councillor Daphne Teale
forty-four

Anthony Staxton-Billing
thirty-eight

Imogen Staxton-Billing
thirty-seven

Lydia Lucas
her assistant, late thirties

Tracey Willingforth
a secretary, early twenties

Mrs Bulley
fifties, voice only

Bruce Tick
thirty-five

Hilary Tick
his wife, thirty-five

Graham Seeds
fifty, voice only

Veronica Webb
forty-eight

Jeremy Pride
fifty-five

Fireman

Eugene Chase
an executive, thirty-five

Motorcyclist

Settings

PART ONE

Prologue

MIDNIGHT. Albert Bridge, SW3

Act One

1: 2.30 a.m. A transport café in Wiltshire
2: 5.00 a.m. The hall, Furtherfield House, Dorset
3: 3.00 p.m. The dining room, Furtherfield House

Act Two

1: 9.30 a.m. Mrs Bulley's offices, Lembridge Tennit
2: 10.00 a.m. A wood near Furtherfield House
3: 10.30 a.m. Bruce Tick's offices, Lembridge Tennit
4: 11.30 a.m. A drawing room, Furtherfield House
5: 4.15 p.m. Bruce Tick's offices, Lembridge Tennit
6: 11.00 a.m. The piggery, the Staxton-Billings' farm
7: 4.45 p.m. Bruce Tick's offices, Lembridge Tennit
8: 5.00 p.m. The hall, Furtherfield House
9: 10.00 a.m. Bruce Tick's offices, Lembridge Tennit
10: 4.00 p.m. A hen house, the Staxton-Billings' farm
11: 6.00 p.m. A wine bar
12: 3.00 p.m. The village green
13: 6.15 p.m. A wine bar
14: 11.00 a.m. A cowshed, the Staxton-Billings' farm
15: 6.30 p.m. A wine bar
16: 7.00 p.m. The hall, Furtherfield House

PART TWO

Act Three

 1: 9.00 a.m. Lembridge Tennit/Furtherfield House
 2: 9.15 a.m. The dining room, Furtherfield House
 3: NOON. Mrs Bulley's offices, Lembridge Tennit
 4: 3.00 p.m. A junior gymkhana
 5: 9.00 a.m. Jeremy Pride's offices, Lembridge Tennit
 6: 7.30 p.m. The lounge of Daphne Teale's bungalow
 7: 9.10 a.m. Jeremy Pride's offices, Lembridge Tennit
 8: 9.30 a.m. The dining room at Furtherfield House
 9: 9.45 a.m. Jeremy Pride's offices, Lembridge Tennit
10: NOON. A drawing room, Furtherfield House
11: 9.45 a.m. Jeremy Pride's offices, Lembridge Tennit
12: DAWN. A wood near Furtherfield House

Act Four

 1: DAWN. A wood near Furtherfield House
 2: 11.00 a.m. A churchyard
 3: 8.50 a.m. Jeremy Pride's offices, Lembridge Tennit
 4: 3.45 p.m. The kitchen of Imogen's farmhouse
 5: 11.30 p.m. The hall, Furtherfield House
 6: 12.30 a.m. The front drive of Furtherfield House
 7: 11.00 a.m. The sitting room of Imogen's farmhouse
 8: 11.00 a.m. Outside the boardroom, Lembridge Tennit
 9: DUSK. The ruins of Furtherfield House
10: 7.00 p.m. The kitchen of Imogen's farmhouse
11: MIDNIGHT. Albert Bridge, SW3

Part One

Act One

PROLOGUE

Midnight.
   Albert Bridge, SW3. Perhaps a little river mist. Distant traffic, a ship's siren. Henry, a man in his early forties, appears in a pool of street light on the bridge. He is wrapped in an overcoat and scarf. He is hunched and miserable. He stares over the edge, deciding whether to jump. From his expression, it's evidently a long way down. He says a little silent prayer, as though asking forgiveness, and makes to climb over the railing. He is uncomfortably straddled across the railing and in some discomfort when he hears a woman's voice from the darkness.

Karen (*calling*) Help . . . Help . . . Please help me . . .

   Henry stops and listens, rather startled.

Please help . . . somebody . . .

Henry (*calling, tentatively*) Hallo?

Karen (*calling back*) Hallo . . .

Henry (*calling again*) Hallo?

Karen Would you stop saying hallo and come and help me, please? I've got myself caught up here . . .

Henry Oh, right. Hang on, there . . . Just hang on . . .

   He starts to clamber back on to the bridge.

Karen I don't have any option. I've been hanging here for hours.

Henry Just one very small second . . .

Henry moves to the source of her voice. As he does so, we make out Karen for the first time. She is in her mid-twenties. She wears a woolly hat and a lightweight coat over an evening dress. She is hanging outside the bridge railing. All that seems to be keeping her from falling is the belt of her coat, which has become entangled with the ironwork. Henry reaches her.

Oh, Lord. How can I . . .?

Karen (*trying to indicate*) Do you see? Something's caught – I think it's the belt of my coat . . .

Henry Oh, yes, yes. Look, I think I'd better . . . (*Flustered*) Look . . . er . . . Yes, yes. I think I'd better try and – er . . . Would you mind if I – tried to lift you . . .?

Karen You can do what you like – just get me off this bloody bridge . . .

Henry Yes, yes, right . . .

He studies the problem.

Karen Can you see? I think it's my belt . . .

Henry Yes, yes, so it is. I think I'd better get that free before I . . .

He starts to untangle the belt.

Karen Careful . . .

Henry Yes. Only I don't want to tear your coat, you see. If I tried to lift you over as you are, I might damage it . . . It's a very nice coat . . .

Karen (*sarcastically*) Well, that's very considerate of you . . . Thank you.

Henry (*finally freeing the belt*) Right. There you go, all free.

Karen Aaaarh!

The sudden release of the belt all but causes her to lose her balance and topple over the edge. She grabs at the first available handhold, which happens to be Henry's scarf.

Henry (*choking*) Hurrgh!

Karen (*screaming*) Hold on to me, for God's sake!

Henry (*with difficulty*) Hould hoo hossibly het ho hof hy harf? Hi han't –

Karen Don't let go . . .

Henry Hi han't . . .

Karen What?

Henry Hi han't heathe . . .

Karen Well, give me something else to hold. (*Angrily*) Quickly, you're so useless . . . You're so totally, totally useless . . . What are you doing on this bridge, anyway?

Henry manages to put his arms under hers and around her middle. Karen releases his scarf.

Henry (*much relieved*) Ah! Thank you. OK, I'm going to try and pull you over. Ready?

Karen Right.

Henry And – heave . . .

Henry hauls at her. Karen reacts.

Karen Aaargh! Careful!

Henry Sorry. It's a question of leverage . . .

Karen Well, could you use another bit of me to lever with?

Henry Yes, I'm sorry, I didn't mean to . . . (*He finds another grip*) That better?

Karen Fractionally. Those are only my ribs.

Henry And two-six! Hup!

He starts to heave her over.

Karen (*reacting*) Hah!

Henry (*another heave*) Hip!

Karen Hoo!

Henry Sorry, is this hurting?

Karen No, it's quite nice, actually. Keep going.

Henry (*a final heave*) Hoy!

Karen Huf!

He finally half lifts, half drags her over the railing. Karen finishes sitting on the bridge. Henry regains his breath.

God! That was terrifying.

Henry Close thing.

Karen It certainly was.

She shudders. She looks around her as if searching for someone.

Henry You all right?

Karen Thank you very much.

Henry Not at all.

Karen You saved my life.

Henry Well . . .

Karen I must owe you something . . .?

Henry No.

Karen Something. A drink, at least?

Henry (*looking at his watch*) It's half past twelve.

Karen Half past twelve?

Henry Yes.

Karen (*angrily*) My God! Half past *twelve*?

Henry Yes.

Karen I don't believe it.

Henry How long had you been there?

Karen Since twenty past eight.

Henry Lord.

Karen Half past twelve! It's unbelievable.

   Pause.

Henry Well . . .

Karen This is Chelsea Bridge, isn't it?

Henry No, this is Albert Bridge.

Karen Albert Bridge?

Henry Yes.

Karen You sure?

Henry Positive.

Karen Sod it!

Henry What?

Karen Nothing.

Another pause.

Henry Er . . . How did you come to get there?

Karen Where?

Henry Where you were. Hanging like that? How did you get there? Do you mind my asking?

Karen Well, obviously, I was trying to throw myself off.

Henry *You* were?

Karen Only I managed to make a complete mess of that, too. Like everything else in my life . . . (*Suddenly despairing*) Oh, God . . .

She hunches up, tearfully, a pathetic huddle on the pavement.

Henry (*ineffectually*) Oh, come on, now . . .

Karen You can leave me, it's all right. Leave me here. I'm just so pathetic . . .

Henry Look, perhaps I could see you home . . .?

Karen Go away. Just leave me here . . .

Henry I can't do that.

Karen I'll be all right. I expect.

Henry I can't leave you here like this.

Karen (*a little cry of self-pity*) Oh . . .

Henry (*soothingly*) Shhh!

Karen Oh!

Henry Please let me . . . at least get you on your feet. You'll catch your – you'll catch your cold sitting there.

Karen lets Henry help her to her feet.

There.

Karen (*holding on to him*) Thank you. You're very kind.

Henry (*slightly embarrassed*) No, not really. I just –

Karen I'm sorry I called you useless. I didn't mean that.

Henry No, as it happens you were right. I am a bit useless, really.

Karen Yes? Is that how you see yourself? Useless?

Henry Most of the time.

Karen Well. That makes two of us, then, doesn't it? (*She smiles a little*)

Henry (*smiling too, despite himself*) I suppose it does.

Karen evidently decides to pull herself together. She scrabbles in her mac pocket and eventually finds a tissue.

Karen Come on . . .

Henry (*startled*) Where to?

Karen I'll take you somewhere for a drink. Come on.

Henry But nothing will be open.

Karen I know somewhere that's open. It's all right, it's not far . . . Do you have your car with you?

Henry I don't have one.

Karen Mine's parked along there . . . Come on, we both need something. Unless you've other things you'd sooner be doing?

Henry (*looking back at the river*) Er, no. No.

Karen Great. (*Turning and extending her hand*) By the way. Karen. Karen Knightly.

Henry (*shaking her hand in turn*) Henry. Henry Bell.

Karen Splendid. Then follow me, Henrybell.

Henry Where are we going?

Karen (*disappearing into the darkness*) Just as far as the bypass, that's all . . .

Henry Ah. (*As he follows her off, puzzled*) What bypass?

The lights dim and almost immediately return to reveal –

SCENE ONE

2·30 a.m.

A table in the corner of a transport café. Faint jukebox music and the sound of an electronic game machine. Chatter from unseen lorry drivers. Henry appears carrying two very large mugs of tea. He sets these on the table. He yawns, something he is wont to do throughout the scene. He removes his coat and scarf and, after a careful examination of two chairs, places the items on one and sits on the other. We see he is wearing a neat, conventional suit. He looks around him. He smiles at someone nervously and looks away self-consciously. He tries his tea and nearly scalds his mouth. The chatter in the room suddenly ceases. So does the game machine. Just the thud of the jukebox. The cause of this lull enters. Karen has evidently been freshening up. She has removed her hat and let her hair loose. She is now carrying her coat, revealing a chic, if somewhat incongruous, strapless evening dress. She seems quite unaware of the effect she has caused. Henry, gaping, rises as she approaches. She really does look quite something.

Karen (*dropping into the chair opposite him*) Sorry I've been so long, Henrybell. Just taken a proper look at myself. I looked frightful. Is this tea? Terrific. Just what I needed.

Henry It's very, very hot. Be careful.

Karen Great.

She takes a great gulp, apparently immune to heat.

Mmm! They don't make tea like this anywhere else but here.

Henry Where exactly are we?

Karen About – twenty miles from Salisbury. Why?

Henry No. No reason. It just seems quite a way to come just for a cup of tea, that's all.

Karen (*sipping her tea*) Worth it, though.

Henry Oh, yes. (*Slight pause*) Glad we didn't decide to have alcohol. We'd probably have finished up at Land's End. (*He laughs a little at his joke*)

Karen (*seriously*) Why, is there a good pub there –

Henry I've no idea.

Karen I'm game to go if you are.

Henry No. No . . .

He sips at his tea tentatively. A silence. The music plays for a second. Karen listens.

Karen Oh, God, this is wonderful, this one. I love it. What is it? The Hollies?

Henry (*blankly*) Pardon?

Karen Or is it Brian Thing and the Thingies?

Henry I don't know, I . . .

Karen (*turning and yelling to someone*) Who's this, do you know? Is it the Hollies?

First Voice (*off*) What's that, darling?

Karen This music. Is it the Hollies?

Second Voice (*off*) It's the Everlys, sweetheart.

Karen The Everly Brothers. Of course it is. Thank you.

Second Voice (*off*) Any time, sweetheart, it's my pleasure.

First Voice (*off*) Make sure that's the only pleasure you give him and all, darling . . .

A lot of laughter. Karen seems amused. She obviously enjoys such attention, unlike Henry, who looks even more embarrassed. He looks at his watch.

Karen Have you got to be somewhere, Henrybell?

Henry What?

Karen You keep looking at your watch, I wondered if you had to be somewhere?

Henry No, I was – I was just wondering – how I was going to get back, that's all.

Karen What's the time?

Henry Half past two.

Karen It's OK. I'll take you back. Don't worry. Where are you? Chelsea?

Henry Er . . . more Fulham, really.

Karen Fulham. Fine. Easy.

Henry (*yawning*) Is that convenient for you? Excuse me.

Karen Anywhere's fine for me.

Henry Where do you have to go?

Karen Me? (*Vaguely*) Oh, the other side of Dorchester.

Henry Dorchester? The one in Dorset?

Karen Have you been there?

Henry Do you mean – do you mean you'd drive me all the way back to London and then drive all the way to Dorset? Tonight? You'll kill yourself . . .

Karen Why not? What else was I going to be doing?

Henry Ah, yes. Point taken.

Karen (*tearful*) God, I'm so unhappy, you know . . .

Henry Yes? (*Pause*) Do you want to talk about it?

Karen (*suddenly angry*) No!

> *They sit in silence. Henry is becoming wary of her
> ever-changing moods. Karen sings along with the
> music. Occasional, wordless, discordant notes with
> no attempt at the melody.*

Henry I – I don't know if this would help at all but . . .

Karen Yes, I'm sure there is a God, Vicar, thank you very much.

Henry No, I wasn't going to say that – what I was going to say is, Karen – you're not alone. That's all.

Karen I know I'm not alone. There's millions of the buggers everywhere. That's half the trouble.

Henry (*patiently*) No, I meant – tonight. When you were trying to – end it all . . . You weren't the only one.

Karen stares at him.

I was just about to do the same thing, you see. Jump off that bridge.

Karen *You* were?

Henry I don't know if that helps at all . . .

Karen I saved your life, then?

Henry I think you did.

Karen Well . . .

She raises her mug.

Henry (*joining in the toast*) Yes.

Karen Would you have really jumped, Henrybell? Really?

Henry (*considering*) Yes. Then I would have done. At that moment, probably. Not now.

Karen The moment's passed?

Henry It has.

Karen Are you glad you didn't?

Henry (*smiling at her*) Yes. Yes, I am.

Karen (*smiling back at him*) So am I.

Henry You're glad you didn't jump?

Karen Oh, yes, that too. But I'm glad you didn't.

Henry Thank you. (*A pause*) It's just everything suddenly conspires against you at once, doesn't it? It all becomes insoluble.

Karen Insuperable.

Henry Right. I don't know how you feel. Every now and then, I just get this overwhelming sense of the futility of it all. Of the sheer uselessness. Do you get that feeling?

Karen No.

Henry Ah.

Karen I don't think I'd kill myself simply because I couldn't think of a reason for living.

Henry You wouldn't?

Karen No. I can always find a good reason for living.

Henry In that case, why would you ever want to kill yourself?

Karen I'd kill myself when I had a very good reason for doing so. A stronger reason than the reason I had for living. There is a difference, I promise you there is.

Henry (*uncertain*) Yes. Yes, I can see there probably is.

Karen Why did you? Want to do it?

Henry As I say. Things. I don't want to bore you with details. My wife – she'd recently left me and – I was just about getting over that . . .

Karen Did she go off with another man?

Henry No. She just went. She found it – me – too much. All of a sudden.

Karen Have you any children?

Henry Yes. One. Well, hardly a child. He's left home, now. Working in Holland.

Karen When did your wife leave?

Henry Oh, a year ago.

Karen You waited that long to jump off a bridge?

Henry No, as I was saying. I'd just about got over her going. I'd come to terms with that. I'd sold the house. Got a little flat. Mastered the microwave. I mean, Marianne and I – we were fond of each other, don't get me wrong – but it was familiar-fond rather than loving-fond – if you know what I mean. A bit routine. Appallingly routine, if you want the truth. We never rowed – we never disagreed – we never – did anything very much except – sit. I wasn't really surprised when she went. Not deep down. It was the . . . I don't know . . .

Karen Loneliness?

Henry Pointlessness. So I hurled myself into my work. I enjoyed my work. I was good at it.

Karen Was?

Henry That's it, you see. I've just been fired. Sorry. Made redundant. Sounds nicer. I cleared my desk this evening – yesterday evening – I had a glass of sherry with the department. And I left quietly by the side door. After fourteen years, and without much home life to speak of, that really did leave a bit of a hole. I had suddenly moved on from a state in which things seemed faintly pointless, to one where I could no longer see any point to them at all.

Karen Where did you work?

Henry Lembridge Tennit. If that means anything.

Karen Can't say it does. What line are they in?

Henry Everything, really. From biscuits to bicycles. You'd know the brand names.

Karen Oh, I see. One of those. Multinationals.

Henry Multi. Multi. Multi.

Karen Polluting the rivers, poisoning the atmosphere and secretly funding right-wing revolutionaries.

Henry Those are the chaps.

Karen Why did they fire you?

Henry Oh. All the jargon. Redefining the job profile. Rationalising the department. Restructuring the management team. Which essentially meant either get promoted or – get out. And, innocent that I was, so certain that I'd been doing a good job, I sat there fully expecting to be promoted.

Karen Being good is never enough in itself . . .

Henry How right you are. (*He pauses*) How right. It's not just a matter of doing a good job. Or even doing the best you can. No. It's no good taking work home with you and sitting seven nights a week ruining your eyesight for no extra money. No point at all in covering for colleagues who aren't doing the job they're paid to do because they're taking three-hour lunch breaks five days a week and rolling in absolutely legless after fifteen double scotches at four thirty in the afternoon. That's never enough. You've also got to be working the system. Chatting up the right people. Buying the drinks that matter. Arranging the cosy little dinner with the boss's PA. Taking the right lift at the right moment with the right people. Going down – hallo, Mr Pride, sir – fancy bumping into you, remember me? Losing the right game of squash. Missing the right putt. Winning the right rubber. Licking the right shoes. Sending the right Christmas cards. Driving the right car. Choosing the right suit. Wearing the right bloody underwear. Screwing the right secretary . . . (*He stops*) Sorry.

Karen (*simply*) It's just a game, that's all.

Henry And you either play by the rules and win, like he did. Or you ignore them and lose, like me.

Karen He?

Henry What?

Karen You said he. Who's he?

Henry (*through grated teeth*) Tick.

Karen Sorry?

Henry (*barely able to say the name*) His name is Bruce Tick. I've never hated anyone in my life, you know. Well, not since I was a child – but then you hate people all the time at that age – but Bruce Tick I actually hate now. He smiled at me and stole my job. Even as he was smiling he was stealing my job. But do you know the worst thing of all? The worst thing was – *everybody knew he was doing it* – and no one – *no one* thought to . . . People I'd worked with for fourteen years. *Friends!*

Karen Yes.

Henry That's what hurt. That hurt more than anything. (*Calming down*) Yes, I came very near to murdering Mr Bruce Tick, I can tell you.

Karen (*seriously*) You should have done. Why didn't you?

Henry (*assuming she is joking*) What? And give him the satisfaction of sitting up there on his cloud afterwards, sipping Glen Whatsit, while I'm down here breaking rocks in a quarry? No, thanks.

Karen Good point.

Henry No, to hell with them all, I say. Except Elaine, of course. (*He yawns*) Excuse me.

Karen Elaine?

Henry My secretary. That was. You know what she did? The minute she heard they were firing me, Elaine marched right in there and handed in her notice.

Karen Was she in love with you?

Henry Elaine? Good Lord, no. Respectable, happily married lady. Six years to go till retirement. Everything to lose and she just didn't care. She marched in there and she told them.

Karen Good for her.

Henry She said to them: 'I can no longer continue to work for a firm who could reward fourteen years of unswerving loyalty with such contemptuous disdain.'

Karen She sounds quite a woman.

Henry She is. Well, at least she's been spared from working for Bruce Tick.

Karen I don't like the sound of him at all.

Henry He's – repellent.

Henry simmers. A silence.

But then, I am slightly prejudiced.

Karen I knew someone like that once.

Henry Really? Bad luck.

Karen Yes.

Pause.

Henry Who was he?

Karen Her name was Imogen Staxton-Billing.

Henry She sounds absolutely appalling.

27

Karen She is. What sort of woman – what sort of wife – would be frigid and inept enough to drive her own husband out of his house into the arms of another woman – a woman who really did appreciate him and gave him love and warmth and comfort and sex – and then, at the very last minute, this wife refuses to let him go. Instead uses all her wiles and cunning and cheap little wifely blackmailings – flaunting their two grotesquely repulsive kids – in order to lure him back into her barren, lumpy iceberg of a bed. What sort of woman do you think would do that?

Henry Sounds like an Imogen Staxton-Billing sort of woman to me.

Karen Right.

A pause.

Henry You don't think that he might have . . . The husband might have . . . been a bit to blame, as well?

Karen Who?

Henry The husband?

Karen Anthony Staxton-Billing?

Henry Yes. You don't think he might have decided, after all, to give the marriage another go? Decided to go back to his wife? Is that a possibility? I mean, I was just hoping to perhaps help you to see her in a better light . . . (*He trails away*)

Karen (*dangerously*) If you don't mind my saying so, that is a very, very ignorant thing to say.

A pause.

Sorry, Henrybell.

Henry That's quite all right.

28

A silence – mainly because Henry can't think of anything to say.

Karen No, you couldn't possibly say that if you'd met the ageing, comatose, bovine Imogen Staxton-Billing. Bouncing, bonny, horsey, dung-smelling niece of one Colonel Marcus Lipscott, DSO, VSOP and twiddly bits. She worked it. Somehow she worked it. She had little Tony running home to Mummy. She cheated. (*She reflects. Calmly*) I was standing at that station with three suitcases. For hours and hours and hours. And he never came. *Three* suitcases. Can you imagine that?

Henry (*yawning, despite himself*) That's terrible. Excuse me.

Karen It was. It was terrible. Wait for me, darling. The trains were coming in. And then the trains were going out. And then they were coming in again. And I was just standing there. Like an old, unwanted – chocolate machine. With three suitcases. Can you imagine how I felt?

Henry Yes. How awful. (*A pause*) Which station was this?

Karen (*furiously*) I don't know which station. I can't remember which bloody station. How do you expect me to remember the station, for God's sake? (*Weeping openly now, as her voice gets increasingly loud*) How could he do that to me? How could he do that to *me*? I'll kill her!

Henry looks around nervously. They are beginning to attract attention.

(*Screaming*) AAAAAAAAAAAAAAAAAAAAAAAAAAHHHHHHHHHH!

A large figure looms into view. It is a Lorry Driver. He stares at Henry suspiciously.

Lorry Driver Spot of bother is there, mate?

Henry No, no, no. We're fine. Don't worry.

Lorry Driver (*to Karen*) Is he giving you any trouble, love?

Karen No, it's all right.

Lorry Driver Sure?

Karen Yes.

Lorry Driver (*a bit disappointed*) All right. (*To Henry*) Don't give her any trouble, mate, all right?

Henry I'm not going to.

Lorry Driver If there's one thing I can't stand in this world it's a man maltreating a pretty young girl, all right?

Henry Absolutely. (*He yawns*) Sorry.

Lorry Driver (*leaning close to Karen*) All right then, love? You all right? You let me know if he causes you any more trouble, all right? I'll come and sort him out for you, all right? You just give me a shout. I'll be just over there if you need me, all right? All right, then?

Karen (*irritated by all this*) Oh, just bugger off, will you? Go away!

Lorry Driver (*outraged*) Oy, oy, oy, oy, oy . . .

Karen Look, go away. We're having a private conversation, all right?

Lorry Driver (*departing truculently*) No need for that. No need for language like that. (*To Henry, threateningly*) You'd better watch her language, mate. If you don't want to get sorted out. All right?

The Lorry Driver goes – a Knight of the Road rebuffed.

Karen I can't stand men like that. Right. (*Shouting in the direction of the Lorry Driver*) Who do they think they are, anyway? (*Pushing aside her mug*) I can't drink any more of this, it's foul. If I don't have a vodka soon, I'll die.

She rises and starts to put on her coat. Henry rises, too, glancing at his watch.

Henry We still won't find anywhere open. It's only just after three a.m.

Karen It's all right, I know somewhere.

Henry Would I be right in thinking it's just the far side of Dorchester?

Karen You got it in one, kid.

She goes out swiftly. Henry, still struggling into his coat and yawning, follows her. He turns in the doorway and nods to the unseen drivers.

Henry Goodnight.

A barrage of abuse and shouting. He exits hurriedly. With scarcely a break, the lights rapidly cross-fade to –

SCENE TWO

5.00 a.m.
Furtherfield House. The hall. Seemingly this is a very large place indeed. The hall is the size of a football pitch. We see some area of it. A couple of chairs or a sofa, to give an idea of the scale. Somewhere, a huge front door is heard to slam. Immediately, Karen enters, pulling off her hat and coat as she does so. Henry follows, totally awed by the unexpected.

Karen (*yelling*) Winnie! Winnie! (*To Henry*) Sling your coat anywhere. I think we'd be better off here in the hall, it'll be freezing in the drawing rooms. (*Yelling again*) Winnie! Wakey, wakey!

Henry It's only five o'clock, maybe people aren't . . .

Karen Winnie!

Winnie appears in her dressing gown. She is the old family retainer, gentle, uncomplaining, with a soft-spoken Dorset accent.

Winnie Just a minute, Miss Karen . . . Here I am.

She gathers up their coats during the next.

Karen Winnie, dearest, could you find us a bottle of nice champagne?

Winnie Champagne. Right, Miss Karen.

Karen (*to Henry*) Anything to eat?

Henry No, not at this time of the morning. (*Yawning*) Excuse me.

Karen No, I'm not hungry either. Just the champagne.

Winnie Right. Just the champagne. Morning, sir.

Henry Good morning. This is very kind of you.

Karen Winnie, this is Mr Henry Bell. Known as Henrybell.

Henry How do you do?

Karen We'll have two glasses, Winnie.

Winnie Right you are, Miss Karen.

Winnie goes off.

Henry What an amazing house. Wonderful. It's yours?

Karen Well, my family's. Yes.

Henry Who lives here? Besides you?

Karen Well, mostly my brother. That's my brother Oliver, he's generally around somewhere – then other people trail in and out from time to time. And then there's people like Winnie and things.

Henry Do you have a lot of servants?

Karen (*vaguely*) No . . . Well. A few. I don't have much to do with any of that side, really.

Henry Your parents don't live here, then?

Karen (*casually*) No, they're both dead. There was an accident. And they died.

Henry Oh dear. What sort of accident?

Karen (*slight pause*) I'm not allowed to talk about that.

Henry Ah.

Winnie enters with a tray, two glasses and a bottle of Dom Pérignon.

Karen This isn't an ancestral home or anything, if that's what you're thinking.

Henry Oh, I see. (*He yawns*) Excuse me.

Winnie Want me to open it, Miss Karen?

Karen Well, we don't want to sit here staring at the bottle, do we, Winnie? (*To Henry*) Some revolting old landowner built it in about 1850. My grandfather bought it in about 1910, spent a fortune doing it up and then promptly died and left it to my father.

Henry I couldn't see it all in the dark. How many rooms?

Karen No idea.

Winnie There's fifty-eight rooms, sir, including the servants' quarters and the old nurseries.

Henry Fifty-eight. Goodness.

Winnie There's twenty-five bedrooms, not counting the master bedroom. Twelve bathrooms. A billiard room, two drawing rooms, dining room, a west study, an east study . . .

Karen Yes, thank you, Winnie. (*To Henry*) You get the idea, anyway.

Winnie (*giving Karen a glass*) Miss Karen.

Karen We don't use half the place. I mean, the billiard room is where Oliver keeps his motorbike.

Winnie He's got a whole race track now and all.

Karen Has he? Oh well, I can't keep up with him these days.

Winnie (*giving Henry a glass*) Sir.

Henry Thank you very much indeed. Delicious.

Winnie Anything else, miss?

Karen No, Winnie, you can go back to bed now. Thank you.

Winnie Nearly time to get up, I think. Sleep well, then.

Henry Thank you.

Winnie goes off again.

Good health.

Karen Good health, Henrybell.

Henry Mmm. Lovely.

Karen studies him for a second.

Karen Henrybell . . . While we were in the car, I had rather an exciting idea.

Henry (*yawning*) Sorry, did I doze off during the drive? I think I did.

Karen You did. You've had your night's sleep. So you can keep awake now.

Henry I'm afraid I'm going to have to go to bed, properly. Very soon. Somewhere or other.

Karen (*ignoring him*) Answer me this –

Henry I presume one of your twenty-five bedrooms is free?

Karen If I hadn't met you – if you hadn't met me – where would you be?

Henry Home in bed, probably.

Karen (*angrily*) Oh, do be serious.

Henry I'm sorry.

Karen I hate silly men. I can't stand them.

Henry What about silly women?

Karen (*ignoring him*) Answer me. Where would you be? Where would we both be? I will tell you. Floating in the Thames. That's where we'd be. Only we're not. Thanks to you, I'm here. And thanks to me, you're here. True? Or false?

Henry Yes. I mean, true.

Karen We've both been given a reprieve. We're playing extra time. I don't know for how long – I may be run over tomorrow. You may drop dead tonight . . .

Henry I probably will, in a minute . . .

Karen But for now, we're here. Alive when we should be dead. And owing that life to each other. And do you know the most crucial thing of all that occurred to me? It must have been *meant*. Something, some force, some power was operating tonight. It saw what you and I were trying to do and it said, not yet, not yet. I need these people. These two people are still necessary. They are still an essential part of the world. They are still in play. They are still there on the board. But the question is, why? For what reason?

Henry (*yawning*) I don't know, no idea.

Karen Think.

A pause.

Well?

Henry I haven't a clue.

Karen We both said it. Back there in that café. We sat there and we both experienced that same feeling.

Henry We did?

Karen Yes.

Henry What feeling?

Karen (*drawing close to him, softly*) Revenge, Henrybell, revenge.

Henry Revenge?

Karen (*excitedly*) That's why we're being kept alive, Henrybell, you and I. Why we weren't allowed to die. We're unquiet spirits, if you like, with unfinished business. The wrongs that have been done to us have got to be put right. We're never going to rest, either of us, until we've done that.

Henry (*intrigued*) You actually believe that?

Karen My psychiatrist told me once that revenge was the most powerful driving force in the human psyche . . .

Henry You're seeing a psychiatrist?

Karen Oh, years ago.

Henry Ah.

Karen I was just a baby.

Henry A baby? You had feelings of revenge when you were a baby?

Karen Well, ten, twelve – I don't know. The point is – you and I – we still have purpose.

Henry Revenge?

Karen Yes. Can't you feel it in you? It's a terrific feeling, Henrybell, if you can harness it. Use it. Creatively.

Henry I don't see how one could possibly do that.

Karen Nor did I. Till just now in the car. Then I had this brilliant idea. Oh, it's so exciting . . . (*Taking up the bottle*) Have some more champagne . . .

She pours some into his glass, regardless.

Henry (*in vain*) Just a drop . . .

Karen What you were saying earlier gave me the idea. You said, if you did what you felt like doing and went into your office and murdered Mr – whateverhisnameis –

Henry Tick. Bruce Tick.

Karen Then your victory would be very short-lived indeed because you'd probably spend the rest of your life in jail.

Henry Quite so.

Karen Similarly, were I to run down Imogen Staxton-Billing on the zebra crossing as she trundled her monstrous brood to school or to put strychnine into her feeding trough, then the finger of suspicion would very rapidly point at me. The same problem would apply.

Henry (*yawning*) Yes.

Karen Keep awake, I'm nearly there. But what – here it is – what if we swapped?

Henry Swapped?

Karen I took on your revenge. You took on mine. I put pay to Mr Tick. You put pay to Mrs Staxton-Billing.

Henry That's ridiculous –

Karen It's brilliant. No motive. No trace. Cold, calculated revenge.

Henry You mean, kill them?

Karen No. Not necessarily. Just – teach them. Give them as good as they gave.

Henry How?

Karen That's half the fun of it. We'd both have to work it out for ourselves. Find a way. Size up our prey and seek out their weaknesses. Choose our method. And – thwunk!

She brings her fingers together like a gin trap.

Henry What's – thwunk?

Karen That's the trap closing on them, Henrybell. Isn't it a brilliant idea?

Henry It's – absurd. I mean how could I – I couldn't –
No. Could you . . .? Honestly?

Karen I could.

Henry You really could?

Karen All I'd need is a way in. Just an intro.

Henry There you are, then. That's impossible to start with.
I couldn't introduce you to Bruce Tick . . . 'Hallo, Bruce,
I'd like you to meet the instrument of my revenge . . .'

Karen No, of course you couldn't, that would ruin the
whole thing.

Henry I don't even know where he lives. It's somewhere
miles out.

Karen You know where he works, though.

Henry So?

Karen I'll get myself a job with the firm.

Henry A job? What sort of a job?

Karen I don't know. A secretary or something.

Henry Have you ever been a secretary?

Karen No.

Henry Well, you can't just walk in and be a secretary,
you know. You need shorthand and typing and degrees
in word-processing. All sorts of things these days.

Karen Oh, I could bluff all that.

Henry Don't be ridiculous. (*Half to himself*) Mind you,
a lot of them seem to.

Karen You don't like the idea, then.

Henry No, I don't.

39

A silence. Karen sulks.

Look, Karen. It wouldn't work. (*Pause*) It really wouldn't.

Karen You're a wimp.

Henry Probably.

Karen What have you got to lose? Nothing. What's the worst that could happen? Imogen Staxton-Billing might slap your face. Better than being fished out of the Thames by the river police any day. But you'd prefer to go on being trodden on by the Mr Ticks of this world, would you? Fine. They'll be happy. They don't expect you to fight back, so they'll hardly be surprised when you don't, will they? (*Pause*) Wimp.

Henry (*tired and angry*) Look, it just wouldn't work.

Karen Wet.

Henry Complete dreamland.

Karen Weed.

Henry Childish.

Karen Wally.

Henry (*shouting*) Look, will you stop that! I'm sorry. I've had enough. I'm sorry. I'm very tired and I want to go to bed. I'm sorry.

A pause. He controls himself.

(*Quietly*) I'm sorry.

Karen Are you frightened because you think you couldn't do it, or because you think I couldn't do it?

Henry I think it's out of the question for both of us even to try.

Karen (*wheedling*) But supposing – supposing – I tried, Henrybell . . . I mean, it needn't involve you at all – no one need trace me to you – Look, say I managed to get in there – into your firm somehow – and say that somehow I got close to Mr Tick – then would you be prepared to give it a try from your side?

Henry (*a slight pause*) Why? Why do you want to do this?

Karen The greatest feeling in the world, Henrybell. Revenge. Pure, unadulterated revenge. Not weedy little jealousy. Not some piddling little envy. But good, old-fashioned, bloodcurdling revenge. Just picture it, Henrybell. What I could do to him, once I got close to your Mr Tick . . . Can't you see it?

Henry My God, I think I can, almost . . .

Karen It'll be him standing on that bridge instead of you . . . And there won't be someone like me there to rescue him, either. I'll just drive past on the other side of the road. And as I go by, I'll lean out and say – by the way, Mr Tick, Henrybell sends you his regards. Isn't that a beautiful thought?

Henry (*softly*) Fairly attractive, I must say.

Karen Think about that.

Henry I will.

He yawns. She refills his glass. Henry is still abstracted.

Karen Did you say your secretary had resigned?

Henry Elaine? Yes.

Karen Presumably they'll have to replace her, won't they?

Henry I suppose so. They'll probably advertise the post, in due course.

Karen When will they get someone?

Henry Oh, weeks. Knowing the pace that place moves.

Karen Big, is it?

Henry Lembridge Tennit? Huge. They've got thirty-two floors in that building alone.

Karen What will they do till they get someone permanent?

Henry I don't know. Probably get a temp.

Karen A temp?

Henry Temporary secretary. From an agency. Just to fill in.

Karen I could do that.

Henry (*yawning*) You couldn't. Believe me. You really couldn't.

Karen Maybe I could talk to your Elaine . . .

Henry What for?

Karen Do you have her address?

Henry Yes, I do actually. Why?

Karen Is she on the phone?

Henry (*yawning again*) Yes, yes . . . I'm sure she is.

Karen Ring her.

Henry Now?

Karen Now.

Henry I'm not ringing anyone now. It's five thirty in the morning, for God's sake . . .

Karen Then later on. Tell her I want to see her. Tell her I need to talk to her . . .

Henry Oh, heavens . . .

Karen Will you do that?

Henry (*yawning*) I'm so tired, you've no idea . . .

Karen Will you do that?

Henry Karen, please let me go to bed . . .

Karen (*slapping him awake*) Henrybell, listen to me . . .

Henry I agree. Yes, I agree to everything.

Karen Will you give me her number?

Henry (*yawning uncontrollably*) Yes, yes, anything. I'll give you anything you want – just let me go to bed . . .

Karen Give it to me . . .

Henry (*producing his wallet*) Here.

Karen Is the number in here?

Henry (*his eyes half-closed*) Yes, in the address book . . .

Karen This is a wallet.

Henry (*yawning*) Oh . . . ooo . . . ot . . . air . . . (*He takes back the wallet and puts it away*) . . . it . . . ear . . . (*He produces an address book from his other inside pocket*) . . . air . . . is . . .

Karen (*examining the book*) What's Elaine's surname?

Henry Oh God, I've told you everything I know . . . let me sleep . . .

Karen Henrybell, what's her surname?

Henry . . . ith . . .

Karen Ith? What, I-T-H?

Henry No . . . Smith . . .

43

Karen Smith (*Finding it*) E. Smith.

Henry (*snuggling up on the sofa*) Mmm . . .

Karen (*keeping the book*) Good. Good. Good boy . . .

Henry (*sleepily*) Good boy . . .

Karen (*helping him up*) Come on, Henrybell. Bedtime now. Don't go to sleep yet. Up you come. Come on. I'll take you up to bed.

Karen starts to lead him off. Henry is reeling with tiredness.

Henry Bedtime . . .

Karen That's it. Upstairs now . . .

Henry Upstairs now . . .

Karen Come on. You can come and sleep in my bed. You can come and sleep with me . . .

Henry Oh, no. Please no. I just need to sleep . . .

Karen Come on. We'll have a nice time now, shall we?

Henry Oh, please no. Not that. Please . . .

Karen Come on, Henrybell, that's it. You mustn't go to sleep yet, we've got to celebrate . . .

Henry (*despairingly, as he is led away*) Oh God, please. Anything but that . . .

They go off. Once again the lights cross-fade swiftly and we move to –

SCENE THREE

3.00 p.m.
The dining room at Furtherfield House. Afternoon
sun is streaming in through large windows. Faint
birdsong from outside. Distant sounds of mowing.
A clock ticks somewhere. The room is dominated by
a (predictably) large table. It is laid for one. Norma,
a young parlourmaid, probably no more than sixteen,
enters. She is evidently waiting to serve breakfast. She
straightens the cutlery a fraction, tweaks the table
arrangement of flowers and walks to the window and
watches whoever it is who is mowing. Winnie enters and
looks at Norma. Norma catches her eye and hurries out.
Winnie moves to the table and restraightens the cutlery
and the flowers. She also has a look out of the window.
In a moment, Henry enters. He has on a large dressing
gown and larger slippers. He looks rather lost.

Henry (*seeing Winnie*) Ah.

Winnie Afternoon, sir.

Henry Ah. Is it?

Winnie Lovely day again.

Henry Yes. You haven't by any chance seen my clothes?

Winnie Clothes?

Henry Yes.

Winnie No, I'm afraid not, sir.

Henry Only they were taken off me – I took them off
me – myself last night and they're nowhere in sight this
morning. It's very odd.

Winnie Very odd, sir.

Henry Yes. Well.

Winnie It might be that Miss Karen took them, sir.

Henry Really?

Winnie It might be. She did have a bag when she went.

Henry Went?

Winnie Out, sir.

Henry Where?

Winnie I wouldn't know at all, sir.

Henry Oh.

Winnie She did take her car, that I do know.

Henry Ah, then she could have gone anywhere, couldn't she? At the rate she drives she's probably in Cornwall.

Winnie A law unto herself, sir, Miss Karen.

Henry Yes. Still, until she gets back with my suit, I'm afraid I have to wear this. I hope nobody minds.

Winnie That's the late master's gown, sir. I'm sure you'll be very welcome to it. Now, would you care for some breakfast, sir?

Henry Well, yes, I think I would. Thank you.

> *Winnie holds out the chair while he sits at the table.*
> *As he goes to sit, a fluttering sound above their heads.*
> *Henry instinctively ducks.*

Winnie Oh, those birds. They fly in here through the windows and then they haven't the sense to fly out again. Shoo! Shoo! There, now.

Henry (*sitting*) Thank you. I'm afraid I'm terribly late down. My watch has stopped. I've no idea of the time.

Winnie It's just gone three ten, sir.

Henry Three ten? Good Lord.

Winnie So long as you slept well, sir.

Henry Yes, I did, I did. Eventually I did, anyway.

Winnie What would you care for, sir? I'm afraid we didn't lay out the sideboard with there just being the one of you here, sir. When we have a house full we have it all laid out there, you see. It's a lovely sight.

Henry It must be, yes.

The bird swoops again. Henry evades it.

Winnie How about eggs and bacon, sir? That suit you?

Henry Oh, well now, that sounds rather . . .

Winnie Or scrambled eggs? Poached eggs? Boiled eggs? Omelette? Kidneys? Kedgeree? Ham? Kippers? A little bit of smoked haddock?

Henry No, no. Eggs and bacon sound just the thing.

Winnie Cornflakes?

Henry Perfect.

Winnie Or Weetabix? Crispies? Puffed Wheat? Shredded Wheat? Sugar Puffs? Rice Krispies? Muesli?

Henry No, no. Cornflakes.

Winnie Tea or coffee?

Henry Tea. (*Quickly*) Indian. Just as it comes. With milk. White toast. Marmalade. Thank you.

Winnie Butter?

Henry Yes, please. Unsalted.

Winnie Or margarine?

Henry Butter.

Winnie Thank you, sir. Won't be a moment. Newspaper is there, sir.

Henry Thank you.

Winnie goes out. Henry takes a deep breath. All in all, he's feeling rather cheerful. The bird dive-bombs him again. He flaps it away with his napkin. He rises and retreats to the window, ducking and weaving. The bird gives up and apparently perches somewhere high in one corner of the room. Henry relaxes. He, too, watches the mowing. He takes deep breaths. He hears the sound of approaching crockery. He hastily resits. Norma enters with a tray with milk, sugar, a silver bowl full of cornflakes and a separate bowl for Henry to eat them out of. Norma is evidently still learning her job. She frowns throughout in concentration, breathing heavily as she goes about her tasks. Her tongue tends to stick out when she attempts anything especially difficult. Winnie shadows Norma throughout, talking her through every action in a low, barely audible voice.

Winnie (*quietly*) Put it down just there.

Norma puts the tray down.

That's it. Now give the gentleman the bowl.

Norma goes to give Henry the large bowl.

No, not that bowl. The other bowl. Give the gentleman the other bowl.

Norma goes to give Henry the smaller bowl.

Henry (*anticipating this, in an encouragingly helpful tone*) Thank you.

48

Winnie No, no, no. Not from that side. You don't serve from that side, ever, now do you?

Norma takes the bowl back and moves round to Henry's other side.

That's it. That's better.

Henry gets the bowl again.

Henry Thank you again.

Winnie Now serve the cornflakes. Serve the gentleman with the cornflakes.

Norma takes up the silver bowl and moves around to Henry's other side.

That's it. Good girl. Good girl. Don't get nervous, he won't bite you.

Norma Cornflakes, sir?

Henry Yes, thank you very much.

Norma now attempts silver service on the cornflakes. It is nail-biting stuff. Each serving gives him about eight cornflakes at a time. She is very nervous. Henry watches her, scarcely daring to breathe. The bird dive-bombs them a couple of times. Winnie continues her back-seat advice in a low monotone.

Winnie That's it, carefully, carefully, carefully. Never mind about the bird.

Norma shoots cornflakes over the table. She attempts to rescue them. So does Henry.

(*Sharply*) No, don't try to pick them up. Leave them there.

Henry and Norma both stop at once.

No point in picking them up now, is there? Keep going.

Henry gets another eight cornflakes.

Norma Is that sufficient, sir?

Henry (*relieved*) Yes, yes. That's perfect.

He stares at his nearly empty bowl.

Winnie Milk and sugar now. Milk and sugar.

Henry Oh, now look, I can easily do that myself. Please.

But Norma is on a pre-programmed course. She carries the tray round to Henry.

Norma (*holding firmly on to the jug*) Milk, sir?

Henry Thank you.

Norma Say when, sir.

Norma attempts another difficult feat, holding the tray in one hand and the milk jug in the other. The milk dribbles out in a thin trickle.

Henry (*waiting till he has enough milk*) Er . . . er . . .

Norma That sufficient, sir?

Henry (*doubtfully*) Yes, yes. Thank you. (*The cornflakes are barely damp*)

Winnie Now the sugar. Serve the sugar.

Norma, like a high-wire artiste, manages to get the milk jug back on the tray and pick up the sugar.

Norma Sugar, sir?

Henry Thank you.

Norma Say when, sir.

She scatters an enormous amount of sugar over Henry's flakes.

Henry (*as she does this*) Yes – right, whoa! Whoa!
Thank you.

Norma That sufficient, sir?

Henry Perfect.

Norma Thank you, sir.

Winnie That's it, now take the rest of that out with you.
Off you go.

Norma I'll serve you your bacon and eggs in a moment,
sir.

Henry Er, look, I think, actually, I've changed my mind.
I don't think I want bacon and eggs, after all.

Norma Right, sir.

Henry Just the tea and toast.

Norma Right, sir.

Winnie (*in her usual undertone*) You better tell cook he
doesn't want it. Tell her the gentleman's changed his
mind.

Norma Right.

Norma goes out carefully, as before.

Winnie (*confidentially*) You'll have to bear with Norma,
sir. She's just learning.

Henry Ah. I see you've had a fire out there.

Winnie Beg your pardon, sir.

Henry The building or whatever it was out there. I see
you've had a fire.

Winnie Oh yes, sir. That'll be the old summerhouse.

Henry Oh yes. What happened? How did it get burnt down?

Winnie (*darkly*) There was a fire, sir. Just a fire.

Somewhere along the hall, the sound of Norma dropping the tray and contents on the parquet floor.

Excuse me, sir. Newspaper's just there, sir.

Winnie goes out. Henry tries to scrape a little of the sugar off his cornflakes. He nibbles at a few but they aren't very appetising. The sound of a sports car outside the window. A scrunch of tyres as it comes to a squealing halt on the gravel drive. Henry looks towards the window, startled. The front door slams, off.

Oliver (*yelling, off*) Winnie!

Winnie immediately hurries through.

Winnie (*as she passes, to Henry*) Excuse me, sir. That'll be Master Oliver.

Henry (*uncomprehending*) Ah.

Norma hurries through after Winnie.

Norma (*as she passes through, to Henry*) Master Oliver.

Voices from the hall. After a second, Oliver strolls in. A tall young man in his early twenties. He is wearing evening dress with a white jacket. He throws himself into the chair at the other end of the table.

Oliver Hi!

Henry (*rising*) Good afternoon.

Oliver Good God! Is it really?

Winnie and Norma re-enter. They are carrying, separately, two halves of a Victorian jardinière.

Winnie carries the top while Norma struggles behind her with the base.

Norma (*as she passes, to Henry*) Tea's just coming, sir.

Henry (*alarmed by her exertions*) Thank you. Can you manage?

Oliver Winnie, run us a bath, will you, there's a sweet.

Winnie (*as she goes*) Yes, Master Oliver.

Oliver Careful with that. I'll have to take it back. When I find out where it came from.

Winnie and Norma go out. Pause.

Found the thing on my back seat. I've been chatting away quite merrily to it all the way home under the impression it was a passenger. Come down with Karen, did you?

Henry Yes. Last night. Early this morning. I'm Henry Bell.

Oliver Oliver Knightly. I'm her bro.

Henry Yes. Hallo.

Oliver Hi. I've just been to this party.

Henry Oh yes.

Oliver Just now. Dragged on and on. Very dull.

Henry Oh dear.

Oliver Still going, I think. They held it in an aquarium.

Henry Really. How unusual.

Oliver I'll tell you one thing. The fish were having a far better time than we were, I can promise you that.

Norma enters with another tray. This time it contains a silver teapot, milk, sugar and teacup, etc.

53

I mean, I don't know your views on dolphin shows but I've just about had them up to here . . .

Henry Well . . .

Norma Tea, sir?

Henry (*vainly*) It's all right, I can –

Norma grasps firmly hold of the teapot.

Oliver I mean, you've seen one. Know what I mean?

Henry I suppose so.

Oliver I mean, nice enough creatures they may be but with a very limited repertoire. I don't care how many nude girls they tow round on rubber rings.

Norma Milk, sir?

Henry Just a little, please.

The bird flutters above their heads. Henry ducks again.

Oliver (*squinting upwards*) Oh, that's a wren. Do you see? Lovely birds.

Norma Sugar, sir?

Henry No. Thank you.

Norma Thank you, sir. Toast is just coming, sir.

Henry Thank you.

Norma goes out, leaving the tray. Henry takes advantage of her absence to adjust the colour of his tea during the next.

Oliver I must have a bath in a minute. I tend to think we have some people coming round.

Henry Oh, really?

Oliver I seem to remember we have. Today's Saturday, isn't it?

Henry (*ducking as the bird apparently dive-bombs him*) Yes.

Oliver Then we definitely have.

Henry Ah. I wonder if you perhaps know where Karen has gone to?

Oliver Haven't the foggiest, sorry. I mean, she disappears for months on end sometimes.

Henry Oh. Does she?

Oliver Looking for her, are you?

Henry It's just that she has my clothes, you see.

Oliver Your clothes?

Henry My suit. And my shoes. And my shirt. So I've nothing to put on. Nothing at all.

Oliver Well, you're welcome to anything of mine. Just help yourself.

Henry That's very kind of you but I'd rather like to get my own clothes back, really.

Oliver (*sleepily*) How come she's waltzed off with your suit? Was she wearing it?

Henry No. I don't think so, anyway. It's a very complicated story . . .

Oliver (*settling back in his chair*) Uh-huh?

Henry We met on this bridge last night, you see. Albert Bridge, actually. And . . . well . . .

Oliver Mwuhuhuh.

Oliver has fallen asleep. He snores very gently.

Henry Ah.

*Henry drinks his tea while Oliver slumbers on.
Norma comes on with her tray, this time containing
toast, butter, marmalade, etc. She sees Oliver and
tiptoes the rest of the way.*

Norma (*whispering*) Toast, sir?

Henry (*whispering back*) Thank you. Now, I know with
this I really can help myself, you see, so don't –

*Another sports car draws up outside at speed. Another
squeal of brakes. Norma freezes. Winnie hurries
through to the hall.*

Winnie (*as she passes through*) That'll be Miss Karen.

Norma Miss Karen.

*She hurries out after Winnie. Henry quickly helps
himself to toast. Voices from the hall. In a moment,
Karen enters. She is now in rather stylish day clothes.
She appears amazingly fresh for someone who can't
have slept at all.*

Karen Hallo!

Henry (*rising*) Ah, Karen, thank heavens . . .

Karen Henrybell. (*She kisses him*) You look lovely. That
suits you. Are they all looking after you?

Henry Yes. Karen, where are my clothes? I can't find my
clothes.

Karen Wait, wait, wait. Just wait and see what I've
bought.

Winnie and Norma enter with innumerable carrier bags and parcels.

(*Indicating her purchases*) Behold! I have not been idle.

Henry Good grief.

Karen (*to Winnie and Norma*) Dump them down, just dump them down. (*Seeing Oliver*) Oh, just look at that. Isn't that sweet? Has he been there long?

Henry Just a moment or two.

Karen He's like a dormouse. He sleeps anywhere. (*Shouting into his face*) Oliver!

Oliver stirs in his sleep but fails to wake.

Hopeless. I'm parched. Winnie, do we have some white wine open?

Winnie I can open one, miss.

Karen Bring us a couple of glasses, there's a dear.

Winnie Yes, miss.

Henry makes a feeble protest. Winnie goes out, followed by Norma.

Karen (*softly*) That was a beautiful night last night. You were fantastic.

Henry Was I?

Karen (*kissing him rather off-handedly*) We must do it again some time. Now, to prove I had not forgotten you . . . (*She rummages among the bags*) Now which one was it? Oh yes. *Voilà!*

From one of her bags she produces a man's suit, new and on a hanger. It is modern and positive in design and colour. Certainly something that Henry would never dream of wearing. She holds it up for him to look at.

What do you think?

Henry (*incredulous*) You're going to wear that to the office?

Karen Of course not. It's for you.

Henry Me?

Karen Do you like it?

Henry I'm not wearing that.

Karen It's gorgeous. I picked it specially. They took it out of the window for me.

Henry I wouldn't be seen dead in that.

Karen (*throwing the suit down, sulkily*) Oh well, walk around naked then, see if I care.

Henry Where's my suit?

Karen I went to a lot of trouble for that.

Henry Karen, where is my suit?

Karen I don't know. In a rubbish bin somewhere. I don't know.

Norma comes on with a tray with a bottle of white wine and glasses. Winnie follows her.

Winnie (*sotto, to Norma*) That's it, just put it down there.

Henry A rubbish bin?

Norma Wine, miss?

Karen Thank you.

Henry What rubbish bin? Where?

58

Karen I don't know. Somewhere in Oxford Street. I wasn't lugging that hideous suit all the way back with me.

Norma (*hovering at Henry's elbow*) Wine, sir?

Henry (*ignoring Norma*) Oxford Street? Why did you take it to Oxford Street?

Karen How else was I to know your size? (*Tearfully*) I got you a shirt and everything to match.

Norma (*patiently*) Wine, sir?

Henry I was perfectly happy with the suit I had.

Winnie (*sotto to Norma*) Other side, girl. You're serving him from the wrong side again.

Henry I was very fond of that suit. I'd had it for years.

Karen Obviously.

Norma (*appearing at Henry's other elbow*) Wine, sir?

Henry No, I don't want any wine. Go away. I just want my suit.

Karen Then you'll have to go to Oxford Street and get it, won't you? I'm not doing any more for you, that's it.

She sits and glares into the middle distance. Henry can't cope with that at all. Oliver snores.

Winnie (*sotto, to Norma*) Ask the gentleman if he's had sufficient, then.

Norma Have you had sufficient, sir?

Henry (*testily*) Yes, yes, yes.

Norma Thank you, sir.

Winnie (*sotto, to Norma*) Clear away, then. Start clearing away.

Norma starts to clear away Henry's breakfast. Oliver snores. Karen sulks.

Henry (*softly, to Karen*) I'm sorry. Look, I'm sorry. I don't want to seem ungrateful. It's just I was – (*Aware of the others*) I was rather fond of that suit. It had seen me through some good times. And yes, it has to be said, some pretty rotten ones as well.

Karen sulks on. Henry perseveres.

You see, I don't think that particular sort of suit would suit me at all. You see?

Karen You haven't even tried it on.

Henry No, but I can pretty well tell just from looking at it, you see. If I was in a shop, shopping, I'd catch sight of it and I'd say straight away, look, that really isn't my sort of suit.

Karen You might at least try it on. I bought it specially.

Henry Yes, OK, OK. I'll certainly go and try it on if you like . . .

Karen You will?

Henry But I'm afraid you're in for a bit of a laugh if I do. It's going to make me look pretty silly.

Karen (*brightening, getting up*) How do you know till you've tried? Come on, try it.

Henry All right, yes. Right . . .

Henry picks up the suit rather gingerly and makes as if to leave the room. During the next, Winnie and Norma go out with the tray.

Karen Wait, wait. We need all the bits. Just a second. (*She rummages in the bags again*) Shirt!

She produces a very jolly shirt.

Henry (*eyeing it*) Ah.

Karen Tie!

She produces a tie in similar vein.

Henry Oh, my God . . .

Karen Not your sort of tie, either?

Henry I didn't say that.

Karen Shoes!

Some very un-Henryish (slip-on) shoes.

Henry Oh-ho! Yes. Those are interesting, aren't they? I'll go upstairs . . .

Karen Here's all right. Why not here?

Henry Here? But –

He indicates Winnie and Norma.

Karen It's all right, there's nobody here. Oliver's sound asleep. I won't look . . .

Henry (*reluctantly*) All right.

He starts to get dressed, rather like a bather on a crowded beach. Karen talks to him as he does this. Henry starts by putting on the trousers under his dressing gown. Only then does he remove this and put on the shirt.

Karen Now, let me tell you what I've been up to. First, I've been to see your Elaine Smith.

Henry (*struggling into the trousers*) You have?

Karen It's all right, I rang her first. She was a little bit suspicious to start with but once she heard the whole story – how you'd nearly jumped off that bridge and how I stopped you in the nick of time –

Henry You told her all that?

Karen Of course. She was horrified. (*Admiring the trousers*) God, those are going to look terrific on you. Elaine said anything I could do to get back at Bruce Tick – and anyone else in that firm come to that – and give him one from her, too. She's ace. No wonder you liked her. Absolutely invaluable. She told me masses about the ins and outs of the firm. Who's having who, who's got their knife into who. My God, the place is an absolute rats' nest. Elaine said it was amazing you survived as long as you did.

Henry Really?

He is doing up the shirt now.

Karen (*as he does this*) Oh, that's gorgeous. You're going to look an absolute knockout.

Henry (*sceptically*) Oh, yes?

Karen Anyway, she gave me absolutely priceless information. And most important of all, the inside secrets of how to cope with the dreaded Mrs Bulley.

Henry Who on earth's Mrs Bulley? Oh, her . . .

He starts to tie his tie.

Karen Mrs Bulley is the key to the whole secretariat. She alone can hire and she alone can fire. If I can win her heart, I can work for anyone in the building. She is the dragon that guards the gates.

Henry Yes, that pretty well describes her.

Karen Her name strikes shivers through the typing pool. But I think I've got the measure of her penchant. Nice, plain, sensible girls with very little make-up in drab wool suits cut just below the knee, plain stockings and flattish shoes. That's her type. Mrs Bulley does not care for the flash.

Henry now has on the trousers, shirt and tie.

(*Applauding*) Oh, yes, yes, yes!

Henry (*coolly*) Socks. Any chance of some socks? Or have you bought me some tartan tights . . . ?

Karen Socks! Damn! I knew there was something. (*Yelling*) Winnie! (*To Henry*) Hang on. The point is Elaine Smith, apparently, was Mrs Bulley's blue-eyed girl. She's going to phone her first thing Monday morning and recommend me.

Henry This is madness . . .

Karen Henrybell . . . Remember our agreement.

Henry What agreement?

Karen The agreement we consummated last night . . .

Henry Oh, that agreement.

Karen Yes. That agreement.

Winnie and Norma enter.

Winnie, can you run upstairs and get me some socks from Master Oliver's room.

Winnie Yes, miss. (*To Norma*) Run upstairs and get some socks from Master Oliver's room . . .

Norma (*going off*) Right.

Karen Better bring a selection.

Winnie Bring a selection.

Norma Yes, miss. I'll bring a selection.

Norma goes off.

Karen (*resuming*) So, anyway, after that I had this shopping trip – you wait till you see *my* suit, it's fabulous – after that, I even had time to call on a couple of friends who've very kindly agreed to give me a reference. And here I am. Not a bad day's work, eh?

Henry How on earth did you find people to give you a reference?

Karen (*smiling evasively*) Oh, they owed me a favour.

Henry finally tries the jacket on. He has everything now except shoes and socks.

Let's have a look at you, Henrybell.

Henry stands self-consciously.

Oh, yes. *Yes!*

Norma returns with two or three pairs of brightly coloured socks.

Ah, good. Thank you. Now then . . .

Karen holds up a couple of pairs and rejects them.

No . . . no . . . (*Finding some that are reasonably appropriate*) They'll do for now.

Henry (*taking the socks*) Thank you. Yes, these should set the whole thing off nicely. All I need now is the crazy car and the bucket of whitewash.

Henry sits and pulls on the socks. Karen sets aside the rejects.

(*Struggling with the socks*) I'm sure this is going to look extraordinary.

Karen Nonsense.

Henry slips on the shoes and rises. The women admire him.

Wonderful.

Henry What?

Karen Turn round. (*Henry does so*) Terrific.

Henry Really?

Karen Really.

Henry Really?

Karen Yes.

Winnie Oh yes.

Norma Yes.

Henry still has his doubts but is rather flattered by their attention. It's doubtful whether so many women have ever given him this much attention at one time before.

Henry Well, I . . . It's certainly not something I would have . . . Still, I suppose . . . (*Smiling at them*) Well.

Karen (*smiling back*) It's the start of a new life, Henrybell. A new life. A new you.

Henry (*preening himself ever so slightly*) Yes, you're absolutely right. What the hell. Ha!

At this point, Oliver snorts and wakes up. The first thing he sees, is the new improved Henry.

Oliver Wah! God! Who on earth are you?

Henry Hallo, again.

Oliver Have we met?

Henry Yes. Henry Bell. I was having breakfast when you dozed off.

Oliver Oh, yes. What have you done to yourself? You seem to have had a new paint job.

Karen Hiya, Ol . . .

Oliver (*seeing her for the first time*) Oh hi, Ka. How're things?

Karen Terrif.

Oliver Good-o. Going to have a bath. Did you run that bath, Winnie?

Winnie Yes, Master Oliver. Be a bit cold now, I dare say.

Oliver Oh, dear. Run another one somewhere else, will you? Use a different tank.

Winnie Yes, Master Oliver. (*Sotto, to Norma*) Come and help run the bath, now.

> *Winnie and Norma go out, taking the rejected socks. They leave the wine tray, which Oliver now spots.*

Oliver Oh great, wine. (*Holding up Henry's unused glass*) This anyone's?

Henry No.

Oliver I'd better get changed. Those people are coming.

Karen What people?

Oliver Oh, you know. All those people. Cheers.

Karen What people? I'm busy.

Oliver The charity fête festival freedom thing committee. You know. The ones who meet here all the time. The one I'm on. They want to use the meadow.

Karen Oh. That committee. Yes.

Oliver They've always got something on. I said we'd lend them the meadow, again.

Karen Isn't Imogen Staxton-Billing on that committee?

Oliver Probably. I think they both are, aren't they?

Karen Anthony as well?

Oliver Think so.

Karen (*to Henry*) Your chance.

Henry What?

Karen To meet them.

Henry You mean they're both coming here? To this house? Him and his wife? With you here? Won't that be –?

Karen Presumably they thought I'd be away . . .

Oliver Yah. I'm sure they did.

Henry All the same . . .

Karen This is the country, Henrybell. You can't stop seeing people just because you've slept with one of them. You'd end up a hermit. It's a wonderful chance for you to have a look at her. See what you make of her.

Henry Yes.

Karen Your first sight of the enemy.

Henry Now, wait a minute. I haven't yet declared war . . .

Karen Just a look. No harm in looking, is there?

Henry No.

Oliver What's all this?

Karen Go and have your bath.

Oliver Right-o. Will you organise some cake or something for them? They usually expect a bun or two.

Karen Oliver.

Oliver Yah?

Karen Listen, when they come, would you mind if we introduced Henrybell as your friend rather than mine?

Oliver Henrybell? Who's Henrybell?

Henry Me. Henry. Bell.

Oliver Oh, yes. Why's that?

Karen I'd just rather they thought he was your friend. And not my friend.

Oliver (*doubtfully*) Well, I don't know. What sort of friend?

Karen I don't know. Any sort of friend . . .

Oliver He doesn't look much like any friend of mine. Not wearing a suit like that. No offence, sorry . . .

Henry That's quite all right. I don't think any friend of mine would wear a suit like this either.

Karen (*beadily*) Well, I know plenty of mine who would.

Oliver Then he'd better be a friend of yours, then.

Karen (*shouting*) I don't want him to be a friend of mine, I want him to be a friend of yours.

Oliver (*shouting back*) Well, he bloody well can't be a friend of mine. I'm damned if I want a friend wearing a suit like that.

Henry (*shouting with them*) Listen, if it helps I'll take the thing off –

68

Karen (*fiercely*) DON'T YOU DARE TAKE IT OFF.

A pause.

Oliver (*calmer*) Tell you what. He could be something else altogether.

Karen (*testily*) What?

Oliver I don't know. He could be from – from our accountants.

Henry In a suit like this?

Oliver Oh, yes . . . Most of them wear suits like that.

Karen That's brilliant. You can be from . . . What are their names?

Oliver Haven't the faintest idea. One of them's called Dennis, I think.

Karen No, the name of the firm.

Oliver Dennis and Co. I don't know. Dennis, Dennis and Dennis.

He laughs.

Karen Don't be stupid. I hate men when they're stupid.

Norma has entered with Winnie just behind her.

Norma Your other bath's run, Master Oliver.

Oliver Oh, yah. Good-o.

Karen I'll tell you who would know what they were called. John would know.

Oliver John?

Karen John Brackett.

Oliver Oh yes. He'd know. He knows everything.

Karen Phone him. Find out what they're called.

Oliver I'm going to have a bath. You phone him.

Karen (*angrily*) Oliver!

Oliver (*as he goes*) They'll all be here in a minute.

He goes out.

Karen Winnie. I want you to phone Mr Brackett, our solicitor. All right?

Winnie Yes, miss.

Karen Ask him could he tell you the name of our accountants. All right? Have you got that?

Winnie Accountants. Right, miss.

She goes.

Karen (*after her*) Oh, and get their address as well. (*To Henry*) You ought to know where you work. In case anyone asks you.

Henry I can't tell lies like that.

Karen All right. I'll tell them you're a failed suicide that I dragged off a bridge to spend the night with me. How about that?

Henry (*weakly*) Oh, God. All right.

A doorbell rings.

Karen They're here. Come on.

Henry Where?

Karen Just say hallo to them.

Henry Now?

Karen Just quickly, come on. It won't take a second.

They're having a committee meeting, you won't have to be with them for long.

Henry What do I say?

Karen Say hallo, that's all . . .

Before they can leave the room, Norma has ushered in two of the guests. First, Lady Ganton, a woman in her sixties. Then Colonel Marcus Lipscott of similar age.

Norma Lady Ganton and Colonel Lipscott, miss.

Karen Hallo, Ursula. How lovely to see you.

Lady Ganton Karen, dear. What a wonderful surprise. We didn't expect you.

They kiss.

You're looking wonderful.

Karen Thank you.

Lady Ganton Wonderful.

Karen Marcus.

Marcus (*slightly less warmly*) Hallo, Karen. (*Kissing her*) Good to see you. Understood you were in London.

Karen No, we – came back . . . last night, suddenly. May I introduce Henry Bell?

Lady Ganton Hallo.

Henry (*shaking hands*) How do you do?

Karen This is Lady Ganton. Ursula Ganton. And this is Colonel Marcus Lipscott. Henry Bell.

Marcus How do you do?

Karen (*pointedly*) Marcus is Imogen's uncle. I may have

71

mentioned her to you, Henrybell. Imogen Staxton-Billing's uncle.

Henry Oh yes, right. That Imogen Staxton-Billing.

Marcus Oh, you know Imogen, do you?

Henry No, I'm afraid not.

Lady Ganton You'll see her in a minute, I expect. She'll be at the meeting. (*To Henry*) Are you coming to the meeting?

Karen No, Henry's from our accountants. He's just here looking at our books.

Lady Ganton Oh, I thought you might have been a sponsor. From the brewery. You look as if you're from the brewery.

Henry No, I'm afraid I'm not from the brewery.

Lady Ganton Pity.

The doorbell rings.

Karen Will you excuse me?

Henry (*panicking at being abandoned*) Er . . .

Karen Won't be a minute . . .

Karen goes out. In a moment, voices are heard outside.

Marcus Did you say you were a turf accountant?

Henry No, no. Just an accountant. I'm looking at the books.

Marcus Really? You look more like a bookie. What sort of firm is it?

Henry Oh, it's a very – trendy sort of place.

Lady Ganton Jolly good. I don't think we can ever have enough of that, do you?

Marcus Enough of what?

Lady Ganton Trendiness. God bless the young people. They brighten up this world, that's what I say. In my day, we all looked dreadfully dull and dressed exactly like our mothers.

Marcus I didn't dress like my mother.

Lady Ganton And then rows and rows of identical men. All in shiny dark blue suits. I mean, whoever decreed that accountants should all wear shiny dark blue suits?

Henry Exactly. That's precisely our policy . . .

The doorbell rings again. In a moment, fresh voices are heard.

Marcus (*suspiciously*) Where is this place you work for?

Henry Oh . . .

He points vaguely at the ceiling.

Marcus What's the name of it?

Henry That's a wren, surely. Up there. Look.

Lady Ganton Oh yes . . . Do you feed them?

Henry Oh yes, rather.

Lady Ganton Well, don't. You'll never get rid of them. They'll be nesting up there next.

Percy Cutting enters – a small unassuming man in his forties in a shiny dark blue suit.

Marcus Ah, Percy. Come over here. Meet Mr Bell. Now that's the sort of suit I expect an accountant of mine to wear. Like the one Percy's wearing. Percy, this is Mr Bell.

Me Bell, this is Percy Cutting.

Percy Hallo.

Henry How do you do?

Marcus Now, Percy, would you believe, this chap's an accountant?

Percy No. I don't think I would necessarily. Not at a glance, certainly.

Henry No, well . . . (*He laughs*)

Percy Where do you work then? Carnaby Street?

He laughs.

Henry (*sharing the joke*) No, no.

Marcus I've just been trying to find that out.

Lady Ganton He's being rather secretive about it.

Henry No, no. There's no secret. No secret at all.

Lady Ganton Who do you work for, then?

Henry Er . . . It's on the tip of my tongue . . .

Lady Ganton I don't think he knows.

At this moment, Winnie arrives at his elbow with a piece of paper on a tray. Marcus and Lady Ganton move away under the next and start talking together.

Winnie (*to Henry*) Excuse me, sir . . .

Henry Excuse me.

Winnie The – information you asked for, sir.

Henry The – Oh yes, thank you. (*He reads it swiftly*) Thank you.

Winnie goes out again.

Percy Not bad news, I hope?

Henry No, no. Where were we? Oh, yes. Where I work. I work with – Ullworth, Gladys and Thrace.

Percy Don't you mean Ullworth, Gledhouse and Thrace?

Henry Gledhouse. Sorry, did I say Gladys? Gledhouse.

Percy I know them well. We used to have dealings with them at one time. You still in the same place then, are you?

Henry Oh yes, you bet. We're still in – in – (*He peeks at the paper but can't read the writing*) Still in good old – Strewth Street.

Percy Really? You used to be in Straight Street in my day.

Henry Oh yes, we are. Don't get me wrong. The main bunch of us are still in good old Straight Street. But a few of us have moved into our new annexe just round the corner in Strewth Street.

Percy Ah well, after my time that must have been. I don't know Strewth Street at all.

Henry No, it's very, very narrow.

Percy Old man Stackwood still soldiering on, is he?

Henry (*affectionately*) Oh yes, yes. Bless his old heart.

Percy Miserable old sod, isn't he?

Henry Oh, yes. And we're mighty glad to be working round the corner in Strewth Street, I don't mind telling you.

Percy I bet. I bet. I can see you've worked with old Stackwood.

Henry You can say that again.

Percy Amazed he'd let you come to work in a suit like that, though.

Henry Well, all sort of things go on in Strewth Street that he doesn't know about, I can tell you.

Percy Tell me now, I've always wanted to know . . .

Henry is rescued from the remorseless Percy by the entrance of more guests. Karen comes in with Daphne Teale, a buxom woman in her mid-forties with bright red hair. Following them, Anthony and Imogen Staxton-Billing. Anthony, in his late thirties, has relied for a fraction too long on his youthful good looks to give him the reputation as the local ladies' man. His wife, Imogen (despite Karen's slanderous description of her) is, at thirty-seven, attractive too – though the trials and tensions of the past few years have left their mark on her. One might describe her as a desperately neglected English rose. She is certainly not at her best this afternoon. She has, after all, just been confronted unexpectedly with Karen.

Karen (*calling to the beleaguered Henry*) Henry?

Henry (*gratefully*) Yes?

Karen Come and meet some more people.

Henry (*hurrying over*) Yes, of course.

Karen Henry. This is Councillor Mrs Teale.

Daphne (*a blunt, plain local speech*) Daphne Teale, how do you do?

Henry Hallo, Henry Bell.

Karen Henry's from our accountants. And this is Anthony and Imogen Staxton-Billing.

She immediately moves away to the other group.

Henry Ah, hallo.

Anthony (*cursorily*) 'Llo.

They shake hands.

Henry (*turning to Imogen*) Hallo, Henry Bell.

Imogen scarcely looks at him but gives him the most peremptory of greetings and handshakes.

Imogen (*glacially*) Hallo.

Daphne Did she say you were an accountant?

Henry (*defensively*) Yes.

Daphne Oh. (*She looks him up and down*) Not local, are you?

Henry No. London.

Daphne Yes, I thought as much. Excuse me, I just want a word with . . .

She drifts away to the other group.

Henry (*charmingly*) Of course. (*Turning to the Staxton-Billings*) Well. A lot of people to meet all of a sudden.

Imogen (*ignoring him, to her husband*) Did you know she was going to be here?

Anthony Who?

Imogen You know who I'm talking about?

Anthony No idea at all.

Imogen I'm talking about that little toad, Karen Knightly. Who do you think I'm talking about?

Anthony Oh, Karen. That's who you're talking about.

Slight pause.

Henry Did you have far to come?

Imogen (*ignoring him still*) God, you bastard. You let me come to this house and walk straight into her. And you never even warned me she'd be here.

Anthony Oh, do put a cork in it . . .

Imogen I mean it's so cruel, Anthony. Don't you realise how cruel it is? Don't you honestly realise?

Anthony Oh, God. It's one of those afternoons, is it?

He starts to move away.

Imogen Anthony . . .

Anthony Goodbye.

He goes to talk to Daphne, who has joined up with Percy. Pause.

Henry (*trying again*) What's this committee in aid of then? Is it for some charity?

Imogen What? Are you talking to me?

Henry Er . . . yes. I was . . . I was just . . .

Imogen Listen, I don't think we have a thing in common, do we? I'm sure you have nothing to say that would be of the slightest interest to me. And there's nothing whatever that I want to talk to you about. So why don't you just run away and practise your small talk with somebody else?

Henry is totally staggered by her rudeness. Before he can even begin to think of a retort, Imogen moves away from him. At the same time, Marcus calls everyone to order.

Marcus Ladies and gentlemen, I think we're all here – are we all here?

Percy Yes, I think so.

Marcus Right. Shall we move through to the library and get under way, then? I understand Oliver's on his way down. If you'd all like to follow on. Tea and biscuits are promised, I am assured, imminently.

Lady Ganton Hooray!

General chatter as the assembly starts to move off. Henry moves away but keeps his angry gaze on Imogen. Karen, having seen everyone out ahead of her, turns back in the doorway to Henry.

Karen (*softly*) Well, what did you make of her? Mrs Staxton-Billing?

Henry (*through gritted teeth*) Mrs Staxton-Billing? Well . . .

Karen So is it on? Our agreement?

Henry (*still smarting*) Oh yes. Most definitely it's on.

Karen (*in a gleeful whisper*) Revenge?

She extends her hand to him.

Henry (*taking her hand, grimly*) Revenge.

Blackout.

Act Two

SCENE ONE

9.30 a.m.

The following Monday morning. The skyscraper offices of Lembridge Tennit. The outer area of the offices of Mrs Bulley (Head of Personnel – Brackets Secretarial). The distant buzz of office activity, fax machines, telex, duplicators, printers, phones, etc. Seated at the secretary's desk is Lydia, Mrs Bulley's secretary. Probably in her mid- to late thirties, she is, in keeping with her boss's preference, very demure and proper. There are a couple of other reception-type seats. On one of these sits Tracey, a very attractive young woman in her early twenties. She is gazing rather nervously at one of the magazines provided. She is here for an interview. Lydia's phone rings.

Lydia (*answering the phone*) Good morning, Mrs Bulley's secretary . . . Oh, hallo, Mr Southland . . . She's just on the other line at present, Mr Southland . . . Would you like to hold or shall she call you back? . . . Right you are, thank you, Mr Southland, she shouldn't be long . . .

She hangs up. She flashes a smile at Tracey.

She won't keep you waiting a moment.

Tracey 'K you.

Lydia busies herself at her desk. In a moment, Karen enters. She, too, is dressed for the interview, but to do so she has somewhat altered her image. She is wearing an unflattering suit, minimal make-up, her hair scraped back and flat shoes. She carries a hefty handbag. The

overall impression is that she has tried to make herself
as plain as possible. Yet, as with all Karen's varying
personas, the impression is of someone ringing the
changes within their own multiple personality, rather
than inventing a totally new character. Karen
approaches the desk. Tracey stares at her faintly
incredulously.

Karen (*in very dainty tones*) Good morning.

Lydia Good morning. Can I help you?

Karen Yes, I hope you can. I have an appointment to see
Mrs Bulley at nine forty-five.

Lydia (*reaching for the list*) Oh yes. Your name is –?

Karen Knightly. Miss Knightly.

Lydia Initial?

Karen K. Just plain K. I believe Miss Smith telephoned
about me earlier?

Lydia Oh yes, of course. Would you like to take a seat
over there?

Karen Yes, I would. I've been here for ages hunting high
and low for this office.

Lydia Oh dear, yes, it is a big building.

Karen It certainly is. I've been going up and down in
that lift like a yo-yo. (*To Tracey*) Good morning.

Tracey (*uncommunicatively*) 'Llo.

Karen You waiting, too?

Tracey Yeah.

Lydia Mrs Bulley won't keep you a moment . . .

Karen Thank you . . .

Lydia (*glancing at her phone*) Yes, she's off the line now.

A voice comes from the intercom on her desk.

Mrs Bulley (*fiercely*) Lydia . . . Lydia, come in here a minute.

Lydia (*pressing down a key and replying*) Coming, Mrs Bulley. (*To the others*) Just one moment . . .

Lydia gathers up her notebook and goes into the inner office. We hear the start of the conversation before the door closes behind her.

Mrs Bulley (*angrily, off*) Lydia, will you please tell me what on earth is going on?

Lydia I'm not quite sure what you mean, Mrs Bulley . . .

The conversation is cut off. Slight pause. Tracey continues to study her magazine.

Karen I don't know why I'm applying for this job. I really don't. I'm the last person who'll get it, I know I am. (*Pause*) I mean, I'm not even remotely what they're looking for. (*Pause*) I know I'm not. (*Pause*) A girl I met in the lift, she described to me exactly what they were looking for and it certainly wasn't my type, I can tell you that. (*Pause*) I'm not remotely what they're looking for at all.

A pause. Tracey refuses to be drawn.

I mean, if you don't mind my saying so, I think you stand a far better chance than I do. (*Pause*) I'm sure you're far more approaching very nearly the type they're approximately looking for.

A pause.

Tracey (*drawn at last*) What type are they looking for?

Karen Oh. You know. Out front.

Tracey Out front?

Karen Apparently this job has a very high public profile.

Tracey Does it?

Karen Apparently. It surprised me, but there you are.

Tracey It's just secretarial, isn't it?

Karen Oh yes. But it's market analysis, you see. Which involves a great deal of entertaining of clients and socialising and so on.

Tracey (*surprised*) Really?

Karen Oh yes. Which of course means they want someone with personality and glamour and buckets of sex appeal. All the sort of things that don't naturally come up my particular alley, I'm afraid.

Tracey Nobody told me that.

Karen (*confidentially*) Well, the point is I don't think we're supposed to know.

Tracey Why not?

Karen They want to see us in our natural state. They don't want us putting on airs. It has to be innate, you see, innate. So this girl was telling me in the lift.

Tracey Well . . .

Karen I'm afraid I'm innately rather quiet . . . Pity. I'd have liked all that overseas travel . . .

Tracey Overseas travel?

Karen Still. (*She sits unhappily*) C'est la vie, n'est-ce-pas?

Tracey Pardon?

After a moment, Tracey goes for her bag. She looks to see if Karen is watching her but apparently she isn't. Tracey checks her appearance in her mirror. She starts to go over her make-up. More lips, more eyes, more blusher. She fluffs her hair. She goes mad with the scent. She hitches her skirt up another inch or so. She practises the odd moue. Lydia comes out of Mrs Bulley's office looking rather flushed.

Mrs Bulley (*off*) . . . Well then, find out who *did*, Lydia.

Lydia Yes, Mrs Bulley. (*Composing herself*) Miss Willingforth?

Tracey Yes?

Lydia Would you go in now, please.

Tracey shimmies to the door. Lydia frowns at her disapprovingly. Tracey winks at Karen, who gives her the thumbs up. Tracey goes into the inner office.

Mrs Bulley (*off*) Ah, Miss Willingforth? Close the door, will you?

Lydia (*half to herself*) Well, I don't know how I'm supposed to know, I'm sure . . .

Karen I beg your pardon?

Lydia Why half these wretched girls haven't turned up for their interviews.

Karen Really?

Lydia I mean, they've all been going back to their agencies and saying that someone here's been telling them at the front desk that they need to speak fluent Russian. I mean, who on earth would tell them that? Ridiculous. (*Sniffing*) I don't think that one's going to last long. If there's one thing Mrs Bulley can't stand it's perfume. She even objects to my talc.

Karen Well, I only hope the aroma of my coal-tar soap's worn off, then. I'm afraid I'm rather addicted to it.

They laugh. The office door opens and Tracey comes out looking rather upset.

Mrs Bulley (*off*) . . . Thank you. I should try the club just round the corner, dear. They're always on the lookout for new hostesses. Next.

Tracey (*muttering*) Old bitch . . .

She glares at Karen, who only smiles at her demurely.

(*In a low tone*) I'll get you for that . . .

Karen (*quietly and sweetly*) Oh, yes? I'd like to see you try, you brainless little bimbo.

Something in Karen's expression makes Tracey hurry out rapidly.

Mrs Bulley (*off*) Next. Come along. Come along.

Lydia Miss Knightly . . .?

Karen Thank you, you've been so helpful.

Karen crosses to the office door, smiles at Lydia and goes inside.

Mrs Bulley (*off*) Miss Knightly?

Karen Mrs Bulley? How do you do? So nice to meet you. I'll close the door, shall I?

The door closes. The voices cut off.

Lydia (*smiling to herself*) What a nice woman . . .

The lights fade and the office scene changes quite rapidly to bring us to –

SCENE TWO

10.00 a.m.

The grounds around Furtherfield House. A wooded part. Dappled sunlight. Birds sing. Henry appears. He is out for a mid-morning walk. He has on another, less extreme, country outfit. One he's presumably found about the house. He has a home-made stick and has been stepping out. He stops now, rather breathless. He sits on a convenient log and looks up at the trees with pleasure and listens to the birds. The life of a country squire is one he's never experienced before. He's enjoying it. His peace is disturbed by the sound of a light motor-bike engine, revving and spluttering as it approaches.

Oliver *(off)* Go on, go on, keep going, keep going, you stupid creature . . .

The engine finally stalls. Silence.

(Off) Oh, knickers.

Oliver enters pushing the bike. Both he and it are very muddy.

(Unsurprised, as ever, at seeing Henry) Oh, hi!

Henry Hallo.

Oliver *(stopping)* Stupid machine keeps stalling. I think there may be something in the fuel. A bit of grit, possibly.

Henry Or a ploughed field.

Oliver Yes. Scrambling. It's great fun.

Henry Looks it.

Oliver When the weather's filthy, then I prefer to race around the house. But today, it's just too good to be cooped up indoors, don't you agree?

86

Henry Absolutely.

Oliver Care for a go?

Henry No, thanks.

Oliver Also a great way to hunt rabbits.

Henry Don't they tend to hear you coming?

Oliver Yah, they tend to. But you can always get the deaf ones. (*He laughs*) Right. See you later.

Henry See you later.

Oliver (*shaping to give his machine a running start*) Come on, you stupid creature . . . Hup!

He trots off and, fairly soon after he is out of sight, the engine bursts into life.

(Off, *triumphantly*) Yee-haw!

The engine revs, recedes a little, then splutters and stops again.

(*Distant*) Oh, knickers.

Henry smiles. The birds resume singing. He stands and is about to resume his walk. He takes a couple of paces and then –

Imogen (*off, urgently*) Whoa . . .! Whoa . . .! Whoa, boy! Easy, Silas . . . Easy! Silas, don't be so bloody pig-headed! Whoa, Silas . . . Whoa! Whoa, Silas . . .! (*A cry*) Sil-a-a-a-a-a-as . . .!

The sound of a body crashing into the bracken. The triumphant whinny of a horse. Silence. Henry stands riveted. Imogen groans in pain.

(*Faintly, in pain*) Oh, shit. Oh, bollocks. You are a bastard, Silas. How could you do this to me? Again? Oh . . . oh . . . Everything's broken . . . Oh!

Henry (*peering into the undergrowth*) Hallo.

Imogen Oh!

Henry Hallo . . . you all right?

Imogen No. Who's that?

Henry (*moving towards the sound of her*) Me. Hallo.

Imogen crawls into the clearing on all fours. She is almost as muddy as Oliver was. She has obviously landed full length on her side. She has mud all down one side from face to toe. She is, of course, in full riding kit.

Imogen (*as she crawls*) Ooo! Eee! Ooo! Aaaa!

Henry (*seeing her*) Oh my word, let me . . .

He takes her arm and tries to help her to her feet.

Imogen Who's that, is that . . .? (*Seeing who it is*) Oh, it's you.

Henry Come and sit over here and get your –

Imogen (*a great cry of pain as she tries to stand on her ankle*) Yarr! Ooh! No. Not on that one. Let me sit down.

Henry Here.

He guides her down. She sits on the log.

Imogen Thanks.

Henry Is your – horse all right? I presume that was a horse you were riding?

Imogen He's been called other things. No, my horse has never been better, thank you. Laughing his head off all the way home.

Henry Oh.

Imogen Take a tip. Never own a horse with a sense of humour. Hallo, you're –

Henry Henry Bell.

Imogen Yes. Imogen Staxton-Billing. We met at the weekend, didn't we?

Henry Yes.

Imogen I – seem to recall being rather rude to you. I'm sorry.

Henry Oh, no.

Imogen It wasn't the best of days. That's my only excuse. (*Slight pause*) It's no excuse at all really, but that's the only one I can offer you.

Henry Please, forget all about it.

Imogen Someone said you were Karen Knightly's accountant. Is that right?

Henry Yes.

Imogen Yes. Well, you see I rather jumped to the conclusion that you and she were together – if you know what I mean.

Henry Oh no.

Imogen You're not?

Henry Not really.

Imogen Not really? What's not really?

Henry Not at all.

Imogen Glad to hear it.

Henry stares at her. Imogen stares back at him for a moment.

(*Suddenly*) Do you think you could possibly help me?

Henry How do you mean?

Imogen Up.

Henry Up. Yes, of course. I'll help you to the house.

He helps her to her feet.

Imogen No, it's quite all right. I'll totter home. It's not far. Ah!

She winces as she tries to put weight on her ankle.

Henry You couldn't possibly totter anywhere. Here.

He lends her his shoulder.

Come on. Up to the house.

Imogen Is Karen there today, by any chance?

Henry (*rather guiltily*) No – she's – in London. I think.

Imogen Ah. OK.

She allows Henry to lend her support.

Henry That's it. That's it. When we get back we can phone a doctor.

Imogen No, it's all right. I'll bathe it, it'll be fine. It's only a sprain . . .

Henry (*as they go*) Now we don't know that necessarily –

Imogen Yes, honestly, I'm sure it is. I've got absolutely pathetic ankles. I'm constantly doing this sort of thing. You always feel such a fool, too . . .

As they go, the lights cross-fade again and we return once more to –

SCENE THREE

10.30 a.m.

The Lembridge Tennit building. This time, the outer area of Bruce Tick's office. In many ways similar to the other office we have seen. The phone on the desk is ringing. Lydia and Karen enter. They stand in the doorway.

Lydia (*evidently concluding a brief tour*) . . . And, finally, this is Mr Tick's office. This is where you'll be working.

Karen Oh, how lovely and light.

Lydia That'll be your desk . . .

Karen It's all so beautifully decorated, isn't it?

Lydia (*rather doubtfully*) Yes . . .

Bruce Tick an overweight, mid-thirties dynamic executive, comes whirling in from his inner sanctum.

Bruce (*yelling to no one in particular*) . . . Three billion profit at the last quarter, you'd think we could afford someone to answer the bloody phones . . . (*Answers phone*) Hallo . . . Bruce Tick speaking . . . Tell me all – Hallo, sweetie. Good morning to you . . . (*Listens*) Uh-huh . . . uh-huh . . .

As he speaks, he gives Karen and Lydia the briefest of glances, failing to note who they are at all.

(*To them*) Sorry, beautifuls, won't keep you a moment. (*Into phone*) Yes, my sweet. Yes . . . yes . . . Well, rest assured it will be with you tomorrow morning. At the latest. This is my first day, I have barely unpacked the briefcase and the place is like early closing day on the *Marie Celeste*. Yes, yes, right. Will do, sweetie. Will do. Love to Helga – Hilda, rather . . . Yes, will do. Bye.

He slams his hand down on the phone and immediately punches up an internal number.

Lydia Mr Tick . . .?

Bruce (*to the phone*) I don't believe this . . . (*As he punches another number, to Lydia*) Just one moment, I'll be right with you, my sweet . . . (*Into phone*) Rachel, I have been trying since nine, I cannot get a reply from Mrs Bulley's office. I think she has finally taken an overdose of formaldehyde and pickled herself. Would you be a sweetie and stick your head out of your office and tell that twelve-ply plank of an assistant of hers that I want a secretary *now*, not tomorrow. I don't care if its stocking seams are crooked and it looks like the rear end of a turnip, I need someone now. OK? Thank you so much, my sweet. Nothing personal. My love to Derek when you see him . . . Dennis, rather . . . Will do.

He puts down the phone.

Lydia Mr Tick . . .?

Bruce My sweetie. I am so sorry. Now, what can I do for you . . .?

Lydia Mr Tick, this is Miss Knightly. She'll be helping you out until we've advertised for a permanent appointment.

Bruce Miss Knightly, you come like the relief of . . . (*He looks at her for the first time*) Relief of . . . (*His voice trails away*)

Karen How do you do, Mr Tick.

Bruce Yes. Welcome. Sit down. Please. Help yourself to a desk.

Lydia Well, I'll leave you then. Anything you want, Karen, just phone me on 961, all right?

Karen Thank you, Lydia, I will.

Lydia Bye.

Karen Bye.

Bruce (*who has been staring at Karen in disbelief*) Er . . .
Linda . . .

Lydia Lydia.

Bruce Lydia. Er . . . (*To Karen*) Excuse me. (*To Lydia,
confidentially*) This is just temporary, I take it?

Lydia Yes, as I say, just until . . .

Bruce Only I don't think I can work with that for long.

Lydia Well, we did the best we could, Mr Tick. Mrs
Smith left very suddenly, as you know . . .

Bruce (*indicating Karen*) I mean, really. Couldn't you
find anything better than that . . . ?

Lydia (*in a fierce undertone*) There was very, very little
choice, Mr Tick. We're very lucky to get her.

Bruce Who's very lucky?

Lydia She's very highly qualified, she has excellent
references and if you lose her we cannot guarantee you
a replacement until Wednesday at the earliest. So please
try and work with her.

Bruce All right. All right.

Lydia (*to Karen*) Bye.

Karen *A bientôt.*

*Lydia goes out. Bruce turns to cope with Karen, who
sits demurely at her new desk.*

Bruce Well now, Miss . . . I suppose we'd better start by
getting each other's names. I'm Bruce Tick. Call me
Bruce. And you're –

Karen Karen Knightly. Call me Karen . . .

Bruce (*a little confused by her pronunciation*) Kieron?

Karen No, Karen.

Bruce Oh, *Karen*.

Karen (*giggling*) Kieron's a boy's name.

Bruce (*laughing*) Yes, of course it is . . . (*Under his breath*) Jesus. (*Briskly*) Right. Now, Karen. I don't know you. You don't yet know me. We're both new here. This is my first day. This is yours. We're going to have to do a certain amount of learning as we go, all right? Thinking on our tootsies, OK?

Karen Yes, Bruce.

Bruce Now, there's a few things you ought to know about me straight away. I work hard and I play hard. All right?

Karen Yes, Bruce.

Bruce I don't like half-measures, pissing about or pussyfooting around, all right?

Karen You believe in calling a spade a spade, Bruce?

Bruce A what?

Karen A spade.

Bruce Oh, a spade, yes. I'm hard but I'm fair. All right? You support me, Kieron, you give me that hundred and five per cent I'm asking for, and I promise you, you will have a ball, baby. But you let me down, Kieron and . . . (*He brings his hand down on her desk*) . . . OK. You know what I mean? (*He repeats the gesture*)

Karen Oh yes, I do, Bruce. (*She repeats his gesture*)

Bruce (*faintly suspicious*) Right. Now this will be our typical day. I shall be here. Day in day out, rain or shine, five days a week at a whisker before nine a.m. You will do the same. I don't want excuses that the tube's broken down or the buses are on strike. Remember, I'll have slogged in from Sunningdale, so that won't wash with me.

Karen No, Bruce.

Bruce At nine sharp we cope with correspondence. Is your shorthand good?

Karen Lightning, Bruce.

Bruce It'll need to be. We'll work a hard, hard morning together until half past twelve. At which point, the demands of this job are such that I need to be out of this office, wheeling and dealing elsewhere. So from then on, back here at homebase, it'll all be down to you, Katherine. All right?

Karen Absolutely, Bruce.

Bruce The next time you see me then will be at half past four to cope with messages, when I'll expect my letters typed and ready for signature. As for going-home time – well, let me say this – (*Significantly,*) Don't ever expect to go home until the day is finished, all right? The boyfriend can wait, the hairdo can wait. Business first. Yes?

Karen Yes, Bruce.

Bruce If you don't like the sound of that, you'd better walk out through that door now.

Karen Oh, no.

Bruce Sure?

Karen No. I think I'll find working with you a tremendous challenge.

Bruce I hope you do. I hope you do, Kerry. All right, shall we get under way? I've a pile of letters on my desk, shall we start with those?

Karen Yes, of course.

Bruce Good girl. I want to make one call, then I'll buzz you, all right?

Karen Yes, Bruce.

Bruce Five minutes. Get yourself a pencil, go to the loo and prepare yourself for a long, hard slog.

Bruce goes into his office. When he is gone, Karen gives a slightly over-the-top shudder of disgust.

Karen Yeerrk!

She then springs into action. Opens her bag and produces a personal cassette player/recorder. Also her address book and a small portable radio phone. She finds a number and keys it in.

Hallo . . . Elaine . . . It's Karen Knightly. Yes . . . I got it . . . Absolute doodle . . . Isn't she . . . Yes – but Elaine, he's *revolting* . . . Yeerrrrk . . . Yes. Listen . . . I can't talk long . . . About the letters – if I bike the tape over to you by about one o'clock can you have them typed and back to me by four fifteen? . . . Yes . . . Sure. (*Opening her desk drawer*) Yes, there's some here . . . fifty sheets of headed paper . . . both sizes. Yeah . . . Please, *yes,* the envelopes as well. I couldn't possibly cope with those . . . Right. (*She opens another drawer*) Yes . . . per letter, yes – do you want it in advance? . . . Yes, sure, either way suits me . . . Yes . . . Bye.

Karen disconnects. On the spur of the moment, she decides to make another call. She punches another number (two keys only) and waits.

Winnie? It's Miss Karen . . . Is Mr Bell there? . . . Is he? *Is* he? Wonderful. Listen, Winnie, don't disturb him then . . . Just give him a message from me, all right? . . .

Are you ready? . . . Karen is condition red . . . red, all right? R-E-D. Yes.

The intercom on her desk buzzes.

OK. Must go, Winnie. Bye.

She puts away the phone in her bag and grabs up a pencil and rummages in the drawer for a notebook.

Bruce (*from his office*) Katie! Come on, come on!

Karen Coming, Bruce . . .

She switches on her recorder, sets it to record, puts it back in her bag and takes that, together with her notebook and pencil, into Bruce's office. As she does this –

Bruce (*yelling once more*) Katie! Shift your bum, girl.

Karen Yes, I'm coming, Bruce. (*To herself as she hurries out*) Yeeeerrrk!

The lights cross-fade to reveal –

SCENE FOUR

11.30 a.m.
A drawing room at Furtherfield House. Imogen is seated. She has removed one riding boot and sock and is resting her injured foot on a stool. Her face is still muddy. Norma is kneeling, dabbing at Imogen's foot with a bag of ice. Henry stands watching anxiously.

Henry Is that any better at all?

Imogen Well, it doesn't hurt as much.

Henry Good, good.

Imogen But then I have lost all sensation in my entire leg.

Henry I think the ice is good for it, though.

Imogen Well, I'll take your word for it. I feel like a deep-frozen chicken.

Henry (*gallantly*) You don't look like a deep-frozen chicken.

Imogen God knows what I look like . . . (*To Norma*) Thank you. Honestly, that's just terrific.

Norma That sufficient, madam?

Imogen Thank you. Ample.

Norma rises and stands a little apart from them, holding the ice bag, uncertain what to do next.

Henry You're sure you won't see a doctor?

Imogen Not unless it gets worse. I may have to ask you for a lift home, though.

Henry Ah.

Imogen That a problem?

Henry I don't drive, I'm afraid.

Imogen Ah. That is a slight snag. Oh listen, if you get someone to phone our place, Anthony should be back for his lunch round about now. He could pick me up.

Winnie enters carrying a tray with a piece of paper on it.

Henry Yes, I'm sorry I couldn't be . . . Ah, Winnie, would you phone Mrs Staxton-Billing's husband and ask him if he'd be so kind as to come and run her home.

Winnie Yes, sir, I will, sir. There's a telephone message here, sir. (*With a look at Imogen*) From Miss . . .

Henry Oh, yes. Thank you.

Henry takes the piece of paper and glances at it briefly.

(*Pretending to make sense of it*) Uh-huh. Uh-huh. Thank you, Winnie.

Norma is starting to shiver badly.

Imogen (*noticing this*) I say. Is this girl here all right?

Henry Norma? Are you all right, Norma?

Norma (*teeth chattering*) Yes, sir.

Winnie It'll be with holding the ice, sir.

Henry Good Lord. For heaven's sake, put it down, girl.

Winnie It's all right, sir. I'll deal with that. (*Sotto, to Norma*) Come on then. In the kitchen. Throw the ice away in the sink and save the bag. Off you go. That's it.

Norma goes out, still shivering.

She's very young, you see, madam. She's still only learning.

Imogen Yes.

Winnie She'll be better when she's older.

Imogen Yes. I hope she makes it.

Winnie I'll telephone straight away, sir.

Winnie goes out.

Imogen (*casually*) Are you staying down for a bit?

Henry (*guardedly*) Yes.

Imogen Good. Well, I must – we must – repay your hospitality. For being so gallant.

Henry (*laughing*) Ha. Well.

Imogen Perhaps you'll come round and have a drink with us.

Henry Thank you. That would be lovely.

Imogen We live just down the hill there. We have the farm.

Henry Ah. Your husband's a farmer?

Imogen Yes. (*Pause*) Amongst other things.

Henry Ah-ha. (*Pause*) I don't know anything about farming.

Imogen No, well. Nor do I really. My family were in textiles.

Henry Oh, were they? Wool?

Imogen I beg your pardon?

Henry Were they in wool?

Imogen (*puzzled*) No, I don't think so.

Henry Cotton?

Imogen No. I think it was mostly sort of nylon, really.

Henry Ah.

Imogen Daddy made an awful lot of money out of it, whatever it was. I'm afraid I never took much interest. He sold the business, anyway, while I was still fairly young. Then he retired.

Henry (*interested*) Uh-huh.

Imogen Then he died.

Henry (*sympathetically*) Ah.

Imogen And left it all to me.

Henry (*brightening*) Oh, well.

Pause.

Imogen And I seem to have given most of it to Anthony. Who's busy spending it as fast as he can.

Henry On the farm?

Imogen (*laughing sarcastically*) Not likely. The whole place is falling down. No, please. Don't get the wrong impression – he hasn't frittered it all away or anything like that. Well, not much of it. No, he's put a lot of it into my uncle's firm. That's my Uncle Marcus. Who was there the other day as well. Did you meet him?

Henry Colonel Lipscott?

Imogen That's him. Anyway, Anthony's a director with his firm. A business which seems to eat money non-stop. God knows how much longer they'll stay afloat.

Henry What do they do?

Imogen They make pipes.

Henry What, briar pipes, you mean? That sort?

Imogen No, concrete pipes. Huge things. Round, you know.

Henry Oh yes.

Imogen Sewage and so on.

Henry I see. Literally throwing your money down the drain, then?

He laughs.

Imogen (*unsmiling*) Yes, I suppose that could be quite funny. In other circumstances I'd probably find it a hoot myself.

Henry Sorry.

Imogen suddenly gives a sob. It is quite unexpected and startles Henry.

Er . . . Anything the –?

Imogen No. No. No.

Winnie looks in.

Winnie Mr Staxton-Billing is on his way, madam.

Imogen Thank you.

Winnie goes.

Henry You all right?

Imogen Yes. I think it's this house. I shouldn't have come here. Whenever I come here it does things to me. It's knowing that . . . You probably know – if you don't then someone's bound to tell you sooner or later – that Karen Knightly is my husband's mistress. Had you heard that? Of course you had. Karen must have told you. She doesn't care, she tells everybody.

Henry (*cautiously*) I heard that she was.

Imogen Was?

Henry But not any longer.

Imogen Who told you that?

Henry That's what I heard.

Imogen They still are.

Henry Are you sure?

Imogen (*snapping*) Of course I'm sure. I'm not a fool.

Henry No.

Imogen I may fall off horses and let other women screw my husband but I'm not a complete fool, you know.

She starts to cry in earnest now.

Henry Oh now, come on . . .

Imogen (*sobbing*) Oh God, my foot hurts – it hurts so much . . .

Henry Your foot?

Imogen (*rocking to and fro*) It's so painful, you've no idea.

Henry Shall I rub it?

Imogen What?

Henry Shall I rub it? Would you like me to rub it?

Imogen I don't care . . . I don't care any more . . .

Henry (*taking her foot*) Here.

He rubs away at her ankle.

That better? That doing the trick?

Imogen suddenly leans forward, seizes him and pulls him to her, hugging him fiercely.

Imogen Oh, hold me. Just hold me, please.

Henry Yes, right, right.

Imogen Please hold me.

Henry Yes, yes, I've got you . . .

Imogen (*a great pent-up cry of grief*) Aaah!

She rocks to and fro in his arms. Henry clings on to her. He has very little option. Slowly the crying subsides.

She stops her rocking and releases him. Henry also lets go.

(*Much calmer*) Thank you. Thank you very much. You're a very understanding man.

Henry (*modestly*) No, it's just . . .

Imogen You don't know how much I needed that cry. It's silly. I hadn't had one for ages. Well, on my own when I'm feeding the pigs or something, but that's not the same thing at all, is it? You really do need someone else, you see. A lot of women I know have girl friends. I'm sure that's one of the reasons they have them. Someone to cry with. I don't have any for some reason. Anthony saw them all off. He either made passes at them or shouted at them. He didn't like me having them, anyway. Now all I can do is sit on my own with the kids while he's off boozing with all his hearty men friends. When he's not here, servicing Miss –

Henry (*gently*) I don't think you'll find he's with Karen, any more.

Imogen (*growing angry again*) Well, he's certainly doing it with someone and it bloody well isn't with me, I can promise you that much. (*She checks herself*) Oh, what's it matter anyway? He can have them all. Who cares? He can have the whole Girl Guide movement, I don't care. (*Feeling her face*) I must look worse than ever now, don't I?

Henry (*totally in love with her*) You look . . . beautiful.

Imogen stares at him.

Quite beautiful. Honestly.

Imogen I warn you, if you say things like that, I shall start crying again.

Henry Please. Be my guest.

Imogen If you're pitying me, forget it.

Henry (*hastily*) Oh, no. Don't worry about that. I'm not the sort to do that. I never pity people. Not in my nature.

Imogen Really? You surprise me.

Henry I kick children. I jostle old-age pensioners. I knock over flag-sellers for the blind. And I go out of my way to run over hedgehogs in the road.

Imogen You don't even drive, you told me.

Henry With my bare feet.

Imogen (*smiling*) God. One of those tough sort of men? I see.

Henry You bet.

Imogen Heavens. I'd better watch my step then.

Henry Unless you want to feel the back of my hand.

Imogen Oh, I don't know. (*Taking his hand in hers*) It looks a very gentle sort of hand really.

> *She kisses it lightly. Henry moves in to return the kiss on her mouth. Imogen evades him gently and easily.*

Now. My husband's car is even now roaring up the drive and I don't know about you but everything's moving a little bit too fast and I need a breather.

Henry OK.

Imogen Sorry. So, to bring you down to earth again, would you help me to put my sock on?

Henry Well . . . It'll have to do instead, won't it?

He takes up the sock and starts to help her on with it.

Imogen I'll leave the boot, I'll never get that on again. Lucky I got it off.

Henry Tell me if I'm hurting you.

Imogen It's OK. I think the worst thing is the frostbite from that wretched girl's ice.

Henry You have a beautiful foot.

Imogen You should meet the other one, it's half the size.

Henry Maybe I will. One day.

He kisses her foot, gently.

Imogen (*sternly*) Stop that! Pull! (*It hurts*) Ah!

Henry Sorry.

Imogen It's all right. Keep going. Aaah!

Henry (*alarmed*) Sorry. I must be hurting you.

Imogen It doesn't matter. I can do with the pain. I'm enjoying it. Go on, don't mind me. Ah! Ah! AAAAH!

As this is occurring, Anthony enters and stands in the doorway, watching them. Winnie hovers behind him. Henry manages to get Imogen's sock back on.

Thank you. (*Seeing Anthony, coolly*) Oh, hallo.

Anthony Hallo. Sorry to interrupt things . . .

Henry (*getting up guiltily*) I was just putting your wife's sock on.

Anthony (*to Imogen*) You coming, then? Only I'm midmouthful through my lunch.

Imogen (*drily*) Yes, darling, I just have this little trouble walking, you see.

Anthony Serve you right. I told you to sell him ages ago.

Imogen I am not selling Silas.

Anthony He's far too strong for you. You want to buy yourself a nice, placid, fat old mare. Something you can handle.

Imogen Well, I won't argue with you, you're the expert on placid mares, aren't you, darling . . .? (*She hobbles to the door and turns*) Goodbye, Henry. And thank you very much.

Henry Goodbye, Mrs –

Imogen Imogen.

Henry Imogen.

Imogen goes out. Anthony gives Henry a look and then follows her. Winnie makes to follow them.

Er, Winnie, just a second . . .

Winnie Sir?

Henry (*fumbling in his pocket*) This phone message you took from Miss Karen . . .

He produces the piece of paper.

Winnie Yes, sir?

Henry I can't quite make it out. Is this – Miss Karen's conditioning rods . . .?

Winnie I think she said condition red, sir.

Henry Oh, condition *red*. I see. Thank you, Winnie.

Winnie Sir.

Winnie goes out.

Henry Condition *red*. My God . . .

*The lights fade on him as Henry follows Winnie out
and the scene changes back to –*

SCENE FIVE

4.15 p.m.
   *The Lembridge Tennit Building. The outer area of
Bruce Tick's office. Karen is sitting at her desk filling in
time by trying to master her electric typewriter.
Unfortunately, even the first principles seem to elude her.*

Karen (*glaring at it*) Stupid machine.

   *Lydia sticks her head round the door. She carries a
large envelope.*

Lydia Hallo.

Karen (*rather forgetting herself*) Oh, hi! (*Remembering*)
Hallo.

Lydia Had a good day?

Karen Wonderful. So exciting.

Lydia Get on all right with old Tick?

Karen Oh yes, he's a very stimulating man. Full of ideas.

Lydia Yes, well. Just watch him. Especially after lunch.
He's got the old roving hands, I'm afraid. Mind you,
I shouldn't think you'll . . . (*Checking herself in time*)
I shouldn't think you'll be the sort of person who won't
be able to cope with him.

Karen Oh, no. Men never try that sort of thing with me.
Well, never more than once anyway.

   She smiles.

Lydia Oh, this just came by messenger for you. (*She holds up the envelope*) It was at the front desk. If it's something you urgently need, then it's best to collect it yourself. They do bring things round but in their own sweet time.

Karen Thank you. I'll give it to Bruce when he comes back from lunch.

Lydia Oh, yes. Only four fifteen, isn't it? It's all right for some people, eh?

Karen (*laughing*) Oh, yes.

Lydia See you tomorrow.

Karen Night.

> *Lydia goes. As soon as she's gone, Karen swiftly opens the envelope and removes a sheaf of letters and their envelopes all neatly typed and ready for signature. Also the original tape cassette which she puts straight in her bag. She drops the main envelope in the bin and arranges the letters neatly by her machine. She starts to put the cover back on her typewriter.*

Oh, dearie me, what a day.

> *At this moment, Bruce rolls in. He has wined and dined well, as he does every day. His manner is more expansive than ever.*

Bruce Good afternoon, my little sweetie. My little petal. How are we coping, then? Keeping our little noses above the water, are we . . . ?

Karen (*playfully*) Just about, Bruce. Just about.

Bruce Phone messages?

Karen Nothing urgent. I left them on your desk.

Bruce (*coming round the back of her*) Splendid, they can keep till tomorrow. Did you finish my letters, then?

Karen Just done the last one.

Bruce (*patting her on the shoulders*) Good. Clever girl. Right, I'll sign them before I go . . .

Karen Shall I bring them in to you?

Bruce No, it's all right, my sweet, I'll sign them here. Shift yourself, that's it.

He helps Karen from the chair, somewhat unnecessarily. She moves rapidly our of his grip and allows Bruce to sit.

Oh, lovely warm chair.

Karen smiles at his playfulness.

(*Snapping his fingers*) Pen, pen, pen, sweetheart. Come along.

Karen is forced to move in to the desk again and leans past Bruce to find a pen for him. As she does this, Bruce pats her bottom. He blows on his fingers as if they had been burnt.

Oooh! That's nice and warm too, eh?

Karen (*handing him the pen and moving away again*) I'm very fortunate. I have excellent circulation . . .

Bruce Oh, oh, oh. Enough said.

He scans the letters cursorily, scrawling his signature on the bottom of each after he's done so. He burps softly.

Karen Did you have a pleasant lunch, Bruce?

Bruce (*still engaged in his task*) Very good. Excellent. There's a first-rate steak house. Just opened round the comer. I'm afraid you'll find, Kieron, after you've been with me for a couple of days. You'll find I have one major weakness . . .

Karen Really, Bruce, you do surprise me . . .

Bruce You know what that is?

Karen I couldn't begin to hazard a guess, Bruce.

Bruce Food.

Karen Food?

Bruce I cannot resist it. Good food, I mean. French, Italian, Chinese, Greek, Indonesian . . . Plain basic English, even. I don't mind. So long as it's good. Do you know what I had today?

Karen No?

Bruce Want to hear?

Karen Oh yes, please.

Bruce We had mulligatawny soup to start with. Then fresh lobster. Then I had whole roast guinea-fowl, all the trimmings, of course, game chips, lovely home-made stuffing, breadcrumbs, beautiful firm Brussels sprouts, roast potatoes and fresh crispy *mangetout*. I love *mangetout* like that. Then, to finish with, we had something I haven't tasted since I was a kid. Steamed treacle sponge. Moist. Plenty of treacle. Coffee. *Petits fours*. And with that we had, what? A bottle of Chablis, a bottle of Nuits-St-Georges, and a glass of magnificent vintage port. That sound all right to you?

Karen Well, I must say the canteen here does a very tasty cheese salad but that's not quite in the same bracket . . .

Bruce No, but you see with my metabolism – I'm very fortunate – I can eat all that and within two hours, literally, I'm going to feel hungry again, you see. Because although I'm putting it in, I'm simultaneously burning it up. My wife hates me for that. She really hates me for it.

Karen Does she?

Bruce I mean, if she eats so much as a water biscuit she's immediately the size of a house. I mean, the kids are like me. They can eat anything, but Hilary – that's my wife – well, we call her Lettuce Leaf Lettie.

Karen laughs merrily.

She can't drink either. Same reason.

Karen What a beastly life for her.

Bruce Oh, I don't know. She gets a few fringe benefits, don't worry. (*He winks at her*) And the one thing she never has to worry about is me. You know what I mean? Because I'm there. She knows I work hard. She expects that, she married me knowing that. And she reaps the benefits of that. She's got a beautiful home, beautiful car, beautiful garden, beautiful kids . . .

Karen I bet she's beautiful, too.

Bruce She's not bad. I have to admit it. I've never kicked her out of bed yet, let's put it that way . . . (*He laughs*)

Karen (*laughing with him*) And even if you did I'm sure you have beautiful bedside rugs too, don't you . . .

Bruce What's that? – No, seriously, she knows – Hilary knows that she has got me one hundred per cent.

Karen She's a very lucky woman.

Bruce (*tapping his chest*) No time-sharing with this one.

Karen Wonderful.

Bruce How many men can say that, hand on heart?

Karen Very, very, very few.

Bruce Exactly. I mean I kid around, sweetie, but . . . as I always tell . . . her every day when I leave home in the morning, I leave my balls back there with her in Sunningdale.

Karen What a wonderful gesture of loyalty.

Bruce So. (*Jokily*) Hands off, all right . . . (*Rising*) Oh, God . . . What's the time? Yes. Listen, sweetie. Can you phone my wife, can you phone Hilary for me now? I gave you the number, didn't I?

Karen Yes.

She takes an address book from her drawer and sits.

Bruce I promised to have a drink with this man from JCC, OK? Phone her and tell I'll be on the later train, if she can meet that. OK?

Karen Yes, I'll do that, Bruce.

Bruce See you in the morning, then. Good girl, you've done well. (*Waving at the letters*) Excellent work. Good.

Karen Thank you, Bruce.

Bruce (*as he goes*) Nine sharp, OK? I'll be waiting.

Karen Right-o, Bruce. You betcher.

Bruce (*seeing someone in the corridor outside, as he goes*) Oh, Ted, Ted. I'm glad I caught you, sweetie. Just a quickie, love . . .

He has gone. Karen looks up the number. She pauses on the point of dialling. She goes into her bag, humming softly to herself as she produces her cassette recorder. She puts it on the table and finds a pre-recorded cassette in her bag. She loads the machine and tests it. A short burst of fairly funky pop. Karen goes to the door and checks the coast is clear. She returns to the desk, sits and dials.

Karen (*humming softly as she does so*) I left my balls in San Francisco . . .

She listens. The phone the other end starts to ring. She starts up her cassette machine and lets it play near to the mouthpiece. She listens.

(*As someone answers, yelling to an imaginary person in an altogether younger, laid-back, sexier voice*) Stop it, don't do that . . . Hallo, sorry about that. Hallo . . . Is that Mrs Tick? This is Karen. I'm Bruce's new sec. Hi! Sorry about the din. Hi! Look, Bruce said can you meet the later train? OK? Because he's been held up here. OK? Got that? Super. What's that? . . . No, I just started today. Yeah . . . If you don't mind my saying so, I think you're frightfully lucky. I think he's just completely fabulous. Yeah. Must dash. Sorry. Bye.

She rings off and switches off the cassette player.

(*With a little secret cheer of malicious delight*) Yeah!

She sits savouring the moment as the lights change again to –

SCENE SIX

11.00 a.m.

The piggery at the Staxton-Billings' farm. A lot of appropriate sounds as Imogen, still limping slightly, comes through with a bucket. She is, again, quite grubby, this time from mucking out. Wellington boots, old jeans and a sweater. Hair tied back with a scarf. Rather sweaty.

Imogen (*shouting at a particularly insistent sow*) Not yet, not yet, you greedy girl. You wait till it's time.

Henry sticks his head round the door.

(*Continuing her conversation*) It's not food, no. Does it look like food, you stupid thing? No. You know it's not. You just wait until . . .

She is suddenly aware that she is being watched. She looks up at Henry.

Oh. God. Hallo, there.

Henry Hallo.

Imogen I was just talking to Sarah.

Henry looks around puzzled.

The sow, there.

Henry Oh, yes. Do all of them have names?

Imogen Oh, Lord, no. Most of them come and go too quickly for that. No, Sarah's a bit special. We've had her quite a time. (*Indicating another sty*) Those over there, do you see . . . Those are all hers.

Henry looks into another sty.

Henry (*smiling*) Oh, yes. (*To Sarah*) Congratulations.

Imogen They're being slaughtered tomorrow.

Henry Oh, really?

Imogen Somebody's breakfast.

Henry Oh, well. (*Philosophically*) That's life, I suppose.

Imogen It is round here.

They stare at each other.

Well. This is a surprise.

Henry Yes. Well, I was out on a stroll. And I thought I'd – see where you lived . . .

Imogen Well, not in here.

Henry Oh no . . . Only I just happened to catch sight of you coming in here. And I thought, well, it would be a bit rude of me not to come and say hallo.

Imogen Well, hallo. (*Slight pause. She self-consciously brushes her face*) We always seem to meet when I'm covered in something.

Henry How's the ankle?

Imogen Oh, perfectly fine. I woke up this morning, I'd practically forgotten about it.

Henry Good.

He smiles at her.

Imogen Anthony's just across the meadow somewhere, I think.

Henry Yes, I did happen to see him.

Imogen I see.

Henry He had some sort of gun with him.

Imogen Yes, I think he's after squirrels.

Henry Oh. You don't eat them as well, do you?

Imogen (*smiling*) No. Not yet, anyway.

Slight pause.

Henry I – I wanted to say – I wanted to tell you . . .
I really did want to tell you . . . to say how . . .

Imogen You don't have to say . . .

Henry No, I wanted to say just . . .

Imogen I know what you wanted to say . . .

Henry You do . . .?

Imogen And you don't need to say it. Really.

Henry It's just I . . .

Imogen All I want to say, from my side, is that I wanted
to say that too.

Henry You did?

Imogen Yes, I did.

Henry That's wonderful.

Imogen No, it's not wonderful at all. It's terrible.

Henry Terrible?

Imogen What are we going to do? It's awful. I never
thought this would happen to me. It's appalling.

Henry I don't think falling in love is appalling.

Imogen I went to bed last night hoping I'd sleep it off.
You know, like a cold. Only I didn't. When I woke up
this morning it was even worse. But you see, I don't
want to fall in love. Don't you understand? Not with
you. Not with anyone. I just want to get on with my life,
feed the pigs and – grow old. If you must know, I'm very
miserable. And I blame you entirely. It's nothing personal.

Henry (*startled by this outburst*) I'm sorry.

Imogen (*fiercely*) Just go away. Go on. Stop bothering me.

Henry (*retreating*) Right.

Imogen (*desperately*) No, don't go away. Please don't go away! Please!

Henry (*moving back to her again*) No, I won't. I won't.

Imogen Hold me. Just hold me.

Henry Right.

> *Henry holds her. She clings to him. He thinks about kissing her.*

Imogen No, don't kiss me. I don't want kissing. I just want holding.

Henry OK. Fine. Fine. Say when.

> *He continues to hold her.*

Imogen (*pushing him away*) What are we doing? What are we both doing?

Henry We're in love. That's what we're doing.

Imogen No, we're not.

Henry We are.

Imogen No.

Henry (*with some passion*) Of course we are. Do you think I'd be standing here holding you in a – pig shed – if I wasn't in love? I don't know about you but I'm in love. I'm forty-two years old, so don't you – try and tell me how I feel, you – you stupid woman. I love you.

Imogen (*affectionately*) Oh. Oh, Henry. (*She holds him again*)

Henry (*feeling this firm line is the one to follow*) That's better. Let's have less of that, please.

A distant gunshot from outside.

Ah, well. RIP one squirrel.

Imogen (*drawing away from him, calmly*) Henry, we're going to have to be very adult about this.

Henry Yes. How do you mean?

Imogen I mean, I don't want anybody hurt.

Henry Who's there to hurt?

Imogen The children.

Henry Oh yes.

Imogen And even Anthony. Though I don't know that he deserves all that consideration. Not after – how he's treated me. Is still treating me, come to that. But I've never believed that because one person behaves badly we all have to start.

Henry But surely if you're unhappy . . .

Imogen But if I left him, I might be even more unhappy, I don't know . . .

Henry Sounds unlikely.

Imogen Anthony'd never agree to let me go. He'd put up a hell of a fight.

Henry Would he?

Another gunshot.

Imogen I know he would.

Henry Even though he doesn't love you?

Imogen I'm afraid Anthony is not what you'd term one of the new men. The fact that he's been fooling around quite openly with Karen Knightly – has been for two years – doesn't automatically give me grounds for complaint. After all, what can I expect? He's a man. He's just pursuing his natural basic urges. I am merely a wife. A woman. No, not even a woman. An ex-woman.

Henry But surely most people would . . .

Imogen Most people here would utterly take his side, I'm afraid. We're not in Earls Court, you know.

Henry (*mystified*) Earls Court?

Imogen Well, wherever. Highgate, then. Wherever it is that women behave as badly as men. I'm out of touch. Round here, women are women and men are men. And ever more shall be so. Sarah there and I – we are not altogether dissimilar.

Henry You're much prettier.

Imogen Oh, do you think so? I think she's rather beautiful.

Two closer gunshots in quick succession.

Henry Grief, there can't be very much left alive out there. He must have slaughtered everything by now.

Imogen Sounds as if he's on his way back. We haven't settled anything, have we?

Henry We're hardly going to. Not here. Not now. We've established we're both in love. That's a major step forward. That'll keep me going for – oh, hours.

Another gunshot.

Maybe he keeps missing them.

Imogen Anthony's an excellent shot. He very rarely misses.

Henry Doesn't he? Well, maybe it's time I was . . .

Imogen (*smiling*) Maybe it is.

Henry Very – wonderful to have seen you.

Imogen Yes. See you in the chicken run some time.

Henry Why not?

They kiss Not for long but with conviction and enjoyment.

Whoo!

Imogen Whoo!

Henry Good.

Imogen Very.

Anthony enters suddenly. He is dressed for shooting and has a shotgun, broken open, over his arm. As usual, he barely seems to notice Henry but addresses his remarks to Imogen.

Anthony (*without stopping*) Somebody's left the bottom gate open and there's about a dozen heifers wandering all over the lane. I thought you might like to know.

Anthony goes out of the door.

Imogen Oh, God. Where's Clem? Can't Clem do it?

Anthony (*off*) Clem's doing the job he's being paid to do.

Imogen All right. (*To Henry*) Here we go then.

Henry I'm sorry, I think that may have been me. The gate. I had trouble with the string.

Imogen (*as she goes*) Don't worry. Come on. You can give me a hand.

Henry (*following her*) Well, I'll do my best. I'm not frightfully good with cows . . .

They both go out. A second and Anthony returns. He stands and watches them for a second as they disappear into the distance. He closes his shotgun abruptly and returns the way he came. As he does so, the lights change back to –

SCENE SEVEN

4.45 p.m.
Lembridge Tennit again. The outer area of Bruce Tick's office. The end of another day. Karen is opening another envelope of letters for signature when Bruce comes back from his lunch. He seems rather more subdued than usual. He also has indigestion. Karen, as she sees him, hastily gets rid of the envelope in which the letters were returned.

Karen Good evening, Bruce. Good lunch as usual?

Bruce (*abstractedly*) Pretty good, pretty good. Thank you. (*Seeing the letters*) These for me? Right.

Karen rises, as before, and allows him to sit in her chair. She is adept now at avoiding his hands. Actually, Bruce seems too abstracted this evening to grope. He starts to sign his letters.

(*Burping quietly*) Excuse me. (*As he signs*) I have to get off home early tonight, sweetie – if you can hold the fort for me . . .

Karen Of course I will, Bruce. You and Hilary going out, are you?

Bruce Er, no, no. Just thought I'd better put in an appearance. Cool the atmosphere.

Karen Oh dear.

Bruce No, it's nothing. It's just . . .

Karen Do you want to talk about it, Bruce?

Bruce Well, it's mad. It's crazy. But she – seems to think I'm up to something.

Karen Up to something?

Bruce You know – I'm playing around. Nooky. You know.

Karen Oh really, Bruce, how can she think that?

Bruce I don't know, it's just a series of . . . (*He burps again*) Excuse me.

Karen Who with?

Bruce Well . . . I hardly like to say this, but – with you.

Karen (*scandalised*) Me?

Bruce I know it's ridiculous.

Karen How on earth could she think that?

Bruce I know, she's just – you've obviously got a very . . . I think that your voice must sound different on the phone. That's all I can think.

Karen Really? I've always been told I have an excellent telephone manner but . . .

Bruce Hilary says you sound like a scrubber.

Karen (*indignantly*) A scrubber?

Bruce A tart, you know. I'm sorry, perhaps I shouldn't have said that.

Karen Well . . .

Bruce It's other things as well, you see. Like, you know I was in Birmingham for that meeting – last weekend.

Karen I know. I booked your hotel . . .

Bruce Exactly. And now I can't find the bill. Did I not give the bill to you? Are you sure?

Karen No, Bruce. If you remember I asked you for it on Monday evening.

Bruce If I had that bill she might believe me.

Karen She doesn't believe you?

Bruce She thinks I was in Dorset for some reason.

Karen Dorset?

Bruce This hotel – I've never even heard of the place – they posted back this nightdress this morning . . .

Karen Nightdress?

Bruce I opened it over breakfast. With a note saying my wife had left it behind last weekend . . .

Karen What was your wife doing in Dorset?

Bruce She wasn't in Dorset. That's the point. Nobody was. But she thinks I was. That's the point. (*He burps*) Excuse me.

Karen With me?

Bruce Probably. And then this nightdress turns up. Bright red frilly thing with bows on . . .

Karen (*disapprovingly*) Oh, no . . . I think I'll stay with my thermals, thank you . . .

Bruce I could almost believe someone was doing it – deliberately, only . . . I can't think . . . (*A thought crosses his mind*) No, he wouldn't do that sort of thing. No.

Karen Who's that?

Bruce No. Forget it. Anyway, you can cut it with a knife back home, I can tell you. At the moment. Here. (*He produces a small gift-wrapped parcel*) Look at that. Peace offerings. Has it come to this, my sweet? Answer, yes it has. (*He burps*) Excuse me.

Karen What is it?

Bruce Just a little pendant thing. Hilary likes to wear them.

Karen How lovely. That will cheer her up, I'm sure.

Bruce I hope to God it does. I'd better sign these and catch the early one.

Karen If you'll excuse me. I'll just pop to the loo . . .

Bruce Yes . . . Sure . . . (*He burps*) Excuse me.

Karen Indigestion, Bruce?

Bruce Just a touch. (*He burps*) Excuse me.

Karen leaves. Bruce takes the phone off the hook. He signs the letters with one hand while punching a number with the other.

Hallo – is that you, Damien? . . . It's Daddy, sweetie . . . Daddy . . . Now come on, Damien, it's Daddy. You want to talk to Daddy, don't you . . .? Yes, of course you do . . . Damey, darling, is Mummy there? . . . Well, is she crying at the moment? . . . Well, when she's stopped talking to Mrs Phillips, will you tell her Daddy's on the early train . . . Will you do that . . .? Damien . . . Dam— Oh God!

He hangs up. Karen has returned, in time to hear the last.

Karen How are things at home?

Bruce I don't know. Everyone seems to be crying. Hilary's crying, the kids are crying, I don't know.

Karen You promised you'd pop across the hall and have a quick word with Mr East before you went home.

Bruce (*glancing at his watch*) No, tomorrow. Tomorrow . . .

Karen You did promise.

Bruce All right. It will be quick, I can tell you. I miss that train, I am dead. Get my coat and briefcase ready, will you?

Karen Yes, Bruce.

Karen trots into Bruce's office. Bruce goes out of the other door.

Bruce (*as he goes, calling*) Ah, Raymond – this is going to have to be a quickie, my sweet . . .

Karen returns immediately. She has Bruce's coat and briefcase. Seeing the room is empty she moves swiftly. Putting down the items on the desk, she removes from her pocket a tiny pair of (bright red) lacy briefs. She takes up the small gift package that Bruce has left on the desk and contrives to attach the lace trimming of the garment to the parcel. She holds the parcel up to inspect her handiwork. The briefs dangle from the wrapping as if caught there by accident. She slips the items into the pocket of Bruce's coat. She steps back behind the desk. As she does so, Bruce returns.

(*Calling behind him*) . . . Yes, well, we'll talk again tomorrow, sweetie. We'll have to talk tomorrow . . . God, that man drives me insane. (*To Karen*) Right. Coat! (*He burps*) Excuse me.

Karen Yes, Bruce.

Karen springs forward and helps him into his coat.

Bruce (*while they do this*) Will you try ringing home again for me once more? I don't know if Damien understood that message at all . . . Tell her I'm on the early one . . .

Karen I will, Bruce, I will.

Bruce Briefcase!

Karen Here!

Bruce (*moving to the door*) Goodnight, see you tomorrow. Wish me luck. (*He burps*) Excuse me.

Karen I do, I do.

Bruce (*stopping*) My God! The present. I forgot her bloody present.

Karen In your right-hand coat pocket, Bruce.

Bruce (*patting his pocket to confirm this*) Clever girl. Well remembered.

Karen If I were you, I should just whip it out the minute you're through the front door.

Bruce (*patting her bottom*) Brilliant. What would I do without you, eh? Night! (*He burps*) Excuse me.

Karen Night!

Bruce goes. As soon as he has gone, Karen does her disgusted routine.

Yeeerrrrkkk!

Purposefully now, she goes to the desk and dials a number, taking out her cassette recorder as she does so. As someone answers, she switches it on as before.

Hallo? Who's that speaking? . . . Oh, you're Damien. (*She switches off her cassette player*) Hallo, Damien . . .

this is someone from Daddy's office . . . Yes . . . That's right . . . Yes, he does . . . Damien, have you got a pencil there? Well, yes, a pen will do . . . Are you big enough to write with a pen? . . . Of course you are, yes . . . Write down this number . . . (*She reaches into her bag and pulls out her radio phone as she speaks*) Are you ready? 0836-213661. All right? Have you got that . . .? Clever boy. Tell Mummy it's very, very important, will you? Right. Bye . . . Bye-bye . . . Bye.

She rings off. She swaps the tape on her cassette player and takes a quick look out of the main door to make sure she'll be uninterrupted. She has barely had time to do this when her portable phone rings. Karen switches on the cassette player and holds it close to the mouthpiece. The music is slightly more slushy and romantic than before. She then answers her phone.

(*In a surburban sing-song*) 213661 Paradise . . . Can I help you? . . . What? . . . I really couldn't say, love . . . I'm sorry, this is a private club, madam, we can't give that sort of information, not to strangers . . . What? . . . Oh, well, just a minute, I'll ask . . . (*Calling to someone*) Maureen . . . is Bruce Tick upstairs still? . . . What? . . . Well, are they still here? . . . Did they? . . . (*Back into phone*) Sorry, love, they both left about half an hour ago . . . I don't know, love, I should ask him . . . Well, try where he works . . . He must work sometimes . . . Goodbye. Please call Paradise again, thank you.

Karen rings off. She switches off the cassette machine and puts both it and the mobile phone away in her bag. The phone on her desk starts ringing as she does so. She answers it in her sexy secretary's voice.

Hallo. Mr Tick's secretary, can I help you . . .? (*Surprised*) Oh hallo, Mrs Tick . . . No . . . He left about half an hour ago . . . No, I've been here at my desk all the time . . .

Yes . . . You did? . . . Well, I don't know where that number came from, I'm sure . . . Paradise? . . . No, I'm afraid I don't at all . . . No, all he wanted you to know was that he'll be on the early train . . . Yes. Bye-ee.

Karen is now very cheerful. She sings to herself as she punches up another number. She wanders round and sits on her desk to make the next call. She shivers suddenly and brings her knees together.

Brrrr! Draughty.

She waits while the number engages. As the phone is answered, a separate light comes up on Henry.

Henry Hallo.

Karen Henrybell . . . it's me.

Henry Oh, hallo. Where are you?

Karen In my office on the fourteenth floor . . . Henrybell, I had to ring you . . . I am near to gold . . .

Henry To what?

Karen Gold. Gold, Henrybell, gold. I have him on the run. The fall of the house of Tick is imminent.

Henry Karen, what are you doing?

Karen Henrybell. It's brilliant. Brilliant. I am brilliant. You're going to be so pleased with me. They're all so stupid, Henrybell. They're fools . . .

Henry Yes, well, some of them . . .

Karen All of them. I could take over this whole place tomorrow if I wanted to . . . I've got them all running in circles . . . None of them has a clue . . .

Henry Yes, Karen, Karen, listen. They may just be pretty busy getting on with their jobs, you see. They wouldn't necessarily be expecting Machiavellian plots from their temporary secretaries . . .

Karen Exactly. That's the brilliance of the whole scheme. How are you getting on, tell me? What stage are you at?

Henry Er . . . oh, quite well. Pretty well.

Karen Are you anywhere near gold?

Henry No . . .

Karen Condition red though, surely?

Henry Yes, sort of – pinkish . . .

Karen (*suspicious*) You are making some progress?

Henry Oh yes.

Karen I don't have to remind you, Henrybell, that this scheme is up and running. You are now committed.

Henry Oh yes . . .

Karen How close have you managed to get to the Pedigree Friesian?

Henry Who?

Karen The cow, Henrybell. The scheming cow.

Henry Oh yes, yes . . . I'm getting closer all the time.

Karen Make her suffer, Henrybell. Punish her and leave her for dead.

She hangs up. The lights go out on Karen but remain on Henry.

Henry Karen . . . Karen . . .

He realises she has gone and hangs up. As he does so –

SCENE EIGHT

5·00 p.m.

The lights spread around Henry and we see he is in the hall at Furtherfield House. He is deeply worried. Winnie comes through. Norma follows her, carrying some logs in her arms.

Winnie Supper'll be ready in a few minutes, sir.

Henry Winnie . . .

Winnie Yes, sir. (*To Norma*) Stop there.

Norma stops patiently.

Henry Can you remember the last time Mr Staxton-Billing came to this house?

Winnie Well, he was here the other day, sir, to collect his wife . . .

Henry Yes, before that?

Winnie And then he was here for that meeting a couple of Sundays back . . .

Henry Yes, but before that when was he here?

Winnie (*straining to remember*) Ohh . . .

Henry When did he last visit Miss Karen . . . ?

Winnie Oh, you mean when did they last stop seeing each other romantically, you mean, sir?

Henry Yes – that's what I meant. Yes.

Winnie Well, that would have been – six months back.

Henry Six months?

Winnie Yes, they had a great bust-up right here in the hall. She threw everything at him. Then she went at him with one of them duelling pikelets . . .

Henry Pikelets?

Winnie Up there on the wall there, see. The bent one. Caught him a cracker.

Henry Good God.

Winnie We got that off her. Then she was in with her fists, like. Took four of us to hold her down. Temper like a tea-kettle, she has. Not one to get on the wrong side of is Miss Karen, if you take my meaning.

Henry No, I do see that. And she hasn't seen Mr Staxton-Billing since?

Winnie Not to my knowledge, sir. Hardly likely after that, wouldn't you think?

Henry Yes, I would, I would. Winnie, do you – happen to know if – I mean, do you happen to have heard rumours about Mr Staxton-Billing perhaps taking up with anyone else? Another woman, I mean?

Oliver enters. He is in evening dress. Winnie gives a glance at Norma, who still stands, patiently and uncomplainingly, sagging slightly under the weight of the logs.

Winnie (*tight-lipped*) I wouldn't know about that, sir, I'm sure. I'm not one for gossip.

Henry No, quite. Quite right.

Oliver Hi!

Henry Good evening.

Winnie Excuse me, sir. (*To Norma*) Come on, then. In here with them. Follow me.

Norma follows Winnie off.

Henry How long's Norma been here now?

Oliver Oh. Months. I don't know.

Henry She seems to be taking a long time to get the hang of the job, doesn't she?

Oliver (*vaguely*) Does she? I suppose so. Still, I believe it is fairly complicated. Well, I'm all ready for the hop. You really not going to come?

Henry No, no. I'd . . .

Oliver I don't know why you're not taking my partner instead of me. You seem to get on better.

Henry No, I don't think that would be a good idea at all.

Oliver No. See what you mean. Hunt Ball. Small village. What do you expect? Her husband really ought to be taking her, oughtn't he?

Henry Why isn't he?

Oliver No idea. Off with somebody else probably, knowing him.

Henry Who?

Oliver Haven't the foggiest. Well, I'd better get the car out. See you later.

Henry Possibly.

Oliver strolls to the front door. As he does so, the bell rings.

Oliver Who the hell's that?

He opens the door. Imogen steps inside. For once, she is done up to the nines for the dance. She is the most beautiful vision that Henry has ever seen.

Oh hi, come in.

Imogen Thank you.

Henry (*incapable of speech*) Ah!

Imogen (*softly*) Hallo.

Henry Hallo.

Oliver I thought I was supposed to be collecting you.

Imogen I thought I'd collect you instead.

Oliver Great. That's the modern way. Yah. Why not?

Henry continues to gape at Imogen adoringly. A pause.

Right. I'll go and sit in your car then.

Imogen Thank you.

Oliver goes our. The two continue to stare at each other. Winnie comes out, followed by Norma.

Winnie Now who could that – (*She stops and takes in the scene immediately*) Ah. Right. (*To Norma*) Back in here then. Come along.

Winnie and Norma exit again.

Henry This is a nice surprise. I didn't expect to see you tonight. I'd resigned myself to a good book.

Imogen I thought you might just like to see that I can look reasonably presentable, when I want to.

Henry You look – stunning.

Imogen Not always covered in half the countryside.

Henry Just so – so beautiful.

Imogen (*rocking self-consciously from one foot to the other*) Oh, well. I don't know about that exactly.

Henry You're just the most beautiful woman I've ever seen in my life. Really.

Imogen (*faintly tearful*) Oh, Henry, you say such lovely things.

Henry I love you, Imogen . . .

Imogen Oh, please don't make me cry now. I'll just run. I'll run all over the place, I always do. I must go. I just had to see you first.

Henry I'll think of you dancing with all those men . . . think of me.

Imogen I'll only be dancing with you really, Henry. You know that, don't you? (*She kisses him lightly*) Goodnight, my darling.

Henry Goodnight.

Imogen goes. Henry watches her leave. He turns in the doorway.

(*A little cry, half pain, half pleasure*) Ah!

As he stands there, the lights cross-fade to –

SCENE NINE

10.00 a.m.
Lembridge Tennit. Karen at her desk. Bruce comes in. He looks ashen and unkempt.

Karen (*brightly*) Good morning, Bruce.

Bruce Morning. (*He burps*)

Karen Miss the train, did we?

Bruce Yes, I . . . yes. It sounds ridiculous but I fell asleep on the platform. At Sunningdale.

Karen Oh dear . . .

Bruce Probably because I didn't sleep at all last night. We had a . . . she had a . . .

He grips the desk unsteadily.

Karen Would you like to sit down?

Bruce Thank you. Nobody had the decency to wake me. You'd think British Rail would have the decency to wake me up. I mean, what are we paying for, that's what I want to know. (*He burps*)

Karen gets up. He sits in her chair.

Someone's doing this to me . . . I know they are . . . This is a conspiracy . . . You've no idea what's happening, Kieron . . . you've no idea . . . Strange women ringing up – nighties . . . knickers in my pocket . . . you name it . . . (*He burps*) I've got this terrible indigestion . . . and I haven't even eaten anything.

Karen Do calm down, Bruce . . .

Bruce We had this ferocious row last night, Hilary and I. Really terrible. And right in the middle of it, this girl in suspenders turns up with a kissogram . . . I mean, who'd do a thing like that? What bastard would do a thing like that to me . . .?

Karen Is there anything I can do to help, Bruce?

Bruce Help? (*He burps*) How? She's leaving me. She's taking the kids and she's leaving me. I'll be going home tonight to an empty house. No supper.

He burps.

Karen If there's anything I can do . . .

Bruce (*with a burst of gratitude, grasping her bottom*) Oh, Kieron – sweetie . . .

Karen (*removing his hand firmly*) Don't do that, Bruce, that isn't going to help, is it . . .?

Bruce Sorry. I just needed – reassurance. I don't know how you can help. The trouble is she thinks you're –

Karen I'm responsible?

Bruce I think she does. It's ridiculous.

Karen Ridiculous. What if I talked to her . . .

Bruce No, she wouldn't listen – she's obsessed . . . She has this image of you. Beautiful, sexy. You know.

Karen Yes, would that I were . . .

Bruce I mean, you know what I mean?

Karen Bruce, if you were to invite her somewhere. For a talk. To thrash things out. And I was to – just happen to wander in . . .

Bruce What, you mean here in the office? I couldn't –

Karen No, no. Somewhere nearby. A quiet wine bar, say. And you could meet her. And then I could just stroll in and say, 'Oh, Bruce, I'm so glad I caught up with you . . .'

Bruce 'Mr Tick.' Better make it 'Mr Tick'. Not 'Bruce'.

Karen 'Oh, Mr Tick, I'm so glad I caught up with you. These urgent papers do need your signature tonight.' You see?

Bruce (*a man grasping at straws*) Yes, yes . . .

Karen And then she could meet me, face to face. You could say, 'By the way, Hilary, have you met . . . Kieron?' And she'd see right away what sort of person I was.

Bruce Maybe. Maybe. (*He burps*)

Karen She'd see straight away there was nothing between us.

Bruce It might work, you know, it might. I mean, if she saw you as you are. I mean . . . don't take me the wrong way . . .

Karen Oh no, Bruce, I'd never take you the wrong way . . .

Bruce The point is, will Hilary agree to meet me? Will she come?

Karen Well, phone her.

Bruce Phone her?

Karen Now.

Bruce Now? Yes. I will. She won't have left yet. (*Rising*) What's my number? No, I know I know my number. It's all right. I'll phone in here. (*He burps*)

Karen You do that. Good luck.

Bruce Thank you.

He goes into his office.

Karen (*to herself*) You're going to need it.

She takes out her own mobile phone, humming as she does so.

(*Getting through, normal voice*) Hallo, is that Jean? It's Miss Knightly. Hallo, darling. I want to make a hair appointment for tomorrow, please. With Martin, yes.

Just a wash and blow-dry. Five o'clock-ish? Super. Bye.

She rings off.

Bruce (*his voice from his office, angrily*) Look don't start on that again, Hilary, for God's sake, sweetie . . . What are you talking about? The woman's about as sexy as a sandbucket . . .

Karen sits at her desk, humming to herself and smiling. As she does so, the scene changes to –

SCENE TEN

4.00 p.m.
   The same day. A hen house. Chicken noises. Imogen, now back in her farm clothes, and Henry crawl inside. The place apparently has quite a low ceiling. From now on the action accelerates and the scenes begin to cross-cut faster and faster.

Henry How long do we have?

Imogen About six and a half minutes, that's all.

Henry God, I want you so much, Imogen . . .

Imogen Well, we can't make love in a hen house, Henry, it's impossible.

Henry (*desperately*) Why not? Why not?

Imogen Well – it's not . . . conducive. And it would probably stop them laying. And all sorts of things.

Henry I love you.

Imogen I love you. So what?

A motor horn sounds.

Oh, that's Betty bringing back the kids. (*Moving out*)
She's early. I must go . . .

Henry (*despairingly*) Imogen . . .

Cross-fade quickly to –

SCENE ELEVEN

6.00 p.m.
*The same day. A wine bar. Muzak behind. Bruce
approaches and sits at a table for two. He has a glass of
white wine and a bowl of appetisers which he starts to
devour compulsively, almost desperately. He burps as he
devours them. His health is deteriorating fast. He looks
about him anxiously. In a moment, Hilary Tick appears.
In her thirties, normally quite attractive, at present she
is drawn, tired and angry.*

Bruce (*calling to her*) Hilary!

Hilary approaches the table.

Thank you for coming, darling. Thank you. Thank you.

Hilary One drink, Bruce, that's all I'm having.

Bruce Yes, yes. OK, sweetie.

Hilary Please don't call me sweetie. You know I hate it.

Bruce I'm sorry. I'm sorry, love.

Hilary I don't think we've anything more to say, have
we?

Bruce I hope we have. I hope we have, Hilly.

Hilary Well, I don't know what to say. I'm still stunned.
That's all. Stunned. I phoned my mother. She was stunned,
too. I phoned your father. He was totally stunned.

Bruce I only wish I could . . . I could . . .

Hilary (*cutting him short*) I'll have a white wine, thank you.

Bruce (*indicating his own glass*) Would you like a glass of this? It's very . . .

Hilary I honestly don't care, Bruce. Just anything . . .

Bruce Right, right. (*He crams the rest of the appetisers into his mouth*) I'll get some more of these.

He goes, leaving Hilary hunched and tense in her chair. A quick cross-fade to –

SCENE TWELVE

3.00 p.m.
The village green. We see only Henry and Imogen in coats standing formally side by side, not touching because they are in public. They seem to be watching some morris dancing. At least, the music suggests they are.

Henry (*fairly irritably*) What is all this prancing about?

Imogen (*also rather tetchily*) It's morris dancing. You must have heard of morris dancing.

Henry Never heard of it.

Imogen Don't be so ridiculous. Everyone's heard of morris dancing.

Henry Well, I haven't. And I think it's awful and I wish they'd go home. I want to touch you.

Imogen Well, you can't. I don't know what you're doing here. (*Calling to a child*) Simon, don't stand there, you'll

141

trip them up. Now come back, outside the ropes. Outside! That's better. (*To Henry, fiercely*) What are you doing here, Henry?

Henry (*sulkily*) What do you think I'm doing? I'm watching this terrific morris dancing.

Imogen You just said you didn't like it.

Henry Yes, I do. I've got the hang of it now, it's tremendous. (*Shouting at the dancers*) Oooh-lay!

Imogen Henry! Anthony is watching, the entire village is watching, now stop it or I'll never speak to you again.

Henry I don't care. I love you . . .

Imogen Oh, this is impossible! What am I going to do . . .

Sound and lights cross-fade back to –

SCENE THIRTEEN

6.15 p.m.
The wine bar again. Hilary is still sitting where she was. Bruce returns with her wine and another bowl of nibbles.

Bruce Here we are. Not a bad wine, this. It's actually German but it tastes not unlike a white burgundy. It's got that same . . .

Hilary I really don't give a damn, Bruce, I really don't.

Bruce Yes, yes. Fair enough, love. Fair enough. (*He burps*) Excuse me.

He takes a handful of nibbles from the bowl. Hilary's glass remains untouched.

(*His mouth full*) Some of these?

Hilary No. What did you want to say to me? I don't want to be here long. Mother's with the children on her own . . .

Bruce (*affectionately*) Oh, bless her. How is Mary?

Hilary She's livid, Bruce. She thinks you're a shit. So do I. Now, what did you want to say?

Bruce That this has all been – a conspiracy . . .

Hilary Oh, not again . . .

Bruce Someone has deliberately broken up my marriage . . .

Hilary Bruce . . .

Bruce It's true.

Hilary But who, Bruce? Who would want to do that?

Bruce (*shouting*) I don't know, do I? Somebody wants to, that's all I know. Them. I don't know. The government. The KGB. The FBI. The CIA.

Hilary Bruce!

Bruce MI5! How the hell do I know? (*Looking round accusingly*) Somebody here. (*He burps*)

Hilary *Bruce!*

A silence. Bruce crams some more food into his mouth.

I think you ought to see someone, I really do. I think you're going mad.

Bruce I probably am.

Hilary And if you eat many more of those, you'll drop dead anyway.

Bruce I don't care. (*He burps*)

Hilary Look, I'm going. There's obviously nothing new to be said, is there?

Bruce (*glancing anxiously at his watch*) No. Hang on. Hang on. Just one minute.

Hilary Why? What for?

Bruce Just for a minute.

Hilary Are you expecting someone?

Bruce No. No. (*Pause*) No.

Hilary looks at him suspiciously. They continue to sit there as the lights cross-fade back to –

SCENE FOURTEEN

11.00 a.m.

A cowshed. Appropriate noises. Henry stands miserably. Apart from him stands Imogen, penitent.

Imogen I'm sorry. I'm trying my best.

Henry Well, it's not good enough.

Imogen Don't be angry with me.

Henry I'm going.

Imogen Where?

Henry Back to London. I've had it with the country. I'm sick to death of all these pigs and chickens and squirrels and cows all happily having each other while we're both standing about . . .

Imogen Henry . . .

Henry . . . waiting to be shot, or made into bacon . . .

Imogen Henry!

Henry What?

Imogen This weekend.

Henry What about it?

Imogen Anthony's going to be away . . .

Henry Where?

Imogen I don't know. There's a meeting or something in London. Something to do with Uncle's firm. So he says, anyway. The point is I'll be on my own. I think I can get someone to look after the kids . . .

Henry You could?

Imogen I think so.

Henry Can you come and stay up at the house?

Imogen Do you think that's wise?

Henry Why not?

Imogen Won't she be there?

Henry No, of course she won't be there . . .

Imogen It would mean I'd be near the kids, wouldn't it? If anything happened. I could tell Betty where I was. She'd never say anything. All right then. Yes.

Henry That's wonderful.

Imogen I thought you'd be pleased.

Henry (*embracing her*) God, that's wonderful.

Imogen Careful, I'm covered in cow muck.

Henry (*still holding her*) I love you, I love you, I love you . . .

They cling to each other. The cows moo in approval as the lights change again to –

SCENE FIFTEEN

6.30 p.m.

The wine bar again. As before. Bruce has nearly finished the second bowl of nibbles. Hilary sits stiffly.

Hilary Right, that's it, I'm afraid. I'm going.

Bruce (*alarmed*) Don't you want your wine?

Hilary No, I don't. You drink it. I'm going. Goodbye, Bruce. I'll talk to Arnold about the divorce. It's all right, I won't be vindictive. I think we can settle it all quite quietly . . .

Bruce Hilly! What are you saying? This is Bruce. This is Brucie baby. (*He burps*) Excuse me.

Hilary gets up.

(*Shouting in desperation*) Remember my promise. I always left them with you, sweetie. I always left them with you, I swear it . . .

Hilary (*icily*) Well, congratulations. All I can say is, you must have a second pair, Bruce.

Bruce (*tearfully*) Hilary. Hilly, Hilly baby, please don't go!

He clings to her.

Hilary Bruce, everyone is staring at us. Come along.

Bruce Don't leave me!

Hilary Bruce!

Bruce You have to stay and meet her. You have to meet her, Hilly. Please.

146

Hilary What are you talking about?

Bruce You've got to meet her . . .

Hilary Meet who?

Karen appears. She has made a very special effort with her appearance. She looks sensational.

Karen Yoo! Hoo! Bruce! Hi!

Hilary Who is that?

Bruce That's Miss . . . (*Looking at her*) Oh, my God. That's Miss . . .

Karen (*reaching them*) Hi! Sorry to trouble you. You forgot to sign these . . . (*To Hilary*) Hallo, you must be Hilary, I'm Karen. Bruce's little helper. (*She smiles fondly at Bruce*)

Hilary (*to Bruce*) You bastard! Is this why you got me here?

Bruce (*staring at Karen in horror*) I don't know what she's . . . Why is she . . .?

He burps.

Hilary That's it, Bruce. Forget it. Gloves off now, darling. Total war. All right? (*To Karen*) You're welcome to him, dear. From the look of you, you thoroughly deserve each other.

Hilary goes. Bruce stares after her.

Hilary Are you going to sign the letters for me, Bruce?

Bruce (*staring at her with horrified realisation*) You little . . . (*He burps*) It was you, wasn't it? It was you all the time. Who are you working for, eh? Who's been paying you to do this to me . . .

He burps. His indigestion is getting worse.

Karen Come along, Bruce, calm down . . .

Bruce (*rising*) I'm going to kill you. You know that? I'm going to kill you right here for what you've done to me. You scheming tart, you . . . (*He doubles up in pain and sits again*) Ah!

Karen Bruce?

Bruce (*gasping for air*) My God! She's poisoned the crisps as well. Help me someone, she's poisoned my crisps.

Karen Will someone get a doctor, please? I think this man isn't well . . .

Bruce (*weakly*) Who are you working for? I have to know. Please tell me . . . The CIA? No? The FBI? The CBI? The EEC? Please tell me. You must tell me.

Karen Very well, I'll tell you.

She leans forward and whispers the name in his ear. Bruce stares at her. Then he starts to laugh.

Bruce I don't believe it? Him? You did this for . . . *him*? I don't believe you. (*A convulsive burp*) Now that's what I call . . . That's what I call . . .

He gives a couple more chuckles and a burp. His eyes glaze over. He slides off his chair. Karen moves to catch him.

Karen Somebody! Please. Help me, please. I think my boss has just dropped dead . . .

The lights change again to –

SCENE SIXTEEN

7.00 p.m.

The hall in Furtherfield House. As the lights come up, the front doorbell rings. Winnie comes to answer it. Henry rushes on in rather indecent haste. He has on a smoking jacket and has made an effort for this weekend. He sees Winnie has beaten him to the door and stands waiting while she opens it. Winnie does so. Imogen steps into the hall. She has her coat on and has also made an effort. She carries a small overnight case. She stops as she sees Henry. They stare at each other. She smiles at him. He smiles. It's the moment they've both dreamed of. Winnie senses she is in the way. She tiptoes out and leaves them. Henry and Imogen move together. They touch each other, almost incredulously.

Imogen (*in a whisper*) I can't believe this is happening.

Henry (*in a whisper*) Nor can I.

Imogen (*in a whisper*) Oh, my darling . . .

Henry (*in a whisper*) My darling . . .

They move to go into the longest kiss ever. Their lips brush. The front door opens. Karen stands there. Henry and Imogen spring apart.

Karen Hi!

They stare at her.

Sorry. Did I . . .? (*Pause*) Carry on. Don't mind me.

Imogen (*recovering*) I'd better . . . I'd better be . . .

Henry Please, no. Don't . . .

Imogen (*hurriedly*) No. Please. Sorry. I have to . . . I have animals to feed. Excuse me.

Imogen grabs her suitcase and rushes out into the night.

Karen Night.

Henry stands crestfallen.

Sorry, Henrybell, you were obviously on the brink of something major. I should have phoned, but I just had to get out of that dreadful place for a bit. Get some fresh air. (*Throwing herself down*) God, I feel better already. I'll have a bath and then I'll feel really clean. I haven't felt clean for days. You never can in London, can you?

Henry continues to stare at her dully.

Well, Henrybell. First, the news in brief. Mission accomplished. Mr Bruce Tick. RIP.

Henry (*dully*) What?

Karen RIP. Deceased. No more. Dropped dead in a wine bar. What more suitable way to go? Leaving behind him a widow and two children all of whom seem totally unaffected.

Henry How did he . . . How did he – die?

Karen Cholesterol. And overexcitement, I think. Don't worry. He died with your name on his lips.

Henry This is . . . I can't believe it. You killed him? You murdered Bruce Tick?

Karen No. I – just nudged him in the general direction of – death, that's all. He was already well on the road.

Henry (*sitting*) I don't know what to say. What are we going to do?

Karen Nothing.

Henry Nothing?

Karen Nothing. Anyway, how about you? You seem to be progressing. You doing all right?

Henry (*still dazed*) What?

Karen Softening her up, I take it. And then that thtutt! (*She makes a chopping motion with her hand*) Yes? That the plan? Brilliant. She looked as if she was cooking nicely to me. (*Getting up*) I'll have that bath . . . (*Yelling*) Winnie! (*As she moves off*) Tell you something. I think I'll hang on with that firm for a bit. I'm rather enjoying it. Be fun to see how far I can get before they rumble me. Bet I can make Managing Director's sec. A bet? Yes?

Winnie enters.

Winnie! Bath!

Winnie Yes, Miss Karen.

Winnie goes off. Karen looks at Henry, who sits motionless.

Karen What's the matter, Henrybell? You look really depressed. You should be celebrating. You've won. We've won. Tell you what, I'll get in my bath. And then you come on up to the bathroom and I'll teach you some water sports you never dreamt of. Have you ever played Dive, Dive, Dive . . . ?

Henry shakes his head.

No? Sailors and Mermaids?

Henry shakes his head again.

Hot Lobsters? No? Henrybell, you've never been in a bath till you've played Lobsters . . .

Henry No, I have to . . . I couldn't, Karen.

Karen What?

151

Henry I'm a bit . . . I'm very . . . I'm sorry.

Karen (*cooling*) OK. Suit yourself. (*She studies him*) I do hope you're intending to keep your side of the bargain, Henrybell. You're not getting seriously involved with the Friesan, are you? Because that's not our deal. Not at all it isn't and you know it. So don't try and double-cross me, Henrybell, will you, because although I'm a loyal friend, I'm also a very bad enemy. Very bad. Awful. Believe me.

> *Henry stares at her.*

(*Softly*) Do you know what I do to people who try to double-cross me, Henrybell? (*In a whisper, almost jokily, but not quite*) I take revenge! Revenge!

> *She puts her finger to her lips and tiptoes off. Off along the passage we hear her shout 'Revenge' once again. Then the sound of her receding laughter.*

Henry (*to himself, in dawning horror*) My God, she's mad! She's completely mad. What am I going to do?

> *As he stands there, the lights fade to blackout.*

Part Two

Act Three

SCENE ONE

9.00 a.m.

Darkness. A single spot comes up on Karen with her mobile phone. She is in a passageway at Lembridge Tennit. She is back in her secretarial outfit, although this has gone slightly up-market since we last saw her. In fact, chameleon-like, she subtly alters to suit whoever she's working for or with.

Karen Henrybell . . .

A single spot comes up immediately on Henry on the phone at Furtherfield House.

Henry Karen?

Karen Wonderful news, Henrybell . . .

Henry Karen, good. I needed to talk to you –

Karen (*excitedly*) . . . Listen, listen, I haven't got much time. I've been promoted. What do you think of that? I've got a new boss. Up four floors, two grades and a thousand a year.

Henry (*dismayed*) Really? You really intend to carry on at Lembridge Tennit, do you?

Karen Of course I do. I'm a mobilely upward special secretarial temp. I'm a MUSST, Henrybell. An absolute MUSST. Isn't it exciting?

Henry Yes, congratulations. Who's the – who's the lucky man this time?

Karen (*consulting a piece of paper*) Er. A Mr Seeds.

Graham Seeds. Head of Transportation – brackets South East. Did you know him?

Henry No, I was North West.

Karen I'm just going to meet him. I'll report back . . . Wish me luck. I must go. Bye . . .

Henry (*urgently*) Karen, wait . . .

Karen What?

Henry Listen, I have to ask you this – I wanted to ask you at the weekend only I – I didn't really get a chance – with being so . . . so . . . (*He falters*)

Karen Tied up is the phrase I think you're looking for, Henrybell . . .

Henry Yes . . .

Karen Wasn't that fun?

Henry Yes, an absolute hoot.

Karen Did someone eventually find you?

Henry Yes. Eventually. Winnie, this morning. Listen, Karen –

Karen Never mind, your turn next weekend . . .

Henry Listen, about Anthony –

Karen In the Red Room. Do your worst, O master . . .

Henry Anthony Staxton-Billing . . .

Karen (*rather impatiently*) Yes? What about Anthony Staxton-Billing?

Henry Are you absolutely certain that he left you to go back to his wife? Back to Imogen?

Karen Of course I'm certain, how many more times?

Henry There couldn't possibly – even remotely – just ever so obliquely and distantly – have been, say – another woman. That he went to? Instead?

Karen Who?

Henry Anthony.

Karen To another woman?

Henry Yes.

Karen No. No. No.

Henry You're sure?

Karen Yes. Yes. Yes.

Henry Would you – would you object very strongly if I made some enquiries . . .?

Karen Look, do what you like. I don't care what you do as long as you keep to our bargain, all right? Keep to that. Or else. OK?

Henry Yes, only if there was another woman, then maybe you're trying to take revenge against the wrong one, you see . . .

Karen Third and final warning. Beep – beep – beep. Bye.

She switches off her phone. The light goes out on Henry, before he can say any more. Karen frowns slightly and puts away the phone. As she does so, Lydia scurries into view.

Lydia Oh, there you are. Sorry to keep you. There was a slight crisis in the – How are you?

Karen Oh, much better. I had a long lie-down over the weekend.

Lydia Oh, how sensible.

Karen Got waited on hand and foot.

Lydia Quite right. Poor you. Poor Mr Tick. Dreadful.

Karen Shocking.

Lydia Poor Mrs Tick.

Karen Indeed.

Karen Were there any . . . ?

Karen Yes, two little Ticks too, apparently.

Lydia Appalling. Was there any prior warning that that might happen?

Karen Well, Bruce had had digestive problems, it has to be said.

Lydia Ah. Yes, I did hear that . . .

Karen But no real warning, no. I'd taken his letters into the wine bar just along the road there for late signature and Bruce just toppled over at the table.

Lydia (*shaking her head*) Well . . .

Karen So.

Lydia It could happen to any of us, I suppose.

Karen Very true.

They reflect for a second on the uncertainty of existence.

Lydia Well, are you ready to meet the new boss? Mr Seeds?

Karen Rather.

Lydia I hope this works out well. I'd hate it if you – I mean, frankly, as Mrs Bulley was saying at the meeting only this morning, you're too valuable to lose, Karen.

Karen (*modestly*) Thank you.

Lydia Now, just a word of warning, between the two of us. Mr Seeds is only just back at work. He's been off sick for – oh, nearly five months.

Karen Oh dear, was it serious?

Lydia I understand it was something very nearly approaching a – (*dropping down to near inaudibility*) nervous breakdown.

Karen No?

Lydia Well, Mr Seeds is . . . he's a rather nervy man. Absolutely brilliant, of course –

Karen Of course. Thank you for telling me. These things are so useful to know in advance.

Lydia I thought you should know. I don't like telling tales but I felt you should be prepared. By the way, I love your new image, I never said. You're looking – decidedly chic, Karen.

Karen (*blushing*) Thank you, Lydia.

Lydia Right-o. Are we ready? Let me introduce you to Mr Seeds.

Lydia knocks gently on the office door. They wait. She knocks again, louder.

(*Calling as she does so*) Mr Seeds! Mr Seeds!

Mr Seeds (*a thin, startled voice*) Who is that? Who's there?

Lydia Excuse me, Mr Seeds. It's Lydia, Mr Seeds. Mrs Bulley's Lydia.

Mr Seeds Well, there's no need to knock the door down, is there?

Lydia (*pulling a face at Karen and then ushering her in ahead of her*) I want to introduce you to Karen, Mr Seeds. Whom we feel sure you'll find a little gift from heaven . . .

Karen (*gushing, as she enters*) Hallo, Mr Seeds. How nice to meet you . . .

As both women go off, the lights change to –

SCENE TWO

9.15 a.m.
The dining room at Furtherfield House. Henry is finishing his breakfast. The sound of the motorbike racing around indoors in the house. Norma enters with an empty tray, shadowed, as usual, by Winnie.

Winnie (*to Norma, in the usual undertone*) Ask the gentleman if he'd care for more toast, then.

Henry (*attempting to anticipate her*) No, thank you, Norma.

Norma Would you care for more toast, sir?

Henry No, thank you, Norma.

Norma Thank you, sir.

Winnie (*indicating the breakfast debris*) Clear that away, then.

Norma starts to clear the table. Winnie watches her.

Henry (*rising from the table*) Delicious. As always.

Winnie Thank you, sir.

Norma Thank you, sir.

Henry moves away to the windows to look out.
A bird flutters above his head. He ducks. In the other
room, the motorbike stalls and stops.

Oliver (*off, angrily*) Oh, knickers.

Henry Pity they never had that building replaced.

Winnie Pardon, sir?

Henry That summerhouse on the other side of the lawn, there. It's a shame they've never replaced it, isn't it?

Winnie Oh no, sir. That building'll never be replaced. Not in our lifetime. Those charred remains are there as a reminder to all.

Henry A reminder of what?

Winnie (*darkly*) A reminder of the fire.

Henry Ah.

Winnie This rain'll be good.

Henry Will it?

Winnie Oh, yes. We need the rain.

Henry Winnie, don't you think . . . I don't want to interfere but . . . don't you feel that Norma is probably up to coping on her own now?

Winnie On her own?

Henry Yes.

Winnie Oh no, sir. She's a long way to go yet, sir.

Henry Really? She seems to have more or less the hang of things. I mean, as I say, it's none of my business . . .

Winnie You see, young Norma, sir, she's being like groomed to replace me. You see. When I retire, then Norma steps in. So she's got to know it all.

Henry I see.

Winnie (*pointedly*) Because once she takes over, I won't be here no more. I'll be retired. With just my pension.

Henry Oh yes, I see.

Winnie So I agreed with Master Oliver, I'd go when I'd got her good and ready. And not before, you see. And with a girl like Norma there, that could take years if you get my meaning.

Henry (*tactfully*) Say no more. I quite understand.

The bird flutters over his head. He ducks. Oliver enters. He wears motorcycle boots, pyjamas, dressing gown and his crash helmet, which he is in the act of removing.

Oliver (*seeing Henry*) Ah! Hi!

Henry Good morning. Have a good ride?

Oliver So-so. I've got quite a circuit laid out now.

Henry Yes, I noticed.

Winnie (*to Norma*) Take that out now.

Norma goes out with the tray during the next. Winnie hovers in the doorway, waiting for a word.

Oliver Hope I didn't wake you. Filthy day, so I'm afraid it's the wet-weather circuit. Billiard room, through the ballroom, then along the passageway, chicane into the library, hairpin round the cabinets, then it's straight all the way to the east study where you can really open up and then you're back in the billiard room – and into lap two.

Henry Terrific.

Oliver Want a go?

Henry No, thank you.

Oliver No? Well, probably wise. It's not as simple as it looks, I can tell you.

Henry I bet it isn't.

The bird flutters over their heads. Henry ducks. Oliver glances at it.

Oliver Blue tit.

Henry Oh, yes?

Winnie Would you care for some breakfast, Master Oliver?

Oliver No, I ate. Out of the fridge. Earlier.

Winnie Very good, sir.

Oliver (*holding out his crash helmet*) Here, you can take this, though.

Winnie, taking the helmet, goes.

Of course, if it wasn't for this rain, I could be out of doors.

Henry Do you ever feel the urge to wander?

Oliver Wander? How do you mean? In the garden?

Henry No, somewhere else? Get away? To new places?

Oliver Where?

Henry Anywhere.

Oliver No. (*A pause*) I can't think of anywhere. (*Pause*) I like it here, actually. It's rather good.

Henry It is. Yes, it is, I agree. Only . . . (*Deciding this is not a fruitful avenue for discussion*) Well, I think I'll brave the rain, anyway. Go for a stroll.

Oliver Why not?

Henry I was just saying to Winnie that it's a pity you've never had that place rebuilt.

Oliver The summerhouse?

Henry Yes. It's a bit of an eyesore, isn't it?

Oliver (*frowning*) Yes. (*Pause*) It's . . . it's difficult really.

Henry How do you mean?

Oliver That's – that's where the parents both died, you see. In the fire.

Henry Oh, I'm sorry. I had no idea.

Oliver They were both keen lepidopterists, you know. Moths, mainly. Always chasing about in the middle of the night together. Smearing trees with treacle and so on. To catch the things, you know. Bunging them in jars, pinning them on boards. They had quite a collection. Really pretty famous. Amongst other lepidopterists, you understand.

Henry Of course.

Oliver I must say they all looked a bit the same to me. A moth's a moth, isn't it? Anyway, one night we all woke up and there was this fire. That whole summerhouse was blazing like a beacon. Moths everywhere. No one could get anywhere near it. They both must have died almost instantly.

Henry How terrible.

Oliver It was. Yes. They were awfully decent people, actually. I mean, I know you're always supposed to think that about your parents but I know a lot of people who loathe the sight of theirs. But I rather rated ours. I thought they were something a bit special.

Henry What did Karen think of them?

Oliver (*evasively*) Karen? No idea. I should ask her.
We're both very different, you see. I can't speak for her.

Henry What caused the fire? Do they know?

Oliver No. Oil lamp possibly, they think. There was no
electricity out there. Not in the summerhouse.

Henry Was Karen – here at the time?

Oliver (*troubled*) Oh, yes. Karen was here. We were both
home on school holiday. Why?

Henry (*avoiding this question*) How old were you both?

Oliver Well, I was about nine or ten. So she'd have been
about thirteen. Difficult age.

Henry Thirteen?

Oliver No, ten.

Henry Oh, yes. The tragedy must have affected you both?

Oliver I suppose it did. Fortunately there was Winnie
and the others to look after us. We coped. (*He's not
enjoying this conversation*) Look, don't let me keep you
from your walk, will you . . .

Henry No. No, I'll . . .

> *He makes to move away. Norma enters again, with a
> tin of furniture polish and a duster. She is followed by
> Winnie.*

Winnie Excuse me, Master Oliver, is it all right if we do
the table . . .?

Oliver Yeah. Sure. Do it away.

> *He makes to move off.*

Winnie (*to Norma*) Start on the table, then.

Norma Right.

Norma starts polishing the dining table, while Winnie watches her and pretends not to be listening to the following conversation.

Henry (*calling him back*) Oliver . . . Sorry. Just one other small question . . .

Oliver Yah?

Henry (*confidentially, drawing Oliver aside*) Look, this may seem like none of my business again – but I do have a reason for asking it . . . There was, I know, a certain friendship between Karen and Anthony Staxton-Billing, wasn't there?

Oliver Oh, sure. Way back, there was.

Henry How long is way back?

Oliver Well. Nine months. A year. I don't know. Karen moped about for ages. Muttering.

Henry Muttering what?

Oliver I don't know. I couldn't hear. Breaking things.

Henry But then – did Anthony Staxton-Billing take up with someone else? Or did he leave her in order to go back to his wife?

Oliver No idea.

Henry Has he got another woman, do you think?

Oliver 'Fraid I couldn't tell you. I really hardly know him. Matter of fact, I don't actually like him very much.

Henry Why not?

Oliver I don't know. I think he's rather stupid. I don't know how he gets all these women. They must be even more stupid than he is. (*Pause*) Sorry. I didn't mean that about . . .

Henry Love can make all of us a bit stupid.

Oliver Really? Don't know. I've never done it. Don't fancy it.

Henry No? It can be – quite a good feeling, sometimes.

Oliver Can it? It always seems to end up with a lot of crying and people trying to kill each other. At least it does in this family. Look, it's clearing up. I should get that walk in. See you later.

Henry Yes, indeed.

Oliver goes out. Norma has finished the table.

Winnie (*to Norma*) Let's do the table in the hall now.

Norma Right.

Norma goes out. Henry is still staring thoughtfully in the direction of the summerhouse. Winnie stops in the doorway.

Winnie If you're looking for the other woman . . .

Henry (*startled*) What?

Winnie I say, if you're hunting for this other woman, sir . . .

Henry Mr Staxton-Billing's other woman? Then there is one, Winnie? She exists?

Winnie Maybe she does. Maybe she doesn't. I'm not one for spreading rumour. All I'm saying is – if she does exist – and I'm not saying she does – then you could do worse than start by talking to Norma out there.

Henry Norma?

Winnie I'm saying no more.

Henry Norma?

Winnie Excuse me, sir.

She makes to leave.

Henry Then I must talk to Norma . . .

Winnie She's rather busy, sir, just at the . . .

Henry Please, Winnie. I must talk to her. Now. Send her in here now.

Winnie Very well, sir. But don't you frighten her, mind.

Henry I wouldn't dream of frightening her.

Winnie goes out. Henry waits. The bird flutters past his head. He ducks.

(*Incredulously, to himself*) Norma? Anthony Staxton-Billing and Norma?

Norma enters nervously. Winnie follows.

Would you leave us alone for a moment, Winnie?

Winnie I don't think I should –

Henry Please.

Winnie I don't care to leave her unsupervised.

Henry Please, Winnie. I do insist.

Winnie (*reluctantly*) Very good, sir. (*To Norma, in an undertone*) You just answer the gentleman's questions, all right?

Norma Yes.

Winnie goes out. Norma is trembling with nerves.

Henry (*aware of this*) Now don't be frightened, Norma. You mustn't be nervous. I just want a little personal talk with you. Would you like to sit down?

Norma (*inaudibly*) No, I can't sit down, sir.

Henry (*straining to hear*) What? What's that?

Norma I can't sit down, sir.

Henry (*rather alarmed*) You can't sit down? Why can't you sit down? Don't be afraid to answer, Norma, I'm a friend. Why can't you sit down?

Norma I'm not allowed to sit down, sir. Not in here.

Henry Oh, I see. Well, you can sit down if I ask you to sit down, though. Sit down, Norma.

Norma No, sir, I can't sit down, sir. Don't make me sit down, sir . . .

Henry (*rather losing patience*) All right! Stand up then, I don't care.

Norma Yes, sir.

Henry (*controlling himself*) How old are you, Norma?

Norma Sixteen and a half, sir.

Henry Sixteen and a half. (*Gently*) Well now, Norma . . . I want you to tell me about Mr Staxton-Billing. Do you know who I mean?

Norma Yes, sir . . .

Henry I want you to answer me honestly, Norma. And don't worry, this will go no further than this room, I promise. It's a secret just between us two, you see? Tell me truthfully, Norma, are you sleeping with Mr Staxton-Billing?

Norma opens and closes her mouth. She makes little
squeaks that grow swiftly into a wail of misery.
Before Henry can stop her, she rushes from the room.
Her voice is heard receding through the house. Henry
stands alarmed. Winnie comes in.

Winnie (*looking at Henry reproachfully*) Now there was
no cause for that, sir, was there?

As they stand there, the lights cross-fade to –

SCENE THREE

Noon.

Lembridge Tennit. The outer area of Mrs Bulley's office.
Lydia enters with Karen, who is clearly distressed.

Lydia How awful for you. How absolutely awful. You
poor thing. Sit down.

Karen Thank you.

She sits.

Lydia Now, look, you really must take the rest of today
off, Mrs Bulley insists on that . . .

Karen That's very good of her.

Lydia Well, dear girl, that's the least . . . Now, look, she
just wants a quick word before you go off, just to say in
person how sorry she is about all this . . .

Karen Thank you.

Lydia I mean, gosh, it's absolutely horrid luck for you –
losing two bosses in less than a week . . .

Karen Yes. Poor Mr Seeds . . .

Lydia Poor man. Now, let me get it absolutely clear, because I don't want you to have to go through the story over and over again needlessly . . . You say that there was the fire drill –

Karen Yes, first thing this morning . . .

Lydia Yes. I remember it. And somehow Mr Seeds got the impression that it wasn't a practice but the real thing . . .

Karen Yes, he just started running up the corridor. Shouting. I tried to run after him to stop him, but . . .

Lydia Yes, I'm sure. So then what happened?

Karen Well, I saw him open the door to the emergency staircase . . .

Lydia Yes. Well, he acted perfectly correctly. He was right to avoid the lifts . . . But why do you think, when he'd taken the stairs, he ran up them, rather than down them?

Karen I think he somehow got the idea that the fire was downstairs . . .

Lydia Oh, I see. So he ran upstairs on to the roof?

Karen Yes. And then jumped.

She sobs.

Lydia And then jumped. How awful. Thirty-two floors.

Karen Yes.

Lydia I suppose he wouldn't have known much.

Karen Well, so they say.

Lydia Anyway, not after the first twenty or so.

Mrs Bulley (*off*) What are you chattering about out there, Lydia?

Lydia Sorry, Mrs Bulley, I was just talking to Miss Knightly.

Mrs Bulley (*off*) Well, bring her in here, Lydia. Bring her in here. I can't talk to the woman out there, can I?

Lydia No, Mrs Bulley. (*To Karen*) Come on in.

Mrs Bulley (*off*) I think you're going gently potty, Lydia, do you know that?

Lydia (*laughing, as she ushers Karen in*) Yes, Mrs Bulley. Here's Miss Knightly, Mrs Bulley.

Karen goes off, followed by Lydia.

Mrs Bulley (*off, jokingly*) Now, Karen, my dear girl, what on earth have you been doing to half our middle management, eh?

She laughs heartily. The door closes, cutting off her laugh. The lights cross-fade to –

SCENE FOUR

3.00 p.m.

A junior gymkhana. Imogen is tense and pale. Dressed sensibly for chilly outdoors, she feigns great interest in the riding events which we hear but don't see. The galloping of occasional hoofs, crowd reaction and an indecipherable PA system commentating cheerfully on the events. Henry hovers, a little apart from Imogen. He, too, is tense.

Henry I say again, you didn't really mean it.

Imogen Oh yes I did. I meant every word of it. (*Calling out*) Well done, Lucy! She's a good little rider, that kid.

Henry What? You never loved me, you found our whole relationship boring . . . ?

Imogen I never said boring. I never said it was boring.

Henry Boring. I have the letter.

Imogen Fruitless. That's what I said.

Henry Boring. That's what you said.

Imogen I said fruitless. I know what I wrote.

Henry So do I, so do I . . .

Imogen It took me hours to write that letter. Do you think it was easy for me? It was agony.

Henry What do you think it was like to get it? (*Pause*) Through the common or garden postal service. (*Pause. Bitterly*) Second class.

Imogen Well, you're only living half a mile away, there was hardly any point in wasting money on stamps.

Henry It still took three days. You were that close, why couldn't you deliver it by hand, for God's sake? If you had to write.

Applause from the crowd as someone wins.

Imogen (*calling out*) Well done.

Henry Or didn't you have the courage to do that?

Imogen No, I didn't. You're quite right.

Henry Why not?

Imogen Because I knew if I faced you, I'd . . .

Henry You wouldn't have been able to say all that, would you?

Imogen (*a small voice*) No.

Henry Can you say it to me now?

Imogen I can't remember what I said.

Henry You just said you could.

Imogen Not every word. I can remember words like 'fruitless'. But not all of them.

Henry Just the cruel ones, eh? Well, come on, do your best. Improvise.

Imogen I can't.

Henry Go on. Of course you can.

Imogen (*yelling*) Well jumped, Simon. I wish I could ride like that. I wish I could do anything.

Henry Don't you think you owe me that, at least? To tell me to my face? Live?

Imogen Go away, Henry.

Henry Come on. Let's hear it, then. 'Dear Henry . . .'

Imogen (*utterly miserably*) Oh, leave me alone . . .

Henry 'Dear Henry . . .' How did it go . . .? 'I'm afraid this is goodbye . . .'? There you are, I can remember it. 'Dear Henry . . .'? Come on . . .

Imogen Why are you doing this to me?

Henry Because I want to hear it. I still love you and I think you love me. And I want to hear it from you. And not from a second-class letter that came via Exeter.

Imogen is now crying openly. But Henry is angry and desperate.

Come on. 'Dear Henry . . .'

Another whimper from Imogen.

(*Relentlessly*) 'Dear Henry . . .' Why can't you say it?

Imogen (*weakly*) 'Dear Henry . . .'

Henry That's it. Go on. Dear Henry, what?

Imogen Dear Henry . . . Dear Henry . . . (*Softly*) Dear, dear, dear Henry . . .

Henry (*gently*) Imogen . . .

With a sudden wail, Imogen rushes from him. Henry looks in alarm. A horse whinnies.

My God! Look out. (*He sighs with relief as some sort of accident is averted*) Whew! That was close.

Henry watches Imogen out of sight. Anthony appears. He is also dressed for the occasion with a steward's badge and a pair of binoculars.

Anthony Hoy! I say . . .

Henry (*alarmed*) Hallo?

Anthony Just a quick word, old boy . . . If you can spare a moment.

Henry (*bracing himself*) Yes, of course.

Anthony From now on, I'm afraid I'm going to have to rule that little number out of bounds as far as you're concerned, old boy.

Henry (*irritated*) What little number are you talking about?

Anthony That one there who's just tried to throw herself under the hoofs of the Under-Thirteens' Selling Plate. She's my wife and she's off-limits, OK?

Henry That's up to her, isn't it?

Anthony No, it isn't. It isn't up to her, at all. It's up to me. And I'm telling you, OK?

Henry I suppose you're going to tell me she's your property?

Anthony Since you ask, yes, she bloody well is. So hands off.

Henry God, you're a nasty piece of work, aren't you?

Anthony Now listen, chummy, I'm being fairly civil to you, all things considered . . .

Henry Civil?

Anthony Fairly civil . . .

Henry You couldn't be more unpleasant if you tried –

Anthony Oh yes, I could be. I could be a lot more unpleasant than this if I tried, I warn you. I can be deeply, deeply unpleasant, chummy, if I choose to be – believe me, so far as you're concerned, at this moment in time, I'm being as charming as you're ever likely to know me, so I should make the best of it. Because I'm not going to be made a public laughing stock by some poncified townie with a hideous taste in suits coming down here and bonking my wife in my own chicken sheds, all right? Now bugger off. Is that loud and clear enough for you?

Henry (*taking a deep breath*) You don't perhaps consider your own behaviour has anything to do with this?

Anthony What behaviour?

Henry Your behaviour with – with Karen Knightly, for one thing.

Anthony Karen Knightly?

Henry Yes, Karen Knightly. I presume you remember her?

Anthony What the hell's she been telling you?

Henry That you had an affair with her . . .

Anthony laughs humorously.

Yes. And then chucked her over, when you'd had enough of her.

Anthony Is that what she told you?

Henry More or less, yes.

Anthony Karen Knightly and I had – well, you could hardly term it an affair – had a bit of sex together, let's say – for all of a month. Well, quite a lot of sex, really. We tried out all twenty-five of the bedrooms in that house of hers over the course of about a fortnight, starting in the attic and finishing up in the master suite. She insisted we dressed in suitable clothes to suit different locations. I remember our night in the nursery as particularly bizarre. When we'd completed the course, she declared that according to ancient law we were now legally engaged. And that at the next full moon I had to sacrifice my existing wife Imogen and change my name to Alric the Awesome. At which point, I realised she was stark staring mad and I broke off the relationship. She then plagued us both for months. Writing anonymous letters, drawing strange runes on our front door, phoning up claiming to be a midwife delivering my illegitimate child. You name it, she did it. Culminating, finally, in a phone call demanding that I be on Chelsea Bridge at eight thirty sharp or she would throw herself in the Thames.

Henry (*suspecting a ring of truth in all this*) My God. And did you go?

Anthony Yes, I did. I stood on that bloody bridge for an hour and a half hoping to see her jump. No such luck. Not so much as a ripple. So I went home again.

Henry She was on Albert Bridge, actually.

Anthony (*uninterested*) Was she? Oh well, that figures. Anyway, that's beside the point. Karen Knightly is totally immaterial. I've forgotten her. We're talking about Imogen. And that one you can forget. You keep out of my chickens. Away from my cows. Off my pigs. And well clear of my wife, all right?

Anthony moves away.

Henry I'm afraid you won't get rid of me that easily.

Anthony Really? Then I'll have to do it the hard way, won't I?

Anthony strides off, leaving Henry brooding and scheming. The gymkhana goes on remorselessly as the lights cross-fade to –

SCENE FIVE

9.00 a.m.
Lembridge Tennit. Lydia is leading Karen into the outer area of Jeremy Pride's office.

Lydia (*looking around*) No, I think they're probably both in the meeting at present. What day is it? Wednesday. Yes. Right. Just time for a quick run down, then. (*Rapidly*) Mr Pride. Mr Jeremy Pride, he's the younger of our two Mr Prides – our other one's Stuart Pride – they're not actually related but they're both directors and it can get rather confusing – but they loathe it if you get them muddled up so try not to. Anyway, Mr Jeremy Pride, whom you'll be working for, is mainly concerned with our building operations in the domestic sphere. Obviously, we've got an overseas building side as well but that's on a completely different floor and really won't bother you and is run by a man called John Hatch, whom you'll probably never meet, nobody ever does. Now, as I said, this is only just a temporary filler for you until we can find you another more permanent job but it will give you a chance to see a whole operation globally, rather than just bits of it – which I think should be really quite fascinating for you, don't you agree? Strictly, of course, you won't be working for Mr Pride but technically you'll be assisting Mr Pride's assistant who's been screaming for help because apparently their paperwork has just got beyond a joke. That all make sense? Great. Can I leave you to introduce yourself then? Only we've got a crisis. It's the flu season come round again, I'm afraid. Always seems to coincide with Wimbledon fortnight for some inexplicable reason. May see you at lunch. I think that'll be your desk there . . . Bye!

Karen Bye . . .

Lydia hurries out. Karen explores the office a little. She examines the other desk. She idly opens one of the drawers. Veronica Webb enters. She sees Karen and stops. Veronica is a woman in her late forties. She is an abrupt, matter-of-fact, no-nonsense sort of woman. She stares at Karen suspiciously.

Veronica What the hell do you think you're doing?

Karen (*jumping guiltily*) Oh, hallo.

Veronica Who are you? What are you doing in here?

Karen I'm Karen Knightly.

Veronica Who?

Karen Karen Knightly. I've been sent here by Mrs Bulley's office. I understand they wanted assistance.

Veronica You got a staff card?

Karen Er, yes.

Karen produces her card. Veronica studies it and her with deep suspicion.

Veronica (*studying Karen's picture*) This meant to be you?

Karen Yes.

Veronica Not a very good picture, is it?

Karen No, I'm afraid I'm not very photogenic.

Veronica You can say that again, you look like a sheepdog. What did you say you wanted?

Karen I'm here to help out, apparently.

Veronica Help who?

Karen Mr Pride's assistant. He apparently wanted some help. Is he around, by any chance?

Veronica (*returning Karen's card*) He certainly is. She's here. I'm Mr Pride's assistant.

Karen (*taken a little aback*) Ah!

Veronica About time. I've been yelling for someone for days. (*Looks Karen up and down*) Well, I suppose you'll do. You're better than nothing. Where do you come from? The pool?

Karen No, I was Mr Seeds' secretary. But unfortunately . . .

Veronica You mean the one who fell off the roof?

Karen That's right.

Veronica Stupid ass. Right. Well, if you're working for me, let's get the ground rules absolutely clear. I work for Mr Pride and I work very hard indeed. You'll be working for me and you're going to work even harder. Up till now I've no doubt you've wiggled your rear end at your boss and got away with murder. Well, that won't cut any ice round here, girl, so forget it. I don't lust after your body and I don't want to listen to your vacuous conversation. You just get your nose down and keep it there, all right? You do that, we'll get along just fine. First hint of trouble and I'll personally boot you straight downstairs again, is that clear?

Karen Yes, Miss . . . Mrs . . .

Veronica Webb. Miss Webb. If you're still here on Wednesday, you can call me Veronica. If you make it till next Christmas you can call me Ronny. That's your desk there.

Karen Yes.

Veronica This is mine. Don't touch it again.

Karen No, Miss Webb.

She prepares to sit.

Veronica (*gathering an armload of folders*) Here you are. Start with these. Can you read?

Karen Yes, I have shorthand and typing . . .

Veronica So long as you can read that's all that matters. Alphabetical by name. All of these, all right? Anything pre-1980 – bin it. OK? When you've finished these, there's a room full of them next door. As you finish each folder, take it along to Janey in the computer room at the end of the corridor there. Too complicated for you?

Karen No, I'm sure I'll manage that, Miss Webb. It looks a real challenge.

Veronica (*looking at her suspiciously*) Yes. Butter wouldn't melt in your in-tray, would it? I bet you're a load of trouble given the chance, aren't you?

Their eyes meet. Karen merely smiles at her sweetly. Jeremy enters. A pleasant, rather shy man in his fifties.

Jeremy (*as he enters*) Ronny, I've been wondering whether we shouldn't be – (*Seeing Karen*) Ah. Good morning. Who have we here?

Veronica (*her manner subtly changing*) Oh, Jeremy, this is Miss Knightly . . .

Karen Karen Knightly . . .

Veronica Karen Knightly, who's been sent upstairs to help us out. Karen, this is Mr Pride . . .

Jeremy Hallo. Jeremy Pride. Welcome aboard the madhouse.

He laughs. Veronica laughs.

Karen (*smiling*) Thank you.

Jeremy Good, right-o then. Anything you want, Ronny will . . . Miss Webb will sort you out, I expect. Give me five minutes, Ronny, and then can we have a chat?

Veronica Yes, right. I put that letter for Taylor's on your desk . . .

Jeremy Oh, Lord, yes. OK.

Jeremy goes into his office. Karen has been watching Veronica. The latter is aware of the look and readjusts her face, which has been smiling non-stop since Jeremy first came in.

Karen He seems very nice.

Veronica (*shortly*) Yes, he is.

Karen I should imagine he's very intelligent, too.

Veronica He's brilliant. Utterly brilliant. This whole place would fall apart without him. He's the only one of the directors with any . . .

Karen Is he married?

Veronica (*sharply*) Why?

Karen I was just curious, that's all.

Veronica Well, you can forget that straight away.

Karen I beg your pardon?

Veronica If I catch you making eyes at him, you'll be straight downstairs, I can tell you.

Karen I'm sure I'd no intention . . .

Veronica Mr Pride only has eyes for his work. He's there at his desk long before anyone else in this building arrives and he's usually the last to leave. He is a happy contented bachelor and that is how he prefers to remain. I should know, I've been with him for twelve years and I know him better than anyone.

Karen (*mildly offended*) I'm sorry, I'm sure. I won't ask again.

Veronica As long as that's clear.

Karen I won't say another word.

Veronica Just – get on with your work, girl. And forget about him, all right?

Karen Yes, Miss Webb.

She opens a folder.

Jeremy (*off*) Ronny, here a second. Do you mind?

Veronica Coming, Jeremy. (*She hurries to the door. To Karen*) And by the way, no smoking and no strong perfumes, OK? I can't stand the smell and they bring on Mr Pride's asthma . . .

Karen Yes, Miss Webb . . .

She starts to hum to herself, thoughtfully.

Veronica (*turning in the doorway*) And we can do without the musical refrain, too, thank you very much.

Karen Yes, Miss Webb.

Veronica goes out. Karen looks up from her work as soon as she has gone. She smiles secretively to herself. A scheme is hatching somewhere. Slowly she begins to rock to and fro and starts to hum softly again. As this happens, the lights cross-fade to –

SCENE SIX

7.30 p.m.
The lounge of Daphne Teale's bungalow. Bright and tasteless. From above, the distant bass thud of pop music from a record player. Daphne leads Henry into the room.

Daphne Come in, please . . .

Henry Thank you. (*Taking in the room*) Oh, ah.

Daphne (*proudly*) Like it?

Henry (*who can't think what to say*) Very much. Very much.

Daphne It's partly the lighting.

Henry Yes, yes.

Daphne You can do a lot with coloured bulbs.

Henry Yes. (*He searches for words*) Yes, they give the place a lot of . . . light and . . .

Daphne Colour.

Henry Colour. Yes. Very interesting.

Daphne Like a drink, Mr –

Henry Henry, please, Henry. No thank you –

Daphne Daphne, then.

Henry Daphne.

Daphne Sure?

Henry Absolutely.

Daphne Take a seat, then.

Henry Thank you. (*Noticing a photograph*) Oh look, this is . . . Is this you in all your . . .?

Daphne That's when I was mayor.

Henry Heavens!

Daphne Fourteen years ago, that was.

Henry Ah. And this is – who's this with you? Surely it's the – Princess . . .?

Daphne (*proud*) Yes. The Duchess of Kent.

Henry The Duchess of Kent, yes, of course it is.

Daphne Opening the new wing of the hospital.

Henry Oh, yes. Must have been an – occasion.

Daphne Oh, yes. She made a speech. I made a speech.

Henry But you're not mayor now?

Daphne Oh no, I served my term.

Henry But you're still a councillor, of course?

Daphne Oh, yes. But I have the business to run as well.

Henry What's that?

Daphne The Beauty Salon. I'm a beautician by profession.

Henry Yes, of course. I think I've passed your – shop . . .?

Daphne Salon.

Henry Salon. The one with the pink curtains?

Daphne Ruched. Right. Well, what is it I can do for you? I take it you don't want a facial, do you?

She laughs.

Henry (*laughing heartily*) No, no . . . (*A slight pause*) This is very awkward really, but . . . Is Norma at home at the moment?

Daphne She's upstairs, listening to her music. Why?

Henry Well, I've come to talk to you. As her mother.

Daphne I'm not her mother.

Henry (*taken aback*) Oh. I'm sorry, I understood –

Daphne She's my sister's child.

Henry Oh, I see. And your sister . . .?

Daphne Dead. Died when Norma was three.

Henry And her father?

Daphne (*dry laugh*) What father?

Henry Oh, I see.

Daphne Could have been any one of a dozen.

Henry Oh. A bit flighty, your sister, was she?

Daphne She was a whore.

Henry Ah.

Daphne (*with satisfaction*) She'll be suffering now, wherever she is.

Henry Well . . .

Daphne Red-hot coals heaped on her navel.

Henry Ah.

Daphne What about Norma? I mean, I'm responsible for her, if that's what you want to know.

Henry Well, it's just that . . . she is, I think you'll agree – at an impressionable age.

Daphne She's only half there, isn't she?

Henry Well, let's say she's yet to develop her personality fully.

Daphne I'd have had her working for me in the Beauty Salon. Only she'd have been a liability. She can't tell face cream from floor polish, that one. Be rubbing all sorts of things into people, wouldn't she? Better off working up there with that old layabout, that's what I say.

Henry You mean Winnie?

Daphne And those two, her and her brother, they just about suit Norma. All about the same level. They make a good household. I don't know what you're doing up there, I'm sure.

Henry No. Nor do I. Altogether.

Daphne That girl – that Karen . . . When we opened that hospital wing, she was a patient in the new ward. Ten years old. She stood up on her bed and sang 'The Red Flag'.

Henry Heavens . . .

Daphne This was with royalty coming round, mark you. Right in front of the Duchess. Should have drowned that child at birth, her parents. But they never . . . Too busy with their butterflies. They paid for it dearly later though, didn't they?

Henry How do you mean?

Daphne (*changing the subject sharply*) What about Norma, then? What's she done? Do you want to see her?

Henry No, no. She hasn't done anything. It's what's being done to her. In a sense. I think she's in danger of being . . . well, to use an old-fashioned phrase . . . corrupted.

Daphne Corrupted?

Henry I don't think it's her fault. Please. In fact, I'm certain it isn't. The man, whom I've been told it is – is . . . well, he's a notorious womaniser. And I think Norma is just another of his – conquests.

Daphne (*rising, grimly*) Who is it?

Henry Now you must promise –

Daphne Who is it?

Henry You mustn't take it out on –

Daphne Tell me his name.

Henry Well, all right. It's Anthony Staxton-Billing.

Daphne stares at him, her face a mixture of emotions.

Daphne (*at length, softly*) Anthony Staxton-Billing?

Henry Yes.

Daphne With Norma?

Henry Yes.

Daphne Anthony. Staxton. Billing. (*Crossing to the door, fiercely*) Norma! NORMA!

Norma (*off*) Hallo?

Daphne (*yelling*) Come down here. Now.

Norma (*off*) Just a minute.

Daphne (*yelling*) Now. Do you hear? Now.

Upstairs, the music stops.

Henry Look, I must ask you not –

Daphne It's all right, thank you. You can leave this to me now, thank you.

Henry But you mustn't take it out on Norma because . . .

Daphne This is a family matter, thank you so much. Now, would you leave, please.

Before Henry can do so, Norma comes down. Out of her maid's outfit and dressed in jeans and a T-shirt, she looks a rather different sight. She also has make-up on and probably plans to go out.

Norma What is it then? (*Seeing Henry*) Oh. Evening, Mr Bell. (*She does an involuntary little bob. To Daphne*) What you want then?

Daphne (*softly*) You just had to have him, didn't you? Couldn't resist him. Somebody else's and you just had to have him.

Norma Have who?

Daphne You know bloody well who. Don't you stand there, madam, like that. I can see the lust steaming off you from here. You cheap little Jezebel. Look at you, coated in tart's make-up and your bust hanging half out, in your tight trousers so you can see every brazen bump that God gave you, you filthy little trollop – why don't you just stick a price tag on it and have done with it, eh?

Norma (*alarmed*) What have I done?

Daphne It just had to be him, didn't it? I knew this was going on. I knew it. It had to be Tony Staxton-Billing, didn't it? Not anybody else? Not someone your own age, oh no. It had to be him –

Norma (*totally bemused*) Mr Staxton-Billing?

Daphne (*approaching her*) I'm going to give you a facial, my girl, you won't forget in a hurry –

> *Daphne swats Norma across the face. The force of the blow sends the unprepared girl flying. She falls backwards into a chair. Daphne follows up the attack by falling on top of her. A brawl ensues. Norma recovers enough to make the contest slightly more evenly matched. Henry, once he's recovered from the shock of this, attempts to separate them.*

(*As this ensues*) You tart . . . you whore . . . you hussy . . . you trollop . . . you bitch . . .

Norma (*simultaneously*) Look, why are you . . . don't you . . . you've gone mad, you've . . . someone get her off me . . . she's bloody off her head . . .

Henry (*simultaneously, getting vocally rather stuck in a groove*) Now, come on. Come on. Come on. Come on – come on– come on. Come on, come on. Come on. Comeoncomeoncomeon.

> *At last the antagonists separate. Probably thanks to exhaustion, rather than to Henry's efforts. They are all on the floor.*

That's it. That's it.

> *Norma is crying softly. Daphne recovers her breath and then starts to get to her feet.*

(*Alarmed*) Now, just a minute, don't –

Daphne It's all right. I've finished with her.

Henry Where are you going?

Daphne I'm going to have a word with him. I know just where Mr Staxton-Billing will be at this time of night. In the saloon bar of the Fox and Hounds, drinking with all the other so-called young farmers. I'll just go and have a little word with him in public. Excuse me.

She marches out.

Henry (*vainly*) Don't you think you ought to . . .

Norma (*muttering*) I haven't had him, what's she going on about?

Henry (*bringing his attention round to Norma*) What?

Norma What she think I want her feller for? I wouldn't want her old feller, anyway.

Henry Her old feller?

Norma Her old feller.

Henry Whose old feller?

Norma Her old feller. Why should I want her old feller? I got my own young feller. I don't even like her feller, I think he's horrible. I don't want her feller, do I? What's my feller going to say if he thinks I've been with her feller?

Henry Wait a minute, Norma. This old feller. Are we talking about Anthony Staxton-Billing? That old feller?

Norma Yes, her feller.

Henry (*dully*) Her feller? He's her feller?

Norma Yes. Who else are we talking about?

Henry Yes. (*Thoughtfully*) Right. Right. I'd better go and try and – (*Turning in the doorway*) Sorry about this. I really am. Oh, God.

Henry goes after Daphne. He doesn't seem to be in much of a hurry to catch her up.

Norma (*miserably*) What's my feller going to say? That's what I want to know . . .

The lights fade on Norma and cross-fade to –

SCENE SEVEN

9·10 a.m.
Lembridge Tennit. The outer area of Jeremy Pride's office. It is empty. Jeremy's and Veronica's voices are heard from his office.

Veronica . . . I think you'll find, Jeremy, they wanted twenty. I'm sure that's what they said in their letter. If you like I'll go and check.

During this, Karen sticks her head cautiously round the outer door. She listens and, seeing the coast is clear, nips in and places a gift-wrapped single red rose on one side of Veronica's desk. She darts out again.

Jeremy (*during this*) No, you're invariably correct on these matters, Ronny. I'm certainly not going to argue with you. I must say, though, twenty does seem an awful lot.

Veronica Well, I thought so at the time but I didn't like to say anything. I heard you agreeing to twenty and I remember saying to myself, is this wise? Aren't we perhaps going to regret this by June?

Jeremy Yes, the answer to that is we certainly are. Well, it's done now. I'll sort it out, don't worry.

Veronica Anything else, Jeremy?

Jeremy No, thanks. I'll give you a yell.

Veronica Right-o.

Veronica comes out of the inner office. She has scarcely done so when Karen comes rushing in through the outer door.

Karen (*breathlessly*) Miss Webb, I'm so sorry. The trains have gone mad this morning . . .

Veronica (*coolly*) Good morning.

Karen You feel so helpless. Just sitting there on that tube. And they never bother to tell you, do they? I –

Veronica (*cutting her off, rather brusquely*) Karen, I'm really not at all interested in your travelling saga. If the journey's that complicated, you'd better set off earlier, hadn't you, dear? And it would be a nice gesture if you paid me back the ten minutes you owe me at the end of the day. That I would appreciate.

Karen (*sitting, suitably mortified*) Yes, course. Of course, Miss Webb.

Without further ado, Karen opens her file and continues with her seemingly endless task. Veronica also sits. In a moment, she comes across the rose. She stares at it, mystified.

Veronica (*holding the box at arm's length*) What on earth's this?

Karen (*looking up*) Sorry?

Veronica Where on earth did this come from?

Karen No idea. What is it?

Veronica (*inspecting the box cautiously*) Looks like a flower. Yes, it's a rose.

Karen How nice.

Veronica A red rose.

Karen Oh-ho.

Veronica (*slightly irritably*) What do you mean, 'Oh-ho'?

Karen Single red rose. You know what that means? An admirer.

Veronica (*putting the box down again, irritably*) Oh, rubbish.

Karen Who's it from?

Veronica I don't know. It doesn't say.

Karen An anonymous admirer!

Veronica I don't even know how it got there.

Karen Was it there when you arrived?

Veronica I don't think so. It may have been. I never noticed. I went straight in to see Jeremy. Like I always do.

Karen The mystery thickens.

Veronica It's a joke by someone.

Karen Lovely joke. I wish someone would play jokes like that on me.

Veronica You can have it. I don't want it.

Karen No, it's yours. Keep it.

Veronica What am I supposed to do with it? Put it behind my ear?

Karen Take it home.

Veronica No point. The cats will eat it.

Karen Do you have cats?

Veronica Four. And they all eat flowers for some reason.

Karen Ah, well. That's because they live in a city.

Veronica Is it?

Karen Well, my father was a vet – well, both my parents were actually . . .

Veronica Were they really, how lovely.

Karen They were in practice together. And he always said, my father, that cats who lived in cities always tried to re-create their natural habitat. And if they couldn't find the real thing – real trees, real grass, real flowers and so on – they'd start to invent them.

Veronica How interesting. How very interesting. I think that might be right.

Karen Cats apparently have tremendous imaginations.

Veronica Oh, I know. They do. They do. Do you keep cats?

Karen Not now, alas, not now. But when I was a child our cottage was just swarming with animals – and there must have been – oh – about ten cats at any one time . . .

Veronica How lovely. Where was this?

Karen Cumbria.

Veronica Cumbria. Oh, beautiful. Well, I must bring you in my pictures. Would you like to see my cats?

Karen I'd love to. Thank you so much, Miss Webb.

Veronica (*smiling*) Please. Veronica.

Karen Veronica.

She smiles back.

Veronica (*admonishingly*) Ah well. Down to work.

Karen You don't think that rose could have been from . . . (*She indicates Jeremy's office*)

Veronica (*in a whisper*) No! Of course not. (*She looks at the rose*) No. He never has done in twelve years, I don't know why he should start now. (*Another look*) No.

Karen Aren't you going to put it in water?

Veronica I haven't got time to put it in water.

Karen You know what they say, Veronica?

Veronica (*irritably*) What do they say?

Karen If you let it wither, then his love will die . . .

Veronica Absolute poppycock. (*She laughs self-consciously*) I've never heard anything so infantile. Romantic twaddle.

A silence. They work.

(*Crossly*) Oh, well, I suppose there's no point in sitting here watching all the petals fall off it. (*Rising*) I'll get a jug or something. This is all a very silly joke by someone. I'm sure it is.

Veronica goes out, slightly flustered. Karen watches her, smiling. She starts to hum to herself again. As she does so the lights cross-fade to –

SCENE EIGHT

9.30 a.m.
The dining room at Furtherfield House. Henry sits finishing his breakfast. A bird flutters past and dive-bombs him. Henry ducks. Winnie comes in, alone, carrying an

*empty tray. There is a slight atmosphere between her and
Henry.*

Winnie Finished, sir?

Henry Yes, thank you.

Winnie Anything more, sir?

Henry No, thank you.

Winnie May I clear then, sir?

Henry You may, Winnie, thank you.

Winnie Thank you, sir.

> *A silence. Henry rises and thinks about leaving the
> room. Winnie clears the table.*

Henry (*unable to avoid the topic*) Winnie . . .

Winnie Yes, sir?

Henry I'm afraid I got – You may have misled me rather
badly yesterday.

Winnie Me, sir?

Henry Yes. You see, I clearly had the impression from
you that Norma was having some sort of relationship
with Mr Staxton-Billing.

Winnie I'm sure I never said that, sir.

Henry Well, you certainly gave that impression, Winnie.
To me at any rate. With the result that the fur is now
flying.

Winnie It certainly is, sir.

Henry Oh, you've already heard?

Winnie Norma telephoned me earlier. To say she wasn't
coming in on account of her injury.

Henry Injury?

Winnie Her black eye, sir.

Henry Oh . . .

Winnie Nothing to the injuries down at the Fox and Hounds, so I've heard.

Henry Well, I arrived too late to stop any of that.

Winnie Five young farmers with broken limbs.

Henry Yes, all right . . .

Winnie I don't know how you ever thought to get that impression from me, sir.

Henry (*angrily*) Well, I did. And it's too late now, isn't it? The damage is done.

The doorbell rings.

Winnie (*huffily*) Excuse me, sir.

Winnie goes out to the hall. Henry paces about agitatedly. The bird dive-bombs him again. He ducks. In a moment, Winnie returns with Imogen.

Mrs Staxton-Billing, sir.

Imogen Henry, what have you been doing?

Henry Oh, don't start, please . . .

During the next, Winnie gathers up the laden tray and goes off to the kitchen.

Imogen The whole village was in pandemonium. Ambulances rushing to and fro, the pub's got half its windows boarded up. What on earth did you do?

Henry (*wretchedly*) I was trying to . . . I was . . . getting hold of entirely the wrong end of the stick. That's what

I was doing, if you must know. (*Angrily, after Winnie*) And it wasn't totally my fault.

Imogen (*tenderly*) Did you do all that because of me?

Henry How do you mean?

Imogen You did. Didn't you?

Henry (*slightly guiltily*) In a – in a way. Possibly.

Imogen That's very touching. (*She smiles*) Well – don't I even get a kiss?

Henry I thought you'd broken off our relationship.

Imogen When?

Henry On Tuesday? At the junior gymkhana? We can't go on, you said.

Imogen Well. I was in one of my moods. Forget it.

Henry I can't keep up with your moods.

Imogen Look who's talking. Look who's got moods.

Henry I'm entitled to moods.

Imogen (*pleading*) Kiss. Please?

Henry kisses her, lightly and without a great deal of commitment. The bird flutters past.

My God. What was that?

Henry Just a bird.

Imogen Oh. I thought it was a bat. Knowing this house, it could easily have been. I'm sorry if I get moody sometimes, Henry. You must see, it's not easy for me.

Henry No. Nor is it for me.

Imogen No. I realise that. And I'm afraid it's going to get even harder for you soon.

Henry How do you mean?

Imogen Well, you don't suppose there aren't going to be repercussions to all this, do you?

Henry Who from?

Imogen God knows. Mrs Teale? Who apparently has fractured her knuckles. Norma? Who may have a chipped cheekbone. Assorted young farmers. Or Anthony, who has mild concussion and a very dented reputation.

Henry Is that all he's got? Pity.

Imogen You can't go around saying things like that about people.

Henry But the man was having an affair after all.

Imogen Yes, but with Mrs Teale. Not with her daughter.

Henry Not much difference, is there?

Imogen There's a hell of a difference. Besides, everyone knew about him and Mrs Teale. It was above board. It's quite another thing to accuse him of being a cradle-snatcher. Mud sticks.

Henry Did you know about him and Mrs Teale?

Imogen No. But then I didn't want to. I didn't want to know he was having a good time with Mrs Teale. I preferred to believe that he was still with Karen. At least if he was with her, I knew she'd be giving him a terrible time.

Henry You think there'll be a backlash, then?

Imogen Didn't you expect one when you started all this?

Henry I – I don't know. I just wanted you – to see what sort of man you were married to –

Imogen (*calmly*) I know what sort of man I'm married to, Henry, you didn't have to tell me –

Henry It might have done the trick and tipped you over.

Imogen Tipped me over where?

Henry Tipped you over in my direction. Made you leave the wretched man, finally and for ever.

Imogen Henry, I'm sorry, I can't go away and live with you in a bedsit. Not with two children. I love my home, too, actually. So do the kids. It's paradise for them. What's more, it's mine. I don't see why I should just give it all up and leave it for Anthony. If anyone's going, it's him. So there.

Henry Then what's keeping him there? He obviously doesn't love you any more. Why doesn't he just buzz off and make room for someone who does?

Imogen I know, I know. It's a dead marriage. The last rites have long been read. I know that. You know that. But unfortunately Anthony doesn't. He will not let go. He doesn't really want me any more but he won't let me go. Why? I don't know. The children, of course. He's fond of them. And, whatever else, I'm very useful to him and he'd find it extremely hard to get another woman to run things the way I do for absolutely no thanks at all. I don't think either Karen Knightly or Daphne Teale would do what I do for him.

Henry Then why do it? Why make yourself so invaluable? I don't see why you bother.

Imogen (*sighing*) I don't know. Because I'm me, I suppose. You're right. I should just let the whole place go to pot. Let the pigs starve, the chickens get bunged up with eggs, the cows fill up with milk and burst . . . I don't know.

Why do I clean the kitchen floor every single evening
once the kids have gone to bed? I don't know . . . Yes,
I do know, actually. Because I can't bear wading through
filth, that's why. I can't bear bits of old bread and Marmite
glued to my instep. God, I loathe Marmite. (*Pause*) I'm
sorry. I don't make it very easy, do I? (*Pause*) Do you
want to pack it in? Us, I mean?

Henry No.

Imogen I'd quite understand, really. I wouldn't be hurt.
I'd cry for weeks on end, but I'd quite understand.

Henry (*gently*) I don't want you to cry any more. Ever.

Imogen smiles at him.

Imogen Well, if you don't, you'd better not say things
like that to me for a kick-off, had you? That makes me
cry immediately. (*Dabbing at her eyes with her fingers*)
God, I'm in such an *awful* state, I don't know what's the
matter with me. It's much too early for the change, isn't it?
I do hope so. I went to the children's concert the other
day, you know. It was absolutely God-awful. I mean
frightful. You've no idea. And our two were just so
embarrassingly bad, it wasn't true. And I sat there crying
my eyes out. As if I was watching some wonderful,
brilliant opera. Or *King Lear* or something. There they
were, all standing in a line singing 'Nick-nack Paddiwack'
and me in floods of tears. God, it was so dreadful . . .

*She trails off, unable to continue. Henry holds her
gently.*

I'm sorry. I'm such a dreary person to be with. I wouldn't
blame you if you went and found someone terribly fat
and jolly . . .

Henry (*softly*) It's OK. It's OK. I'll think of something.

The doorbell rings.

Oh God, who's that now?

Winnie comes through to answer it.

Winnie (*eyeing them both disapprovingly*) Excuse me, please.

Imogen (*weakly*) I must go.

Henry Yes, all right.

Imogen gets to her feet. Henry kisses her lightly on the cheek. She moves to the door. Before she can reach it, Winnie ushers in Marcus. He stops as he sees Imogen.

Winnie (*with some satisfaction*) Colonel Lipscott, sir.

Marcus Ah!

Imogen Hallo, Uncle.

Marcus Hallo, Imogen.

He stares at her intently.

Imogen (*avoiding his stare*) Excuse me, I was just off, I have to . . . Excuse me.

Imogen hurries out, followed by Winnie.

Henry Hallo.

Marcus We have met.

Henry Yes.

Marcus You had a different suit on, I remember.

Henry That's right.

Marcus (*extending a hand*) Marcus Lipscott.

Henry Henry Bell.

They shake hands.

Would you prefer to move into the –

Marcus No, here's fine. Here's absolutely fine.

Henry Fine.

Marcus How are things in Strewth Street?

Henry Oh, pretty brisk.

A pause.

Marcus I couldn't help noticing she'd been crying. My niece.

Henry Oh, yes . . .

Marcus Not really fair on her. All this, you know.

Henry I agree.

Marcus She's a nice girl. A damn nice girl.

Henry She is.

Marcus In a country which, in my humble opinion, is running pretty short of nice girls just at present.

Henry (*intrigued by this theory*) Really?

Marcus I haven't met any. All too busy taking their clothes off and selling cornflakes. Anyway. Imogen means a lot to me.

Henry And to me.

Marcus Maybe. Maybe. We shall see.

Henry (*defiantly*) We certainly shall.

A pause. Marcus is evidently impressed by Henry's vehemence. The bird flutters overhead.

Marcus (*momentarily startled*) Good God . . .

Henry (*apologetically*) Sorry.

Marcus That's a green woodpecker, isn't it?

Henry Is it?

Marcus Shouldn't keep it indoors. He'll have your panelling for breakfast. Anyway. Why I'm here. You're probably aware you've stirred up a hornets' nest?

Henry Yes.

Marcus Managed to slander half the neighbourhood. Including my – nephew-in-law. Anthony.

Henry Most of what I said was true. I may have got the wrong woman. But the principle remains. It was essentially, give or take a few details, the truth.

Marcus I don't give a tinker's whether it was true or not. You still can't go around saying things like that. Not in this village.

Henry Why not if it's true?

Marcus For the love of Mike, man, if we all went around shouting out the truth every time we felt like it there wouldn't be a building left standing in the county. It's just not on. It really isn't. You've spread accusations about a chap, some of which were as it happens entirely false and now he's demanding some sort of satisfaction from you.

Henry What sort of satisfaction? Money?

Marcus Have you got any money?

Henry Not much.

Marcus Then don't be ridiculous.

Henry What does he want then? An apology?

Marcus He wants a bit more than that, old chap.

Henry What, then?

Marcus What do you suppose? He wants to fight you.

Henry Fight me?

Marcus A duel, man, a duel.

Henry A duel? What sort of duel?

Marcus He suggests guns.

Henry Guns? He wants to fight with guns?

Marcus Have you another preference?

Henry Well . . . swords . . . ?

Marcus Can you use a sword?

Henry No.

Marcus Then don't be so ridiculous. Neither can he. Both of you waving swords about indiscriminately – you'd be an absolute liability to everyone. No, guns are safer. They're also cleaner. Take my tip.

Henry Don't be absurd. We can't fight a duel. Not in this day and age.

Marcus Why not?

Henry People just don't do it any more.

Marcus They do round here. You know when the last duel was fought around here?

Henry No idea.

Marcus Go on. Have a guess.

Henry Seventeen-fifty.

Marcus Last June.

Henry Good God. What did the police have to say?

Marcus They said what we wanted them to say. Accidental death.

Henry You mean you bribed the police?

Marcus Of course not. No need to. Listen. A group of like-minded chaps arrange a shooting party. Amongst them are the two protagonists and their seconds. They set off at dawn to shoot a few rabbits, grouse, whatever. Depending on the season. They even bag a brace or two, just to make it look above board. They reach a quiet spot – say, a clearing in the middle of a wood – and the two rivals get on with it. Ten paces, turn and fire and the slowest man buys it . . .

Henry I'm having a spot of trouble with this . . .

Marcus One of the party, an innocent member, rushes for help. Officer! Officer! So-and-so – blithering idiot – just ran right in front of the guns . . . killed instantly. Terrible tragedy, sir. Happens all the time. Flowers to the widow. Rest in peace.

Henry You've actually done this?

Marcus When things reach a certain stage between two chaps, it becomes more or less inevitable. I don't know, I expect women will be doing it, too, before long.

Henry There must be another way.

Marcus What way's that?

Henry Well, lawyers . . .

Marcus Lawyers? Good God, man, you're better off taking a chance with both barrels.

Henry I'm sorry, I can't accept this. I'm sorry. Besides, Anthony Staxton-Billing's an experienced – gunsman. I've never fired a shot in my life. What sort of contest is that?

Marcus You never know. You might have beginner's luck.

Henry Thank you. That's very reassuring.

Marcus You're within your rights to refuse, of course. So long as you don't care what people think of you.

Henry I don't give a damn. They don't think much of me round here anyway.

Marcus You presumably care what Imogen thinks of you?

Henry I don't honestly think that my not fighting a duel is going to alter her view of me.

Marcus Not fighting it mightn't. But fighting it might.

Henry Sorry?

Marcus Look at it this way. If you win, that makes her a widow. The way's clear to marry her. A free idyllic farmhouse. Built-in family. There'll even be a vacancy on the board of my company if you fancy it. So there's a job promised, as well. What more could you want?

Henry This is monstrous. Do you think I'd risk getting killed just for that?

Marcus People have done it for a damn sight less than that. Come on. Do you want the girl or don't you?

Henry Yes.

Marcus Well, then. Where's your problem?

Henry What if I lose?

Marcus You've got no problem at all then, have you?

Henry And what if I refuse?

Marcus Then I suggest you leave the district immediately. Because you won't be welcome here, I can tell you.

Henry I could take Imogen with me.

Marcus Always providing she'd agree to go.

A silence.

Well, you don't have to answer straight away. Twenty-four hours will do. (*Producing his wallet*) Here's my card. Better do things correctly. You can generally get hold of me at one or other of those numbers. It's all right, I can find my way out.

Marcus moves to the door.

Henry (*with sudden determination*) Colonel . . .

Marcus Yes?

Henry Tell Mr Staxton-Billing that I accept his challenge. And that I retract nothing.

Marcus Splendid. Good man. I take it firearms are acceptable?

Henry (*bravely*) Yes. Firearms are perfectly acceptable.

Marcus Excellent. Good day to you, sir.

Henry Good day, sir.

Marcus, just before he leaves, turns in the doorway.

Marcus (*almost as an afterthought*) Oh, by the way, if you take my tip you'll get yourself a second who can teach you how to fire the thing.

Marcus goes out. Henry takes a deep breath and looks rather worried. The bird swoops. He ducks nervously. As he does so, the lights cross-fade to –

SCENE NINE

9.45 a.m.

Lembridge Tennit. The outer area of Jeremy Pride's office. Karen is at her desk going idly through her folders. After a second, Veronica enters, looking rather flushed.

Veronica Oh, I'm so sorry I'm late . . . I mean, I've never been as late as this, I mean *ever* . . . I am sorry, I . . .

Karen (*reassuringly*) Don't worry, Veronica; no flap, really.

Veronica (*anxiously*) Is Jeremy . . .?

Karen He's at the finance meeting . . .

Veronica Oh yes, of course, that's today, isn't it? I should have been there, too. Honestly, I don't know if I'm coming or going . . .

Karen Sit and get your breath. Don't worry.

Veronica Yes, I'll . . .

Veronica sits. There is another red rose in the middle other desk.

Oh, look! Another . . .

Karen Yes. I noticed.

Veronica That's – five days in a row. This is getting beyond a joke, isn't it? And do you know, when I got home last night, the woman in the flat next door – she sometimes feeds the cats if I'm away – she's very helpful – she'd taken in this parcel. And guess what it was?

Karen I've no idea.

Veronica (*in a whisper*) Chocolates.

Karen Really?

Veronica A beautiful, beautiful huge box of chocolates. I mean huge. I was quite overwhelmed. I mean, I've never ever – in my life . . .

Karen Who do you think they were from?

Veronica It didn't say. No note, nothing. Posted locally. That I did see.

Karen Must be the rose man again.

Veronica It could be, couldn't it? Oh, and wait. That's not all. The reason I was late in this morning. I was just leaving and there's this Interflora man. With a huge bunch. Huge. For me. The woman next door must wonder what's going on.

Karen Flowers?

Veronica Roses.

Karen Red?

Veronica A dozen.

Karen Oh. Well. You're as good as engaged then, aren't you?

Veronica Oh, really . . .

Karen If you only knew who he was.

Veronica Well, I do have one small clue . . .

Karen You do?

Veronica Whoever it was certainly knows me. It's not a complete stranger, anyway. Not some crank who's just picked me out of the phone book.

Karen That's a relief.

Veronica No, I was thinking on the bus . . . He knew exactly the sort of chocolates I liked.

Karen Ah-ha!

Veronica Remember, I was telling you the other day over lunch . . .

Karen Were you? I don't remember.

Veronica Dark chocolates with soft centres. I'm very particular. Now who would have known that? Eh? Tell me that.

Karen Well . . . (*She indicates Jeremy's office*) You know who? Would he have known?

Veronica Yes. I think it has to be . . . I think it really has to be . . . (*She indicates Jeremy's office*)

Karen Oh, well.

She shakes her head.

Veronica What is it?

Karen Nothing.

Veronica What? Tell me.

Karen Oh, well . . . Since you've guessed already, I suppose it doesn't matter . . .

Veronica What are you saying?

Karen Promise you won't let on? You must promise.

Veronica What? (*Pause*) Come on. What?

Karen All right. I got here a little early this morning, anyway. And – of course Jeremy was here – and he came in and asked where you were – and we conjectured that you'd probably been held up . . .

Veronica (*agitated*) Oh, he did notice? He did notice, then?

Karen It didn't matter. Anyway, I happened to remark on that rose on your desk . . .

Veronica Oh, you shouldn't have done that . . .

Karen Well, he was sort of standing there looking at it . . .

Veronica Was he? I see. I see.

Karen So I said something like, 'Oh, isn't that lovely, she's got another rose.' And before I knew, he sat down there where you are now . . .

Veronica (*touching the chair*) Jeremy did? Here?

Karen Yes. And he just poured his heart out to me. Went on and on and on.

Veronica (*suspiciously*) What about?

Karen You.

Veronica Me?

Karen Veronica, he's absolutely besotted with you.

Veronica Jeremy is?

Karen Yes. It's very worrying. I don't know what you're going to do . . .

Veronica Worrying?

Karen He's quite obsessive.

Veronica (*frowning*) Yes, that is worrying, isn't it?

Karen What are you going to do?

Veronica I don't know. I don't know.

Karen You won't say anything, will you? He begged me not to tell you.

Veronica Why on earth should he do that?

Karen He's obviously terrified of openly declaring himself. You know how some men fear rejection . . . ?

Veronica Yes. Do they? Yes . . .

Karen I think it depends what *you* want to happen. You could confront him and frighten him off. That's often a good way.

Veronica (*unenthusiastically*) Yes . . .

Karen Or you could ignore him. Hope it dies out naturally . . .

Veronica Yes . . .

She considers this option.

Karen It depends really what you want, doesn't it?

Veronica Yes.

Karen I think those are your safest options.

Veronica Yes.

Karen That is unless you want to start gently encouraging the wretched man . . .

She laughs.

Veronica (*laughing*) Yes . . .

Karen (*laughing*) Maybe you do?

Veronica (*laughing*) No, no, no, no, no, no no . . .

Karen Well.

Veronica Heavens.

They stop laughing.

What did you mean by gentle encouragement?

Karen Oh, you know – little signals a woman gives off to a man – message received and understood, you know. Safe to proceed into harbour. Standard stuff.

Veronica Oh yes. (*Pause*) What sort of little signals? I mean – I'm sorry – I haven't, I've never – well, certainly not for . . . not since . . . Oh, dear, it's very hot . . . it's this dreadful air-conditioning . . . What are these signals one's supposed to give off?

Karen Well, you know, you smile at him a lot. That tells him you're happy in his company . . .

Veronica Yes, yes . . .

Karen You get a little girlish occasionally . . .

Veronica Girlish?

Karen Make him feel masterful . . .

Veronica Do you think I could get away with being girlish?

Karen There's a little girl inside every woman, Veronica.

Veronica Possibly.

Karen You wear your prettiest clothes.

Veronica I don't know that I've . . .

Karen Or you buy pretty clothes. Just for him. A little perfume.

Veronica No, no. Jeremy's asthma . . .

Karen Oh, yes. Well, slap on a bit of make-up . . .

Veronica Oh, I never wear make-up.

Karen Well, men appreciate it. It says to him – 'See, I have made the effort for you.'

Veronica Oh, I don't know about all this . . .

Karen Well, otherwise where's the signal, Veronica? Where's your signal?

Veronica Oh yes, I see, I see. Of course. No signal. But I haven't worn make-up since I was seventeen . . .

Karen Excuse me. May I . . .?

Karen dives into her bag and produces a very large bulging make-up bag. She places the bag in front of Veronica.

Veronica Heavens! What's all this?

Karen Discovered! My secret weakness. I'm afraid I buy make-up by the ton. Take that lot home with you and experiment – it's the only way . . .

Veronica Well, I – er – I . . . Are you sure you can spare it?

Karen That's just my emergency kit . . .

Veronica (*opening the bag and looking inside*) Well, I don't know . . . Some of this is very vivid . . .

Karen Experiment. Have fun.

Veronica I'll have to get up at three in the morning to put all this on.

Karen (*coyly*) Many women do to please the man they love.

Veronica The cats aren't going to be very happy – being woken up at that hour. Still, I suppose if I –

Karen (*hearing someone approaching*) Shh!

Veronica What? Oh!

She hastily conceals the make-up bag. Jeremy comes in, rubbing his eyes. He is rather tired this morning.

Karen (*mouthing to Veronica*) Smile . . .

Veronica (*flashing him a deep smile*) Morning, Jeremy.

Jeremy (*without so much as a glance at her*) Oh. Morning, Ronny. Give me five minutes, will you?

Veronica (*holding her smile, gamely*) Right-o, Jeremy.

Jeremy goes into his office. Veronica seems a little disconcerted.

Karen (*in a whisper*) Don't give up. If at first you don't succeed . . .

Veronica (*whispering eagerly*) Try, try again . . .

They smile at each other. As they do so, the lights cross-fade again to –

SCENE TEN

Noon.
    A drawing room at Furtherfield House. Oliver sits in a chair, staring thoughtfully at the wall. Henry enters.

Henry Ah. Oliver . . .

Oliver (*thoughtfully*) Mmm?

Henry Could you spare a minute?

Oliver (*not moving*) Yah.

Henry waits for a second but Oliver still remains deep in thought.

Henry (*plunging in*) I was just wondering if you –

Oliver (*cutting in over him*) You see, if that wall came down. If we bashed that one out . . .

Henry Sorry?

Oliver I don't think that wall's important, do you? That one there?

Henry Well. It depends what you mean by important. I suppose that, in so far as it separates this room from the next, it's fairly vital.

Oliver (*impatiently*) No, no, no, no, no. Structurally.

Henry Structurally? I've no idea.

Oliver I had a look upstairs, briefly. It doesn't appear to be holding anything up. Not that I could see.

Henry Except the roof, perhaps?

Oliver No. That'll be the wall on the floor above the floor above this one that'll support the roof.

Henry (*accompanying this with a few unhelpful hand gestures*) Yes, but something must in turn be supporting the floor that's supporting the wall – that's – supporting the floor – that's supporting the – wall above that – which in turn is supporting the roof.

Henry pauses. Oliver considers.

If you follow me.

Oliver (*nodding appreciatively*) Good point. You've studied architecture, then?

Henry No. Only from the street. What were you planning on doing then?

Oliver I was wondering, if I knocked that wall down there, whether I could combine these two rooms to make a squash court. But that's shot that idea in the head.

Henry Pity. Do you play squash?

Oliver Not at all. But I was thinking, if I had my own private court here on the premises there'd be no more excuse not to learn, would there?

Henry True. (*Looking about*) If you did that, you wouldn't leave yourself anywhere much to sit down though, would you?

Oliver (*irritably*) I wouldn't want to sit down, would I? I'd be playing squash, for God's sake?

Henry (*giving up*) Yes. Absolutely true. (*Trying again*) I wondered if I could . . . ?

Oliver Oh yes, sure. What was it you wanted?

Henry Do you have . . . ? I wondered if you had anything in the house like a gun?

Oliver A gun?

Henry Yes.

Oliver A shotgun? That sort of thing?

Henry Exactly.

Oliver Got a whole room full of them, why? Want to shoot something, do you?

Henry Yes. Yes, I do.

Oliver What you after? Rabbit? Pheasant? Partridge?

Henry Actually. No. A person.

Oliver A person?

Henry Yes.

Oliver You mean a person as in people?

Henry Yes.

Oliver You mean generally? I mean, are you simply planning on blazing away at the public in general or at someone specific?

Henry Oh, someone specific.

Oliver Oh, that's OK, then. Sure. I hope you didn't mind my asking?

Henry No, no.

Oliver Only obviously you can't hand out guns willy-nilly just like that, can you?

Henry Absolutely not.

Oliver The gun room's along the back there. Past the kitchen, about the third door along. Help yourself.

Henry Thank you.

Oliver Who were you planning on shooting?

Henry Anthony Staxton-Billing.

Oliver Bloody good idea. Good luck. Does he know you're planning to?

Henry Oh, yes, yes. We're actually – we're going to be actually fighting a sort of duel. Actually.

Oliver A duel? With Anthony Staxton-Billing?

Henry Yes.

Oliver He's a pretty good shot, you know.

Henry Yes, so I've heard.

Oliver Are you?

Henry I've never fired a gun in my life.

Oliver I see. (*He reflects*) Look, I don't want to stick my nose in but do you think you've settled on the right choice of weapons?

Henry I don't really think it matters a damn. Swords, pistols, blowpipes, pointed sticks, what's the difference? I've never fought with anything more dangerous than a school ruler in my life.

Oliver Perhaps you'd like me to give you a few tips. On guns. Loading and aiming and that sort of thing. I mean, if you didn't think I was interfering.

Henry I was secretly hoping you'd offer. I really need someone to help me rather a lot. And possibly even come with me. See fair play and so on.

Oliver You mean a second? You'd like a second?

Henry Yes. Oh, yes.

Oliver Why didn't you say so before?

Henry Would you mind?

Oliver Absolutely delighted. I'm your man.

They shake hands.

(*Enthusiastically*) Right. Let's get cracking, then. When is this duel, do you know?

Henry It hasn't yet been decided.

Oliver Good. Well, we'll try and get you in a bit of practice. To the gun room. (*Remembering*) Oh, it'll be locked, won't it? We'll have to get the key from Winnie. I have to keep it locked. Prowlers and servants and so on. Follow me.

Henry Lead on.

Henry follows Oliver out as the lights cross-fade to –

SCENE ELEVEN

9.45 a.m.
Lembridge Tennit. The outer area of Jeremy Pride's
office. Karen at her desk. Jeremy comes out of his office.

Jeremy No?

Karen Not yet, Mr Pride.

Jeremy Dear, oh dear. This is getting to be rather a habit, isn't it?

Karen (*shrugging*) Well . . .

Jeremy I've known her – what? – over ten years. She's never been late like this before.

Karen No?

Jeremy Mind you, she's . . . No, I mustn't talk about her. I mustn't talk about her behind her back. Ronny's been absolutely first rate, I couldn't have done without her. A pillar of strength. A rock. An absolute foundation. An ally, a loyal friend and a colleague. (*Pause*) She is behaving very oddly, though. Very, very oddly. Have you noticed?

Karen Well, I haven't been here that long, Mr Pride –

Jeremy No, no . . .

Karen – so I don't really know what might be termed her norm.

Jeremy She's growing increasingly . . . kittenish. I think that's the word.

Karen (*sympathetically*) Yes, yes . . .

Jeremy Do you think it's . . . something to do with women? You know . . . glands? That sort of thing?

Karen Glands?

Jeremy Yes, you know . . .

Karen Well, I don't really know Veronica well enough to pass judgement on her glands, Mr Pride . . .

Jeremy No, no, no. I'm sorry. I mustn't involve you, Karen. Very naughty of me. Oh, look at the time. This is ridiculous. What are we going to do? I want to read my letters.

Karen Can't you read your letters?

Jeremy No, you see. I can't open them. Unless Veronica's here, I can't open them.

Karen Are they tricky to open?

Jeremy Well, yes, you wouldn't think so, but they are. Very. Apparently whenever I do try to open them on my own, I put envelopes in the wrong bins and letters in the wrong trays and that confuses the system. I don't quite understand it – all these bins and trays – but Ronny made me promise never to open my letters personally, so I never do.

He has moved to Veronica's desk. He picks up the boxed rose that is waiting there, as usual.

Here's another of these flowers. Where does she get all these flowers? She seems to get them every morning.

Karen I think she does.

Jeremy Has she some admirer, do you think? It doesn't sound very likely. I asked her the other day if she had one. She just sort of winked at me. At least, I think it was a wink. She's putting so much stuff on her eyelashes these days, they seem to be in danger of getting glued together permanently. (*Still holding the rose*) Who do you think these can be from?

Karen Well, I hate telling tales but I have a sneaking feeling that she may be sending them herself.

Jeremy Herself?

Karen Yes. Though I loathe telling tales.

Jeremy To herself? (*Gravely*) Oh dear. Oh dear. That doesn't sound so good, does it?

Karen No.

Jeremy What do you think we should do?

Karen I don't really know. Humour her? Hope it will pass?

Jeremy Yes. That's the best course to take perhaps.

Karen Oh, I despise and detest telling tales.

Jeremy You're a very sensible young person – Karen.

Karen Thank you, Mr Pride.

Jeremy Jeremy.

Karen (*smiling*) Jeremy.

> *Veronica enters in a rush. She has on a rather too bright dress and is vividly made-up. While the result is far short of plain ludicrous, it has to be said that it doesn't really work.*

Veronica Good morning. Good morning. Oh . . .

> *She looks at Jeremy and Karen suspiciously. Jeremy, who has still been holding the rose in its box, puts it down absent-mindedly on Karen's desk and moves away from her.*

Jeremy Really, Ronny. It's ten to, you know. This really isn't . . .

Veronica I'm sorry. (*Looking at the rose*) What's that doing on there?

Jeremy I beg your pardon?

Veronica My rose. What's it doing on her desk?

Jeremy Oh, I'm sorry. I must have put it there.

Veronica (*tense*) Why did you put it on her desk?

Jeremy I'm sorry, I put it there accidentally.

Veronica Why isn't it on my desk?

Jeremy It was on your desk. I just picked it up and put it on her desk . . .

Veronica Why? Simply because I was late? Is that why?

Karen Look, I'll put it back on your desk . . .

Veronica I don't want it back on my desk. If he wants to put it on your desk, I don't care.

Karen (*crossing with the rose*) I'm putting it back on your desk, all right?

She puts it on Veronica's desk.

Jeremy I don't see what the fuss is about. I picked it up from your desk and I walked over here with it –

Veronica (*snatching the flower off her desk*) Don't put it on my desk. I don't want the thing on my desk. You can have it on your desk . . .

She slams it down on Karen's desk.

Karen I don't want it on my desk, honestly.

She picks it up and plans to return it again.

Veronica (*shouting*) Don't you dare, don't you *dare* to put that *thing* back on my desk . . .

Karen (*also raising her voice*) Well, what am I supposed to do with it?

Jeremy (*with sudden, uncharacteristic anger*) Right. That's it. That's enough.

He takes the rose from Karen.

I don't want another word from either of you. This – (*he brandishes the rose*) – is going in – here.

He drops it into the waste bin.

And that is where it will stay. We all have a good deal of work to do, I suggest we get on with it. Ronny, as soon as you've pulled yourself together, I'd like you in here, opening my letters. Thank you.

Jeremy stalks back into his office. A silence.

Veronica (*at length*) Well, what a lot of stupid fuss about nothing. (*Pause*) I got up rather early. (*Pause. Anxiously*) Do you think this is really working, Karen? Are you sure it's working?

Karen Oh yes, Veronica.

Veronica Well, he does look at me slightly more than he used to, I suppose.

Karen Believe me, Veronica, it's working like a dream.

Veronica (*softening*) Please. Ronny. I think it's time for 'Ronny', don't you?

Karen Thank you, Ronny.

Veronica goes into Jeremy's office, rather brighter. Karen gets out her mobile phone and dials. A bright laugh from the next office from Veronica.

Hallo. It's Karen Knightly again. Yes, that's right . . . Absolutely fine . . . Thank you . . . Yes, I wanted to order

some more flowers . . . Yes . . . No . . . Two dozen . . .
Yes, it's a very special occasion . . .

As she speaks, the lights cross-fade to –

SCENE TWELVE

Dawn.

A clearing in the wood. Birdsong. A group of men arrive together. First, Marcus with Anthony and Percy Cutting. Following them, Henry and Oliver. All carry guns. Percy also carries a couple of dead rabbits. They stop.

Marcus Right you are, gentlemen, this looks an ideal spot. Will this suit you both?

Anthony (*grimly*) Perfect.

Marcus Mr Bell?

Henry opens and shuts his mouth but manages to make no sound.

Oliver Fine. Absolutely perfect.

Marcus Splendid. Well, just to go over the rules once again. Both seconds will load the combatants' weapons to ensure they're using the correct cartridges. The seconds will retire, the combatants will stand, traditionally, back to back. Mr Cutting here, as the neutral observer, will count out the regulation ten paces, at which point, gentlemen, you will turn and fire. Is that clear? Any questions?

Anthony Perfectly clear.

Oliver (*for Henry*) Crystal.

Marcus Very well, gentlemen. Mr Cutting, will you take up your position?

Percy Yes, Colonel.

He stands to one side, at a central vantage point.

Marcus Seconds will now prepare the combatants.

Marcus, Percy and Oliver set aside their own weapons. Marcus takes Anthony's gun and loads it. Oliver does the same for Henry. Anthony makes to take his coat off.

I'm afraid you'll have to keep your coats on, gentlemen. For all our sakes, this needs to look like a fatal accident . . .

Henry gives an involuntary whimper of fear.

Oliver You all right?

Henry makes another little noise.

(*Quietly, to Henry*) Better with your coats on. It'll slow him down.

Henry What about me?

Oliver Ah yes, but you're slow anyway. It'll make it more even. Incidentally, just a tip . . .

Henry (*eagerly*) Yes?

Oliver I appreciate I haven't been an awful lot of help to you these past couple of days . . .

Henry You've been splendid . . .

Oliver I'm afraid I wasn't able to teach you as much as I'd hoped but – well, if I were you when you shoot – I should keep your eyes closed –

Henry Closed?

Oliver It's just that you seem to be a lot more accurate when you shut them.

Marcus (*calling to them*) Ready, gentlemen?

Oliver (*calling*) Ready.

Marcus Then take your places, please.

Oliver (*handing Henry his gun*) Incidentally, I had a fiddle with this trigger mechanism – it's pretty responsive. So don't, for God's sake, touch it unless you mean business. Good luck.

Henry and Anthony take up their back-to-back stance. Marcus and Oliver retire to their corners.

Marcus Are we prepared? Good luck to you both. Mr Cutting, please proceed.

Percy Ready, gentlemen? And . . . one . . . two . . . three . . . four . . . five . . . six . . . seven . . . eight . . . nine . . . ten.

Henry and Anthony turn together. Their faces are left in single spots as the rest of the lights fade. A swift freeze and then a quick blackout.

Act Four

The same. A few seconds earlier. We hear Percy's voice as the lights come up. Soon we see Henry and Anthony are in their back-to-back stance. Marcus and Oliver have retired to their corners.

Percy Ready, gentlemen? And . . . one . . . two . . . three . . . four . . . five . . . six . . . seven . . . eight . . . nine . . . ten . . .

Henry and Anthony turn together.

Henry (*suddenly, lowering his gun*) Just a minute. I'm sorry, just a minute. This is totally mad.

Anthony stares at him in amazement, uncertain whether he should fire or not.

Marcus (*to Henry*) Shoot, man, shoot . . .

Henry (*exploding with pent-up, nervous fury*) No, I'm sorry this is totally – totally ludicrous – this is stupid and foolish and crass and – insane . . . And this is the twentieth century and not the Dark Ages and we are grown up and we should know a damn sight better and I'm having nothing to do with it, so there!

He hurls his gun down on the ground in anger. There is a loud bang which startles everybody, especially Henry. Anthony spins and falls to the ground with a cry. A stunned silence. Anthony moans.

Oliver Good shot.

Henry I'm – I'm – that was a complete – accident. I'm . . .

Marcus and Percy move to Anthony. Anthony tries to sit up. They support him.

Marcus You all right, old chap? (*To Percy*) How is he?

Percy gives a slight shake of his head.

Henry (*to Anthony*) It was an accident. I'm really most dreadfully sorry. Do you hear me? It was an accident. Honestly . . .

Anthony makes a strange croaking sound.

Marcus What's he saying?

Percy I think – I think he's laughing . . .

Anthony (*with his last breath, still laughing*) Some . . . bloody . . . accident . . .

He dies laughing. They lower him to the ground.

Percy May he rest in peace . . .

Marcus Hear! Hear!

A moment's respectful silence. Henry is in a state of shock.

Well, I think we all witnessed that, didn't we? A clearer accidental death than that I never saw . . .

Henry (*dazed*) It was an accident . . .

Marcus Absolutely. My very words. (*To Henry*) It's all right, old man. You've absolutely no worries. We three witnessed the whole shooting match. Between us, you've got a landowner, a JP and a member of Rotary. You can't get more reliable witnesses than that.

Henry It was an accident . . .

Marcus Oliver, old chap, take him home and give him a brandy – try and persuade him to lie down . . .

Oliver OK. Will do. Come on, Henry.

He takes Henry's arm.

Marcus Leave his gun there. It's evidence. You'll both need to have a word with the police later on – but it's a sheer formality. Absolutely open and shut case.

Oliver Come on, Henry. Cheer up. (*As they go*) Look at it this way. It could have been you, old boy, it could have been you . . .

Henry It should have been me . . .

Henry and Oliver leave. Marcus picks up Anthony's gun, which has fallen by him.

Marcus Chap's taken it rather badly, I'm afraid . . .

Percy Yes.

Marcus I thought for one ghastly moment he wasn't going to fire.

Percy That crossed my mind . . .

Marcus Nice enough chap, though.

Percy Very pleasant.

Marcus Don't think I'll take him shooting with me, though, not on a regular basis . . . Still, he'll suit Imogen down to the ground. Don't imagine he'll give her such a bad time as this monkey did, anyway.

Marcus holds Antony's gun up to the sky as he is speaking, squinting along the barrel. He pulls both triggers. There is a double click but no explosion.

(*Unsurprised*) Good Lord, Percy, what do you think are the chances of that? Two dud cartridges at once. What are the odds on that happening?

Percy (*smiling*) Almost astronomic, I should imagine . . .

Marcus opens the gun, removes the dud cartridges and slips them into his pocket.

Marcus (*producing two more cartridges from his other pocket*) Better give the poor fellow some decent ones then, hadn't we?

During the next, Marcus reloads Anthony's gun and replaces it where it was.

Percy Would you like me to go on ahead and telephone, Colonel?

Marcus Oh yes, would you, Percy, that's a good chap. I'd better hang on here with the remains. Try and get Chief Inspector Rogers, if he's there. He tends to deal with these sorts of things rather tactfully . . .

Percy Chief Inspector Rogers. I'll do my best . . .

Percy goes off, carrying both their guns with him. Marcus, on his own, wanders over to inspect the body.

Marcus (*jabbing the body with his foot*) Well, that ought to keep you in your own bed for a bit, anyway . . .

He wanders away from the body. As he does so, the lights cross-fade to –

SCENE TWO

11.00 a.m.
A churchyard. A bell tolls. Marcus is joined by Imogen, dressed in black. He takes her arm to comfort her. Others, also sombrely dressed, join them. They gather in a circle. There is no dialogue, merely the bell and maybe a few birds. It is as though we are watching the scene in long

*shot. Oliver stands with Henry. Percy stands with Daphne
and Norma. Winnie stands alone. As from a distance,
Karen appears and watches them. She is dramatically
dressed in a long black coat and a big black hat. She
looks rather like a ghost. The mourners start to disperse,
without noticing Karen. Last to leave is Henry, who
takes one rather apologetic glance back at the grave. He
sees Karen and is startled. Karen puts one black-gloved
hand dramatically to her lips and blows Henry a silent
kiss. Then she is gone. Henry is rather alarmed by this.
He looks round nervously and then hurries after the
others. As he does so, the lights cross-fade again to –*

SCENE THREE

8.50 a.m.
   *Lembridge Tennit. The outer area of Jeremy Pride's
office. It is empty. Jeremy comes out of his office. He is
looking for something. He roots about on Veronica's
desk and finds what he is looking for – a pencil.*

Jeremy (*slightly irritably, to himself*) There was once a
time when I was supplied with pencils . . . I didn't used
to have to go grubbing about for them . . .

   *He goes back into his office. A slight pause. Karen
comes in through the other door, having just arrived
for work. She carries a huge bunch of red roses
wrapped in cellophane. She is humming loudly. Seeing
no one is in there she stops and listens. She looks
cautiously through the door of Jeremy's office.
Contenting herself that he is indeed in there, she starts
humming again even more loudly. She makes another
entrance from the doorway. Jeremy comes out of his
office again.*

(*Crossly*) Who's that? Who on earth is that? Oh – Karen, good morning. Do we really need the musical overture first thing?

Karen (*irrepressibly cheerful*) Mr Pride, I'm so sorry . . . Good morning.

She holds the flowers in front of her rather conspicuously.

Jeremy Good morning. You're especially bright and early.

Karen Yes.

She rustles the flowers slightly.

Jeremy Let's hope one or two of your colleagues will follow suit, eh?

He laughs.

Karen Yes. I believe I saw Ronny just behind me on her way up.

She rustles the flowers again. Jeremy still fails to notice them.

Jeremy Well, I must . . . I've got a mountain to get through in there . . .

Karen Yes, right . . . (*Sniffing her flowers vigorously through the cellophane*) Ooo! Ooo! Ooo!

Jeremy (*genuinely seeing the flowers for the first time*) Good heavens above. What on earth have you got there?

Karen Oh – just some – roses . . .

Jeremy Ah. A special occasion?

Karen Actually – it's my birthday . . .

She smiles modestly.

Jeremy Well . . . Many happy returns.

Karen Thank you.

Jeremy (*playfully*) I won't ask how old . . .

Karen (*equally playfully*) No. Better not.

Jeremy A secret admirer?

Karen No, I think I know who they're from. I'm not completely sure. It could be one of three boys but I'm pretty sure it's Johnny. This is a typical Johnny gesture.

Jeremy Well, you'd better be sure. You don't want to get them mixed up, do you?

He laughs. Karen laughs.

Start saying thank you to the wrong one. (*He laughs*)

Karen (*laughing*) No. .

Jeremy Oh, look. (*Indicating the flowers*) There's a card with them. See, here's a card.

He indicates the slightly larger than average card attached to the wrapping.

Karen Oh, yes. I never noticed that. We can find out. Could you possibly . . .?

Jeremy What?

Karen (*with a glance towards the door*) Could you possibly read it to me . . .?

Jeremy Oh, I don't think I should read it, should I?

Karen No, it's quite all right, I'm sure . . . It's just that I have my hands full and –

Jeremy (*doubtfully*) Well . . .

Karen If it's Johnny, I promise you it'll be perfectly clean . . . (*She laughs*)

Jeremy (*enjoying this*) Well, I hope so, I hope so. (*Opening the card and reading the message*) Ah! Ah! Well, it's very – well, sort of personal but . . . very sweet . . .

> *He chuckles romantically. It is round about now that Veronica, unseen by either of them, arrives in the doorway. She stops and stares at the tableau, thunderstruck.*

Karen Well, read it, then. Go on.

Jeremy I'll do my best. Oh dear. (*He is still giggling a lot with embarrassment*)

> Just to say
> Happy day
> And to pray
> You will stay
> Just the way
> You are today
> From Great Big J
> To Special K.

Karen Oh, that's lovely. How lovely. Thank you.

Jeremy Don't thank me.

Karen You read it so beautifully.

Jeremy Thank you.

Karen (*seeing Veronica*) Oh, good morning, Ronny.

Jeremy Ah, Ronny.

Veronica (*coldly*) Good morning. Sorry I'm early.

Jeremy No, no. You're not early . . . It's Karen's birthday, Ronny. Someone's sent her these flowers. Look.

Veronica Yes, I heard. From Great Big J, apparently. Whoever he may be.

Jeremy What's his name? Johnny, did you say?

Karen That's right. Johnny. John – Bell, really.

Veronica Well, that's the first we've heard of him, isn't it? And where did John Bell spring from all of a sudden, I wonder?

Karen (*smiling at her*) Croydon.

Jeremy Oh, Croydon? That's quite near us.

Veronica Well, let me put these in water for you.

She takes the flowers from Karen.

Karen No, I can do it . . .

Veronica No, I insist. You can't waste your day putting flowers in water, can you? Mustn't ruin your little hands on your birthday.

Veronica sweeps out with the flowers.

Jeremy She really is in the most extraordinary state, isn't she? I have to say it. I think I'm going to have to have a quiet word with her. Privately.

Lydia appears in the doorway. She has a loosely wrapped parcel in her hand.

Lydia Excuse me, Mr Pride – Karen, dear, is this yours? I think you left it on my desk when you were with me this morning.

Karen (*mortified*) Oh, how awful. I completely forgot them. Isn't that awful? I'm sorry. Thank you.

238

Lydia Well, we forgive you. Seeing it's your birthday. Here.

Karen Thank you. I wish they wouldn't send them to the office. It's so embarrassing. I've told them . . .

Jeremy What's this, then? Another gift from Johnny?

Karen No – if I'm not mistaken – if it's what I think it is . . . (*She opens the parcel*) Oh, it is. It's chocolates. My favourites. Yes, it must be from him.

Jeremy Johnny?

Karen No. These are from Jimmy.

Jeremy Jimmy?

Karen Yes.

Jeremy (*laughing*) Johnny and Jimmy. All the Js, eh?

Karen Yes, so they are.

Jeremy I'd better watch out, eh? I could be next on the list. (*He laughs*)

Karen (*laughing*) Yes, of course. Jeremy! Of course.

Lydia (*enjoying the joke*) Oh, Mr Pride . . .

All three laugh.

Jeremy (*enjoying the joke enormously*) Oh, this is much, much better than working . . . Where are your flowers? I hope she hasn't walked off with them. (*He laughs*) Karen had this lovely bunch of flowers, Lydia –

Lydia Yes, I saw them earlier . . .

Jeremy Beautiful red . . . What were they? Roses? (*A sudden thought*) I say – I've just had a thought. Do you think Ronny may have got hold of the wrong end of the stick?

Karen How do you mean?

Jeremy It just occurred to me – Ronny's been getting all these anonymous flowers sent to her, Lydia . . .

Lydia Yes, I'd heard she had . . .

Jeremy I'm wondering. Perhaps they weren't meant for her at all. Perhaps they were intended for you, Karen. What do you think?

Karen Well, it's possible, I suppose. I'd never thought of that. How stupid of me. Of course. It's just the sort of thing Johnny would do . . .

Jeremy Sounds like Johnny's work to me.

Karen Either him or Jason, that's for sure.

Jeremy (*roaring with laughter*) Jason! Did you hear that, Lydia? She's got a Jason as well. The girl's incorrigible. I don't know when she finds time to come to work . . .

Lydia (*laughing at this*) Oh, Mr Pride . . .

Jeremy playfully chucks Karen under the chin. As he does so, Veronica enters and takes in this jolly scene, frostily. She has the flowers. Or what's left of them. She has separated the heads from the stalks. The heads she has saved and wrapped in the original cellophane. The stalks she has stuck into an impromptu 'vase' – the bottom half of a lavatory-brush holder.

Veronica I'm sorry to have taken so long. I'm afraid I had a disaster with your flowers, Karen, and all the heads fell off. But I'm sure you'd still like to sniff the stalks, though, wouldn't you? There.

She thumps the 'vase' down on Karen's desk.

Lydia Oh, dear . . .

Jeremy (*shocked*) Oh, good Lord.

Veronica Never mind, I saved you the heads. You can float them in your bath. If you ever take one.

Karen (*hurt*) Oh.

Jeremy What on earth has come over you, Veronica? Look what you've done to Johnny's flowers. What on earth is the matter? I demand an explanation . . .

Karen It doesn't matter, Jeremy . . .

Jeremy Oh, yes, it does. I'm afraid I don't believe your story about an accident, Ronny . . .

Karen Jeremy, please. It is my birthday. Chocolate, anyone? (*Offering the box*) Lydia?

Lydia (*wrestling briefly with temptation*) Well . . .

She dithers over which one to take.

Jeremy And quite apart from the damage you've done to these blooms, Ronny, you may care to know that for several weeks you've been appropriating flowers that were intended for someone else . . .

Karen Oh, Jeremy, please, don't tell her that . . .

Veronica (*dangerously quiet*) What?

Jeremy Those roses that were arriving every day, I think you might have realised that they weren't meant for you . . .

Karen It really doesn't matter, Jeremy . . .

Jeremy They were obviously intended for Karen here. Only she was too kind to say anything.

Karen (*offering him a chocolate*) Chocolate, Jeremy?

Jeremy No, no, thank you. Not just at present.

Karen Oh, go on. They're lovely . . .

Jeremy No, I can only cope with soft centres, Karen, I don't think I'll risk . . .

Veronica (*taking the box from Karen*) Please. Allow me . . .

Before anyone can stop her, she walks a little way away from them, carefully replacing the lid of the box as she does so. Then she puts the chocolates on the floor and calmly jumps up and down on them a couple of times. The others watch her, dumbfounded. Veronica picks up the box and prises it open again.

(*Offering the box to Jeremy*) There you are. Now they're all soft centres . . . (*Icily*) Help yourself.

Jeremy stands looking at her as though hypnotised.

Jeremy I . . . I . . . I . . .

Veronica (*suddenly screaming*) COME ON! EAT THEM, YOU LECHEROUS BASTARD!

She makes to squash his face between both halves of the chocolate box. He retreats in terror. Lydia attempts to restrain her.

Jeremy Get away, get away. Someone get her away. She's gone mad. She's gone completely mad . . .

Lydia (*simultaneously*) Miss Webb! For heaven's sake! What do you think you're doing? What's come over you? Miss Webb!

Veronica (*simultaneously*) I'll make you eat every one of these and your filthy flowers. Do you think I want your flowers? I don't want your revolting flowers . . .

Jeremy is driven back so he is lying across a desk. Karen sits on her desk and watches, amused. Lydia, who seems to have some rudimentary grasp of self-defence, finally manages to restrain Veronica.

Lydia It's all right, I've got her. I've got her. Don't hurt her, Mr Pride, there's no need to hurt her . . . .

Jeremy I wasn't going to hurt her . . .

Lydia All right. I can take her now . . .

Veronica is making low growling noises in her throat.

I'll take her down to the nurse. She may be able to give her a sedative.

She indicates Jeremy, who is still sprawled across the desk.

Karen, will you see to Mr Pride . . .

Karen Yes, of course. You bet . . .

Lydia goes out with Veronica. Jeremy tries to stand but is unable to do so. He is breathing noisily. Karen has picked up the chocolates. She watches him. As she does so, she dips her fingers in the squashed chocolates and licks the cream fillings off them.

Jeremy I'm afraid I can't . . . I can't . . . Karen, would you . . .?

Karen (*not moving*) Just a tick, Jeremy.

There's an – an inhaler – an inhaler in the – bottom right-hand – drawer of my desk in there . . . would you mind . . .?

Karen (*still not moving*) Of course I will, Jeremy . . .

Jeremy I think I'm having one of my – a little trouble breathing . . . Karen . . . please. (*He slips down behind the desk*) Karen, are you there? Where are you?

Karen Yes, I'm looking for it, Jeremy. Hold on. Won't be a sec. Coming up.

The phone rings.

(*Answering it*) Hallo, BES. UK Department. Mr Pride's assistant. How can I help you? No, I'm sorry, Mr Pride is unavailable at this time. I'm presently in charge, can I help you at all? . . . Yes . . . yes, of course . . . (*Laughing*) No problem . . . Karen Knightly . . . What's your name? . . . Hey . . .

As she laughs and chatters on, Jeremy's laboured breathing continues from behind the desk. The lights cross-fade to –

SCENE FOUR

3.45 p.m.

Imogen's farmhouse kitchen. A room that obviously serves as the main living area. Cosy and a little untidy. Evidence of children. Imogen comes in with some washing that has evidently been drying. During the next, she folds it roughly for ironing later. Henry follows her in. He has clearly been trailing about after her. He seems troubled. Imogen seems determined and practical.

Imogen (*after a silence*) So. What do you say?

Henry You don't feel it's a bit soon?

Imogen Soon for what?

Henry For . . . respect. For Anthony.

Imogen Why should I respect Anthony? He never respected me.

Henry No, but he's dead and it's usual to wait a proper . . . a respectful time . . .

Imogen But that's only if you're in mourning . . .

Henry But you are in mourning. If we were in the Mediterranean you'd be walking around in a black sack . . .

Imogen Well, thank God we're not, that's all I can say. How can I possibly mourn a man I didn't like?

Henry You did, though. At one time, presumably . . .

Imogen Yes. I did. And if he'd dropped dead then, I would have mourned him. I'd have worn endless black sacks. But he's died too late for that, hasn't he? Hard cheese.

Henry You're very – tough, aren't you? I never realised you were quite so tough.

Imogen Does that put you off me?

Henry No. It's just I have to reassess you.

Imogen I'm going to have to be tough, aren't I? No point in lying around looking helpless, is there, with a farm to run, two children to feed and no husband? (*Slightly beadily*) No prospect of one, either.

Henry What makes you say that?

Imogen You've just said no.

Henry I didn't say no.

Imogen You did. I said, what about it then? And you said, no thanks.

Henry I didn't say no thanks, I said – Anyway, I'm supposed to be doing the proposing, not you. What are you doing proposing? You just wait till you're asked.

Imogen Right. Sorry I spoke.

A silence. Imogen huffily continues with her tasks. She looks out of the window as she does so.

(*In her Snow White voice*) Goodness! It is nearly dark and still he hasn't returned to propose to me. Will my Prince ever come? What do you think, Sneezy? Maybe he will ask me tomorrow. I will put on my prettiest dress and braid my hair and stand at the door and wait for him . . . Oh look, Grumpy, look, Dopey . . .

Henry Oh, shut up. Just shut up. (*Pause. Sulkily*) I'm not proposing to you today anyway. So don't sit around waiting for it. (*Glancing at his watch*) It's too late now. Maybe in the morning.

Imogen (*drily*) Gosh! Will I sleep?

Henry I just feel we ought to wait. People will . . . I mean, it's not going to look very good, is it? I only shot the man a fortnight ago. Now here I am getting engaged to his wife. (*Pause*) What's another week or two either way? I'm thinking of you, you know. I am. (*Pause*) Perhaps you – would you like me to come and stay here with you? I could move out of Furtherfield House right now. I could do that. Be here with you at nights. Help during the day. With the kids. If that'd be any help.

Imogen I'm not living in sin. If you want your cake you can bloody well eat it as well, mate.

Henry (*grudgingly*) Oh, all right, then. Have it your own way. Will you marry me, then?

Imogen (*grumpily*) All right.

Henry Is that a yes? Does that mean yes?

Imogen Yes, it means yes. Thank you. Yes.

Henry Good. OK? Happy? (*Pause*) Great Romantic Moments in History, Number one-two-seven.

Imogen relents and comes and kisses him gently.

Imogen Do you really want to marry me?

Henry Of course I do.

Imogen I'm sorry I proposed. That was terribly rude of me. I just assumed that was what we'd . . . It was terrible. Terrible of me. Sorry. (*Pause*) Do you want to leave it and propose again tomorrow?

Henry No, I certainly don't, thank you. I'm not going through all that again.

Imogen You're happy?

Henry Yes. Over the moon.

Imogen (*frowning*) Good.

Henry My only conditions are that I won't eat lunch, I never do. And I refuse to shoot squirrels.

Imogen Well . . . The lunch bit's all right. I think with the squirrels you may find you have to. When they're sitting on the end of our bed chewing at our toes, you may feel the need for action.

Henry If it gets to that stage, I promise to have a pretty serious word with them, OK?

Imogen Super.

Marcus enters. He sees them and retreats in embarrassment.

Marcus Oh, sorry . . .

Imogen Hallo, Uncle. Come in . . .

Marcus Sorry, I didn't think. Just barged in the front door, never thinking . . . Sorry . . .

Imogen Please, honestly. Come in.

Henry Please.

Marcus Well. Just for a minute. Just wanted to see how you were.

Imogen Oh, we're fine. (*To Henry*) Aren't we?

Henry Yes.

Marcus Good.

   Pause.

Imogen (*holding Henry's hand*) Do you want to tell Uncle the good news?

Henry Yes.

Imogen Or shall I?

Henry No. OK. Fine.

   Pause.

Marcus (*waiting expectantly*) Well. What's the news?

Henry (*muttering, without enthusiasm*) We're getting married.

Marcus (*to Imogen*) What did he say?

Imogen He said, we're getting married.

Marcus Oh. Good. Good. (*He looks enquiringly at Imogen*) Isn't it?

Imogen Yes, I thought it was pretty good. I'm pleased.

Marcus Good. (*To Henry*) What about you?

Imogen Henry's over the moon.

Marcus Oh, good. So long as you're both happy. That's the main thing, isn't it?

Imogen I think so. (*Frowning, she gathers up the washing*) Excuse me just a moment.

Imogen leaves.

Marcus You want to marry her, don't you?

Henry Yes, I do. Very much. It's just . . . Well, two things really. First, I wish it wasn't quite such a foregone conclusion. I mean, I always think it's good to have at least the illusion of freedom of choice.

Marcus Yes, I appreciate that. But I do feel if you don't marry her, people will tend to take rather a dim view. I mean, it's one thing getting rid of her husband for her, but you really can't stand the girl up afterwards, can you? Not when you've wiped out her breadwinner in the first place.

Henry Literally a shotgun wedding, isn't it?

Marcus Yes, that – pretty well sums it up. What's your other problem?

Henry It's more complicated. It involves – other people. Promises I made . . .

Marcus You haven't got a wife already, have you?

Henry No. We've split up. Divorced.

Marcus Mistress?

Henry Not – in the strict sense.

Marcus Well, take my tip. Get rid of her – strict or not.

Henry I'll try.

Marcus (*indicating Imogen*) I don't want her heart broken again, you see.

Henry (*with feeling*) No. Nor do I. I promise.

Marcus (*satisfied*) Good. Now, about this other thing.

Henry What's that?

Marcus As you may know, Anthony was on the board of my company. So now we've got a vacancy. What about it?

Henry Well . . .

Marcus It won't entail too much. Occasional meetings. It's just that a lot of Imogen's money is tied up in the firm, money that will technically be yours as well, so maybe you'd like to keep an eye on things. We're not that huge so it's not a vast undertaking, as I say. Shouldn't interfere with your other interests in Strewth Street at all. But between you and me, I think our board could do with a spot of new blood. And, of course, your being an accountant isn't at all a bad thing either.

Henry I'm not . . . I'm technically not really an accountant –

Marcus I thought you were. I understood you were the Knightlys' accountant?

Henry No, not really . . .

Marcus Well, what are you?

Henry (*picking his way*) I was acting for – as the representative for the Knightlys' accountant.

Marcus Really? Trust the Knightlys to have grand accountants like that. They've got a damn sight more money than they know what to do with. Well, anyway, you've got a business head. That's what I'm getting at.

Henry Oh, yes.

Marcus And that's what my board needs. Desperately. So let's see you at our next meeting, OK?

Henry Right.

Marcus I can't for the life of me remember when that is but I'll give you a ring and let you know . . .

Imogen enters, putting on her coat.

Imogen I have to collect Lucy from school . . .

Marcus Ah, well, I must be off . . .

Imogen Do stay if you want. I'll only be a second. I'll make us some tea . . .

Marcus No, no. I'm off. Other furrows. Other burrows. (*Smiling at them both*) I'm delighted. Absolutely delighted.

He kisses Imogen on the cheek.

(*As he goes, to Henry*) I'll call you.

Henry Fine.

Marcus goes out.

Imogen Do you want to come with me? To collect Lucy? It's only up the road.

Henry Yes, of course.

Imogen Since you're going to be her father soon.

Henry Yes.

Imogen I do wish you'd look a bit happier about all this. I'm beginning to feel guilty. Please don't marry me if you don't want to. Please, Henry.

Henry I love you more than anything in the world. I want to marry you. I want to look after your children. And if you want to some time, we could even have our own children. I love you.

Imogen Then what's the problem, Henry?

Henry I'm . . . nervous.

Imogen Of me?

Henry Of course not.

Imogen What, then?

Henry I don't know precisely. I'm just nervous. Come on, then.

> *They go out. Henry still frowning, Imogen looking at him very concerned. As they do so, the lights cross-fade to –*

SCENE FIVE

11.30 p.m.
Furtherfield House. The hall. Winnie is in her dressing gown and night attire, doing her rounds with an electric torch. She checks the front door and is heading for the stairs when Henry wanders in, carrying a book.

Winnie Oh. Evening, sir. I thought you were in bed.

Henry No, Winnie. I couldn't sleep. Things on my mind, you know.

Winnie (*not very interested*) Oh yes, sir? I was just locking up for the night. You didn't want to go out, did you? Only the front door isn't locked if you want to go out.

Henry Really. Do you find you needn't lock it around here?

Winnie Well, I normally would, sir. But not on the anniversary. I never lock it on their anniversary.

Henry Oh? Whose anniversary's this?

Winnie Theirs, sir. Miss Karen and Master Oliver's parents. It's the anniversary of the night they both died, you see, sir. I always make a point of leaving the front door on the latch. Each year I do it. Off my own bat, like. Just in case their spirits are wandering abroad, poor things. Feel like visiting the old place.

Henry Ah.

Winnie Silly superstitious old woman, you're saying . . .

Henry No, no. I'm not saying that.

Winnie Will you be going out again tonight, sir?

Henry No, I'll just – go for a walk in here for a bit. Perhaps read my book. Master Oliver in bed, is he?

Winnie Yes, sir. I took him up his milk and biscuits.

Henry Oh?

Winnie Always has his milk and biscuits when he's at home. Well, goodnight. I hope you sleep.

She switches on her torch and starts to move off.

Henry Do you find the torch necessary?

Winnie It is where I'm going, sir.

Henry Where's that?

Winnie The servants' wing, sir. Not many light bulbs still alive down there, not these days.

Henry Doesn't that make you nervous?

Winnie Nothing for a God-fearing person to be afraid of in this house, sir, I can promise you.

Winnie goes off. Henry stands and looks around for a moment. Outside, the wind moans. He feels nervous. He pulls himself together and sits down, preparing to read. Somewhere, upstairs, a clatter. Henry jumps. He stands. Listens. Reassures himself and settles again. Another sound. This time outside the front door. He moves towards it cautiously. Unseen, Karen appears at the top of the stairs. She is dressed in a long black gown, something rather exotic. She seems rather pale. Tonight she is playing Edgar Allan Poe's weird Mistress of the Manor.

Karen (*in sepulchral tones*) Henrybell!

Henry (*jumping*) Oh, good grief!

Karen Good evening, Henrybell.

Henry Karen, please. Don't do that to me again. Ever.

Karen (*approaching him*) You haven't phoned me lately, Henrybell, and you won't answer my calls. I wanted to know how you were. How are you?

Henry I'm – very well, thank you. How are you?

Karen Me? I'm having a simply wonderful time. You've no idea. I never dreamt big business could be so much fun. You never told me.

She reaches Henry and kisses him.

(*Softly*) Hallo, Henrybell. I've missed you.

Henry Thank you.

Karen I've missed you terribly. I hope you're not tired tonight because I've missed you terribly.

Henry Ah. Well, yes, that's . . . You're looking very . . . very . . .

Karen Thank you. I thought we should celebrate.

Henry Celebrate?

Karen Our revenge. Both our achievements. I'll have some champagne sent upstairs. (*Yelling*) Winnie!

Henry No, please, Karen, wait . . .

Karen (*yelling again*) Winnie!

Henry (*loudly*) Karen! Please. Don't wake Winnie, please. We don't want champagne. There's nothing to celebrate, there really isn't.

Karen Nothing?

Henry No. Even if you feel there is, I can assure you there really isn't. Not from my side. Not as far as you're concerned.

Karen Henrybell, you're just being modest . . .

Henry No, really –

Karen What about Anthony? That was brilliant. I mean, I came down here for the day, just on the off-chance to see how you were doing, and there was this funeral in full swing. 'Whose funeral might this be, my good man?' I enquired. 'That be Mr Staxton-Billing's funeral, ma'am. Gunned down in his prime by that furren gentleman from Lunnen.' I consider that rather a brilliant achievement, even if you don't.

Henry You're not sorry?

Karen Why?

Henry That Anthony's dead?

Karen No.

Henry I thought you loved him?

Karen I never said that.

Henry You were upset when he left you, though?

Karen Not really.

Henry Upset enough to want to try and kill yourself . . .

Karen I wasn't upset because he left me, I was upset at her for taking him back. But I can see your plan. It's very clever. Better than killing her, far better. Leave the Friesian to pine till her milk turns sour. Now, that is what I call really poetic. Henrybell, you are a true artist. And that is a compliment, believe me. Because it comes from a true artist herself. Do you think there's a chance she'll die of grief? She might, I suppose.

Henry Karen, she didn't even like her husband. Imogen didn't take Anthony away from you. Anthony took himself away from you. Imogen had nothing to do with it. She is not to blame in any way for him leaving you. He left you for another woman . . . altogether.

Karen Who?

Henry Councillor Mrs Daphne Teale.

Karen Who? Norma's mother?

Henry Right.

Karen Nonsense. No one would leave me for Mrs Teale. Mrs Teale? That old tart? No one would leave me for that fat old tart.

Henry I'm afraid Anthony did.

Karen Bollocks. It was that wife of his. You're defending her. Why? Why are you trying to defend her, Henrybell?

Henry Because . . .

Karen Why? I want to know. Why?

Henry Because . . . because, if you must know, we're engaged to be married. Imogen Staxton-Billing and I are going to be married. I'm sorry I have to tell you quite as bluntly as that, but there it is. You'd have found out sooner or later. I'm sorry. I'm sorry if I've upset you.

> *Karen stares at him. When she speaks, it is not the reaction that Henry expects at all. Instead, she sounds faintly puzzled.*

Karen (*frowning*) I don't get it.

Henry You don't?

Karen Why you're marrying her. I don't see the point.

Henry Well, why does anyone ever marry anyone?

Karen To make her miserable?

Henry No. Course not. To make her happy.

Karen (*incredulously*) Happy?

Henry Yes.

Karen Why?

Henry Because I love her.

Karen You love Imogen?

Henry Yes. I've just said. What's the matter with you?

Karen (*smiling in disbelief*) You can't love Imogen. *Imogen?* How dare you stand there and say things like that? You're joking. *Imogen.* No, that is out. Sorry. That is out.

Henry What do you mean, 'out'?

Karen That is entirely contrary to what we agreed. I'm afraid you're not able to do that, Henrybell, that is breaking the rules. I'm sorry, I can't allow you to break the rules. Out. Fault. Out.

Henry Karen, I'm not talking about rules. I'm talking about real life – this is real life –

Karen (*blazing*) And I'm talking about rules which are a bloody sight more important –

Henry Karen, Karen. This is reality. Real, do you understand? It is not a game. Life is not a game, Karen.

Karen (*quietly*) Who told you that?

Henry It happens to be the case. There's a much bigger board, for one thing. People keep stealing your counters and changing the rules. Life's a lot more complicated and a good deal harder to play. Take it from me.

Karen Wrong, Henrybell. Wrong. It's easy. Easy-peasy. You play by the rules and it's easy . . .

Henry But who makes up these rules in the first place?

Karen You do. You make up your own rules. That's the joy of it. But you see, Henrybell, once you've made them up, you must keep them. You really must. Otherwise life *is* difficult. If you're finding things difficult, it's only because you're breaking your own rules –

Henry But what we're talking about were never my rules, those were your rules . . .

Karen They are *our* rules. We agreed them. We made a pact. We started a game together, both of us. It was called revenge. And I insist that you play it to the end. I demand that you do. Now you go over there now and you tell her that the engagement is off, all right? Destroy her. I don't care what you do but you have to destroy her somehow. Now go. Go now.

Henry (*impatiently*) Oh, come on, Karen. Don't be so ridiculous.

Karen starts to try and shove him towards the front door.

Karen (*pushing*) Out. Go on. Out now. Out.

Henry (*resisting her*) Now, stop that . . . Karen!

Karen (*pushing him quite savagely*) Do you hear me? I want you out, do you hear? Out, out . . .

Henry (*pushing her away from him*) Look, just stop that, will you?

The shove he gives her is harder than he meant. She is also caught off-balance. She staggers back and sits on the ground. Nothing really hurt except her dignity, she sits there startled, like the school bully who's been unexpectedly punched in return.

I'm sorry, Karen. I didn't mean . . .

Karen stares at him. When she speaks, her tone is quiet and very dangerous.

Karen (*getting up and dusting herself down*) How dare you do that to me, you piddling little – clerk. I make a very bad enemy, Henrybell. Beware. You don't want to play against me, I promise. Never, never try and play against me.

Henry I'm not playing at all. I'm finished.

Karen Oh no, you're not.

Henry does not reply.

All right. We'll see. (*Screaming at him suddenly*) We'll see!

Oliver enters in his pyjamas and dressing gown.

Oliver What the hell's going on down here? Oh, hi, Ka.

Karen does not respond. Oliver assesses the situation.

What seems to be the problem?

Karen runs to him and buries her head in his chest. From the sounds that emanate from her we can judge that she is crying very angrily, very privately.

(*Who has seen all this before*) OK. OK. That's it. No problem. Come on. I'm here.

Henry watches, startled. Oliver holds up a reassuring hand.

(*To Henry*) It's OK. Nothing serious. This happens. (*To Karen*) There we are. There. There. Come on, then. It's only Olly.

Oliver sits on a chair and Karen sits on his lap. He rocks her gently like a small child.

Do you want to go to bed, then? Shall I put you to bed?

Karen (*muffled*) No . . .

Oliver No? What do you want to do then? Want to play a game?

Karen (*muffled*) No.

Oliver (*to Henry*) Sorry, she'll be all right in a tick.

Henry Do you want me to . . .?

Oliver No, she's fine, honestly. (*To Karen*) What's the problem, then? Tell me the problem?

Karen (*muffled*) He's cheating.

Oliver What?

Karen (*muffled*) He's cheating. I hate him . . .

Oliver No, you don't hate him. You don't really hate him. Old Henry? He's a nice man. You don't hate old Henry.

Karen (*muffled, vehement*) I hate him.

Oliver Come on. Stop crying and we'll find you something nice, all right? All right?

Karen (*nodding*) Mmmm.

Oliver Tell you what – would you like to have a ride on my bike? What about that? Would you like to do that?

Karen (*nodding*) Mmmm.

Oliver Yes, of course you would. (*He gets up*) Come on, then. I'll get it started, then you can race all over the house. You'd enjoy that, wouldn't you?

Karen (*nodding*) Mmmm.

Oliver Come on, then. Come with Olly. (*To Henry, quietly*) Back in a tick.

Oliver takes Karen out, his arm round her shoulders. Henry shakes his head incredulously. In a second, a roar as the motorbike starts up in the billiard room nearby.

Karen (*off, a cry of pleasure*) Hey!

Oliver (*off*) There you go. Off you go. Mind the billiard table . . .

Karen gives distant cries of glee as she motors off, all upsets apparently forgotten. Oliver returns. The

*motorbike sound continues under the next for a time,
receding and approaching as Karen does a few laps of
the circuit. Then, unnoticed by the men, it stops.*

She'll be all right now. Always does the trick. Just take
her mind off it with something. Used to do that whenever
she fell over as a kid.

Henry She's not a kid now, though, is she?

Oliver Well, at heart she is. I suppose we both are,
really. You mustn't blame her. It's not her fault she
behaves like that.

Henry Whose fault is it?

Oliver Oh, circumstances, you know. All sorts of things.
Growing up here, in this house. Big Wendy house really,
isn't it? God, we used to have some good games. She's
brilliant, you know. At inventing games. Always told her
she ought to be working for John What's-his-name's.
You know, those games people. Dressing up. Lot of that.
She made us pretend to be different people for days on
end. She was terrific. I was no earthly good. I mean, you
can do what you like, stick me in a frock, put as many
funny hats on me as you like – I'm always exactly the
same. Useless. But Karen. Sometimes you couldn't
recognise her. Should have been an actress, I suppose.
No, not an actress. Nobody else would ever have got a
word in, would they? You see, I think the only trouble
with Karen is she gets bored rather quickly. She got
bored with playing here, eventually. Had to look for new
amusements. Other women's husbands. That sort of
thing. That's the difference between us. Me, I'm perfectly
happy staying here. I'll stay here for ever. No problem.
Smaller brain, probably, I don't know.

Pause. They are aware of the silence.

Henry Quiet, isn't it?

Oliver She's stopped. Probably stalled. Or run out of petrol. (*Slight pause*)

Henry (*looking at Oliver*) Petrol?

Oliver (*a nasty thought*) Petrol. Oh, my God. Quickly.

They hurry to the door. Before they can reach it, Winnie enters, coughing.

Winnie Master Oliver! Master Oliver! There's smoke everywhere . . .

Oliver Winnie, are you all right?

Winnie Thank God you're up . . .

Henry (*who has been looking off towards the billiard room*) We can't go that way, the whole corridor's alight . . .

Oliver What about that way?

He indicates the way that Winnie's just come.

Winnie I wouldn't go that way. I only just got through in time. The whole building's ablaze . . .

Oliver (*shouting*) Karen! Karen!

Henry (*shouting*) Karen!

Winnie Is Miss Karen here, then?

Oliver Of course she's here. Who else do you think would have – Oh, never mind. Come on. We'd better get out of the front door. We might be able to get to reach her through the back . . .

Henry Shouldn't we phone the fire brigade?

Oliver Well, you can stay and phone if you like. I'm going to stand outside on the hill and wave. It's a damn sight safer.

Oliver goes out with Winnie. Henry hesitates for a second, considering whether to phone. The room starts to glow red. He decides against it and follows the others out. The flames increase and the roar becomes very loud indeed. Then the sound of fire engines arriving. Maybe some smoke. As this occurs, the location shifts to –

SCENE SIX

12.30 a.m.

The front drive of Furtherfield House. Henry, Winnie and Oliver stand watching, their faces lit by the fire which rages fiercely some thirty feet away. Oliver, especially, looks totally dazed. Above the roar of the flames, the sound of fire engines working the pumps. A Fireman rushes past them with a hose.

Fireman (*over the din*) Mind your backs, now! Keep well clear!

Henry It's hopeless. The whole place is alight. Look at it.

Winnie (*agitatedly*) Miss Karen, is she still in there?

Henry I – don't know . . .

Winnie She may be trapped in there. What are we going to do?

Henry It's all right, Winnie, it's very unlikely she's still in there . . .

Winnie How do we know that for sure?

Henry We don't know for sure, Winnie, I'm afraid. But there's nothing we can do to help even if she is.

Winnie Oh!

Henry If it's any comfort, she does seem to have a very strong instinct for self-preservation. Just pin your hopes on that. That's all we can do.

Oliver (*suddenly*) Oh my God, she's still in there . . .

Henry No, Oliver, we've just been saying –

Oliver (*very agitated*) She's still in there. I can't leave her in there –

He moves forward.

Henry (*restraining him*) Listen, Oliver, we just don't know if Karen's in there or not . . .

Oliver Not Karen, she'll be OK. It's my bike. My bike's still in there. I can't leave my bike.

Oliver breaks free from Henry and rushes off in the direction of the flames.

Henry (*vainly trying to stop him*) Oliver . . .!

Winnie Master Oliver, you can't go back in there . . .

A commotion, and Oliver reappears, being physically restrained by the Fireman.

Fireman Now, come on. Back, back, back, I'm sorry. You can't go back in there. There's no way anyone can go back in there . . .

Oliver (*at the same time*) It's my bike, you see. My bike's still in there. It's very valuable. Great sentimental value. I have to get back in there. I must rescue my bike.

Fireman (*shouting Oliver down*) Look now, listen. Listen. (*To Henry and Winnie*) Look, could you hold him back for me please, I've got a fire to fight there.

Henry and Winnie do so. Oliver slowly relaxes.

Listen, even my own lads can't get near that. Not even with special clothing and breathing apparatus. You get within twenty feet of that you'd go up like a bloody Roman Candle. If there's someone in there, we'll do our best for them. What did you say his name was? Mike, was it?

Henry No. Bike. I think he was anxious to rescue his bike.

Fireman His bike? You mean he tried to get back in there for a bloody bike? I don't believe it. What about your roller-skates? You want us to have a try for them as well? I don't know. (*Calling to one of his men*) Take that one round that way. Where Harry is. Link up with Harry. Try and keep it off them outbuildings there. (*To them*) We're not going to save a lot of this, I'm afraid.

Henry No?

Fireman Too late, you see. Time we got the call. Lucky someone in the village saw the blaze. Or we wouldn't be here still.

Henry Yes, yes.

Fireman Mind you, we nearly weren't anyway. Halfway up the hill. This maniac coming the other way in an open sports car. I ask you. Open sports car, middle of the night. Nearly had us in the ditch . . .

Henry Did you happen to see if it was a man or a woman?

Fireman Don't know. Couldn't tell. Had a crash helmet on. We'd better get you people somewhere safe . . . Got anywhere we can take you? Otherwise we'll knock up the hotel . . .

Henry Well, I . . .

*Imogen appears, anxiously. She has her coat on over
her night things.*

Imogen Henry? Oh, Henry . . .

Henry Imogen?

Imogen (*rushing to him*) Darling, you're safe?

Henry (*holding her*) We're OK. We're all all right. Don't
worry. We're all safe.

Imogen (*slightly delirious with relief*) Thank God! I
woke up and I saw the whole sky was alight. I knew
what it was at once. And I knew you were here and I
was so frightened.

Henry (*reassuringly*) It's all right. We're perfectly safe.
Nothing to worry about.

Imogen I was so frightened. How did it start? Do you
know?

Henry (*with a glance at Oliver*) We're – not a hundred
per cent sure . . . (*Looking at her feet*) Darling, you've
got no shoes on, what are you doing?

Imogen (*vaguely*) Oh, no. Nor I have.

Henry You're shivering . . .

Winnie I should come nearer the fire, miss . . .

Henry Darling, is there a chance you could put us three
up? Just for tonight . . .

Imogen Yes. Of course. Yes. We'll have to improvise a
bit. There may not be quite enough beds.

Henry Well, maybe we could squeeze up a bit . . .

He smiles.

Imogen (*smiling*) Yes. That would be nice.

Henry Good. (*Calling to the Fireman*) Excuse me! I say.

Fireman Hallo!

Henry We're OK. We're fixed up. We'll be down at the farm there. When you need us . . .

Fireman Right. Tomorrow morning. Someone'll need to talk to you tomorrow morning.

Henry Right. Thank you for everything. All you've done. (*To Imogen*) One doesn't need to leave something for firemen, does one?

Imogen No, I don't think so.

Fireman (*moving off*) Bring that round. Bring that right round now, Ray. On to the base. The base of it . . . That's it!

The Fireman goes off.

Imogen Poor Oliver! That's his home, isn't it, gone for ever.

Henry (*concerned*) Yes. (*Calling gently*) Oliver.

Oliver (*who has been staring at the fire throughout*) Hallo?

Henry Imogen wondered if you wanted to – come back to the farmhouse . . .

Imogen For the rest of the night, anyway. Have a cup of tea or something . . .

Oliver Terrific. That'd be terrific. Do you happen to carry any hot milk . . .

Imogen Yes. We can run to that.

Oliver Terrific.

Winnie (*gently*) I'll bring it up to you, Master Oliver.

Oliver Terrific.

He still continues to stare, fascinated, at the flames.

Henry (*to Imogen, indicating Oliver*) You wait in the car.

Imogen OK. It's just down the drive a little way. They wouldn't allow me any closer. Don't be long.

Imogen and Winnie go off towards the car.

Henry Oliver? Olly?

Oliver Yah?

Henry You all right?

Oliver Oh, yah. It's just a bit . . . A bit, you know . . .

Henry Yes.

Oliver Hell of a blaze. Oh, well. It's only a building, isn't it?

Henry That's a very healthy way of looking at it . . . Are you coming?

Oliver Yah, sure. (*Looking back at the building as he goes, half to himself*) I'll have to find somewhere else to go, I suppose . . .

Oliver and Henry go off to the car. As they do so, the lights cross-fade to –

SCENE SEVEN

11.00 a.m.
The sitting room of Imogen's farmhouse. In a second, Marcus enters, followed by Henry, who seems very abstracted throughout.

Henry After you.

Marcus Thank you. (*Continuing their conversation*) Yes, as I say, I spoke to Percy Cutting yesterday and he said he'd be very honoured to be a witness for you.

Henry Oh, good. Thank you. I'd hoped to persuade Oliver Knightly to do it but I can't seem to trace him. No one's seen him for at least a fortnight.

Marcus Probably spending all his money somewhere.

Henry Do you think so?

Marcus Well, that house was pretty well covered, I believe. Miraculously, they paid up. That was all his, of course.

Henry Not hers?

Marcus No, no. They both had money in trust – the parents were pretty sensible in that respect – but the house was Oliver's. I haven't seen either of them, actually, come to think of it. Have you seen her at all? Karen?

Henry (*troubled*) No. No, I haven't.

Marcus Well, good riddance . . .

Henry She's – around, though . . .

Marcus Around?

Henry Yes.

Marcus Here?

Henry Not far away. I don't know, it's just a feeling.

Marcus I should forget her, if I were you. This time in a fortnight you'll be married to Imogen. A new life.

Henry (*unenthusiastically*) Yes.

Marcus Did you have a look at those figures?

Henry (*blankly*) What?

Marcus The ones I gave you? My company books?

Henry Oh, yes. Sorry. Yes, I did.

Marcus What's your verdict?

Henry Well, it's – er – I mean, as I say, I'm not an accountant – but I would say, from a very cursory first glance – without in any way committing myself to a definite judgement . . .

Marcus The firm's in a spot of trouble, is that it?

Henry I'd say a fairly big spot.

Marcus Yes?

Henry Desperately big.

Marcus Yes. (*He worries*) I was hoping that the – whatjercallit – general upsurge in trade that's been apparently happening of late – might have carried us with it . . . But we seem, as a firm, to have been left a bit high and dry . . . Very disappointingly.

Henry The thing is, you see – it would appear to me that your basic problem – please, this is just one man's opinion.

Marcus No, carry on. Carry on . . .

Henry Your basic problem is that you're producing something – much more expensively than anyone else is producing it . . .

Marcus Ah well, there are sound reasons for that, of course . . .

Henry And on top of that, you're not really producing enough of them . . .

Marcus (*recognising the truth in this*) Yes, yes . . . That's an excellent point.

271

Henry And, if that wasn't enough, nobody seems to want them anyway.

Marcus Yes. I think you've put your finger on it. This is just the sort of talk I wanted to hear . . .

Henry So far as I can see, the only reason you haven't yet been declared bankrupt is that the Inland Revenue and the Customs and Excise are in nearly as much chaos at present as you are.

Marcus (*thumping the furniture*) I said it, you see, I said this – almost these exact same words – at our last board meeting. We need substantial capital investment. We need to modernise the plant, drastically reduce the cost per unit and on top of that –

Henry – make sure you're producing something that people want . . .

Marcus Oh, don't worry about that. As my grandfather said to me, 'Don't worry. People will always need pipes.' So long as there's a civilisation they're going to need some way of pumping it in and then some way of pumping it all out again afterwards. No, it's capital, that's what we lack. We're crippled without it.

Henry How much do you need?

Marcus About a million and a half.

Henry Well, we can't help you. You've had most of Imogen's money.

Marcus She'll get that back, don't worry . . .

Henry Oh, I'm sure . . .

Marcus With interest. Don't you worry about that. Maybe not immediately but – never fear. No, I've got – feelers out. In the City.

Henry Really?

Marcus In the next day or two – I'm fairly confident we'll get a nibble from someone.

Imogen comes in.

Imogen OK. We're there. Coffee's coming. Sorry for the delay.

Marcus Oh, grand.

Henry (*nodding towards the kitchen*) All right?

Imogen (*inexpressively*) Yes.

Henry Good.

They all sit down and wait. No one speaks.

Marcus (*after a pause*) Er . . .

Imogen Sorry?

Marcus Where is it? The coffee?

Imogen Winnie's bringing it.

Marcus Winnie? The woman who used to work for the Knightlys?

Imogen That's right. She came to us the night of the fire. And we seem to have – inherited her rather.

Henry She's jolly useful.

Imogen (*with less conviction*) Oh, she is.

Henry Doesn't cost us much. Board and lodging.

Marcus Good arrangement then.

Imogen Yes.

A pause.

Henry What's she doing?

Imogen I don't know. I made the coffee. I just left her to bring it in.

Winnie appears in the doorway, empty-handed.

Winnie Excuse me, madam?

Imogen Yes?

Winnie (*confidentially*) Could I have a word . . . ?

Imogen (*rising and going to her*) Yes, Winnie, what is it?

Winnie It's just that I'm finding the tray just a little too heavy to carry, you see, madam . . .

Imogen Yes, all right . . .

Winnie It's just my left wrist, you see, madam. My right one's as strong as an ox . . .

Imogen (*shooing her out*) Yes, come on, then. Come on.

Imogen and Winnie go out.

Marcus Have you decided where you're going for your honeymoon?

Henry Yes. Here, I think.

Marcus Here?

Henry Yes. We thought, you know, with the children. And the animals. More trouble than it was worth. We thought, why sit and be miserable in a hotel when we could be . . . be here? Instead.

Marcus Pleasant enough, here.

Henry It is.

Marcus (*staring at him*) You're looking rather pale, Henry. If you don't mind my saying so.

Henry Am I? Oh. I'm not sleeping perhaps as well as I should . . .

Marcus Oh dear. Why's that? Guilty conscience?

He laughs.

Henry (*smiling feebly*) Possibly.

Imogen returns, carrying the coffee tray. Winnie shadows her.

Imogen Here we are.

She starts to unload the tray on to the table.

Winnie (*in an undertone*) I'd put the coffee pot just there, madam . . . And then the milk just next to it there . . .

Imogen (*irritably*) Yes, all right, Winnie. Thank you . . .

Winnie The cups can go along here then, madam . . .

Imogen (*in a sharp undertone*) I said thank you very much, Winnie. I can manage, thank you.

Winnie (*a little hurt*) Thank you, madam.

Winnie goes out. Imogen pours the coffee.

Imogen White, Uncle?

Marcus Fairly dark, thank you. (*To Henry*) How are you coping with the farmer's life? Keeping your head above the muck?

Henry Yes, I think I'm . . . I'm coping, aren't I?

Imogen Henry's especially good with chickens.

Marcus Chickens? Really?

Henry Yes, we seem to have an affinity. I can chat to them for hours.

Imogen Don't get too friendly. We may have to get rid of a few soon.

Henry Oh, Lord. Couldn't we possibly wait till they die naturally?

Imogen (*admonishingly*) Henry . . .

Henry Sorry.

Imogen He's completely hopeless. He can't bear to kill anything.

Henry sags. A pause.

(*Smiling awkwardly*) Much. (*Looking at the coffee tray, irritably*) Oh, there's no spoons. She hasn't brought any spoons.

Marcus Oh, we don't need spoons . . .

Imogen Of course we need spoons . . .

Henry I'll get them. Don't worry. I'll get them.

Henry goes out to the kitchen.

Imogen (*muttering*) If I was only allowed to do this myself, we'd have spoons in the first place.

The doorbell rings.

Now who is that? The front door. Excuse me a moment.

Imogen goes out of the other door. Henry returns almost at once with some teaspoons.

Henry (*to Winnie, who is apparently following him*) It's all right, Winnie. I can carry them. Thank you. (*Looking round the room, concerned*) Where's Imogen?

Marcus She's –

A clatter of somebody tripping over a tin in the hall.

Imogen (*from the hall, angrily*) Oh, for heaven's sake . . .

Henry puts down the spoons and runs to the door.

Henry (*alarmed*) Imogen?

Imogen enters before he can leave the room. She carries a square parcel about the size of a biscuit tin.

You all right, darling?

Imogen Yes, I just fell over that damned can. I meant to take it out to the barn.

Henry Can?

Imogen Yes. Petrol can.

Henry Petrol can?

Imogen Yes.

Henry In the hall?

Imogen Yes.

Henry What's a petrol can doing in the hall?

Imogen Well, it wasn't in the hall until I put it there. It was on the front step.

Henry The front step?

Imogen Yes. This morning. When I opened the front door. It was just sitting there. Someone must have left it.

Henry Who?

Imogen I don't know.

Henry Someone must have done.

Imogen Yes, I said, someone obviously did.

Henry Who?

Imogen I said. I haven't the faintest idea.

Henry Who'd leave a petrol can on the front step?

Marcus (*helpfully*) A passing motorist?

Henry Was it full?

Imogen No, empty.

Henry Empty? (*In fresh panic*) Then where's the petrol gone?

Imogen Henry! What's the matter with you?

Henry What have they done with the petrol?

Marcus They possibly put it in their car, old chap.

Henry (*laughing, slightly hysterically*) A likely story.

　　Imogen and Marcus exchange glances.

Imogen (*soothingly*) Well, let's have our coffee, shall we?

Marcus (*adopting her tone*) Good idea.

Imogen Did you get the spoons, darling? Oh good, you did. Thank you, darling.

Henry (*calming slightly*) They're the right ones, are they?

Imogen They're lovely, darling. Perfect spoons.

　　Handing a cup.

Uncle?

Marcus Thank you.

Imogen Help yourself to sugar. Darling?

Henry (*taking his cup*) Thank you.

Imogen Well. (*She sips her own coffee*) That's better.

Marcus Very nice. What's in your parcel?

Imogen I don't know. I'd better see. It's addressed to me, anyway.

Henry (*alert*) Parcel?

Imogen Yes. Probably an early wedding present.

Marcus Oh, that's nice.

Henry (*tense again*) Where did that parcel come from?

Imogen I just brought it in here, just now.

Henry Just now?

Imogen You saw me bring it in here. Just now.

Henry Where did it come from?

Imogen Out there. The postman brought it – darling, what is the matter with you?

Henry How do you know he was a postman?

Imogen Because I opened the door to him . . .

Henry (*shouting*) What proof did you have he was a postman? Did you ask him for proof?

Imogen (*shouting back at him*) No, I'm afraid I didn't ask him for his birth certificate. He was wearing a postman's uniform, a postman's hat, a postman's badge, driving a postman's van and delivering parcels as he has been doing for the past ten years. That seemed good enough to me, all right? (*Calmer*) Now, really . . .

> She shakes the parcel. It rattles.

What on earth can it be?

> She starts to untie the string.

Henry (*in a low, urgent tone*) Imogen, just put it down there. Very gently.

Imogen (*startled*) What?

Henry Do as I say, please. Put it down. (*Sharply*) Now, please.

Imogen (*doing so, alarmed*) What's the matter?

Marcus What's wrong, old chap?

Henry moves to the parcel, cautiously.

Henry I'm . . . just . . . going to . . . take this . . . outside . . . (*He takes up the parcel*) All right?

Imogen What on earth are you doing? Where are you taking my parcel?

Henry (*moving to the door, very carefully*) Trust me darling. Don't try to follow me, anyone. And please keep away from the windows . . .

Imogen (*indignantly*) But Henry, it's for me. It's addressed to me.

Henry Please!

Henry goes out slowly to the front door. Slight pause.

Marcus Imogen, do you think – just before you finally tie the knot – you might – he might be persuaded to have a medical? I mean, it's just . . . If you were . . . Children. Hereditary and so on . . . Just a thought.

Imogen (*rather dazed*) I don't know what's come over him.

Marcus Poor old darling. You've not had an awful lot of luck with your men so far, have you? One libertine and one lunatic. Not a good score.

Imogen He's . . . Henry's changed. He's got some terrible problem he doesn't seem to want to talk about . . . And he's so jumpy . . . He's hardly sleeping . . .

Marcus No, he said he wasn't.

Imogen When he does, he has these terrible dreams. During the day, he spends most of his time patrolling the yard with that gun of Anthony's. I don't know why, he can't fire it anyway. And at night we have to have all these buckets of water round the bed . . .

Marcus Buckets of water?

Imogen Yes?

Marcus Does he get very thirsty?

Imogen No, in case of fire.

Marcus Oh, fire. I see. He worries about fire.

Imogen Yes. I thought it was – just a reaction to the fire up at the house but it's been going on for weeks. (*She rises and goes to a window*) I don't know why, but I have this feeling that Karen Knightly might have something to do with all this . . .

Marcus Karen Knightly, but how –

Imogen (*looking out of the window*) Dear God, what on earth is he doing now?

Marcus Imogen, he asked us to stay away from the windows. Don't you think you ought to humour him?

Imogen (*watching*) I think he's gong to shoot my parcel.

Marcus What?

He rises to join her.

Imogen Yes, look. He's put it on the wall there, see? He's going to shoot at it.

Marcus Good Lord, so he is . . . Duck! He's going to shoot!

Marcus and Imogen crouch below the window. From outside, a shotgun is fired, followed immediately by a clang. They both peer cautiously back over the window ledge.

Good God, he hit it. Better not stand here. He'll see us.

They sit. As they are doing so, Winnie comes in.

Winnie I heard a shot, madam. Was that a shot?

Imogen It's all right, Winnie, it was just Mr Henry again.

Winnie (*darkly*) Oh, yes? I see.

Winnie goes out again.

Marcus What makes you think Karen Knightly's behind this?

Imogen I don't know. It's just a – feeling. (*Suddenly, very anxious*) Uncle, I've got the most dreadful fear I'm going to lose him, somehow. I think I'll die if I lose him.

Marcus (*uncertain*) It'll be all right. I'm sure it'll be all right.

Henry comes in. He carries a crumpled gift card in one hand and a 13-amp plug attached to a short length of tattered flex in the other.

Henry (*casually*) Hallo.

Imogen Hallo, darling.

Marcus Hallo, there.

Pause.

What was in the parcel, then? Anything nice, was it?

Henry Yes, it's . . . It was an electric toaster. (*Handing the card to Imogen*) From Betty and George.

Imogen Oh, lovely. How kind of them.

Henry Yes. I – (*Holding up the flex*) I saved the plug.

He smiles at them rather feebly. They smile back, encouragingly. As they do so, the lights cross-fade to –

SCENE EIGHT

11.00 a.m.

Lembridge Tennit. The waiting area just outside the boardroom. Eugene Chase, a young executive, is waiting with his briefcase. Percy enters. He too carries a briefcase.

Eugene Ah! Good morning. Are you one of the gentlemen representing J. W. Lipscott's?

Percy Indeed I am. How do you do? Percy Cutting's the name. (*They shake hands*)

Eugene Eugene Chase. How do you do? Welcome to Lembridge Tennit, Mr Cutting.

Percy Thank you, Mr Chase.

Eugene Are your colleagues with you, Mr Cutting, or –

Percy Yes, yes, they're just behind me, Mr Chase. I took an earlier lift . . .

Slight pause.

Eugene Good trip up, was it?

Percy In the lift?

Eugene Well, I meant on the train really, but . . .

Percy Oh, on the train? Yes, splendid. Bang on time.

Eugene Oh well, that's nice. Makes a change, doesn't it?

He laughs. Percy laughs.

Nice and warm today, anyway.

Percy Yes, indeed.

Eugene Was it warm down there?

Percy Oh, it was very warm down there.

Eugene Mind you, it's warm up here.

Percy Yes, yes. It certainly is warm up here.

Eugene Makes a change, anyway.

He laughs. Percy laughs with him.

(*Seeing someone along the corridor*) Ah, these look like your colleagues now, Mr Cutting.

Marcus and Henry enter. Both carry briefcases.

Welcome to Lembridge Tennit, gentlemen. (*Extending a hand*) Eugene Chase. How do you do?

Marcus How do you do? (*Taking his hand*) Marcus Lipscott.

Eugene (*taking his hand*) Eugene Chase. Oh, you're the Mr Lipscott in person. How do you do?

Marcus Colonel Lipscott.

Eugene Colonel Lipscott, I beg your pardon. Must get that right, mustn't we? I'm Eugene Chase. Part of the Lembridge Tennit negotiating team. I'm sure we'll be seeing a lot of each other over the course of the next few weeks.

Marcus You've met my colleague, have you? Mr Cutting?

Eugene Indeed I have met Mr Cutting.

Marcus My general manager. And this is Mr Bell. One of our directors.

Eugene (*staring at him*) Ah, you're Mr Bell. Yes. How do you do? Eugene Chase.

Henry How do you do?

Eugene Just to fill you in, gentlemen. Just as soon as the rest of our negotiating team arrive, we'll be going into the boardroom there in order to commence our discussions. (*Glancing at his watch*) I think, in essence, you may just be a shade early.

Marcus Yes, we are. I think. Just a fraction. Thank British Rail for that.

Eugene Makes a change, anyway.

He laughs. They all laugh.

I think – I don't want to anticipate, obviously, what's going to be said in there – but I think we'll be discussing the general outline of how control is to be satisfactorily transferred.

Marcus You talked in your last letter about personnel changes. What are you anticipating there, exactly?

Eugene Well, as I say, let's not pre-empt the meeting itself, shall we?

Marcus Are you talking about management? Or the workforce? Or what? I mean, some of those chaps have been with us practically from birth. I don't want to see them on the scrapheap, you see.

Eugene I'm sure none of us want to see anyone on the scrapheap, do we, if it can possibly be avoided? There may inevitably be an element of purely unavoidable wastage as a result of rationalisation, but then – I regret to say that can happen to anyone at any point in time, can't it?

Henry (*grimly*) Oh, indeed it can.

Eugene Indeed.

Henry Especially at Lembridge Tennit, I seem to remember.

Eugene Ah. Yes, I read you'd . . . Of course, you were once one of ours, weren't you?

Henry Yes, I was.

Eugene Yes.

Henry Now I'm one of theirs.

Eugene Yes, yes . . . (*Seeing rescue*) Ah. Here they come. Here are my colleagues now.

Karen arrives. She is the very essence of a top executive. She is followed by Jeremy, who carries her briefcase.

Karen Good morning, Eugene. Good morning, gentlemen.

Henry (*softly*) Good God!

Eugene I don't know if you already know any of these gentlemen, Miss Knightly . . . ?

Karen (*nodding at them all but not shaking hands*) Yes, I think I know everyone. Hallo, Percy.

Percy Percy Cutting, yes. Hallo, Karen.

He shakes hands.

Karen Colonel Lipscott.

Marcus Hallo, Karen. This is a surprise.

Karen Mr Bell . . .

Henry Miss Knightly . . .

Karen May I introduce my assistant, Jeremy Pride.

Jeremy Hallo.

Karen Well, this is all very exciting, isn't it?

Marcus Oh, yes.

Karen A new era, gentlemen, don't you agree? Well, shall we go on in?

Eugene Yes, indeed . . .

Eugene holds the door open. Karen sweeps in. She is followed by Percy, Henry and Jeremy with Marcus bringing up the rear.

Karen (*as she goes*) Did you have a pleasant trip up?

Percy Oh yes, thank you. Arrived bang on time.

Karen Oh, good. That does make a change, doesn't it?

She laughs. Percy and Jeremy also laugh. Marcus is about to follow them in when Eugene stops him.

Eugene Just a warning. I didn't like to say anything in front of your colleagues, but be warned, I think she's going to insist on a great deal of strengthening at board level.

Marcus Oh, yes?

Eugene I think she feels that people like, say, your Mr Bell, for instance, could usefully be replaced by someone with a shade more technological know-how . . .

Marcus Henry's a very good man, you know . . .

Eugene Ah yes, no doubt. Would that goodness were enough in itself, Colonel. But sadly not . . .

Karen (*off*) Are you coming in to join us, Eugene, or would you prefer us all to meet in the passageway?

A lot of appreciative male laughter.

Eugene Coming, Miss Knightly. (*To Marcus*) Whatever you do, don't underestimate her, will you? Or she'll have you for breakfast.

Marcus (*grimly*) Yes, I can well imagine she might.

As Marcus and Eugene enter the boardroom, the lights change to –

SCENE NINE

Dusk.
The fire-damaged remains of Furtherfield House. Henry stands in what was once the hall. He stares about him for a moment. Suddenly Oliver appears from somewhere within the house.

Oliver (*unsurprised to see him*) Oh, hi.

Henry Oliver! Good Lord. Haven't seen you for a bit.

Oliver No. I was just – taking a last look at the old place.

Henry Yes.

Oliver Hell of a mess. Not a lot left really. I tried going upstairs but it's far too dangerous. I wouldn't advise it.

Henry I won't try.

Oliver Terrible mess. What are you doing these days, then? Busy?

Henry I'm – Well, I was working for Marcus – for Colonel Lipscott's firm but – I've just been removed from the board, so . . .

Oliver Oh? Oh, bad luck.

Henry So. Sort of unemployed really.

Oliver Aren't you getting married? Didn't I hear that?

Henry Er . . . I'm not sure about that, either. Probably. I don't know.

Oliver Oh. Mine of misinformation, aren't I? Comes of – I don't know what it comes of, really.

Henry What are you doing then?

Oliver Well . . . Not a lot, like you. I've been settling the insurance on this place. Persuading them to smile and pay up.

Henry They have, I hope?

Oliver Oh, yes. Eventually. After a good deal of argy-bargy. And then I've been selling the place.

Henry This place?

Oliver Well, what's left of it. The land, you know.

Henry All of it?

Oliver Yes. I didn't want to stick around here any more. Too many memories. Thought I'd go and settle somewhere else entirely. No idea where. And I was offered a pretty fair sum for this lot actually.

Henry Who's bought it?

Oliver Oh . . . God, I never remember their name . . . Somebody. Something.

Henry Lembridge Tennit, by any chance?

Oliver Lembridge Tennit. Absolutely. Got it in one.

Henry What are they going to do with it? Do you know?

Oliver Oh. A factory, I think. A plastics factory.

Henry Here?

Oliver Yes. Be absolutely ghastly, I should think.

Henry Yes, it will. Not very nice to live next door to, either.

Oliver I believe they're putting a slip road through the wood just along there. And then . . .

Henry Down past the farm?

Oliver Yah. They need to go that way because, of course, all down there they want to build the new industrial estate.

Henry Industrial estate?

Oliver Yah.

Henry Where the meadow is now?

Oliver That seems to be the scheme. I've told them, I don't think they stand a hope in hell of getting permission for the heliport but they're going to try.

Henry Oh, I dare say they'll get it. I dare say they will.

Oliver Anyway. All I can say is, I'm glad I'm moving.

Henry Yes. I bet.

Oliver Well, I'll see you around, I expect.

Henry Yes, I've no doubt, Oliver.

Oliver Think I'll stroll gently down the hill. I don't like it here at night. Gives me the creeps. Too many ghosts, you know. Just – full of ghosts. Bye.

Henry Bye.

Oliver strolls off into the night. Henry stands and shakes his head. A man finally admitting defeat.

Suddenly, there is the sound of a motorbike nearby.
In the darkness, it is quite eerie. It startles Henry. He
looks about him to see if he can locate it. It seems to
be circling round him but he can't see it. He runs one
way. Then another. But the bike sound is all around
him, getting louder and closer. He is on the verge of
panic. Suddenly, as suddenly as it had started, the
noise stops. Henry stands listening. Silence, then the
sound of footsteps slowly approaching. Heavy feet
crunching over the debris. Henry stands alarmed.
A figure appears. A tall Motorcyclist all in black.
Sinister and menacing in his gleaming helmet with
impenetrable tinted glass. The figure stops as it sees
Henry, then starts to approach him. Henry draws
back but doesn't dare turn and run. He braces himself
as the Motorcyclist reaches him and stops. He reaches
in his pocket and Henry watches terrified, expecting
the worst. The Motorcyclist produces an envelope and
hands it to Henry, without a word. Henry takes it.

(*Hoarsely*) Is this for me?

The Motorcyclist does not respond. Henry opens the
envelope and reads the note. Despite his nervousness,
he gives a brief laugh and shakes his head.

Motorcyclist (*in a perfectly ordinary sort of voice*) Any
reply at all?

Henry No. No reply. Thank you.

The Motorcyclist turns and goes off the way he came.

(*Laughing slightly hysterically*) No reply.

He starts to move off as the lights cross-fade to –

SCENE TEN

7.00 pm.

Imogen's kitchen. She enters with some toys which she is evidently tidying away. She treads in something and looks at her feet in disgust.

Imogen Uggghh! It's Marmite. I know it, it's Marmite. God, I hate it.

She dumps down the toys, finds a floor-cloth and scrubs at the floor.

I hate it. How I hate it.

She is scrubbing away when Henry enters. He stops when he sees Imogen. She eventually straightens up and sees him.

(*Angrily*) Henry, where have you been? Where the hell have you been?

Henry What?

Imogen I've been frantic. I thought you were in an accident or something.

Henry How do you mean?

Imogen You don't say anything, you just vanish all day. I thought you'd been hurt –

Henry Hurt?

Imogen Knocked down or something. I don't know what I thought. God, why do you do this to me, Henry?

Henry (*shrugging*) I'm sorry . . .

Imogen I've been worried sick. Don't you care?

Henry I'm here now, anyway.

Imogen Well, thank you. Thanks very much. (*Composing herself slightly*) Do you want something to eat then?

Henry No.

Imogen You can't have eaten since this morning, can you?

Henry I don't know, I can't remember. Probably not.

Imogen You didn't have much then, either.

Slight pause.

Where have you been?

Henry Oh, just walking around.

Imogen All day? Where?

Henry I don't know. Up at the old house.

Imogen Furtherfield?

Henry Yes.

Imogen Why were you up there?

Henry Just looking.

Imogen I see. (*Slight pause*) Are you going to take your coat off or are you going to sit in it all evening?

Pause. Henry slowly takes off his coat.

What are we going to do, Henry? Please talk to me. What are we going to do? You won't tell me what's worrying you . . . I feel so helpless. I don't know what to do for the best. (*Pause*) Tell me. Do you want to leave me? Is that it? Do you want to go? (*Slight pause. More urgently*) Henry. Tell me! Please, talk to me. I don't care what you want to do, but you must talk to me about it.

Henry (*slowly*) You see, everything that's happened between us is based on – lies, really.

Imogen Us? Our relationship, you mean?

Henry Yes.

Imogen Based on lies?

Henry Yes.

Imogen (*coldly*) Oh, thank you. Terrific.

Henry No, I didn't mean . . .

Imogen Bloody terrific. Thank you.

Henry Imogen . . .

Imogen Great. Thank you. You . . . pillock!

Henry (*going to touch her*) Imogen . . .

Imogen (*moving away, savagely*) Go away! Get away from me!

They stand apart.

(*Tearful*) What did you mean, lies? How can you say lies? How can you say that to me? I never lied to you. Ever.

Henry I didn't mean you were lying, Imogen. It was me. I was the one who was lying . . .

Imogen How? What were you lying about?

Henry Oh, almost everything.

Imogen You mean you didn't love me?

Henry No, of course I loved you. I still do love you. It's just – the reason I came here – why I got to know you – how I came to be engaged to you – all of it's based on a deceit.

Imogen It's that bloody girl, isn't it? Karen Knightly?
I don't know what she's done to you, what she's holding
over you, but . . . What is it, Henry? What is there
between you two? There's something, isn't there? You're
not lovers, I know that much.

Henry (*alarmed*) No.

Imogen But it's something almost as strong as that.
Stronger. Because it's pulling us apart, isn't it? She's
doing that. Not you.

Henry It's . . . We had an arrangement. An agreement
between us. And I can't break it. I've asked her to release
me from it and she won't. The problem is that if I stick
to the letter of our agreement, hers and mine, then it's in
direct conflict with what I feel for you.

Imogen What are you talking about? What sort of an
agreement?

Henry It's a pact. It's – revenge.

Imogen Revenge?

Henry Oh, it all sounds so ridiculous now – but, six
months ago – seven months – I don't know – it was the
lowest point in my life and I decided the only thing left
for me, frankly, was to jump off a bridge.

Imogen Jump off a bridge? Which bridge?

Henry What does it matter which bridge –

Imogen I want to know. Which bridge?

Henry Albert Bridge. Anyway, there I was. And there
was Karen Knightly also busy apparently jumping off.

Henry (*disbelievingly*) Karen Knightly?

Henry Well, I – Maybe she wasn't, I don't know. Anyway –

Imogen Wait a moment. Was this the same night she dragged Anthony up to town in order to stop her?

Henry That's right, it was.

Imogen Then she certainly had no intention of jumping. If you're really seriously considering it, you don't issue invitations, I can promise you that.

Henry Well. Whatever. The fact was we were both very low, she and I. And we both felt that our respective worlds had treated us very badly. So we decided to – hit back at them. Get our revenge. Only the twist was – and it did seem a brilliant idea at the time – we'd swap revenges.

Imogen Swap?

Henry I'd take her revenge and she'd take mine.

Imogen I see. And who was your revenge to be against?

Henry Oh, just people in my office, that's all. People I felt had done me down. Pathetic really.

Imogen And has she taken your revenge?

Henry My God, she has. She's decimated the building. Lembridge Tennit is operating on a skeleton staff.

Imogen You mean she killed people?

Henry Only one or two.

Imogen One or two?

Henry Well, she didn't kill them, I don't think. No, she just – caused them to die.

Imogen I can't quite see the difference, but never mind. So that was your revenge. What was hers? Who were you supposed to kill?

Henry No one. I wasn't supposed to kill anyone . . .

Imogen I'm sorry. I'll rephrase that. Who were you supposed to cause to die then? (*A slight pause*) Anthony? Was it Anthony?

Henry I swear to you that was an accident. You have to believe that.

Another pause. The truth sinks in.

Imogen (*staring at him*) It has to be me, then, doesn't it?

Henry No . . . .

Imogen (*feeling weak*) Oh, my God . . .

Henry Imogen . . .

Imogen (*sitting*) I feel sick. I actually feel sick.

Henry Imogen, listen. Listen to me.

Imogen (*her hands to her head*) You'd better go. You'd better leave now, Henry, please.

Henry Imogen, you have to believe that . . .

Imogen (*screaming*) Henry, please go away. Please. I am very frightened. I am terrified. Now, please go! Now! (*Pause*) Now!

Henry stares at her.

Henry (*at length*) Yes. OK. I'll – may I just – I'll just pack a couple of things – May I?

Imogen (*huddled*) Be quick. Be quick. Be quick.

Henry Yes.

*Henry leaves the room. Imogen gives a shudder. She is
shivering from the shock of all this.*

Imogen Oh.

She clasps her arms round herself.

Oh. Oh, dear.

She gets to her feet, uncertain what to do for the best.

Oh! Oh, dear. Oh.

*Her teeth chatter slightly. Rather more for something
to do than for any other reason, she picks up Henry's
coat and prepares to put it tidily over a chair. She sees
the corner of the note Henry received earlier, sticking
out of one of the pockets. She puts the coat down so
that the note is uppermost. She attempts to look at it
without touching it. Then she flicks it casually once or
twice, hoping to open it enough so she can read it.
Finally, she takes it by the corner and twitches it
clear of the pocket and on to the floor. She ambles
past trying to read it as it lies there, but it remains
obstinately folded. She gives up, retrieves it and allows
it to fall open in her hand.*

(*Reading*) 'Henrybell. The game proceeds until I choose
to stop it. Admit defeat and I may show you mercy.
Meet me where it all began at midnight. K.'

Imogen looks thoughtful as the lights change to –

SCENE ELEVEN

Midnight.
  *Albert Bridge, SW3. As before at the start of the play.
Henry wanders on to the middle of the bridge and
contemplates the murky depths.*

Karen (*off*) Henry! Henrybell!

Henry Karen?

Karen appears at the other end of the bridge. She is dressed in evening dress.

Karen Good evening, Henrybell, I hoped you'd come. I really hoped you would.

Henry (*wearily*) What do you want, Karen? Just tell me.

Karen I told you that in my note, Henrybell. Did you like my messenger I sent? I chose him specially.

Henry Terrific. Terrific bloke. We had a load of laughs together.

Karen Now don't be sulky, Henrybell. I came to show you mercy. I told you. I bring you a choice.

Henry Oh, yes? What might that be? Pistols or poison?

Karen Choice number one. We continue to play the game as we're doing at present . . .

Henry No. No more.

Karen (*smiling*) No. I didn't think you'd choose that one. In which case, Henrybell, you have to stand by the agreement, don't you?

Henry Listen, Karen . . .

Karen Wait! In which case you have choice number two, don't you? If Imogen loves you – as you say she does and I'm sure it's true – then it's obvious what you do next, isn't it?

Henry Nothing's obvious to me any more, Karen, I'm sorry.

Karen You jump, Henrybell, you jump.

Henry (*incredulously*) What?

Karen Jump and break her heart. Isn't that brilliant?

Henry You're joking.

A pause. She waits.

Is that the choice? Is that all? Thanks very much.

Karen (*slowly*) Not – quite all.

Henry Well?

Imogen's voice is heard in the distance.

Imogen (*calling, off*) Henry!

Henry (*surprised*) Imogen?

Karen What the hell's she doing here? Why did you bring her?

Henry I didn't bring her, she must have . . .

Imogen (*closer*) Henry!

Karen Oh, well. It doesn't matter. All the more fun, really.

Imogen appears at the other end of the bridge from Karen.

Imogen Henry, what are you doing?

Henry Imogen, I'm . . .

Karen Ignore her, Henrybell.

Henry (*to Imogen*) Just a second, wait there.

Imogen Henry!

Henry (*to Imogen*) Wait there! I won't be long.

Karen And so to your third and final choice, Henrybell. All the best things come in threes, isn't that the case?

Henry What is it, then? Come on.

Karen You change sides and join me.

Henry What?

Karen We play on the same side. For ever. As a team.

Henry A team.

Karen You and me. (*She holds out her hand*) I'm inviting you to join me, Henry. For ever. Isn't that the best? It's a great, great honour.

Henry stares at her.

What do you say? Wouldn't we be fabulous? Just think of it . . .

Henry You and me?

Karen Me and you.

Henry That's my third choice, is it?

Karen Yes.

She smiles at him.

Imogen (*anxiously*) Henry, please. I'm sorry . . .

Henry In that case, I unhesitatingly choose to jump off the bridge . . .

He starts to climb up on to the parapet.

Karen What?

Imogen Henry!

Henry I'm sorry, it's the only choice that's even remotely attractive . . .

Karen (*outraged*) What are you talking about?

Henry All in all, I think jumping sounds by far the best.

Karen (*incredulously*) You'd rather be dead than with me . . .?

Henry I didn't want to put it as crudely as that, but absolutely, yes . . . Cheerio, then!

He appears to be about to jump.

Imogen (*screaming*) Henry!

Karen (*yelling*) Henry . . .!

Henry (*stopping*) What?

Karen Henrybell, you can't.

Henry Why not? What's to stop me? It's what you wanted, isn't it?

Karen No. No, I didn't.

Henry Why not?

Karen Because . . . (*In a small voice*) Because . . . I love you, Henrybell.

Henry You what?

Karen (*a little girl*) I love you.

Imogen Don't believe her.

Henry I don't. Not at all.

Karen Of course you do. You know I do. It's true. It's true, Henrybell. It is, I swear it.

Henry You don't love me. You just want to take me away from Imogen, any way you can. You don't love me, you just want to hurt her . . . That's not love . . .

Karen I love you.

Henry I'm sorry, Karen, no, you don't.

Karen (*angrily*) I don't care about hurting her. Do you think I care about her? I love you for you.

Henry Wait a minute. Are you saying you don't care whether we hurt Imogen?

Karen I love you.

Henry And you don't care if that love hurts her or not?

Karen No. Why should I care?

Henry You don't even care if you hurt Imogen any more or not?

Karen I've said no. No.

Henry And so you no longer care if I hurt her or not? You won't even mind if I don't hurt her?

Karen She's irrelevant . . . Forget her. I don't want to see or hear about her ever again. I just want you, Henrybell.

Henry And that's all you want?

Karen (*shouting*) Yes, yes, yes!

Henry (*with a cry*) Terrific! Well, that's settled then.

Karen Is it?

Henry Game's over, isn't it?

Karen (*blankly*) How do you mean?

Henry You no longer want me to hurt her. Then I'm free to love her . . .

He starts to climb down.

Imogen (*in breathless admiration*) Oh, Henry, you're brilliant.

Karen (*realising*) Oh, now wait. Oh, no . . . Oh, no . . .

Henry Oh yes, Karen. Oh yes . . .

Karen You can't do this. I forbid you to do this.

Henry Now, now, we play by the rules, Karen, remember? You taught me that. There's nothing you can do. It's all strictly legal, I've stuck to the letter.

Karen What are you doing?

Henry I love you, Imogen. Forgive me.

Imogen Oh, Henry . . . I love you too much to care.

Karen (*outraged*) What are you doing? You can't let her do this . . . You can't do this.

Henry (*falling into Imogen's arms*) Oh, Imogen . . .

Imogen (*blissfully*) Oh, Henry . . .

They kiss.

Karen This is disgusting! This is revolting! Get back on that bridge at once, do you hear me? I'd sooner you jumped.

Imogen Are you coming home?

Henry Take me home, now . . .

Henry and Imogen walk slowly away from Karen.

Karen (*screaming after them, as they go*) If you do this . . . if you do this to me . . . I swear you'll never sleep again without dreaming of me – you'll have me on your conscience for ever . . . for the rest of your lives . . .

She climbs up on the bridge, the better to shout after them.

Oh, yes. Go on then. Go home to your cosy little country cottage with your pigs and your cows and your hideous children. You'll never be free of me. You'll remember me with guilt in your hearts for ever. For ever . . . Ever . . . Henrybell!

Imogen and Henry have evidently vanished from her view. Karen stands perched on the bridge, undecided what game to start next. She seems momentarily at a loss.

(*In her little voice*) Henrybell.

She pouts. Then, slowly, a smirk crosses her face. She laughs to herself with childish delight as she thinks up a new game.

(*Delightedly*) Of course. Of course!

She looks at the water, then in the direction in which Imogen and Henry have gone. She braces herself to jump.

(*Softly*) Revenge. (*A little louder*) Revenge!

As she jumps off the bridge, with a great triumphant cry:

Rev-e-e-e-e-n-n-g-e!

She vanishes out of the light. As she hits the water, a distant splash and, almost simultaneously, blackout.

THINGS WE DO FOR LOVE

Things We Do for Love was first performed at the
Stephen Joseph Theatre, Scarborough, on 29 April 1997.
The cast was as follows:

Barbara Trapes Joanna van Gyseghem
Nikki Wickstead Sally Giles
Hamish Alexander Cameron Stewart
Gilbert Fleet Barry McCarthy

Director Alan Ayckbourn
Designer Roger Glossop
Lighting Mick Hughes
Music John Pattison

The play was revived in a new production at the Yvonne
Arnaud Theatre, Guildford, on 10 February 1998. This
transferred to the Gielgud Theatre, London, on 3 March
1998. The cast was as follows:

Barbara Trapes Jane Asher
Nikki Wickstead Serena Evans
Hamish Alexander Steven Pacey
Gilbert Fleet Barry McCarthy

Director Alan Ayckbourn
Designer Roger Glossop
Lighting Mick Hughes
Music John Pattison

Characters

Barbara Trapes
forties

Nikki Wickstead
her friend, late thirties

Hamish Alexander
Nikki's fiancé, forties

Gilbert Fleet
forties

Sections of three flats
at 56 Bloom Street, London SW

Twelve days in October

Act One

SCENE ONE

6 p.m., Monday 10th.
  56 Bloom Street, London SW.
  A side-on view of this early Victorian terrace house.
The building is now divided into flats. To one side, the
front door from the street leading to a small hallway
with stairs up to the first-floor flat and another flight
down to the basement flat.
  There is a front door leading off this hallway to
Barbara's ground-floor apartment.
  In view in her flat is the main sitting room. This serves
as her living and dining area. The room is adorned with
numerous knick-knacks, many of them arranged on a
home-made shelf unit attached to one wall. The overall
impression is of order and cleanliness. A tasteful,
feminine, male-free, child-free zone; a room with small-
scale, fastidiously selected furnishings chosen to suit its
fastidious single owner.
  Leading from the living room are three further doors:
one to the bedroom, one to the bathroom and one to a
small, galley-style kitchen.
  Upstairs, we can see part of the corresponding flat
above Barbara's. However, our view of this is cut off at
about knee level. This is therefore the view we are
afforded of any occupant.
  As far as we can see, this flat is more basically
furnished: a utility carpet, the legs of an old-fashioned
bedstead, an armchair, a couple of upright chairs and
an all-purpose table.
  Downstairs in the basement, below Barbara, we can see
even less of Gilbert's flat. A foot or so of the ceiling of his

bed-sitting room is all that is visible, together with the top of a stepladder supporting a trestle. Gilbert appears to be decorating his ceiling.

At the start, Gilbert is not in his own flat but upstairs in the top one. We can see him now and then, his bag of tools on the floor nearby, lying on the floor wrestling with an old-fashioned radiator valve. Gilbert is probably in his mid-forties, but he is one of those people whose age is hard to guess. As he works, Barbara's feet (for that is all we can see of her) are clopping backwards and forwards across the upstairs room as she tidies, cleans and lays things out. Gilbert chats away happily as he works. Barbara barely seems to be listening to him but this doesn't seem to bother Gilbert at all. It is quite usual.

Gilbert (*as he works*) . . . No, you see, what you've got here, Barbara, is a basic, good old-fashioned gravity system which is effectively responsible for pumping hot water to all parts of the building: this flat, your flat downstairs, my flat in the basement there . . . but it's not very efficient . . .

Barbara (*absorbed in her own tasks*) No, it certainly isn't . . .

Gilbert . . . not if it's installed wrongly, like this one was. It never could have been, you see. Because what you're asking the water to do is, you see, Barbara, is to lift itself by its own heat. You get me?

Barbara Goodness . . .

Gilbert You see, hot water, Barbara, hot water is actually lighter than cold water. Did you know that?

Barbara (*not particularly interested*) No, I didn't. How fascinating.

Gilbert It has a lower specific gravity, hot water. You get me?

Barbara Easier to carry, then?

Gilbert No, no, no. I don't think that, no, but . . .

Barbara I must bring some tea towels up before I forget . . .

Gilbert . . . what's intended in a system like this, you see . . .

Barbara I'm just getting some tea towels, Gilbert. They won't have tea towels.

Gilbert . . . is that as the water, Barbara, is heated, it rises up the pipe from your downstairs boiler . . .

Barbara Won't be a second, this is fascinating, Gilbert, carry on . . .

> *She leaves the flat and goes downstairs and into her own, the door of which is open. During the next, she goes into her kitchen and returns with a handful of neatly folded tea towels which she will bring upstairs again. We see now that she is a small, neat woman of about forty; precise, organised, contentedly living alone in an ordered if slightly antiseptic domain of her own creation.*

Gilbert (*continuing as if she were still in the room*) . . . and as this water rises . . . (*To a recalcitrant radiator part*) Come on, get off, get off, you bastard . . . (*Resuming*) . . . As your water rises up your flow pipe it circulates through your rads and then, in turn, the cooler water from the rads – once it's cooled – with its higher specific gravity, you get me? – will drop down and back into your tank and that's your circulation. That's how you get your circulation, Barbara. (*Raising his voice as he realises she has gone*) You get me?

Barbara (*yelling from the flat below*) Keep talking, I can hear you, Gilbert.

Gilbert Because this is interesting, Barbara, what you've got in this instance – is that someone in their wisdom, or rather lack of wisdom in our case – has installed a single-pipe system. Now for various reasons too complicated to go into, a single-pipe system is never going to be as efficient as your two-pipe system. You get me? Because with your single pipe your water is being circulated through one rad out of that into another rad . . . get me? So the net result is that the water at the end of your loop is going to be cooler than at the beginning, so what you end up with is UDH. Unevenly distributed heat . . .

Barbara (*returning to the upstairs flat with her towels*) I know. Don't tell me.

Gilbert You get me? I mean, it should never have been put in like this. You get me?

Barbara Don't blame me. Blame my father . . . He put it in . . .

She has moved into the upstairs bathroom though we can see nothing of it.

Gilbert Well, they saw him coming, your father. That's all I can say. I mean, a single-pipe system . . .

Barbara He was probably broke. He usually was. He probably couldn't afford more than one pipe. I hope this towel rail's still working. My God, they left this place in a tip. How can people live in such a tip? She said she'd cleaned it. She hasn't touched it. Look at the state of this shower. Just look at this shower tray! I mean, how can people walk away from a shower tray and leave it like this? It's unbelievable. It's black . . . What have they been doing in here? Storing coal?

Gilbert They'd need to up here to keep warm. If you want my tip, you'd be better off taking all this lot out and starting again . . .

Barbara I mean, they both worked for solicitors, for heaven's sake . . .

Gilbert Well . . .

Barbara I despair of people sometimes, Gilbert. I despair.

Gilbert (*sympathetically*) Ah . . .

Barbara I can't bear to look under the bed.

Gilbert Looks all right from here . . .

Barbara I'll have to clean the whole place myself. I don't know when I'm meant to do that. They're moving in tomorrow. What's the time? They'll be here in a minute. They'll probably take one look and bolt.

Gilbert It's a very nice flat, Barbara.

Barbara It was. Once. This used to be my bedroom when I was little, you know. (*A fresh horror*) Oh, God, I can't bear it! I cannot bear it! Will you look at the state of this lavatory bowl . . .

Gilbert Not everyone's got your high standards, Barbara. Alas.

Barbara Well, they could at least aim straight . . .

Gilbert . . . Would that they had.

Barbara I don't know why men have to spray up the wall like cats . . .

Gilbert Once I get this heating working it'll make all the difference.

Barbara I'll have to spend all night doing it, I suppose. I've no time tomorrow. I have to be at work at the crack of dawn.

Gilbert They push you too hard, that firm.

Barbara (*with a last look at the room*) Uggghh! It's disgusting. This door-handle's sticky, as well. Just turn the light out and shut the door when you've finished, will you, Gilbert?

Gilbert Right, I'll do that, Barbara.

Barbara starts downstairs again.

You see, if you replaced this whole system, what you'd actually be doing in the long run is saving money. On your running costs. Do you get me? I mean, you've got water rising from the tank at what, ninety degrees centigrade in order to come down through the top rads at about seventy degrees . . .

Barbara's doorbell rings.

Barbara (*who has just re-entered her own flat, over Gilbert*) Oh, they would be early. That's typical. When you'd prefer people late they come early. When you want them on time they're invariably late . . .

Gilbert (*ploughing on, oblivious*) . . . So by the time the water reaches the lower rads, yours and mine, Barbara, it's going to be significantly that much cooler. You get me?

Barbara Just a moment, Gilbert, there's someone at the door . . .

Gilbert Right. I'll leave you in peace, Barbara.

Barbara goes to the door and opens it. Nikki is on the doorstep. She is a pretty, rather superficial woman, a few years younger than Barbara. As soon as she sees Barbara, she bursts into song.

Nikki (*singing*)
Girls of St Gertrude's,
Where e'er you be,
Strong in your virtue,
Come join with me!

Barbara joins in with her.

Both
You in the classroom,
You on the field.
We shall not weaken
Nor shall we yield!

They fall into each other's arms with cries of affection.

Nikki (*as they embrace*) It's so good! It's just so, so wonderful to see you again, Barbs.

Barbara You've not changed at all!

Nikki Oh, I have. I have. Look at me! I'm fat! Fat!

Barbara Nikki, you're not!

Nikki I am. Look at me. I'm terribly, terribly fat. I'm gross.

Barbara Nonsense.

Nikki *You're* not! You're – I don't know how you do it. You never change. You still look seventeen.

Barbara (*mirthlessly*) Ha! Ha! Come in, it's freezing, come in. Oh, where's –?

Nikki Hamish is coming. He went via the house. He had to have a word with the architect.

Barbara (*as they enter*) Let me take your coat. How's it coming along? The house? I want to hear everything.

Nikki (*removing her coat*) Oh, well. The house. For ever. Hamish says we'd have been better off starting from scratch and building a new house. Every time they strip the plaster off, there's another tale of disaster. The whole place is held together with willpower . . .

Barbara (*examining her coat*) This is nice. Where did you get it? In Norway?

Nikki No, Harvey Nichols.

Barbara Oh, it's lovely.

Nikki Hamish gave it to me. An unbirthday present.

Barbara Yes, I want to hear all about him, too.

Gilbert (*calling down*) You'll never believe what they've done here, Barbara . . .

Barbara Yes, Gilbert. I'm just shutting the door, I've got someone here now.

Gilbert Right-o. You would not credit it . . .

    Barbara closes her flat door.

(*To himself, examining the shoddy workmanship*) Dear, oh, dear.

Nikki (*sotto*) Who's that?

Barbara Oh, that's Gilbert. He lives downstairs. He's – having a look at the heating for me.

Nikki Oh, really? He's not –?

Barbara Not what?

Nikki I mean, you're not a unit or anything, are you?

Barbara Certainly not. Good Lord!

Nikki Sorry, I just wondered if you'd been keeping him a secret . . .

Barbara No. Certainly not. Heaven forbid! No, he just rents the basement flat from me. He's been here for ages. I must have mentioned him, surely? He does odd things for me. He's very helpful but – no, nothing like that.

She wrinkles her nose in mild distaste at the very thought.

Nikki What is he? A plumber?

Barbara No. He's a postman, actually.

Nikki Golly.

Barbara So he's up at dawn. And then spends the rest of his time doing odd jobs. He's very useful. His wife died very young. He moved in below. I mean, it's good to have a man around occasionally, isn't it? But certainly nothing like that.

Nikki So you're still – fancy free?

Barbara Happily. Are we waiting for Hamish? Would you like a cup of tea or something?

Nikki I'd kill for a cup of tea.

Barbara goes to the kitchen.

This is lovely. You've made this place beautiful.

Barbara (*off*) Thank you. I'm very happy here now. I love it.

Nikki I can't even remember what it used to look like. You've turned it all into flats, obviously . . .

Barbara (*off*) Well, after Mummy died . . .

Nikki (*snooping around*) So what have you got now, you've got . . .?

Barbara (*off*) Well, there's not much more to it. Have a look, you're welcome. I think the place is probably a tip but –

Nikki A tip? You should see our place! (*Sticking her head through the kitchen door*) Oh, this is lovely. Barbs! What do you mean, a tip? It's gleaming. Like a ship. There's not a saucepan in sight.

Barbara (*off*) No, well, it's tiny. I have to keep it straight. Otherwise it's a nightmare. I'd never find anything.

Nikki Look at all those knives standing to attention. Like they're on parade. Oh, it's all beautiful, Barbs.

Barbara (*off*) Thank you. You see those shelves out there? I put them up myself. I'm very proud of them.

Nikki (*looking*) What, these? Brilliant.

Barbara (*off*) Gilbert says they're going to fall down any day but I put that down to pure male jealousy.

Nikki I didn't know you were practical as well. I mean, at school you were always the brains, but I didn't realise you were practical . . .

Barbara (*off*) You live on your own you just get on with it, don't you? Can't call someone in every time you need to change a light bulb.

Nikki (*wandering away towards the bedroom*) I have to.

Barbara (*off*) No, you don't.

Nikki I can't do anything. I just lie on the floor and scream.

Barbara (*off*) Then you're just playing helpless little woman, Nix. Shame on you. I can't be doing with that. Lapsang Souchong or Earl Grey?

Nikki Not fussy.

Barbara (*off*) Come on, quickly. Which? Which? Which?

Nikki (*pulling a face*) Earl Grey, please, senior prefect. (*Inspecting the bedroom from the doorway*) Oh, this is sweet. What a pretty little bedroom! I love it, everything here's so diddy.

Barbara (*emerging from the kitchen*) Diddy?

Nikki You know. Like a doll's house. Diddy.

Barbara Why shouldn't it be? I'm quite diddy.

Nikki I suppose when you're used to living with men, you get used to everything on a massive scale. *Huge* chairs and *vast* beds. Great big cupboards filled with *enormous* trousers.

Barbara (*returning to the kitchen*) Well, I couldn't have a man here. There's no room.

Nikki There certainly isn't. It makes me feel even more vast. (*Inspecting the other door*) And this is the bathroom. Look at this dinky winky little bathroom. And look at that little bath. Can you actually bath in that?

Barbara Yes. I can bath in that. Every morning. Very comfortably. I wish you'd stop trying to make out I'm some sort of mini-freak.

Nikki I'm not! I love it. I'm terribly jealous, Barbs. Mind you, I could never keep the place as tidy as this. I never could. It would be total chaos in ten minutes. I think you're terribly lucky.

Barbara comes out of the kitchen with a tray of tea things.

Barbara It's not luck. It's simple choice. I chose. I chose to live alone. I can choose how I live. Better let this brew for a second. No, we all have a choice. Live alone or compromise. Take your pick. You want to compromise, that's your choice.

Nikki I don't necessarily want to compromise. It's just that I can't live on my own.

Barbara Of course you can.

Nikki I can't. I've tried it. I – wilt.

Barbara (*irritably*) Nonsense. That's just pathetic.

Nikki (*meekly*) We aren't all as strong as you, Barbs. (*Looking at her affectionately*) You're just the same, aren't you?

Barbara How do you mean?

Nikki You know. Spikey.

Barbara Spikey?

Nikki You were like that at school, too.

Barbara At St Gert's? No, I wasn't.

Nikki You were even known as Spike. That was your nickname. Spike.

Barbara Spike? What are you talking about? Nobody ever called me Spike.

Nikki Not to your face they didn't. You were a prefect. We were just fourth-formers.

Barbara And you called me Spike?

Nikki Yes. It was meant affectionately.

Barbara Doesn't sound it.

Nikki Well, it was. We were all madly in love with you.

Barbara Who were?

Nikki The fourth form.

Barbara In love with me?

Nikki You know. Only crushes. We thought you were wonderful. We all had wild dreams of being carried off by Spike.

Barbara I'm glad I never knew.

Nikki God, we'd never have told you. We were all far too terrified.

Barbara Of me?

Nikki You were so fierce. And clever. And strong. And honest. We adored you. We'd have died at your feet. The whole of St Gert's, practically.

Barbara (*dubious*) They really were terribly unhealthy, those single-sex schools, weren't they? Thank God they're dying out. Lemon?

Nikki Please. (*Sadly*) Yes, poor old St Gertrude's. All closed up now.

Barbara Yes.

Nikki Once Miss Tong died . . .

Barbara (*recalling*) Miss Tong. Yes . . .

Nikki Remember Miss Tong? (*Chanting*) Good morning, Miss Tong . . .

Barbara What have they done with the building, do you know? Pulled it down?

Nikki No. It's a Centre for Business Studies or something now, I think. Something like that.

Barbara Good job, too. Good riddance.

Nikki Oh, come on, Barbs. It was great fun.

Barbara I didn't realise I was an object of fourth-form lust, I must say.

Nikki Oh, really! It was a phase. If it hadn't been you it would have been somebody else.

Gilbert has come downstairs and now knocks on the door.

Barbara (*calling*) Hallo?

Gilbert (*calling through the door*) It's all working now, Barbara. It should be all right now.

Barbara (*rising and opening her door*) Oh, thank you, Gilbert. You're brilliant.

Gilbert holds up a tiny piece of plumbing.

Gilbert There he is, you see. The guilty man. That's the guilty party. This little fellow. Return valve. You get me? Jammed solid.

Barbara Oh, yes, horrid.

Gilbert I've by-passed it temporarily, Barbara. I'll pop in the shop on the way back from work, get you a new one tomorrow.

Barbara I don't know what I'd do without you, Gilbert.

Gilbert Oh, you're not that hopeless, Barbara. Don't give me that. (*To Nikki through the doorway*) She's not that hopeless, look at her shelves there, eh?

Nikki Hello.

Gilbert How do you do? Gilbert Fleet.

Barbara Oh, Gilbert, this is Nikki. Nikki – what do you call yourself these days?

Nikki I'm back to my own name. For the time being. Nikki Wickstead. Hallo.

Gilbert Hallo. You're taking the flat upstairs, so I understand?

Nikki Yes. With my – fiancé. Just until our house is ready.

Gilbert Right. Right. That's nice. See a bit of you then, I expect.

Nikki I hope so.

Gilbert Nice and warm up there now, anyway. Will be in half an hour. Moving in tomorrow, are you?

Nikki Yes. Sometime in the afternoon. We have to check out of our hotel at noon. Pick up the rest of our stuff from the store . . .

Gilbert Good bit of luggage, then?

Nikki Quite a bit.

Gilbert Bang on my door. I'll give you a hand with your luggage. I'm home by one.

Nikki Well, there's no need for –

Gilbert My pleasure. We are on this earth but once . . .

Barbara That's very kind, Gilbert, thank you.

Gilbert It's a lonely old world if we can't help each other along the way.

Nikki Yes . . .

Barbara Well. (*Attempting to close the door, gently*) Till tomorrow then.

Gilbert Oh, Barbara, I'll be going past the charity shop Friday. If you've got any stuff for them, I can drop it off for you.

Barbara Yes, I have as matter of fact. I've just been chucking out some of my summer clothes. I'll leave them out for you.

Gilbert Just sling them in a bag as usual.

Barbara I will.

Gilbert Just bung them in a bag, Barbara.

Barbara Yes. Night-night, Gilbert. See you later.

Gilbert goes off downstairs. Barbara closes the door. The women look at each other and laugh.

Nikki (*giggling*) Yes. I can see he might not be quite your type.

They laugh some more.

I'm so pleased to see you, Barbs. I've really missed you, you know.

Barbara Yes, I've – I've missed you, too. Letters aren't the same, are they?

Nikki No. So you're entirely a hermit, then.

Barbara No, I'm not a hermit, not at all. Don't keep on about it. I just don't want some heavy relationship. I've been very lucky. I've never felt the need.

Nikki Don't you get lonely sometimes?

Barbara I have my work. I have Marcus to look after.

Nikki Oh, yes. The famous Marcus. Still the same boss then?

Barbara I suppose you could call him that. Technically. We're more of a team, really. The fact is, Marcus can't move without me. He says these days I actually get his thoughts just before he does. It's extraordinary.

Nikki How old is he?

Barbara (*airily*) Heavens, I don't know. Forty-five – fifty. I don't know. (*Slight pause*) I think he's forty-eight. Next April. The sixteenth. He's an Aries. Why?

Nikki Nothing.

Barbara Oh, don't be so corny, Nikki. For goodness sake. He's got this beautiful young wife. He has Miriam. He has three children. He's got everything in the world he could possibly want –

Nikki And he has you looking after him at work. Lucky old him.

Barbara That's my job. Anyway. Enough of me. What about you? Are you over it all now? It sounded a nightmare.

Nikki Oh, God. Don't. I've been through hell, Barbara. It was absolute unmitigated hell. I don't want to talk about it. I wrote you everything, anyway. In boring, boring detail.

Barbara I did warn you.

Nikki Everybody did, Barbs. My mother warned me. All my friends warned me. But, you know what it is when you're in love like that – No, you probably don't, do you? You've been lucky. Well, it blinds you. Like they always say it does. No, it really does, Barbs. Stop looking like that. It does. I knew Micky was violent. That he had this terrible temper – he was in a fight the very first time I met him.

Barbara Micky was?

Nikki He was always – getting into quarrels. He'd drink and then he'd lash out. But never – never with me.

Barbara I thought that was the point. He did.

Nikki Well, only later. Yes, eventually he did. He broke my jaw and put me in hospital for three weeks but – that was only towards the end.

Barbara I hope so.

Nikki He was only mentally cruel to start with. He'd lock me in cupboards and things. You know, Barbs, I still ask myself: Was it partly me? Did I provoke him somehow? Was some of it my own fault?

Barbara (*angrily*) Oh, for God's sake, Nix . . .

Nikki No, no. Listen. I'm serious. Am I a born victim, Barbs? That's what I ask myself sometimes. Do I bring out the worst in people? I mean, it happened before Micky with other men, in minor ways. Not as violent as him. But they used to throw things at me. I'm wondering if it's me.

Barbara God, this makes me mad. I'm sorry this sort of talk just makes me absolutely hopping mad, I'm sorry. No, you are not a born victim, Nix. You do not deserve to be struck by any human being, male or female. Or indeed have things thrown at you or be shut in cupboards. There is no excuse for anyone ever to strike another person, and certainly not in a relationship which is supposedly based on trust and respect and love. There, end of lecture.

Nikki But it all happens *because* of love, Barbs. Don't you see?

Barbara (*impatiently*) Where's this man of yours? Is he coming or isn't he?

Nikki I'm sorry. Have I made you cross?

Barbara No, no, not at all. I just don't want to talk about it.

Nikki I have. I've made you angry, I'm sorry. Please don't be cross with me.

Barbara I'm not cross.

Nikki I always hated it when you got like this. Come on, we haven't seen each other for eleven years, you know. Please, Barbs.

Barbara Is it really eleven years?

Nikki You came and saw us off at the airport.

Barbara Yes. You and that –

Nikki Micky. Yes. (*A little tearfully*) We were so happy then . . . I did try, Barbs. Really I did. I put up with it for six years, you know.

Barbara Well, you're all right now, aren't you? You've got – thingumabob, haven't you? Hamish. So come on. Brighten up.

Nikki Oh, I'm so pathetic sometimes, aren't I? No wonder people punch me. Never mind, Barbs, it's all going to change, I promise. You're right. I've got dear, sweet Hamish now. I have to keep pinching myself to remind me I've got Hamish. I've been rewarded, Barbs. I wake up in the night and there he is. On the pillow beside me. God, he smells so beautiful. I look at it this way, Barbs. I've been through the valley of pain and unhappiness. I've lived in the shadow of loneliness for so long. Now at last the sun has started to shine for me again.

Barbara I think you've been living iri Norway far too long if you ask me. Is Hamish Norwegian, by the way? I never asked.

Nikki Oh, no.

Barbara He sounds more Scottish.

Nikki He is sort of Scottish, yes. Both his parents were Scottish.

Barbara I think that makes him Scottish then, doesn't it?

Nikki Well, he doesn't sound Scottish. Not terribly Scottish, anyway. But he's so gorgeous, Barbara. He is, he's really, really dishy. He's kind and he's gentle and he's patient with me. He's got this wonderful tender humour. And he's everything that Micky wasn't.

Barbara He hasn't shut you in the wardrobe yet. Let's put it that way.

Nikki Of course he hasn't. Don't even say that. He treats me like – royalty. He says I'm his porcelain princess.

Barbara Oh, yes?

Nikki Don't tell him I told you.

Barbara I wouldn't dream of it. If a man called me that, I'd knock his teeth out.

Nikki Oh, Barbs!

Barbara 'Porcelain princess'. You're both batty. How old is he?

Nikki About – about your age.

Barbara And he's never been married before?

Nikki (*guardedly*) Yes. But they're separated.

Barbara And why did they separate? Do you know?

Nikki Well, yes. Me. He left Sonja for me.

332

Barbara I see.

Nikki She was Norwegian. It was a dead marriage.
I didn't break it up or anything. It was totally dead. She
was horrible to him. You've no idea.

Barbara Just so long as you're sure. Don't go through all
that again, Nix. Be very certain this time, won't you?

Nikki I am, Barbs. This time I really, really am. Wait till
you see him. You'll understand. I really do love him.

Barbara Enough to marry him?

Nikki Oh, yes. Yes, yes, yes. Have you never been in
love, Barbs? Ever?

Barbara I don't think so. If I have been, I haven't
noticed.

Nikki Oh, you'd notice. I promise. You'd notice.

Barbara Too late now.

Nikki What?

Barbara Past all that, thank you very much. Give me a
nice book, a hot water bottle, a bit of good music, that's
all I want.

Nikki What do you – I have to ask you – have you
never had – never –?

Barbara If you're asking if I've ever had sexual
intercourse, Nix, the answer is yes. And it really wasn't
worth the time or effort.

Nikki How often?

Barbara Enough. Enough to know. Once or twice . . .

Nikki No, I mean was it ongoing or just the odd one-
night stand?

Barbara I can't remember, Nix. Why are you asking all this?

Nikki I just think you probably haven't given it a proper try, that's all.

Barbara Well, once was at St Gertrude's with the caretaker's son. That was the first time.

Nikki What, with the Coote? With Barry Coote?

Barbara I think that was his name.

Nikki He said he had. He told us he had. We wouldn't believe him.

Barbara He told you?

Nikki 'I've had 'er. I've had 'er,' he said. 'I had your Spike.' And we said, 'Bollocks, Barry. Go and screw yourself.'

Barbara I can't believe he told you.

Nikki That's amazing. Was he any good?

Barbara He had a nosebleed in the middle, I think. It was all very messy. I've wiped it from my memory completely.

Nikki And the other time?

Barbara Other time?

Nikki You said once or twice. What was the twice?

Barbara (*after a moment*) That was it.

Nikki Just Barry Coote?

Barbara Yes.

Nikki Oh, Barbs, that's so sad. The sum of your whole love life is Barry Coote. That's so, so *sad*.

Barbara What's sad about it? Don't you start pitying me, Nix. It's you who ought to be pitied. Wasting your life ducking plates and being beaten up. I'm fine. Don't worry about me.

Nikki There are other times. Good times . . .

Barbara I'll do without them. I've got this far. The only reason would have been to have had children and I can't stand them, so that's fine. My role in life is to stay single and take care of romantic little fools like you.

Nikki (*smiling happily*) We used to talk like this in the old days, didn't we? Before I went away. You used to tell me off then. You used to get so cross with me. Nothing's changed, has it? (*Taking Barbara's hands*) Nothing's changed between us. Isn't that wonderful?

 The doorbell rings.

Oh. That'll be Hamish. Shall I let him in? (*Excitedly*) Wait till you see him.

 Nikki goes out of the flat and opens the outer front door. Barbara moves to her mirror and, despite her apparent indifference to all this, checks her appearance. Hamish is on the doorstep. If he can't quite live up to Nikki's build-up (who could?) he is both charming and good-looking.

Hamish Hi! Sorry, darling. Traffic. I couldn't get a cab.

 Nikki nuzzles up to him at once. They kiss.

Nikki Missed you, big bear.

Hamish Missed you, princess.

 They both go through their little semi-secret loving mantra.

Nikki Love you, love you, love you!

Hamish Want you, want you, want you!

Nikki Need you, need you, need you!

They kiss again. Barbara is now in her doorway, looking on rather disapprovingly. Hamish finally sees her over Nikki's shoulder.

Hamish Oh, I'm sorry.

Barbara Hallo.

Nikki Barbs, this is Hamish.

Barbara Hallo.

Nikki Hamish, this is Barbara, my very, very, very best friend.

Hamish (*charmingly, taking Barbara's hand*) Hallo, I've heard a lot about you.

Barbara (*smiling*) Jolly good. Do come in.

Hamish Thank you.

They all go into Barbara's flat.

(*As they do so*) What a lovely area round here. I don't really know this part of London. It's really very peaceful.

Barbara Not too bad. It can get rowdy. On Saturdays, mainly. If there's football. We're not far from the ground. Then we get all those drunks.

Hamish Oh, this is beautiful. What a lovely room.

Barbara Thank you.

Nikki (*proudly*) It's all Barbara. All of it's Barbs.

Barbara With a little help from Peter Jones.

Nikki Is he your architect?

Barbara No, he's a shop.

Hamish Peter Jones, darling, you know.

Nikki Oh, yes, I know. Sorry. That Peter Jones.

Hamish I must congratulate you.

Nikki She's brilliant. She put those shelves up herself as well, darling.

Hamish Amazing. That's impressive. More than I could do. You'll have to forgive me, Barbara, I'm particularly interested at the moment in looking at other people's ideas. Everywhere I go I find I'm checking their wallpaper. (*He laughs*) As Nikki probably told you, we're right in the middle of decorating our own house.

Barbara Yes, she's told me all about it.

Hamish Yes, I feel this place is your centre. You must feel very centred here.

He goes to sit on the upright chair.

Barbara (*sharply*) No, not there if you don't mind.

Hamish jumps up.

I'm afraid that won't take any sort of weight. Sorry.

Hamish Right. Understood.

Nikki (*puzzled*) What's it there for, then?

Barbara Well, not for sitting on.

Nikki But it's a chair.

Barbara Yes, it's a chair for – putting things on.

Nikki That's silly.

Hamish No, no. I can see that, darling. It's more an ornament than a chair. It's a – it's a chornament. (*He smiles*)

Nikki (*laughing*) A chornament.

Barbara (*unamused*) You want to look at the upstairs flat?

Hamish Oh, yes, thank you. It's so kind of you to – I hope Nikki explained. As soon as the builders are out we'll be moving into our place, but there are the usual delays. In the meantime, thank you. Really.

Barbara You are paying, of course. For the flat.

Hamish Oh, yes. All the same . . .

Barbara I mean, it's not free . . .

Hamish No, of course not. That's understood . . .

Barbara I mean, I didn't want a misunderstanding . . .

Nikki No. We're paying, Barbs, we're paying. It's all right.

Barbara You're not paying very much but . . . Mind you, once you've seen it, you might decide you don't want it at all.

Nikki No, we'll love it, I'm sure. If it's anything like this . . .

Barbara It isn't. I have to warn you it's disgusting. It's absolutely filthy. But I will give it a thorough clean tonight, I promise.

Hamish Oh, there's no need.

Barbara There's every need. Wait till you see it.

Hamish Barbara, may I just say this? This is a beautiful house. We're both very grateful to you for sharing it with us, and of course we want to pay our share. You've also been a great friend and support to Nikki at a very difficult time in her life. I don't want to break a confidence, but I can tell you she did read me parts of your letters to her. They were really a tremendous help. I love her very dearly and I want to thank you for that on behalf of us both.

Nikki takes Hamish's hand.

Barbara (*unimpressed, smiling*) Yes. Well, this time I'm here to keep an eye on her personally, aren't I? Shall we go up? (*Waving Hamish ahead*) Please. Lead on. It's the door at the top of the stairs.

Nikki After you, darling.

Hamish starts up the stairs, leading the way. Nikki follows him.

(*Turning back to Barbara, in an excited whisper*) Isn't he gorgeous?

As they continue up the stairs, the lights fade.

SCENE TWO

5 p.m., Tuesday 11th.
Gilbert and Hamish are struggling up the stairs with a trunk.
Nikki's feet are seen upstairs as she busily unpacks things. She is wearing her jeans.
The most noticeable change is that the upstairs bed now sports a new, brightly coloured bedspread.
The men pause for breath on the stairs, putting down the trunk.

Hamish (*breathless*) Just a minute. Out of condition. I'll have to start playing squash again.

Gilbert Did you play squash in Norway, Hamish?

Hamish Not a lot, Gilbert, no. Right. Here we go again. Ready?

Gilbert Right.

Hamish One, two . . . hup . . .

They lift the trunk again.

Gilbert (*as they struggle*) What is it you do then, Hamish? What line are you in?

Hamish Well, I'm technically an oceanographer . . .

Gilbert Oh, right . . .

Hamish I was over there attached to the university . . . but I've got sidetracked into other things of late.

Gilbert Deep-sea diving. Submarines. That sort of thing?

Hamish No, more sitting behind a desk really. I'm about to work for the government . . .

Gilbert Oh, dear. (*He laughs*)

Nikki appears at the top of the stairs.

Nikki Do you need a hand?

Hamish No, no. We're all right, darling. If you don't mind my asking, though, what the hell have you got in here?

Nikki Everything I own in the world.

Hamish (*as they struggle up*) I thought you said you didn't own anything.

Nikki That trunk and a few cardboard boxes . . .

Hamish I ask you, what a dowry, eh? All right – to me . . .

They squeeze through the door of the upstairs flat.

Gilbert To you . . .

Hamish Up a bit . . . mind the door . . .

Nikki (*ineffectually instructing them*) Through you go. That's it . . . Keep straight on . . . that's it . . . straight on, keep straight . . . that's it . . .

Hamish (*only mildly irritated by this*) Yes, all right, darling. We've got it. It's OK.

Nikki That's it, that's it! Down here.

They set the trunk down.

Hamish Whooorr!

Nikki Well done. You all right, darling?

Hamish Yes, I'm fine, darling.

Nikki Only I don't want you to do your back again . . .

Hamish No, I'm fine. Really.

Nikki He's got a bad back.

Hamish No, I haven't got a bad back, darling. Not any more.

Gilbert You shouldn't be lifting that. Not with a bad back. You should have said. I'd have done it on my own. I'll change that plug for you next, Nikki.

Hamish No, I can do that, Gilbert, really . . .

Gilbert (*leaving*) Just get my tools.

Nikki (*after him*) I've put it on the side here. I bought the plug. Though I wasn't sure about the fuse. It's a hair-drier.

Gilbert (*going downstairs*) Don't you worry, Nikki. I've got fuses.

341

Gilbert goes down to his flat and disappears for a time. Nikki kneels and starts to try and unlock her trunk.

Nikki (*as she does so*) He's so kind, isn't he?

Hamish Oh, yes.

Nikki You forget how kind people can be sometimes. Look, darling.

Hamish What's that, darling?

Nikki The bedspread we bought. Look. Doesn't it look good?

Hamish Oh, yes. Makes a great difference. Lightens the place up a bit.

Nikki It is a bit pokey here, isn't it? After Oslo. But I think we'll cope.

Hamish It's only for a day or two.

He sees she is in difficulty with the trunk keys and kneels beside her.

Here. Let me do that.

He takes over the job of unlocking the trunk.

Nikki (*kissing him*) Thank you, darling. Barbs should be home in a minute.

Hamish Mmm. Mmm.

Nikki I'll ask her about that electric meter.

Hamish I think you need a new lock on this, darling.

Nikki You didn't really take to her, did you? Barbs?

Hamish She's all right.

Nikki No, you disliked her, big bear. I could tell.

Hamish I didn't. I just . . . didn't instantly warm to her. She's quite hostile, isn't she?

Nikki She can be, I suppose. No, not really.

Hamish Maybe it's just men. She certainly didn't warm to me. As soon as we met she seemed to want to put me down.

Nikki No . . .

Hamish That's the impression I got.

Nikki She liked you.

Hamish (*unconvinced*) Really?

Nikki Yes. She said she thought you were gorgeous.

Hamish (*disbelievingly*) Oh, yes. (*Opening the trunk*) There you are.

Nikki Well done.

Hamish I wouldn't try locking it again.

Nikki No, I won't. I'd love you and Barbara to get on. She's been such a good friend. My only real friend now. I've lost touch with the rest.

Hamish I appreciate you're both very close. I wouldn't want to damage the friendship. I just can't see what you can like in the woman.

Nikki It's just her manner, darling. She doesn't mean it. And she's let us have this flat, hasn't she?

Hamish For a price.

Nikki Quite a small price.

Hamish It's quite a small flat.

Nikki Not for London, it isn't. Pity about having no bath, though.

Hamish Well, we'll shower. We can shower, can't we?

Nikki I love being in the bath together.

Hamish We can shower together instead. Let's be adventurous. Let's get vertical for a bit. (*He kisses her*)

Nikki Oh, you big gruffly bear . . . You're all prickly . . .

Hamish growls and gently lays her on her back.

What are you doing?

Hamish (*growling*) Big bear's here to eat the princess . . .

He growls again.

Nikki No. No, big bear, not now. Not now. Don't eat the pwincess now. No, no, no, no . . .

Hamish growls again and stifles her protests with a kiss.

(*Makes muffled sounds*) . . . We mustn't. (*Ineffectually*) No . . . no . . .

Hamish starts the awkward task of removing her jeans whilst unfastening his own.

As this is happening Barbara lets herself in through the front door. Simultaneously Gilbert comes out of his flat with his toolbox. Barbara is dressed for work.

Gilbert Evening, Barbara.

Barbara Oh, hallo, Gilbert. Are they . . .?

Gilbert Yes, they're moved in. Upstairs unpacking. I'm just going to do their plug. (*He starts up the stairs*)

Barbara (*as she lets herself into her flat, calling after him*) Super. Tell them there's a cup of tea down here if they'd like one.

Nikki and Hamish stop and listen, frozen.

Gilbert (*calling down*) I'll tell them, Barbara . . .

Hamish Shit!

The two scramble hastily to their feet, adjusting their dress. Barbara meanwhile goes into her bedroom removing her coat. Gilbert knocks politely on the upstairs flat door and enters.

Gilbert Only me. Back again.

Hamish Come in, come in.

Nikki Hallo.

Gilbert Do your plug, then you're all set, aren't you, Nikki?

Nikki Thank you. It's just my hair-drier.

During the next, Barbara comes out of the bedroom and goes into her kitchen.

Gilbert Can't do without your hair-drier, Nikki, can we? Barbara says there's a cup of tea downstairs if you'd like one.

Nikki Oh, really? How kind. Did you hear that, Hamish?

Hamish Mmm?

Nikki Barbs is making us a cup of tea.

Hamish Oh, great.

Nikki Want to go down? Leave Gilbert in peace?

Gilbert Don't mind me, Nikki.

Nikki Coming then, darling?

Hamish Yes, all right, darling.

Nikki We'll see you in a minute, Gilbert.

Gilbert All right, Nikki. You carry on.

Nikki (*softly, as they go down the stairs*) Do you think he saw us?

Hamish shrugs.

We'll have to thank him somehow, you know.

Hamish How do you mean?

Nikki You know. Thank him.

Hamish We do. We do nothing else but thank him. We've been saying thank you to him all afternoon.

Nikki You know what I mean, darling.

Hamish You mean money?

Nikki No, I don't think so. He'd probably be very hurt.

Hamish Why should he be hurt?

Nikki Well. He's a postman. (*Knocking on Barbara's door, coo-ing*) Hallo!

Barbara (*off, from the kitchen*) Come in. Kettle's just boiling.

Nikki (*softly again to Hamish*) No, I didn't mean money. I meant possibly offer him a meal or something.

Hamish A meal. My God! Couldn't we make it a snack? Listen, we're not going to make a habit of coming down here, are we?

Barbara comes out of the kitchen.

Barbara Hallo. Welcome. Come in. (*Embracing Nikki*) Hello, Nix darling.

Nikki Hi, Barbs darling. Mmm, you smell good.

346

Hamish watches this, expressionless.

Barbara The usual old pong. (*Rather more formally*)
Hallo, Hamish. How are you?

Hamish (*likewise*) Very well, thank you, Barbara.

Barbara Do sit down, both of you.

Hamish Thank you. (*Indicating the sofa*) Safe to sit
here, is it?

Barbara Sorry?

Nikki Sit down, darling.

Hamish and Nikki sit together on the sofa.

Barbara I can see I won't hear the end of that. Tea won't
be a second. It's just boiling. Moved in all right, have
you?

Nikki Yes. Wonderful.

Hamish We were just wondering about the electric
meter, Barbara. It seems to be set a little high.

Barbara Really?

Hamish It appears to be charging about two pounds a
minute. And that's just with a sixty-watt bulb burning.
We're a little nervous about opening the fridge in case
the light goes on.

Barbara Well, I'll have a look. Nobody else has
complained. I think you're beginning to talk a little like
a true Scotsman, Hamish.

Hamish No, I think I'm just talking a little like a man
on a finite income, Barbara.

They laugh.

Barbara I'll have a look.

Nikki Thank you so much. We were just saying how –

Barbara (*indicating Nikki's jeans*) Darling, your zip's undone.

Nikki (*flustered*) Oh, yes. Sorry. (*She does up her zip*) It's always doing that.

Hamish (*winking at Barbara*) I prefer it that way. Ease of access.

Nikki gives a shocked giggle. Barbara is not amused.

Nikki You had a good day, Barbs? Good day at work?

Barbara No, I didn't as a matter of fact. Kind of you to ask, but if you must know it was an appalling day. I have a new assistant who frankly should be taken out and shot.

Hamish Poor chap.

Barbara She's a woman, actually. Well, a girl. Her name's Devonia Hargreaves. Says it all really, doesn't it?

Nikki You can't help your name, can you? Look at me. Nikki Wickstead. Nix Wicks. (*She laughs*)

Hamish Is that what you were called at school? (*He laughs*) Nix Wicks?

Barbara I think it was No Nix Wicks at one stage, wasn't it?

Hamish Still is.

Nikki (*giggling, loving to be teased*) Oh, stop it. Stop it, both of you.

Hamish Yes, I'm only kidding, darling.

Nikki I wear knickers.

Barbara Just as well you do. Oh, there's the kettle. Excuse me. (*She goes out*)

Hamish (*under his breath*) Jesus Christ!

Nikki What, darling?

Hamish Nothing, darling.

Nikki Anyway. It'll soon be Nix Alexander, won't it?

Barbara (*off, from the kitchen*) Earl Grey all right for everyone?

Hamish You don't have ordinary by any chance?

Barbara (*off*) What do you mean by ordinary? I've got Lapsang Souchong.

Hamish Er – no, thanks. (*Sotto*) An ordinary bloody Tesco tea bag, what does she think I mean?

Barbara (*off*) Herbal? Peppermint? Raspberry?

Hamish (*loudly*) No. Earl Grey's fine, Barbara.

Barbara (*off*) Right. Won't be a second.

Nikki (*sotto*) Darling, don't be naughty now. (*Loudly*) Hamish likes plain ordinary tea, Barbs. You know, good old Assam. Hot and strong.

Barbara (*off*) Oh, workman's tea, you mean? Well, jolly good, why not?

Hamish stares at the ceiling. Barbara enters with the tea tray.

Here we are. Those are cinnamon biscuits. They're quite nice. Home-made.

Nikki Did you make them yourself, Barbs?'

Barbara No, of course I didn't, I bought them. I've no time to make biscuits. Lemon?

Hamish Milk, please.

Barbara Milk. Right. I'll get some.

Nikki No, I'll get it, Barbs.

Hamish No, please. Lemon's fine.

Barbara You sure? It's no trouble. (*As she pours*) Now, I was going to say to you, you must come and have dinner one evening. Perhaps towards the end of the week. Yes?

Hamish Er . . .

Nikki Oh, that would be lovely.

Barbara Super.

Nikki We really ought to be taking *you* out though, Barbs.

Barbara No, no, no. I'd love to cook you dinner. I insist.

Nikki Well. Thank you. We'll just have to be careful as far as Hamish is concerned.

Barbara Why's that?

Nikki He's vegetarian.

Barbara Oh my God, he's not? You're joking. Really? You can't be?

Hamish Why not?

Nikki What's wrong?

Barbara Well . . .

Nikki What?

Barbara Oh, I don't know. It just sort of generally irritates me, that's all. I mean, I'm sure you have very good reasons, Hamish, but I don't believe half the people you read about these days are vegetarians at all. It's a trend. They just love being trendy, don't they? I think most of it's affectation.

Hamish Affectation? What do you mean? What's affected about choosing not to eat animals?

Barbara Well, for heaven's sake, if we weren't meant to eat animals, then there wouldn't be any animals, would there?

Hamish There wouldn't be any animals specially bred for food, no.

Barbara No, I mean nature wouldn't have made any animals in the first place, would she?

Hamish I'm not following this at all . . .

Nikki Now, now, now . . .

Barbara Well, what else are animals there for? If not to eat? Tell me that?

Hamish I don't believe I'm having this conversation . . .

Nikki Barbs . . .

Barbara I mean, what earthly use is a cow except to eat? I mean, they just stand there, don't they? Devouring grass. What else are they there for?

Hamish Look, I don't want to get into this.

Barbara (*warming to her task*) Well, honestly. I ask you. Or a pig. What possible use is a pig to anybody? A pig is a totally pointless animal . . .

Nikki Do let's change the subject, please.

Pause.

Hamish I just can't get over those shelves of yours, Barbara. They're quite an amazing piece of engineering.

Barbara (*unsure of this compliment*) Thank you.

Hamish They practically defy gravity. Breathtaking. The Forth Bridge of shelf design.

Nikki laughs nervously. A pause.

Barbara No, it can't be good for you, whatever they say. Most of the vegetarians I know are covered in spots.

Nikki Gilbert was telling me he paints as well.

Pause. Upstairs, Gilbert has finished the plug and is packing up his tools.

So he was telling me.

Barbara Apparently he does. I've never seen anything he's painted. Then I've never been inside his flat. But he claims to paint. Wobbly watercolours, I expect.

Nikki Man of many talents. Postman. Plug putter-on. Painter.

Hamish A regular Renaissance man.

Pause.

Barbara No, I think it's all right for women to be vegetarians. I mean, they have to be sometimes. For health reasons. Or for their figures. But I think men need meat, don't they? A man never looks right sitting behind a plate of vegetables.

Hamish I'm sorry, I'm not discussing this.

Nikki (*softly*) Barbara, please.

Barbara No. Just let me say this, then I'll shut up. I think vegetarian men – I mean, don't take this personally, I'm sure you've got very good reasons for being one, Hamish – but I mean in general, I think vegetarian men always come over as rather wimpish. If you know what I mean. All wispy beards and limp wrists.

Pause. Gilbert is coming downstairs.

Nikki What about this dinner? What about Friday? Is that a good evening? Only we're busy on Saturday, aren't we, darling?

Hamish Are we?

Nikki It's our – (*mouthing the word*) anniversary.

Hamish Oh, yes.

Barbara Your what?

Nikki It's our anniversary.

Barbara Really? Have you known each other a year?

Nikki Eight months.

Barbara Oh. (*She is faintly puzzled by the logic of this*)

Pause.

Hamish Well, I think we'd better get on, hadn't we, Nikki? Finishing unpacking.

Nikki Yes.

They rise.

Barbara Oh, you haven't had a biscuit. No animal fat, I promise.

Hamish declines. Gilbert knocks on the door.

(*Calling*) Hallo?

Nikki opens the door.

Gilbert All finished, Nikki.

Nikki Thank you so much.

Barbara Oh, Gilbert. Before I forget. I must give you those things for the shop.

Gilbert Right. I'll take them now, Barbara, if you like.

Barbara Just a second.

She goes into the bedroom momentarily.

Hamish We were just saying, Gilbert – we'd – Nikki and I'd like to thank you for all you've done to help.

Nikki Yes.

Gilbert It was nothing, Hamish. A pleasure. If you can't help someone along life's long highway . . .

Hamish The point is we're all three of us having a small dinner party on Friday.

Gilbert Oh, yes?

Hamish And we wondered if you'd like to come along as well?

Nikki (*admonishingly*) Hamish!

Barbara has appeared in the bedroom doorway with a large plastic sack of clothing.

Gilbert Oh. Well . . .

Hamish I'm sure Barbara would love to include you, wouldn't you, Barbara?

Nikki Hamish!

Gilbert You mean dinner here? At Barbara's?

Hamish Yes. (*He looks at Barbara*) Isn't that right?

Barbara (*aghast at the idea*) Yes.

Gilbert (*completely overcome*) Oh. Well. If you're sure. I'd love to. If you're quite sure, Barbara.

Barbara Yes, of course. (*She gives him the sack*) You'd be most welcome, Gilbert.

Gilbert Right. Thank you very much. Friday, you say?

Barbara Yes. Shall we say about half past seven for eight?

Nikki Lovely.

Gilbert Half past seven to eight. Yes, right-o, Barbara.

Barbara No, *for* eight, Gilbert. Half past seven *for* eight. We may need more than half an hour to eat it. (*She laughs*)

Gilbert I'll be there, Barbara. Any particular dress code requested?

Barbara Just come as you are, Gilbert.

Gilbert Right. Will do. I'll drop these in the shop tomorrow for you, Barbara.

Barbara Thank you. Oh, Gilbert . . . ?

Gilbert Barbara?

Barbara You're not vegetarian, are you?

Gilbert Oh, no. Anything you care to throw at me, Barbara. Anything at all.

Barbara Splendid.

Gilbert goes down to his flat with the sack.

Nikki (*embarrassed*) Hamish, honestly . . .

Hamish What?

Nikki Well, just inviting him like that, darling. It's Barbara's party.

Barbara Oh, that's perfectly all right. The more the merrier.

Hamish (*innocently*) Oh, I'm sorry. I thought that was the whole idea.

Nikki Of course it wasn't . . .

Hamish To say thank you. I thought you wanted to say thank you to Gilbert.

Nikki Yes, I did but . . . honestly . . .

Barbara (*smiling*) Think no more of it.

Nikki Honestly . . . (*Sotto*) Bad bear.

Hamish I obviously got hold of the wrong end of the stick. I'm sorry. Well, cheerio, Barbara.

Barbara (*smiling*) Bye-bye.

Hamish (*smiling*) Thank you so much for the tea.

Barbara (*smiling*) My pleasure, Hamish.

Nikki Bye, Barbs.

Barbara closes the door and goes back to clear the tea things. Hamish and Nikki start to climb the stairs.

Barbara God, what a wimp.

Hamish Fucking bitch.

Nikki Darling!

Hamish and Nikki go into their flat, closing the door. Barbara goes into the kitchen.
Downstairs, Gilbert appears for the first time on his trestle. He holds a small paintbrush and a palette. He lies on his back and starts work on his ceiling mural, one we will never see.

Gilbert (*still working it out*) . . . Half past eight for seven. No, half past seven . . . half seven for . . . eight for half past seven. No, seven for half past eight . . . that's it . . . I'll be there, Barbara . . .

He works on this, whistling happily as he does so, until the lights fade.

SCENE THREE

8.30 p.m., Friday 14th.
Barbara is dressed for her dinner. She is moving about rather restlessly. Nikki, also dressed up, sits holding a sherry. She watches Barbara nervously.

Barbara (*slightly drunk*) Half past seven for eight. Where are they?

Nikki I don't know. Hamish should be back. He was meeting the builder at six up at the house. But he should be back by now.

Barbara And where on earth's Gilbert? He's not in his flat. Where is he?

Nikki No idea.

Barbara (*picking up her own glass*) Well, he can't have forgotten, surely?

Nikki No.

Barbara They never consider anyone, do they? Anyone but themselves.

Nikki Hamish does.

Barbara (*sharply*) Then where is he?

Nikki I don't know. Please, Barbs, don't blame me. I don't know. He may have been run over for all I know.

Barbara I shouldn't think so. Not on a Friday. (*She drinks*) We've practically finished this sherry. We're both going to be under the table at this rate.

Nikki Speak for yourself. I'm still on my first.

Barbara Well, have some more then.

Nikki No, thanks.

Barbara Well, I will. (*She refills her own glass*)

> *Pause. Under the next, Hamish lets himself in the front door.*

I mean, here you are, you've dressed up, you've made an effort. I've dressed up. I've made the effort. I've made this wretched vegetable casserole which will be quite revolting because I had to use aubergines instead of leeks – and where are they –?

> *The doorbell rings.*

(*Going for the door*) Thank God for that. At last. At last.

Nikki Now, Barbs . . .

Barbara Mmm?

Nikki Calmly, darling. Try your best.

Barbara Yes.

> *She takes a deep breath and opens the door.*

(*Rather too joyously*) Hamish, my dear. Come in, come in.

Hamish (*jovially*) Hallo, Barbara! Sorry. Traffic, would you believe?

Barbara I would. Never mind. You're here.

She goes to kiss him on the cheek. It takes Hamish entirely by surprise and the result is a clumsy collision.

Whoops, sorry.

Hamish Sorry. Here. (*He holds out a bottle*) Some wine.

Barbara Oh, lovely. Looks good.

Hamish You may need to pop it in the fridge.

Barbara (*as she goes*) Will do. You didn't see Gilbert, did you?

Hamish No, is he –?

Nikki We don't know where he is.

Hamish How odd.

Barbara goes into the kitchen. Nikki takes the opportunity to embrace Hamish.

Nikki (*sotto*) Hallo, big bear.

Hamish Hallo, princess.

Nikki (*pressing herself against him, urgently*) Love you, love you, love you!

Hamish (*likewise*) Want you, want you, want you!

Nikki Need you, need you, need you!

Barbara comes out of the kitchen. The two move apart. She surveys them rather coolly.
A slight pause.

Barbara Oh dear. Sorry. Sherry?

Hamish Lovely.

Barbara It's sort of medium. But it's more or less drinkable, isn't it?

Nikki Delish.

Barbara (*pouring*) We've both enjoyed the ten glasses we've had so far. No – correction, sorry, Nikki. The nine glasses I've had and the one glass Nikki's had – we've enjoyed those . . .

Hamish Do you have many dinner parties, then?

Barbara No. No, I don't. The place is a bit small really. I mean, it's all right for us, but . . . Marcus was going to come once. With his wife, of course. Miriam. She's quite stunningly beautiful. Only she was ill at the last minute.

Nikki Marcus is Barbs's boss, darling.

Hamish Right.

Barbara Cheese straw?

Hamish Thank you. Home-made, no doubt.

Nikki gives him a signal.

(*Taking his cue*) You're looking very nice this evening, Barbara.

Barbara (*rather sharply*) Why?

Hamish I mean, you're looking very – attractive. In that dress.

Barbara Oh. Really? Thank you. It's terribly old. Completely out of fashion. The colour's all wrong on me as well. I don't know why I bought it really. It's never recovered from that dreadful dry cleaner's. And I think the hem's coming down.

Hamish Well. Looks good.

Barbara Thank you. (*Laughing*) I wish I could say the same about your tie.

Hamish What?

Nikki Barbara!

Barbara What on earth is it? It's revolting. Not your colour at all.

Hamish rips off his tie and tosses it into the corner of the room.

Hamish There you are. It's gone. That better?

Barbara Great improvement.

Hamish What about the trousers, shall I lose those?

Barbara I thought you were about to, a minute ago.

Nikki Tell us about Marcus, Barbara.

Barbara Marcus? Why?

Nikki I mean, what does he do? I still don't know exactly what he does.

Barbara Marcus is a leading investment consultant. He's a senior partner in our firm. *The* senior partner. He travels a great deal all over the world to advise clients. I'm his assistant. I try and keep his diary up to date, which is impossible because he's always on the move and constantly changing his plans. Still, that's the job. I also run his office on a day-to-day basis while he's away. And most of the time while he's there as well. Until last week I had my own assistant called Sandra who was absolutely brilliant, but then went and got herself pregnant so that was the end of that. I now have Devonia Hargreaves who may last till the end of next week if she's very, very lucky. What else can I tell you? Marcus is married, as I said. To Miriam. His second wife. She's younger than him and quite devastatingly beautiful. And he has three children, James, Emily and Katherine. Two from Miriam.

And James from his first wife. They're an extremely happy, friendly, outgoing family and they all live in this wonderful huge house near – (*She is starting to come apart*) Near – Godalming – I'm sorry – near Godalming. It has a swimming . . . pool . . . and . . . a . . . tennis . . . court . . . and a . . . Excuse me.

She runs into the kitchen. Nikki and Hamish stand somewhat bemused.

Hamish (*softly*) Has she been drinking?

Nikki Yes, but she's in – quite a funny state. All round. Generally.

Hamish Clearly. What is it, her job?

Nikki I don't know. She won't talk about it at all. She used to tell me things in the old days, but now . . . I think she's just terribly unhappy. That's what I was trying to tell you the other day, darling, but – you wouldn't listen. You were such an angry bear.

Hamish I had a bloody right to be an angry bear. What about that business with my tie just now, for God's sake? I'm doing my best, cranking up a smile for her and she . . . I mean, OK, I'll try but it's a two-way thing . . .

Nikki I know. Please try. For me.

Barbara returns, apparently back to normal.

Barbara More sherry?

Hamish Why not?

Barbara Why not? Bugger that little postman, I say.

Hamish So you were senior to this one at school, I understand, Barbara? Keeping her in order. At St Geraldine's –?

Nikki St Gertrude's. Shall we give him the song, Barbs? (*Without waiting for Barbara to reply*) Yes! (*To Hamish*) This is the clean version. There's a dirty version as well.

Nikki sings the school song again. Complete with what were presumably regulation movements of a sort learnt by young ladies undergoing old-fashioned private education.

(*Singing*) Girls of St Gertrude's,
Where e'er you be,
Strong in your virtue,
Come join with me!

(*Speaking*) Come on, Barbs, join in . . .

Barbara joins her, reluctantly at first, then with a fervour that eventually overwhelms her.

Both
You in the classroom,
You on the field.
We shall not weaken
Nor shall we yield.

Come join with me, girls,
Lag not behind.
Pure in your body,
Healthy of mind.

St Gert's! St Gert's! St Gert's!
St Gert's . . .

Barbara is clearly distressed, has stopped singing and has started crying again.

Nikki (*stopping singing, too*) Barbs?

Barbara Oh God, why do we have to get so old? Excuse me . . .

She goes into the bedroom this time.

Hamish I think we ought to go.

Nikki We can't just walk out, can we?

Hamish It's you singing that stupid song. You just set her off again.

Nikki It wasn't my fault.

Hamish Then it's me. She's obviously allergic to vegetarians. I'll be upstairs. You sort her out, she's your friend.

Nikki Hamish!

Hamish makes to leave. As he does so, Gilbert comes in the front door. He is dressed in his best, but is evidently very drunk. He has a battered bunch of flowers.

Hamish (*coming face to face with Gilbert*) Oh. Hallo.

Gilbert Good evening, Hamish. Good evening, all. I am here. (*He lurches into the room*) My dear, good evening.

Nikki Good evening, Gilbert.

Gilbert You're looking a picture. A positive picture.

Nikki Thank you.

Gilbert Look at her. Isn't she a picture? Your lady should be on a postcard. She's fit for a postcard. A picture postcard. You're marrying a postcard, Hamish, did you know that?

Nikki laughs nervously.

Hamish (*slightly alarmed at Gilbert's condition*) Are you OK, Gilbert?

Gilbert My late wife was never a postcard, you know.

Nikki No?

Gilbert Oh, no, no, no. You could never class her as a postcard. She was more of a parcel. Still, all the best things come in parcels. That's what they say, isn't it? Eh? Eh?

Hamish Been having a drink or two, have you, Gilbert?

Gilbert Just to get in the mood, Hamish. Big occasion for me this, you know. The first time I will have crossed these portholes as a guest. It's a great honour for me. Brought some flowers. For the lady of the house.

Nikki Lovely.

Gilbert Where's the lady of the house? Where's her beauteousness – her beautiness?

Hamish Gilbert, don't you think you ought to . . .

At this point, Barbara comes out of the bedroom.

Barbara Oh, there you are. I thought I heard you.

Gilbert Ah, here she is! Here she is! Barbara! My dear Barbara . . .

Barbara Is he drunk?

Gilbert Barbara . . .

Barbara He can't be drunk. I don't believe it.

Gilbert Barbara. Barbara, my dear. I was saying to these good people that this evening is a great honour for me. Living in this house, with a person such as you, Barbara, has been a privilege and a joy.

Barbara Thank you, Gilbert.

Gilbert No, no, listen. Barbara, Barbara. Listen. Listen. When my dear, darling, late wife died, I thought, this is

365

the end of the world. I thought, I have nothing left to live for. Life for me is an empty space. A lonely ballroom where once we had danced through life together . . .

Barbara Oh, dear God . . .

Hamish (*trying to move Gilbert aside*) Gilbert, why don't you . . .

Gilbert No, wait, wait, wait. I need to say this. I have to say this to Barbara. When the lights in that ballroom went out, Barbara, I found myself in the dark. The orchestra had gone and that glittering ball had stopped its spinning. I was alone and lost, Barbara. And then, dear Barbara, into my life came you. Not a dancing partner, for my dancing days were over. Don't get me wrong. But someone to whom I could look up to and admire. A face in which I can relive all my memories. Barbara, if I say I love you, my dear, do not misunderstand me. Do not take that in the wrong way. I wouldn't want you to take that the wrong way.

Barbara No.

Gilbert You don't take that the wrong way, do you, Barbara?

Barbara No I don't, Gilbert.

Gilbert 'Cause I wouldn't want that, Barbara. I would never ever want that. I would never want to embarrass you, you know that. I never would.

Barbara I know. Gilbert, will you do something for me?

Gilbert Yes, Barbara.

Barbara Go home and go to bed.

Gilbert (*after a second*) Right, Barbara. I'll go to bed. Quite right.

Barbara Good. (*Taking the flowers from him*) Are these for me? Lovely.

Gilbert moves to the door. Hamish holds it open for him.

Gilbert (*pausing anxiously in the doorway*) I haven't hurt your feelings, Barbara? I haven't embarrassed you, have I?

Barbara No, you haven't, Gilbert. Not at all. Goodnight.

Gilbert Night-night.

Barbara Night-night.

Gilbert goes out and stands in the hall swaying about for a moment. Hamish closes the door.

It's all right. He does have a slight drink problem. I've seen him like that before.

Nikki He seems terribly fond of you.

Barbara That's me. St Barbs, the patron saint of drunks –

Hamish Will he be all right?

Barbara He'll be fine.

At this point, Gilbert tries to take the stairs down to his flat. He stumbles and falls down them with a cry.

Nikki Oh, heavens . . .

Barbara Oh, Lord . . .

The three of them run into the hall, Hamish goes down the stairs to where Gilbert is lying groaning. Nikki goes halfway. Barbara remains in her doorway. Hamish examines Gilbert.

Hamish Gilbert! You all right, Gilbert?

Gilbert (*dazed*) Sorry about that, Barbara.

Nikki Is he all right?

Hamish I think so. Gilbert. Come on, Gilbert. Up you get now.

Barbara How is he?

Gilbert Sorry about that . . .

Gilbert lurches, causing Hamish to stagger.

Hamish Darling, give me a hand. Give me a hand with him, will you?

Nikki (*hurrying to help*) Right.

Barbara Do you want me to . . . ?

Hamish Barbara, you go back inside. Just go back inside, it's all under control.

Barbara Right. (*Angrily*) Oh God, oh God, oh God. Isn't this typical?

Barbara goes back into her flat leaving the door ajar. She pours herself another sherry and sits. Nikki assists Hamish.

Hamish Have you got your key, Gilbert?

Gilbert My key?

Hamish Your front-door key. Darling, see if you can find his key in his pocket.

Hamish and Nikki search Gilbert.

Gilbert Was I on time? I wasn't quite sure about half eight for seven.

Nikki (*finding the key*) Here.

Hamish Right, let's get him inside and into bed.

Gilbert I could have been a minute or two late, I'm sorry . . .

They open Gilbert's front door and disappear into his flat.

Nikki (*off, a cry of alarm*) Oh, dear Lord! What on earth is that?

Hamish (*off*) Oh, God! Come on, get him on the bed.

Nikki Darling, what is it?

Hamish It's a painting, isn't it?

Nikki Who is it meant to be? Is it meant to be Barbara?

Hamish Presumably. There!

They are heard dropping Gilbert on to his bed.

Nikki Barbara? But she's all over his ceiling with no clothes on. She's enormous.

Hamish Yes, I can see, darling . . . Now you go upstairs, I'll take it from here. I'll just get Gilbert undressed.

Nikki Hamish, look at her . . .

Hamish I'd prefer not to, darling. Now go upstairs, please. Leave this to me.

Nikki What about all this other stuff, too? These are her clothes, aren't they? What's he doing with her clothes?

Hamish (*quite sharply for him*) Darling, will you please go upstairs . . .

Nikki (*meekly*) Right.

Hamish And don't say a word about this. Please. Not to Barbara. Not to anyone.

Nikki No?

Hamish Especially not Barbara. Now go on.

Nikki comes upstairs. She sticks her head into Barbara's flat. Barbara is seated, as before, sipping her sherry, getting very drunk.

Nikki Barbs . . .

Barbara Mmmm?

Nikki All right?

Barbara Fine. The senior prefect is fine.

Nikki I wish there was something I could do to help. There are so many people who love you, you know, Barbs.

Barbara Name three.

Nikki Well. Me. And . . . (*She pauses*) I'll leave you in peace.

Nikki goes upstairs and into their flat. Hamish appears at the top of the ladder in Gilbert's flat. He examines the ceiling.

Hamish My God. There's acres of the woman . . .

Hamish goes down the ladder again and disappears.
Barbara has put down her sherry glass. She curls up on the sofa.
In a moment, the lights go off in the basement. Hamish comes out of Gilbert's flat, closing his door. He starts up the stairs and stops outside Barbara's flat. He knocks softly. Getting no reply, he gently pushes open the door.
He sees Barbara curled up asleep. He goes briefly into her bedroom and returns with a duvet.
As he does this, Nikki's bare feet appear upstairs as she clambers into bed in her nightdress.

Hamish covers Barbara with the duvet, having first removed her shoes. He checks the kitchen briefly. He then tiptoes out of the flat, switching off the main lights as he goes. He climbs the stairs and enters his own flat.

Nikki Hallo.

Hamish You're in bed?

Nikki I was cold.

Hamish Don't you want something to eat? We haven't had anything.

Nikki I'm not very hungry. Are you?

Hamish Not very.

Nikki Did you look in on Barbara?

Hamish She's asleep.

Nikki Oh. Hamish, what's going on down there? What was that all about? That huge painting. And her clothes laid out. It's like a museum.

Hamish It's – it's just a harmless obsession. That's all.

Nikki Harmless?

Hamish The man obviously has a thing about Barbara. We should probably feel sorry for him. No, it happens. People get obsessed with people. It happens.

Nikki Yes, I know. I mean, you once said you were obsessed with me but you don't hang my underwear round the room, do you?

Hamish No, well. I don't need to. I mean, I have you already in it. All right, yes, he's a bit over the top, I grant you that. But he's doing no harm, is he? I mean, think of it, he could be out serial killing, couldn't he?

Nikki You don't think he's a serial killer?

Hamish God, no. No, no.

Nikki (*in a panic*) He's a postman. He could murder everybody.

Hamish He's not a serial killer, for God's sake! Calm down, Nikki!

Nikki If Barbara ever finds out . . .

Hamish She mustn't. If she did it would probably – tip her over completely.

Nikki You think so?

Hamish Don't worry. I'll have a talk to Gilbert. Try and straighten him out.

Nikki You must. Oh, hold me, big bear.

Hamish does so.

That's it. Oh, I feel so peculiar tonight. Everything's so unsettled somehow. I don't know what it is. It all feels uncertain.

Hamish I'm certain.

Nikki Yes?

Hamish Very certain . . .

Nikki Oh, big bear . . .

Hamish Oh, my darling . . .

Some activity on the bed. Then:

Nikki (*gently but firmly*) No. No. No, darling.

Hamish No?

Nikki Not that. Not now. Not at the moment. I just feel a bit . . .

Hamish You feel a bit . . .

Nikki I feel a bit . . . You know . . . And then it hurts.

Hamish Yes, right. Right. Right.

Nikki At the moment. You understand, don't you?

Hamish Oh, yes.

Nikki You're so sweet, you always understand, don't you? I won't always be like this, darling. I'll relax. One day . . . I promise. I'll relax. Are you upset? Are you cross with me?

Hamish No. No. God, no. (*Pause*) Hell. No.

Nikki It's probably, you know, the time of the month as well. God, you're wonderful. There's not another man like you in the world. Who'd understand. No man who'd be as patient with me as you are.

Hamish (*unhappily*) No. Probably not, no.

Nikki (*kissing him rapidly*) I love you so much. So much. So much. So much.

Hamish Mmm-mmm.

After a second he gets off the bed.

Nikki Where are you going?

Hamish I feel a bit hungry. I'm just going to make a sandwich.

As he goes off into their kitchen, the lights fade.

373

SCENE FOUR

9.30 p.m., Saturday 15th.
  The lights are out in the top flat but Barbara's is lit and there is also a light on in Gilbert's.
  The phone rings in Barbara's flat.

Barbara (*from off in the bathroom*) Oh, for crying out loud!

The distant slosh of water as she gets out of her bath. In a moment she appears, swathed in a towel. She answers the phone.

Hallo . . . What? . . . Who is this? Devonia, for heaven's sake, girl . . . What time is this to call? It's after nine o'clock . . . What? No, of course he isn't . . . Well, it's a bit late if he was, isn't it? . . . Marcus goes to Rome next weekend, Devonia. That's why we have a diary. In order to look in it . . . No, the twenty-first . . . Devonia, assuming you have one, try using your brain, girl, before making unnecessary phone calls. You'll make all of us a good deal happier. Goodnight. I'll see you on Monday morning. (*She slams down the phone*) Phoning from a nightclub from the sound of it. I don't know. Give me strength.

She starts back to the bathroom. Gilbert has come up the stairs from his flat and now knocks timidly on her door.

Now what? (*Sharply*) Yes?

Gilbert It's only me, Barbara. It's Gilbert.

Barbara Well, I can't talk to you now, Gilbert, what do you want?

Gilbert I just wanted to apologise, Barbara. I want to apologise for last night.

Barbara Yes, I'm sure you do. But not now. I'm busy.

Gilbert Barbara, I need to apologise. I behaved like an animal, Barbara. Like a beast of the field . . .

Barbara You certainly did, Gilbert . . .

Gilbert I ruined your dinner party. I was a drunken disgrace. You have every right never to speak to me again . . .

Barbara I'll talk to you tomorrow . . .

Gilbert Barbara, I only want to tell you that I would never wittingly have done anything to hurt you . . .

Barbara All right, Gilbert.

Gilbert You are my star, Barbara. The bright star in my firmament . . .

Barbara (*screaming through the door*) Gilbert! GO AWAY!

> *Gilbert stops.*

Gilbert (*quietly, half to himself*) Right-o, Barbara, right-o.

> *He sits on the stairs. After a second he starts to cry softly.*
> *Barbara listens for a second to satisfy herself that Gilbert has gone away. Then she goes back into the bathroom.*

Barbara (*to herself, as she goes*) This is all I need on a Saturday night. What gets into them? What on earth gets into people?

She has gone. Gilbert sits miserably. In a moment, the front door opens and Nikki comes in. She is also in some distress, bent over with stomach cramps. She shuts the door and goes upstairs without seeing Gilbert. She enters their flat and as she closes the door, she lets out a moan of discomfort. She sits on the bed and kicks off her shoes. She bends almost double in pain so that we see the top of her head for a moment. She lets out a stream of little sounds.

In a moment, Hamish comes in through the front door. He is in slightly less of a hurry and so sees Gilbert.

Hamish Gilbert? Is that you, Gilbert?

Gilbert (*attempting to pull himself together a bit*) Oh, yes. Only me. Good evening, Hamish.

Hamish You OK?

Gilbert Yes. Just having a sit down.

Hamish Yes. (*He waits*)

Gilbert I was – hoping to apologise to Barbara in person, but she was otherwise engaged this evening.

Hamish Yes.

Gilbert For last night.

Hamish Yes.

Gilbert I was a bit over the limit, Hamish, I think. You put me to bed, did you? I seem to recall.

Hamish Yes. Nikki and I brought you down.

Gilbert Oh. I see. Nikki . . .

Hamish Listen. About . . . (*He hesitates*)

Gilbert Yes. You noticed, did you? My picture?

376

Hamish Yes. Well, it's about twenty foot square. It was hard not to, Gilbert. We also couldn't help noticing all the – the clothing. Barbara's clothing.

Gilbert Yes. Did you think badly of me, Hamish? Seeing all that?

Hamish No. No. Not at all. That's a private matter between you and – Barbara.

Gilbert (*alarmed*) She doesn't know, though.

Hamish No.

Gilbert She must never know. I mean. If she ever knew . . .

Hamish She'll never know, Gilbert. Not from us. I promise. I think it's better she never knows, frankly. All I will say, though, is . . . Gilbert . . . it might be better . . . it might just . . . I know the love and deep respect you have for Barbara . . .

Gilbert I do, I do, Hamish. That woman is . . .

Hamish (*gently*) Yes, well, don't you think you would give her even more respect and love if you painted a few clothes on her, Gilbert? I mean, that's not a dignified picture, Gilbert, let's be honest. That's Barbara reduced to page three. Sprawled out like that . . . she deserves better than that, doesn't she? Don't you think? She's an intelligent woman, with human dignity, Gilbert. And that demeans her. It really does.

Gilbert Yes, I see. I see. It could be seen that way.

Hamish I mean, can you imagine in reality, Gilbert, Barbara behaving like that in real life? Truthfully?

Gilbert No, no . . . I could paint a dress on, do you think?

Hamish Yes, I think that would be brilliant. You may have to rearrange her limbs a bit but –

Gilbert Yes, I could do that.

Hamish Good. Good. And while we're on the subject, Gilbert . . .

Gilbert Yes, Hamish?

Hamish Her clothes. Now, all her clothes down there. That's not very nice either, is it? I mean, some of those are highly personal garments, Gilbert. They shouldn't be draped around on show like that.

Gilbert You think that's demeaning too?

Hamish Yes, I do. To be honest. Tell me, just between us. Do you like to wear them, Gilbert? Or just keep them around the place?

Gilbert Generally, I just keep them around the place. Generally. (*Sadly*) I'll pack them up, shall I? Take them down the shop?

Hamish I think that would be best. Frankly.

Gilbert Everything? Do I have to get rid of everything?

Hamish Well, maybe you could keep hold of a dress maybe and a pair of shoes – no, not shoes – a scarf or something.

Gilbert Her angora stole . . .

Hamish Yes, that's a good one. That's a great garment, Gilbert. You go for that. OK?

Gilbert (*rising*) Right.

Hamish Well, I must get upstairs. Excuse me. Sorry to have . . .

Gilbert No. Thank you, Hamish. Thank you very much.

Hamish No problem.

Gilbert goes down to his basement, considerably brighter. Hamish goes up to his own flat. Nikki's legs have now disappeared. She is presumably lying on the bed.

Sorry, darling.

Nikki (*feebly*) Did you get some?

Hamish Yes. Sorry, I got talking to Gilbert. Disprin. Is that all right?

Nikki Anything.

Hamish Right, I'll just . . .

He moves away. We hear him filling a glass with water.

Nikki I'm sorry, darling.

Hamish You can't help it, can you?

Nikki It's really bad this time. Right on our anniversary, too. I'm sorry.

Hamish Never mind. We've plenty more anniversaries yet, I hope. (*Giving her the glass*) Here.

Nikki Thank you, darling. (*She drinks*)

Hamish Did you pack your bottle? Your hot water bottle? That sometimes helps a bit, doesn't it?

Nikki I don't think I did. I meant to. It's in the other trunk. What I really need is a bath, you know.

Hamish Ah. Shower's no good, is it?

Nikki No, no. When I lie in the bath it relaxes me, you see.

Hamish Hang on, hang on. I'll tell you what I'll do. I'll go down and ask Barbara if she'd let you have a bath down there. How about that?

Nikki Oh, no.

Hamish Yes, why not? I'll ask her. You're her best friend, for God's sake. It's the least she can do for you. You get undressed. Won't be a tick. (*He leaves the flat*)

Nikki (*feebly, after him*) I don't think you should disturb her on a Saturday . . .

During the next, Nikki gets up slowly and undresses, putting on her night things. Hamish has gone downstairs and now knocks on Barbara's door.

Barbara (*off, angrily from the bathroom*) What *now*?

She emerges from the bathroom. She now has on her night things and dressing gown. She is obviously just finishing a beauty treatment. She is in the process of drying her razor on a small hand towel.

If that's you back again, Gilbert, I shall be very, very angry indeed.

Hamish (*calling through the door*) No, Barbara, it's me. It's Hamish.

Barbara Hamish?

Hamish I've got a small request from Nikki. I wonder if you could possibly help?

Barbara Just a minute. (*She opens the door to him*) Come in.

Hamish does so. She closes the door.

What's the problem?

She is aware she is holding the razor. Rather self-consciously she wraps it in the hand towel. Hamish tries not to notice.

Hamish It's nothing too serious. It's just that Nikki – she's a bit under the weather and – her stomach, you know – and the only thing that really helps when she's like that is a bath. And she was wondering whether you could possibly let her have a bath down here.

Barbara A bath?

Hamish If you wouldn't mind.

Barbara Just for her, is it?

Hamish Oh, yes.

Barbara Well. I think that would be all right. I've just had one myself, actually. But there's always plenty of water. Tell her to come straight down. I'll run her one.

Hamish Thank you so much. (*He starts to leave*)

Barbara I haven't properly cleaned it. It'll be disgusting.

Hamish I'm sure it won't, Barbara. Won't be a second.

Hamish bounds upstairs. Barbara prepares to go back into the bathroom. She catches sight of herself in a mirror.

Barbara God, I look a positive fright.

She goes back into the bathroom. The sound of the bath being rinsed round and then finally starting to refill. Hamish arrives back in their flat.

Hamish She says, fine.

Nikki She doesn't mind?

Hamish She's more than happy. She's running it now. Come on, put your slippers on. Down you come.

Nikki Yes, all right. (*She does as she's told, obediently*) I hope she's not cross.

Hamish She's not cross at all. She says it's no problem.

He starts to lead her.

Nikki (*laughing a little*) It's all right, darling, I can manage. I'm not that ill.

Hamish All right. All right.

Nikki Honestly.

They progress downstairs to Barbara's flat.

Hamish (*as they do so*) I had a word just now with Gilbert, by the way.

Nikki Oh, good.

Hamish I think I've straightened him out.

Nikki He is getting rid of everything, isn't he?

Hamish Yes. He promised.

He rings Barbara's bell. Barbara emerges from the bathroom.

Nikki Painting over that awful picture?

Hamish Yes. Yes. He's painting that over.

Nikki Good.

Barbara opens the door.

Barbara Oh, come in, you poor thing.

Nikki Sorry about this . . .

Barbara Heavens, not at all. Look, it's running. Just help yourself. There's plenty of soap and bath essence. And shampoo as well, if you need it.

Nikki No, just a bath. Just a glorious bath, that's all. Thank you. (*She hurries towards the bathroom*)

Barbara The lever's broken on the plug, but don't worry. I'll fiddle with it later.

Nikki goes into the bathroom, closing the door behind her.

Oh, has she got a towel? She'll need a towel.

Hamish Oh, I forgot. I'll get one.

Barbara It's all right, I have masses.

Hamish No, no, please. So have we. (*He lingers in the doorway*) Thank you for this. She gets these – best thing for them.

Barbara Yes. Well. That's a woman's lot, isn't it?

Hamish Oh, yes.

Barbara Still, look on the bright side. It's only a few days a month, isn't it?

Hamish Yes. Though in Nikki's case it's slightly more than that. She has these other – difficulties.

Barbara Oh, God. Does she have problems ovulating, as well?

Hamish Apparently.

Barbara I didn't know. That must be recent. Poor thing. How dreadful. I suppose I've been very lucky.

Hamish Yes?

Barbara I once read an article somewhere that said that if you had regular sex it helped. But I don't really believe that, do you?

Hamish No, no. Well, I wouldn't really know.

Barbara I think I've disproved that one anyway.

Hamish Yes?

Barbara According to that theory I ought to have spent my entire life doubled up on the floor, twenty-eight days a month. (*She laughs*)

Hamish (*laughing rather awkwardly*) Yes. I'd better get that towel. Excuse me.

He leaves her flat door ajar and practically sprints up the stairs to his flat. He closes the door. Barbara takes two or three short breaths and blows on her own forehead. This presumably serves as her own personal relaxation exercise.

(*Once inside the safety of his own domain*) Jesus!

Barbara (*catching sight of herself in the mirror*) God, I look an absolute nightmare. (*Calling through the bathroom door*) Are you locked in?

Nikki (*from within*) No. Come in.

Barbara opens the bathroom door a crack.

Barbara Everything you want?

Nikki This is heaven. Sheer heaven. I could lie here for ever.

Barbara You enjoy it. Take your time. Hamish is just fetching you a towel.

Nikki Oh, God, yes. Thanks. This is *heaven*.

Barbara closes the door and goes swiftly into the bedroom. At the same time, Hamish comes downstairs with a bath towel.
    He re-enters her flat and, seeing no sign of Barbara, goes to the bathroom door.

Hamish (*calling*) Darling.

Nikki (*from within*) Hallo.

Hamish Brought your towel. Can I come in?

Nikki Come in, it's not locked.

Hamish opens the bathroom door and places the towel inside.

Hamish I'll leave it just here for you. You OK?

Nikki This is heaven! It's sheer heaven!

Hamish See you in a minute. I'll close the door.

He closes the bathroom door and stands for a moment, reluctant to leave even though there is little reason for him to stay.
Barbara emerges from the bedroom. In the brief time available she has wrought a few changes to her appearance. She has combed her hair and applied a little rudimentary make-up.

Barbara Like a cup of tea?

Hamish No, thank you.

Barbara It's Earl Grey again, I'm afraid. Sherry? I've got a tiny bit left.

Hamish No.

Barbara Wine? I've got your wine from last night. A glass of that?

Hamish No, thank you.

Pause.

Barbara Well. That's all I have on offer.

Hamish Right.

*From the bathroom Nikki starts singing rather
untunefully. This serves as somewhat inappropriate
background music to the romantic encounter that
follows.*

*Hamish slowly approaches Barbara. She stands her
ground.*

*He stops close by her. She waits as if defying him to
touch her.*

*He steps back a pace. She moves away a little. He
watches her. She turns to face him. She moves towards
him.*

*Hamish again backs away, as if fighting for self-
control. He retreats until he reaches a wall. She stands
very close to him. Waiting, her hands by her sides.*

*Hamish's hands very slowly run up her body without
touching her. She seems aware of this, though, for she
trembles slightly.*

*They are both breathing more deeply and gradually
more swiftly.*

*During this, in the bathroom, Nikki starts to sing
the school song, humming a verse first and then:*

Nikki (*from the bathroom*)
Girls of St Gertrude's,
Where e'er you be,
Strong in your virtue,
Come join with me!

You in the classroom,
You on the field.
We shall not weaken
Nor shall we yield.

Come join with me, girls,
Lag not behind.
Pure in your body,
Healthy of mind.

St Gert's! St Gert's! St Gert's!

On the last 'St Gert's', with a sudden, violent movement, Hamish grabs Barbara. Almost simultaneously she pulls him to her. They fall on each other in a fierce, ferocious kiss.
They emerge briefly for breath.

Barbara (*breathless*) Oh, God . . .

Hamish (*likewise*) Oh, shit . . .

They kiss again. They surface. Hamish starts to drag her towards her bedroom.

Hamish (*softly, urgently*) Come on, come on, come on . . .

Barbara (*likewise*) No, no . . .

Hamish (*incredulously*) No?

Barbara Upstairs. Let's go upstairs.

Hamish hesitates.

Come on! She'll be in there for hours. Come on!

Hamish gives in. They both head for the stairs in a rush. Nikki sings on, wordlessly, as she sploshes about in the bath.
Barbara and Hamish practically hurl themselves into the attic bedroom. They land on the bed and in a moment we see items of their discarded clothing strewn on the floor.
The bed becomes very agitated. We never see either of them clearly but occasionally parts of their respective anatomies come into view: legs, arms, Barbara's head in some contorted upside-down position.
It is obviously a very passionate and uninhibited session if prone, through unfamiliarity, to the occasional misunderstanding.

387

Barbara (*as this happens*) Yes!

Hamish Oh, yes!

Barbara Oh, yes!

Hamish Oh, yes!

Barbara Oh, God!

Hamish Oh, yes!

Barbara Oh, please!

Hamish Oh, yes!

Barbara (*with a great cry*) Oh, dear GOD!

Hamish Shhh! Shhh! Shhh! (*A similar yell*) AAAAhh!

Barbara Shh! (*Another sharp sound*) Hah!

Hamish Sorry!

Barbara No, that's good! That's *good*!

Hamish Good? Good?

Barbara (*gradually louder*) Hah! Hah! Hah! HAH! NOOOO!

Hamish No?

Barbara YES! YES! I mean YES!

Hamish Yes.

Barbara HAAAAAH!

At this point Barbara, entangled in a sheet, falls off the bed altogether and lands on the bedside rug with a thump. She is breathing deeply from their exertions. Nikki has paused for a moment in her song.
  Hamish's head appears beside her, equally breathless.

Hamish You OK?

Barbara (*regaining her breath*) You're a lot better than Barry Coote.

Hamish Better than who?

Barbara Never mind.

Hamish Come on.

He makes to haul her up on to the bed.

Barbara (*holding back for a second*) Listen. There's one thing we have to get clear.

Hamish Yes?

Barbara This is a one-off, that's all it is. We're both out of control and we're old enough to know better. But this has got to be a one-night stand.

Hamish Definitely.

Barbara Agreed?

Hamish Absolutely agreed.

Barbara Right. Then come here, you gorgeous bastard . . .

Hamish You beautiful bitch!

Barbara God, I'm out of condition . . .

Hamish hauls Barbara back on to the bed and they resume their love-making. Nikki's singing has resumed but this time with the 'dirty' version. In the basement, Gilbert has climbed his ladder and started repainting.

Nikki (*singing bawdily*)
Boys of St Alfred's,
We're after you.
We like to snog, boys,
We love to screw.

Open your legs, girls,
Not just your minds,
Show both your tits, girls,
Bare your behinds.

Come, girls! And lift your skirts!
St Gert's! St Gert's! St Gert's!

Let's do it till it hurts!
St Gert's! St Gert's! St Gert's!

As this rousing chorus reaches its own climax, the lights fade to:

Blackout.

Act Two

6 p.m. Monday 17th.
   The house appears deserted. Hamish lets himself in the front door, somewhat furtively. He listens for a minute, then rings Barbara's doorbell. He waits. There is no answer. He looks at his watch. He sits on the stairs and waits.
   Gilbert comes out of his flat with a large black bin liner stuffed with clothing.

Gilbert (*seeing Hamish*) Ah! Evening, Hamish.

Hamish (*a little embarrassed at being caught sitting there*) Hallo.

Gilbert Just taking another load down to the shop. Clothes.

Hamish Yes.

Gilbert Doesn't close till seven.

Hamish Ah.

Gilbert You locked out? Nikki gone off with your key, has she?

Hamish No, I'm just waiting to have a word with Barbara.

Gilbert She's not back yet. Late for her.

Hamish Yes.

Gilbert Mind you, she sometimes works late. All hours they work her. I tell her they take advantage. Crack of dawn some mornings. Up earlier than me. Then nine, ten

391

o'clock at night. She's a frazzle sometimes, Hamish. I wouldn't work those hours. I wouldn't. Not if you paid me.

Hamish Yes, well, she's dedicated.

Gilbert She is. She's a very special person, Hamish. She's a living saint.

Hamish Right.

Gilbert Incidentally. You were right. She looks a lot better with her clothes on.

Hamish What?

Gilbert In my picture. I'm painting a dress on her. Calf length, maroon. Very demure. Long sleeves.

Hamish Yes.

Gilbert Just a hint of decoltage, that's all. You get me? But nothing vulgar, Hamish. She looks a million dollars.

Hamish Good.

Barbara comes in the front door.

Barbara Oh. What are you both doing out here?

Gilbert I'm just off, Barbara. Just off to the shop with this lot.

Barbara I thought you took those in last week.

Gilbert No, I didn't get down there last week, Barbara. I'm doing it now. Excuse me. See you later.

Barbara Bye.

As Gilbert goes out of the front door, Barbara opens the front door to her flat.

(*To Hamish, rather coolly*) What are you doing here? I thought you were up at your house.

Hamish I need a word with you.

Barbara I thought we agreed we wouldn't –

Hamish I need a word.

Barbara (*sighing*) Well, you'd better come in. But only for a minute, all right?

Hamish All right.

Barbara I hope that's understood.

They go into the flat. She closes the door.

(*As she does so*) I give Gilbert all these old clothes of mine. God knows what he does with them. Sits down there trying them on for all I know.

Hamish laughs rather unconvincingly. Barbara goes into the bedroom briefly, removing her coat as she does so.

I had to give Devonia her final warning today. She came in half an hour late wearing a skirt that was practically under her armpits and then she took an hour and a half for lunch whilst some of us have to make do with twenty minutes. Well? What do you want?

Hamish You said we only had one option. Never to see each other again.

Barbara Except in company. Yes. Never alone. We'll have to see each other socially occasionally otherwise it would get ridiculous. But never on our own. It'll only lead to more bedrooms. You shouldn't even be here now, Hamish. Go away.

Hamish Look, there is another option, you know.

Barbara What?

Hamish That we – get together. I break it off with Nikki and – we become a unit.

Barbara A unit?

Hamish Partners, lovers, husband and wife if you like.

Barbara You'd marry me?

Hamish Yes.

Barbara On the strength of twenty minutes wrestling together on a bed you'd be prepared to spend the rest of your life with me?

Hamish I would, yes.

Barbara Then you're utterly batty, that's all I can say.

Hamish What do you mean –?

Barbara Hamish, for heaven's sake, we don't even like each other.

Hamish What?

Barbara You're not that bright, you've got a ghastly clothes sense, an awful schoolboy sense of humour, you're a vegetarian and you're Scottish! What more is there to dislike about you?

Hamish What's wrong with being Scottish?

Barbara Nothing. It's just I can't stand them. It's nothing personal. Or the Welsh. Or the Irish for that matter. As for the French . . .

Hamish Oh my God, who have I got into bed with here? A candidate for the National Front? You just say these things, Barbara, you don't mean half of them. I know you don't.

Barbara Look, go away, Hamish. Go back to nice, simple, uncomplicated Nikki. I'm a cantankerous, bad-tempered old woman. Just go away.

Hamish You're not old. Stop saying that. God dammit, you're not old, so shut up about your age. You're young and you're beautiful and you're the most exciting woman I've ever met in my life. And I think you're barking mad and you drive me up the bloody wall but I love you. All right?

Barbara stares at him for a moment.

Barbara Did you know what my nickname was at school? At St Gert's? I was known as Spike. Because I was so spikey, apparently. I used to think I was rather popular, but it turns out I wasn't at all. Everyone was clearly terrified to death of me. Except the fourth form who seemed to harbour this extraordinary mass crush unequalled since the Beatles.

Hamish Including Nikki? Nikki had a crush on you?

Barbara So she told me.

Hamish I think she still does. You know, when I first met you I thought you were a lesbian.

Barbara Really? Why was that, do you think? Because I didn't look as if I was gasping to leap into bed with you? That's the common male conclusion. (*Reflecting*) Perhaps I should have been a lesbian. God, no, I'd probably have finished up with Devonia Hargreaves.

Hamish I think it was only that I saw how fond Nikki was of you. I got a bit jealous. Trouble is now, I think I'm a bit jealous because you're so fond of Nikki. (*Worriedly*) Do you really think I'm not very bright? I'm quite good at my job, you know.

Barbara I don't know. I don't want to talk about you, Hamish. Not at all. I don't even want to think about you. I've made a fool of myself once, I couldn't go through it again, I'm sorry.

Hamish Who with?

Barbara It doesn't matter. What difference does it make now?

Hamish With Marcus?

Barbara Brilliantly deduced.

Hamish I'm not that stupid.

Barbara I never thought you were, really. I'm sorry. I get frightened. That's all. I shout and snarl and snap at poor defenceless people and all the time I'm terrified. I'm like a jellyfish. A useless, shapeless drifting lump that stings anyone that comes within range.

Hamish Well. That's a little harsh on jellyfish. They can also be extremely beautiful, you know.

Suddenly they are all over each other again.

Barbara (*kissing him*) God, I want you so much.

Hamish (*kissing her*) Yes, yes.

Barbara We must stop this, you know.

Hamish Yes.

They start to remove each other's clothing.

You're so beautiful.

Barbara You think so?

Hamish Yes, yes . . .

Barbara It unfastens there, don't tear it . . .

Hamish Right.

Barbara I love you so much. I want you inside me . . .

Hamish (*kissing her*) My God, you've got the most beautiful body . . .

They are moving towards the bedroom, strewing clothes as they go.

Barbara (*as they enter the bedroom*) This is the last time. It has to be the last time . . .

Hamish The last time, yes . . . You're so fucking beautiful . . .

Barbara The very last time . . .

Hamish The very last time, yes. Let's make it the best . . .

He kicks the bedroom door shut, cutting off their sounds.
  A second later, Nikki enters through the front door. She runs up the stairs and enters the flat. She is evidently in a great hurry. She is here to collect two large books of wallpaper samples.
  As she is doing this, an enormous cry from Barbara in the bedroom.
  Nikki stops and listens. She comes out of the flat, down the stairs and knocks tentatively on Barbara's door. She knocks again louder.

Nikki (*tentatively*) Barbara . . . Barbs . . .

Finally Nikki rings the doorbell. The noises from the bedroom stop abruptly. Barbara's head and naked shoulder emerge tentatively.

Barbara (*cautiously*) Hallo? Who is it?

Nikki It's only me, Barbs. It's Nikki.

Hamish (*from the bedroom*) Oh, shit . . .

Barbara (*going back into the bedroom briefly*) All right. Don't panic. Don't panic.

Hamish (*off*) Oh, my God . . .

Barbara Don't panic. (*Appearing again, loudly*) Just a second. I'm on the phone.

Nikki Right.

Hamish (*off*) Oh, my God . . .

Barbara (*going back in, fiercely*) Hamish! Pull yourself together, for goodness sake! Get dressed and stay in here.

She comes out, half clothed. Simultaneously, while throwing Hamish his clothes, she struggles into her dressing gown.

(*Angrily, as she does so*) I was perfectly fine before all this happened, I was perfectly happy, you bastard . . .

She is more or less presentable, if hardly her normal immaculate self, as she opens her front door to Nikki.

Nikki! Hallo . . .

Nikki I'm not stopping, Barbs, I just heard you down here . . .

Barbara Yes, I was – on the phone to Devonia. You know the wretched, *wretched* Devonia. *Stupid* girl. I just really had to bawl her out.

Nikki Yes. I heard. Wow. Sooner her than me.

Barbara What can I do for you?

Nikki (*realising that for some reason Barbara is barring the door*) Well, I can't stop, I heard you down here and I haven't seen you since Saturday and . . . you know. I hope you're OK, that's all.

Barbara Oh, yes, yes. I'm fine.

Nikki I was passing. Just checking. I feel I need to look after you for a bit, Barbs. That makes a change, doesn't

it? Normally the other way round. You look a bit –
distressed. Have you been crying?

Barbara No. No, no . . .

Nikki You can always share it with me, Barbs. You
know that. Whatever it is. We can share it. Yes?

Barbara (*weakly*) Yes.

Nikki I just wanted to give you a big loving hug, that's
all. (*She clasps Barbara to her in a swift, fierce embrace*)
And I think you're fabulous. Bye. Must dash. Hamish is
waiting for me up at the house. I left these behind. Had
to fetch them or he'd murder me. Bye.

> *Nikki races out of the house, slamming the door
> behind her. Barbara stands appalled.*

Barbara What are we doing? What are we doing to that
poor, dear woman? She's my best friend.

Hamish (*sticks his head out of the bedroom*) Has she
gone?

Barbara I've never behaved like this. I am an honourable
person. I do not betray my best friend. I do not hide
other women's naked fiancés in my bedroom. Other
women do that. I do not do that. I refuse to come down
to their level. I am a civilised woman. A caring, loving
member of the human race. I will not have you reduce
me to less than an animal. (*Furiously*) How dare you
do this to me, Hamish! (*Silence. She sits*) God, I'm so
confused. What are we going to do?

> *Hamish sits beside her.*

Hamish (*gently*) I think we're going to have to tell her.

Barbara It would kill her.

Hamish No, it wouldn't.

Barbara She adores you. You saw how happy she is. I couldn't do this to her. What's more she adores me. That's even worse.

Hamish It happens. It's the old triangle. Corny as hell, but it happens. There's no point in ducking it, Barbara. One way, someone's going to get hurt.

Barbara Then it has to be me. You stay with her.

Hamish Then I'll be unhappy.

Barbara No, you won't. Well, for ten minutes you might.

Hamish That doesn't say much for me, does it? I happen to love you.

Barbara A week ago you loved her, what guarantee is that?

Hamish No. A week ago I thought I loved her.

Barbara God, you men. You can argue anything round to suit yourselves, can't you?

Hamish It's the truth.

Barbara What is to say that next week you won't be saying to Devonia Hargreaves or someone that you only thought you loved me?

Hamish Because I've never felt like this about anyone in my whole life. I swear.

Barbara (*torn*) Oh, God. Who's going to tell Nikki then?

Hamish I will, if you like.

Barbara No, we both must. It's the right thing to do. We'll tell her together. It's the only way. Sooner the better. Tonight? No, I couldn't face it tonight. (*She has taken her diary from her bag*) What about tomorrow evening? The eighteenth?

Hamish (*taking out his own diary*) Oh, God, no. We've got dinner with my boss-to-be and his wife. At Quaglino's.

Barbara What, the four of you?

Hamish Yes.

Barbara You're sitting down and having dinner with Nikki at Quaglino's? When you're planning to tell her it's all over? What kind of man are you, Hamish?

Hamish I just –

Barbara No, don't answer that. Wednesday? No, not Wednesday. That's the board meeting. Marcus has an evening board meeting.

Hamish Do you have to attend board meetings?

Barbara No, of course not. But I have to be on hand. In case. We'll have to make it Thursday. I'm free as a bird Thursday evening. If you're planning to go to a football match then cancel it. Thursday 20th. Seven o'clock. Write it in. 'Tell Nikki.'

Hamish has taken out his mobile phone.

What are you doing?

Hamish (*dialling*) Just a minute.

Barbara (*still in her diary*) God, and I must remember I've got the airport trip with him first thing Friday. He's in Rome again for the weekend. But he always likes to do office things on the way.

Hamish I think I've got your pants on, you know. These are cutting me in half. (*Into phone*) Hallo, Harry. It's Hamish . . . just to say, I'm on my way. If Nikki gets there before me can you tell her I've been held up . . . Yep . . . See you . . . Cheers, mate. (*He rings off*)

Barbara Have you done this sort of thing before?

Hamish No.

Barbara You're suspiciously smooth at it, I must say.

Hamish (*making to kiss her*) That's me. Suspiciously smooth.

Barbara (*drawing back*) Don't touch me.

Hamish Why not?

Barbara Because we'll only start again. I can't cope at the moment. Just go away.

Hamish (*opening her door*) I love you.

Barbara Go away.

Hamish I love you, I love you, I love you.

Barbara picks up a cushion and makes to throw it at him. Hamish hastily closes the door. In the hallway, he smiles to himself and takes his mobile phone from his inside pocket. He is dialling a number as he lets himself out of her front door. Barbara meanwhile is inspecting the room and tidying it. Her phone rings.

Barbara Now what? (*She answers*) Hallo? . . . I said go away, Hamish!

She slams down the phone. She picks up the cushion from the floor and hugs it to her. She laughs a little.

(*Realising what she is doing*) Oh God, what's happening to me? (*As she goes into the bedroom*) What on earth's happening to me?

As she goes the lights fade.

SCENE TWO

7 p.m., Thursday 20th.

    Barbara is ready and waiting. She has laid out sherry and nibbles as before. She is very nervous. Upstairs, we see Nikki's feet moving to and fro rather busily. Hamish is sitting on the bed. In the basement, Gilbert is happily engrossed in his ceiling mural.

Hamish It's seven o'clock.

Nikki All right, darling, I'm being as quick as I can . . . I'm sorry. Oh, look at this. It's terribly creased. I can't wear this.

Hamish It really doesn't matter. It's only for – a drink.

Nikki I can't go down to Barbara's wearing this. Look, you go ahead, darling, you go on. I'll be down in a second.

Hamish Well . . .

Nikki Can you bear to face her on your own?

Hamish Yes.

Nikki I'll be as quick as I can. Promise.

Hamish Yes. (*He gets up and goes to the door*)

Nikki I don't think I've got any tights now . . .

Hamish Quick as you can, darling.

Nikki Yes, yes, promise.

    Hamish goes out of the flat and down the stairs. He rings Barbara's doorbell. She jumps, then composes herself. She opens the door.

Barbara (*in a fittingly grave manner*) Hallo . . .

Hamish Hi!

Barbara Where is she?

Hamish She's coming. She's got problems with tights.

Barbara Come in. (*She closes the door*) I thought you were coming down together?

Hamish God, this is so heartless and clinical, all this. I mean, it's all laid on. Look, you've even got nibbles.

Barbara It's not heartless. It's civilised. How else do you want it to happen? Wait for her to be told by a third party? Till she finds love letters or contraceptives in your pockets?

Hamish No . . .

Barbara Something sordid like that?

Hamish No, it's just . . .

Barbara Or should we both be cowardly and run off together and write her a letter? Or a fax? Contact her through the internet?

Hamish No, this is the right way. Of course it is. I think it's just the nibbles.

Barbara Then I'll put them away. We'll have tea if you prefer.

Hamish No. No more of that bloody Earl Grey . . .

Barbara Well, I don't know. I don't do this sort of thing regularly. I don't know how one's supposed to do it. You tell me. You've obviously done it before.

Hamish Usually, it just sort of happens.

Barbara You wait for her to find out. That's typical.

Hamish Not always. No. It gradually becomes – apparent.

Barbara Well, I think this is the honourable way. I mean, if this were business, if I was firing Devonia Hargreaves, say, which I'm about to do, I'd bring her in, I'd sit her down and I'd offer her a cup of tea and I'd say, 'Devonia, you're a sweet charming girl but I'm afraid you're not up to this job and you're going to have to go.' Then she'd probably have a little cry and I'd give her a motherly hug and that'd be that. I mean, this is not that different, is it?

Hamish You're going to tell Nikki she's not up to the job?

Barbara No . . .

Hamish I don't think it's going to be quite as cut and dried as that, Barbara.

Barbara Do you want to back out, then? I mean, we don't have to tell her. We can stop it now. We can all sit down, have a sherry and indulge in small talk. Sing the school song again. And incidentally in the process we, of course, forget all about us because I refuse to go on the way things are at present. Carrying on behind her back. So which is it to be?

Hamish I don't know.

Barbara It's your choice. Which one do you want? Me or her?

Hamish Why do women always say that?

Barbara You *have* done this before.

Hamish Only once.

Barbara When? When did you do it before?

Hamish When – when I left my wife for Nikki.

Barbara Oh, God. Of course.

Pause.

Hamish Listen, Nikki probably knows already.

Barbara How can she possibly?

Hamish They do. Women do. They have an instinct for these things. I mean, with a man – a wife can sometimes deceive him for the whole of their married life and he never has the slightest inkling –

Barbara Because most of them are stupid . . .

Hamish But – wait – but women – they *know*. They sense the change.

Barbara Nikki would have to be brilliant. We've only been together five days. I mean, she's my best friend, but no one could call her brilliant.

Hamish Take it from me. Nikki knows. In here. Maybe she hasn't put it into thoughts yet. But somewhere inside her, she *knows*. I'm sure of it. What I'm saying is, she's not going to be completely gobsmacked.

Barbara I hate to contradict you, Hamish, but it sounds to me like you're whistling in a coal cellar. She hasn't the faintest clue.

Nikki closes the upstairs door. They both look up.

That's her. Should we both sit on the sofa with her on the chair?

Hamish Yes, that's good.

Barbara Or is that too contrived? Should it be me on the chair and you two on the sofa.

Hamish I can't sit next to her.

Barbara Well, I don't think I should . . .

The doorbell rings. They stop.

Here we go then.

*Barbara opens the door. Nikki steps inside. She has a
leather scrapbook under her arm.*

(*In the same grave tone as before*) Come in, Nikki.

Nikki (*cheerily*) Hi! Sorry. I'm all at sixes and sevens
today. Hallo. (*She looks at them both expectantly. To
Barbara*) You look nice, Barbs.

Barbara So do you.

Nikki This is the only thing of mine that isn't creased.
(*She laughs*)

Barbara Oh, I'll lend you a . . . (*She checks herself*)
Shall we sit down, then? You want a sherry, Nikki?

Nikki You bet. (*She sits on the sofa*) Oh, darling, I
meant to tell you. I spoke to Harry. Those tile samples
have come at last.

Hamish Great. (*He sits in the armchair*)

Nikki Barbs, you'll never guess what I've got here.

Barbara Oh, what's that? Here we are.

*She gives sherry to Nikki and Hamish. She then takes
her own glass and, finding there is only a choice of
sitting next to Nikki, opts for the small 'ornamental'
chair in the corner.*

Nikki Thank you. No, I was looking for something in
one of the packing cases which they've delivered to the
house and I came acr— (*Noticing Barbara*) What are
you doing?

Barbara Sorry?

Nikki Why on earth are you sitting there?

Barbara I – I – just thought the chair needed – using.
I mean, it's silly. It just – sits here, doesn't it? Hamish
was absolutely right. Carry on – you were saying?

Nikki Yes. Look, what I found, Barbs. It's my old scrapbook. With masses of stuff from St Gert's. Look. Old show programmes, look. *The Pirates of Penzance.* You were in that, weren't you?

Barbara (*in the grip of some strong emotion*) Mmm.

Nikki Look, look, come and look, Barbs. Don't sit over there. Come and sit here.

Barbara gets up and sits next to her.

That's better.

Barbara Mmm.

Nikki You all right?

Barbara Mmm.

Nikki (*back to the scrapbook*) Look, Barbs, look. Remember that? It's *the* dance. You remember *the* dreadful annual dance. (*Giggling*) That's me. Look at that dress! How could I have worn that dress? Not surprising I couldn't find anyone to dance with.

Barbara Mmm.

Nikki Look, look. That's us. Together. Look. Look, Hamish, this is really funny. That's Christine . . . can't remember who that one is . . . Alison, remember Ali? . . . and Kath . . . and there's you with your arm round me. I didn't wash my shoulder for a month, you know.

Barbara (*now crying visibly*) Mmmmmm!

Nikki Barbara, what's the matter?

Barbara rushes into the bedroom and slams the door. A silence.

(*Softly*) I'm worried to death about her, Hamish, I really am. There's something terribly wrong.

Pause. Hamish looks at her.

I thought this would cheer her up. What are we going to do about her? (*Pause*) She needs help. (*Pause*) Don't you think so?

Hamish Nikki, I have something to tell you.

Nikki Yes, darling, in a minute. But what about Barbs? What are we going to do about Barbs? We have to find out what's wrong with her, surely?

Hamish Nikki, listen. Principally . . . primarily . . . essentially . . . what's wrong with Barbs . . . with Barbara is . . . she's in love with me. That's it – chiefly.

Nikki takes this in.

Nikki (*giggling*) Barbs is in love with *you*?

Hamish In a nutshell.

Nikki But she can't stand the sight of you, darling.

Hamish Did she say that?

Nikki No, but . . . It's obvious. You two don't get on at all, do you? I mean you can't stick her, can you? I mean, you called her an – an f. b.

Hamish Yes. Well, that might have been a fraction misleading. You see, the other chief point is – the other – chief point is I'm in love with her. I love Barbara.

Nikki (*blankly*) What are you saying?

Hamish I think you know what I'm saying, Nikki.

The door to the bedroom opens very gently. Barbara stands and watches them both.
  Nikki looks at them both in turn.
  She laughs.
  Neither of them reacts.

Nikki looks at them again.
She laughs again. A little less convincingly. Her
world is caving in.

Nikki (*eventually, in a little voice*) What about me?

They stare at her.

(*To Hamish*) What about us? (*To Barbara*) Barbs?

Hamish I'm afraid it's over, Nikki. I'm dreadfully, so
dreadfully sorry. I can't say how sorry I am.

Nikki, still on the sofa, appears to be losing her breath,
at first shallow panting and then doubling up as if she
has been punched in the stomach. She starts to make
short staccato cries of pain, growing in volume and
intensity.
The other two watch her, transfixed at the effect the
news is having on her.

(*At length, recovering and rising as if to touch her*)
Nikki . . .

This has the effect of causing Nikki to rise and plunge
from the room with a terrible cry. She rushes upstairs
and into their flat. She slams the door and locks it and
then flings herself on the bed. Her crying continues
into her pillow. The other two are rather lost for
words.

Barbara As you said, she obviously knew about it all
along, didn't she?

Hamish All right. Don't start . . . I'll – I'd better see if
she's – I'll go and talk to her.

He rises.

Barbara We should have kicked her in the face and had
done with it really . . .

Hamish I'll be back.

Barbara I've no doubt you will.

Hamish goes out of her flat, leaving the door ajar. He goes up to his own flat.

(*To herself*) No one else is going to have you, are they? No one else is going to have either of us.

Hamish tries the door of his flat and finds it locked. He knocks. Barbara remains motionless in her bedroom doorway.

Hamish (*calling through the door, knocking*) Nikki . . . Nikki, darling . . . come on. Let me in, please, Nikki. Nikki, I need to talk to you, please. Please, Nikki. Come on, darling. Nikki. (*He waits*) Nikki. (*He knocks again and waits*)

Gilbert has come out of his flat during this and climbed the stairs. He stands outside Barbara's flat listening to Hamish above. Gilbert peers cautiously through Barbara's half-open door and sees her.

Gilbert Oh, hallo there, Barbara.

Barbara (*muted*) Gilbert?

Gilbert enters her flat a little.

Gilbert (*confidentially*) What's going on up there? Is it a domestic? Little tiff?

Barbara No, Gilbert, it's quite a major tiff.

Gilbert Really?

Barbara Miss Wickstead – Nikki, has just learned that her fiancé is carrying on with another woman.

Gilbert Good gracious! Oh dear, oh dear, oh dear. Do we know who it is?

Barbara Yes. It's me.

Gilbert (*stunned*) You? You and – you and Hamish, Barbara?

Barbara Yes. I thought you should know, Gilbert.

Gilbert (*seemingly losing his power of speech*) I . . . I . . . I . . . I . . . (*Incredulous with the shock*) Oh, Barbara! Oh! Barbara!

   He walks slowly back to his flat. A man in deep shock. He closes the door.

Barbara (*a little puzzled at the strength of his reaction*) Gilbert . . . ?

Hamish (*one last try*) Nikki . . . Nikki . . .

   Nikki is now silent on the bed. Hamish gives up and comes downstairs. He enters Barbara's flat.

I'll leave her – for a moment or two. (*Silence. An attempt at jollity*) Had the best of the day, really, haven't we?

Barbara I've just told Gilbert.

Hamish Well, why not? Everyone's going to know sooner or later.

Barbara He seemed surprisingly shocked.

Hamish Yes . . . Anyway. What about a nice cup of Earl Grey, then?

Barbara Is this going to work out, Hamish?

Hamish How do you mean?

Barbara Us. You and me? I just hope we haven't done all this for nothing. We've just caused someone the most appalling pain and hurt and I'm not sure now whether it was worth it. Are you?

Hamish (*shrugging hopelessly*) Time will tell.

Barbara Please God it does.

Barbara continues to stand there while Hamish goes into the kitchen.
Simultaneously, Gilbert appears at the top of his ladder. He sits there gazing at his ceiling portrait.

Gilbert (*sorrowfully*) Oh, Barbara, Barbara, what have you done?

As all this happens, the lights fade.

SCENE THREE

7 a.m., Friday morning.
Upstairs, Nikki has been busy. The bed is surrounded by shredded material. She is evidently executing the classic revenge and cutting up or generally destroying all Hamish's clothes. A small suitcase can be seen by the door, packed and ready to go.
In Barbara's flat, the sherry is finished as is the bottle of wine that Hamish brought the previous week.
Hamish lies on the sofa. The crumpled vision of a man who has been up all night.
There is no sign of Gilbert in the basement.
Barbara is outside Nikki's door, having another try at gaining admission.

Barbara (*wearily*) . . . Nikki . . . Nix . . . It's Barbs . . . Come on, now . . . You can't keep this up for ever, darling, can you? . . . Come on . . . Nix. This is silly. Nix. (*She sighs and finally gives up*)

Barbara comes down the stairs and re-enters her flat. Nikki continues calmly with her destructive activities. Hamish sits up as Barbara enters.

Hamish What's the time?

Barbara Just gone seven.

Hamish Hell. Where did the night go?

Barbara At least you slept.

Hamish I didn't sleep. I haven't slept.

Barbara You have.

Hamish I have not.

Barbara You dozed.

Hamish I may have dozed. I didn't sleep, though.

Barbara What's the difference between dozing and sleeping?

Hamish (*irritably*) There's a hell of difference.

Barbara (*snapping back*) All right! (*Pause*) I haven't slept. Not a wink.

Hamish You snore while you're awake, do you?

Barbara (*choosing to ignore this*) I don't know what she's doing up there. I heard her moving about.

Hamish God knows.

Barbara If she doesn't come out soon we may have to break the door down.

Hamish Good luck.

Barbara Well, we may have to. She may be planning to harm herself.

Hamish No, not Nikki. She wouldn't try that. Women like Nikki never –

Barbara Oh good, this is some more of your famous female psychology, is it? If you're too feeble, I'll ask Gilbert. He can unscrew it.

Hamish Unscrew it?

Barbara Yes.

Hamish Unscrew what?

Barbara The door.

Hamish How the hell do you unscrew a door?

Barbara I don't know. Presumably they can be unscrewed.

Hamish They can't.

Barbara Then how do you screw them up there in the first place if you can't unscrew them?

Hamish (*exploding*) You can only unscrew them when they're open, woman! You can't unscrew them when they're shut, can you? Otherwise what would be the bloody point? People would be going round unscrewing doors everywhere. So there'd be no bloody use in having a fucking door in the first place, you stupid bitch!

Barbara All right! All right! All right! (*Pause*) God, you're a testy man, aren't you? Another side of you, this is.

Hamish I'm sorry. I've had no sleep. I'm sorry.

Barbara Oh yes, you have.

Hamish gives her a sharp look.

Nor have I. But I don't go around shouting and swearing.

Hamish I'm sorry.

Barbara We can see the true Scottish coming out now, can't we?

Upstairs Nikki now starts destroying the bedding. There is a great quantity of feathers and mattress ticking. Simultaneously, Gilbert appears on his ladder and studies his painting. He is wearing one of Barbara's old evening frocks.

Gilbert (*gazing at his picture, sorrowfully*) Oh, Barbara, Barbara . . .

Barbara I don't think Gilbert's gone to work either. I could hear him moving about earlier. I listened outside his door.

Hamish Why did you do that?

Barbara I thought I heard him crying.

Hamish Oh.

Suddenly, loudly, Barbara's phone rings. They jump.

Barbara Who on earth can that be at this time? (*Answering*) Hallo . . . Who? . . . Devonia, dear, it is 7.15 in the morn— What? . . . (*She listens*) Oh . . . Oh, dear God . . . How is he? Is he furious? . . . No, well, I had – tell him I had a – family crisis . . . (*To Hamish, appalled*) I'm supposed to be at the airport . . . (*Into the phone again*) Now listen, Devonia, this is what you must do. First of all, make sure Marcus is safely on the plane and then . . . He what . . . With him? . . . I see. No. No. Right. Yes. Well, if that's what he wants . . . Yes, have a good trip . . . I will. Yes . . . Goodbye. (*She is stunned. Bitterly*) Well. Lift your skirt high enough, the sky's the limit, apparently. Marcus is taking Devonia to Rome. The rest of us have to make do with the departure lounge at Heathrow. I think I've probably lost my job as well.

Hamish Oh, come on. You're exaggerating. They wouldn't get rid of you just for that . . .

Barbara No. But she might. Given time. Well, what else can happen? My best friend, my job . . .

*A crash from upstairs. Nikki is smashing an upright
chair by the look of it. They listen.*

I think she's breaking up my flat, now . . .

*Hamish and Barbara run for the door and up the
stairs. Gilbert begins to peel back a corner of one of
the strips of his ceiling's lining paper on which his
masterpiece is painted. Hamish bangs on the upstairs
door.*

Hamish Nikki . . .

Barbara Nikki! Stop that at once! That is just wanton
destruction! Nikki!

Hamish (*simultaneously*) Nikki! Come on, darling.
Nikki. That won't do any good!

Barbara (*to Hamish*) Break it down! Break that door
down, at once!

Hamish Right. Stand back. (*Calling*) I'm breaking this
door down, Nikki.

*He takes a pace or two back and hurls himself at the
door. He rebounds off it.*

(*Reacting*) Ahhh! (*He clutches his shoulder*) What did
I do that for?

Barbara You're pathetic. If only you'd eat steak like any
normal man . . . (*Calling*) Nikki! Nikki! Stop that at
once!

*Sudden silence from the flat as Nikki stops, more of
her own volition than as a result of anything the
others may have said.
Silence.*

That's better.

Gilbert chooses this moment to rip off the piece of lining paper he has loosened. It is a dramatic two-handed tug. In the process he loses his balance and topples off his ladder, still clutching the paper which peels away from the ceiling as he falls.

Gilbert Barbarrraaaaaaaaaaaaa!

There is a crash and clatter as Gilbert lands, followed by a cry of pain. The others hear this.

Hamish What the hell was that?

Barbara It sounded like Gilbert.

They both rush downstairs again, this time to Gilbert's flat.

(*Banging on Gilbert's door, calling*) Gilbert! Gilbert! Are you all right?

They both listen. There is a faint groan from Gilbert.

I can hear him. (*Calling*) Gilbert!

Hamish Gilbert!

More groans from Gilbert.

Barbara What's he doing? Can you hear?

Hamish I think he's just maybe crying . . .

Barbara Crying? What's he got to cry about? (*Calling sharply*) Gilbert! Let us in at once! That is a rented flat. This is your landlord!

She stands, unsure what to do next.

Hamish Well, I'm not hurling myself at any more doors, I tell you.

Barbara All right! We'd better leave him for a bit.

She leads the way back to her flat.

It's probably for the best. Sometimes it's good to have a cry. I mean, why shouldn't men be allowed to cry? Women do it all the time. It's very therapeutic. Far healthier than bottling it all up. That's why we have less heart attacks, did you know that?

Nikki now has her coat on. She picks up her suitcase and during the next she unlocks the door and comes downstairs. She is very pale and drawn but has reached a state now of near catatonic calm.

Hamish We only get heart attacks because you lot won't stop crying.

Barbara Rubbish. I feel like some breakfast. I'm starving.

Hamish Breakfast? You're seriously going to eat breakfast?

Barbara (*going into the kitchen*) Why not? Eggs and bacon? No. Of course not. Eggs and mushrooms, what about that?

Hamish Certainly not.

Barbara (*off*) Egg, tomatoes, mushrooms and fried bread? I'm a whizz with fried bread. Come on. A real old fry-up. Do you good. I always eat when I'm miserable.

Hamish I don't know how you can.

Barbara (*off*) What else is there to live for? Eat, drink and be merry, I say, for tomorrow we –

She is cut off by the doorbell. Nikki stands outside with her suitcase, waiting. Barbara comes out of the kitchen cautiously and moves to the front door.

(*Tentatively*) Who is it?

Nikki Nikki.

Barbara (*in an undertone*) It's Nikki.

Hamish Should we let her in?

Barbara Do you think she could be dangerous?

Hamish Dangerous?

Barbara Do you think she might attack us?

Hamish No, she'd never do that. Not Nikki. You know her better than that surely? In these situations, women rarely if ever –

Barbara (*cutting him off*) All right. Let her in.

Hamish makes to do so.

No. Wait!

Barbara ducks back into the kitchen and re-appears with a large kitchen knife.

All right!

Hamish Barbara!

Barbara What?

Hamish Put that away. Come on.

Barbara She could be dangerous.

Hamish If you're nervous of her then get yourself a blunt instrument, then. Not a damn great knife, for God's sake.

Barbara (*reluctantly*) All right.

She disappears again and this time comes back clutching a rolling pin.

Hamish All right.

He opens the door. He steps back as he sees Nikki.

Hallo, Nikki. How are you feeling?

Nikki (*flat*) I'm leaving now.

Hamish Darling, where are you going? Where will you go?

Nikki You'll never see me again.

Barbara Nikki –

Nikki Enjoy your pastry, Barbara.

She turns and goes out of the front door, closing it behind her.
Silence.

Barbara We'd better go and see what damage she's done.

They both troop upstairs again. Nikki has left the flat door slightly ajar. Barbara pauses at the door.

Wait! She may have booby-trapped the room somehow.

Hamish (*a trifle impatiently*) Oh, come on.

He pushes past her and opens the door.

Barbara (*surveying the room*) Oh, no!

Hamish (*a pace behind her*) Oh, God. My suits!

Barbara Look at this bed!

Hamish She's trashed every one of my sodding suits!

Barbara What has she done to this chair?

Hamish Look at this! She's even cut the feet off my socks.

Barbara How could she do this? How could anyone do this?

Hamish Oh, hell. Leave it. New life, new wardrobe. (*He starts to leave*) Oh, God . . .

Barbara It's all right for you. What about my chair? It was a Victorian nursing chair. It was priceless. Oh, it's so spiteful.

Hamish Come on. Leave it. We'll clear it up later.

They troop down again. As they reach the front door, Hamish calls down to the basement.

(*Calling*) Gilbert! Gilbert! Are you OK, mate?

Silence.

Barbara If he doesn't come out soon, we may need to call the fire brigade.

Hamish Oh well, why not? Let's make a party of it.

They re-enter her flat and close the door.

Barbara I can't tell you how upset I am about that chair. I'm really heartbroken.

She sits on the sofa.

Hamish You going to make this breakfast, then?

Barbara No, I'm not hungry any more.

Hamish What, all because of a chair?

Barbara No, it's not that, it's . . . I was simply trying to take our minds off things for ten minutes. Comfort eating. That's all. It's too late now.

She has picked up the scrapbook which Nikki has left. She starts to turn the pages.

(*Tearfully*) Look, this is her little scrapbook.

Hamish Yes.

Barbara We're never going to be happy again, are we? It's all gone, hasn't it?

Hamish No, it hasn't.

Barbara We'll never be able to go on as we were. We've caused so much unhappiness, so much misery . . .

Hamish It happens, that's all . . .

Barbara Well, it shouldn't happen. We've destroyed someone's life because of our own selfish needs.

Hamish Listen. Yes, sure, feel bad. We should both feel bad about it. But we shouldn't let it destroy everything we've got, should we? Otherwise what's the point? Life has to go on. You get hurt, too bad, you get up, you lick your wounds, you go on. You find your happiness over again. Somewhere else. And maybe someone else gets knocked down in the process. Sorry, hard luck. Listen, Nikki came into my life and out went my wife. Ten years together and suddenly it's Nikki. Next week it could happen to me, I don't know. Are you listening to this?

Barbara (*tearfully, gazing at the scrapbook*) Look at her here, bless her. All dressed up for her dancing class, her little dancing shoes . . .

Hamish Yes, OK. Sure . . .

Barbara She looks so happy . . .

Hamish Listen, can you hear what I'm saying, Barbara? If we let this go, this – thing between us – whatever it is, then all this'll have been for nothing. Don't you see? Nothing positive will have come out of it at all. And what sort of waste will that be?

Barbara Oh, God. Look. It's the junior debating society . . . All in their little . . .

Hamish (*losing it completely*) Look, leave the bloody book alone, will you?

423

He snatches the scrapbook from her and throws it across the room. It unfortunately hits Barbara's home-made shelving unit which collapses spectacularly, spilling the contents on to the floor. A stunned silence.

Barbara (*furiously*) How dare you? How dare you destroy my home? Get out! Go on, get out!

She pushes him rather violently.

Get out of my house, you animal!

Hamish (*trying to keep calm*) Don't push me, please, Barbara.

Barbara (*pushing him*) Do you hear me? Out.

Hamish Barbara, I said don't push me. I'll go if you want. But don't push me. I'm warning you.

Barbara (*little vigorous pushes*) Get out! Get out! Get out! Get out!

Hamish (*pushing her in turn*) Barbara! Stop it, now!

Barbara You push me again and I'll kick you in the balls so hard you . . .

Hamish You touch my balls, I warn you I'll punch the tits off you . . .

Barbara (*totally losing control*) You . . .

She grabs hold of the rolling pin which is conveniently to hand and lands him a glancing blow on the head.

Hamish (*recoiling*) Jesus . . .

Barbara comes at him now, swinging the rolling pin like she means business. Hamish initially wards off the blows with his forearms and finally manages to catch her wrist. They now engage in a session of close combat.

Hamish at first does his best to contain her but Barbara's unrelenting onslaught of kicks, punches, bites and attempted scratching eventually forces him to employ countermeasures.
They lose their balance and crash to the floor.

Barbara (*in some pain*) Aaaaaah!

Hamish (*likewise*) Aaaaarrgggh!

At length they fight themselves to a standstill. It is an awesome, reasonably evenly matched battle.
They sit separately breathing deeply, both completely exhausted. Each of them inspecting and gradually discovering the injuries the other has inflicted.

Barbara (*wincing*) Ah!

Hamish Oh!

Barbara Ooooh!

Hamish Aw!

Barbara I think you may have broken my arm. I'm going straight to a battered women's refuge and I'm going to have you put in prison for assault.

Hamish You can show them my head while you're there.

Barbara (*scornfully*) Your head? Why, what's the matter with your –? (*Examining the wound*) Oh, Lord. Was that me?

Hamish With a little help from the rolling pin. You could have killed me. You're a very dangerous woman.

Barbara (*in sudden pain*) Ah! You have! It's broken. Look! (*She waves her limp arm about to demonstrate*)

Hamish I don't think you'd be able to do that with it. (*Trying to get to his feet and swaying*) Seriously, though, I think I may have concussion.

He sits down on the sofa. He looks at Barbara, who is still sitting on the floor.

You all right?

Barbara Possibly.

Hamish No hard feelings and I'm very sorry but I think you did have that coming.

Barbara So did you.

Hamish It's incredible. All through my childhood, all through my young adult manhood, I managed successfully to get right through it all without ever once striking my fellow man. Let alone my fellow woman. All through ten years of marriage to that manic-depressive Viking transvestite. I never raised a hand in anger. And you've undone all that in less than a week. I'll never be able to look myself in the eye again, you know that?

Barbara Good. How do you think I feel? You've utterly destroyed me. You've turned me into an animal. I'm so ashamed of myself. What's happened to us, Hamish? We used to be wonderful people. I did.

Hamish I think it's what's called being in love.

Barbara Love? What do you mean, 'love'? You can't call this love. It's not my idea of love . . .

Hamish (*extending his hand to her*) Come here?

Barbara What?

Hamish Here.

Barbara (*suspiciously*) What are you doing?

Hamish pulls her up beside him on the sofa.

(*As he does this*) Ow!

Hamish That's it! (*He puts an arm gently around her*)

Barbara Ooo! Careful! Careful!

After a second, she relaxes against him.

Hamish Better?

Barbara (*very muted*) Mmm.

Hamish All right?

Barbara Mmm.

They sit there, if not re-united, at least together. Downstairs, Gilbert's door opens and Gilbert emerges. He is crawling and in some pain. He has broken his leg in the fall.

Gilbert (*as he tries to crawl upstairs*) Help . . . help, someone . . .

He falls by Barbara's door and scrabbles on it like a dog.

Barbara (*hearing this*) What's that?

Gilbert Help me·. . . please . . . help . . .

Hamish It's Gilbert!

Hamish gets to his feet and totters to the door. He opens it. Barbara, still in some pain, follows.

(*Seeing him*) Gilbert?

Gilbert Morning, Hamish. Morning, Barbara. I'm very sorry to trouble you, but I think I've broken my leg.

Barbara Why is he wearing my Nicole Farhi?

As Hamish and Barbara move to help Gilbert, the lights fade.

SCENE FOUR

6.30 p.m. Friday 21st.

Everything is comparatively back to normal. The debris upstairs has gone. Barbara's flat is more or less straight again, though her shelves hang at sorry angles.

Barbara is finishing vacuuming. She is moving rather stiffly and has the makings of a fine black eye.

She is coiling up the cable as the front door opens and Hamish comes in. He is leading Gilbert, now in normal clothes, who has one leg in plaster and is using a crutch.

Hamish has a professionally applied head dressing. He is also moving quite stiffly.

Barbara goes into the kitchen to put away the cleaner, under the next.

Hamish (*assisting Gilbert*) Can you manage?

Gilbert Yes, I'm all right, Hamish, thank you. Soon get the hang of this thing. Not to worry. There!

Hamish Will you cope with the stairs down on your own or do you need some help?

Gilbert No, I need to get used to it, don't you worry about me, Hamish. I've had worse than this. (*As he goes down*) I've had a collar bone . . .

Hamish Really?

Gilbert I've had two separate fingers . . .

Hamish Heavens!

Gilbert A dislocated thumb.

Hamish Lord!

Gilbert And three cracked ribs.

Hamish Dear, dear.

Gilbert So what's a leg, eh?

Hamish Exactly.

Gilbert I'll see you around I expect, Hamish.

Hamish Probably. Oh, Gilbert?

Gilbert Yes?

Hamish If I were you, I wouldn't wear that dress again.

Gilbert No. Good advice. Point taken. Did Barbara . . .?

Hamish I told her you were probably using it as a sort of painter's smock.

Gilbert Ah.

Hamish She took quite a dim view. It was apparently a designer number of some sort.

Gilbert Yes, it was a good fabric.

Hamish Now don't you go falling off things again.

Gilbert No, no. A momentary aberration, that's all that was. All over now. (*Opening his front door*) I'll probably start on the painting again sometime, but I think I may have to forgo it for a bit. Not really equipped for climbing ladders at the moment, am I? See you soon, then.

Gilbert goes in and closes his door behind him.
Hamish hesitates, then rings Barbara's doorbell.
Barbara comes out of the kitchen and opens the door.

Barbara (*muted*) Oh, hallo.

Hamish Hi.

There is a coolness between them.

Barbara Come in.

429

Hamish Thanks. (*He closes the door*) Just dropped in to see if you were OK.

Barbara Yes. Yes. (*A pause*) Can I offer you anything? A cup of tea?

Hamish No. No, thank you. You've got a bit of an eye there.

Barbara You should see the rest of me.

Hamish Yes. I've got a few beauties.

Barbara You been round to your house?

Hamish Yes. I dropped in. And set the wheels in motion.

Barbara How do you mean?

Hamish To sell it.

Barbara Oh. You're selling it? That's rather a pity, isn't it? After all that work.

Hamish It's no use to me. I'll sell it and split the money with Nikki. It's only fair.

Barbara Yes.

Hamish She put a lot into it, you see.

Barbara Yes.

Hamish My architect's not too pleased. All this work for nothing. Still, he's being paid, what the hell.

Barbara Yes.

Hamish You been to work today?

Barbara Yes. Briefly. I told them I'd had a fall. They were all very sweet. Someone went out and bought me some chocolates.

Hamish Oh, that was nice.

Barbara Unfortunately, I went and left them in the taxi on the way home.

She thinks about crying but doesn't.

Hamish Oh, dear.

Barbara (*pulling herself together*) I don't usually take taxis but . . . with all this. Marcus phoned in. They seem to be enjoying themselves.

Hamish Good.

Barbara Oh, I hope you don't mind. I tidied upstairs.

Hamish You needn't have done that –

Barbara Well, it was a terrible mess. I thought I'd better. I'm afraid she did a pretty good job on your clothes . . . I've put them all in a bag but I don't think there's very much that's salvageable . . . You might be able to make a quilt.

Hamish Ah well. I may have to hang on to your underpants for a day or two longer, if you don't mind.

He laughs.

Barbara (*laughing rather forcibly*) You're very welcome. (*Silence*) Did you find out where Nikki went?

Hamish To her mother's.

Barbara Ah. Traditional refuge for . . . Unfortunately mine's dead.

Hamish I'm sorry. I just brought Gilbert home. It's a clean break, fortunately, so he shouldn't be in plaster for too long.

Barbara Good. He did look quite bizarre in that dress of mine. Everyone suddenly seems to have taken to wearing my clothes. (*She laughs rather feebly*) Is your head any better?

Hamish Yes. Good job I had it looked at, though. I needed a couple of stitches. She said a few millimetres deeper I could have . . . Well. If you're OK, I'll get on upstairs.

He moves. She makes no effort to stop him.

Listen, what I thought I'd do is, if it's OK with you, is I'll hang on here for a day or two while I look round for somewhere else. I'll get out of your hair as soon as I can . . . If that's what you'd like. If that's OK with you.

Barbara Fine. If that's what you want to do, fine.

Hamish So, I'll try not to disturb you any more. I'm certainly happy to settle for any damage that Nikki did. I mean, I don't think you should be paying for that.

Barbara Thank you. Very generous.

Hamish Just to show we Scots are not all close-fisted caricatures.

He laughs. Barbara gives a strained smile. Hamish can think of no more excuses to stay there.

Well. I'll say cheerio, then.

Barbara Goodbye.

Hamish Bye. Bye. (*Just before he closes the door*). I think – this is all definitely for the best, isn't it? For us both? As you say, there really isn't a future, is there? I mean, I gather that's very much your feeling, isn't it?

Barbara (*almost inaudibly*) Yes.

Hamish I mean, saving your presence, we're both middle-aged people and we're really past the stage of plunging into destructive relationships, surely? Smashing up the place. You'd agree with that?

Barbara Yes.

Hamish Hell! It's about time we both grew up, isn't it? We're sane, adult, responsible human beings, for God's sake. Come on. Get a life! Yes. Right. Absolutely.

He goes out, closing the door. Barbara stands silently as Hamish climbs the stairs.
Quite suddenly she gives a little cry of unhappiness that almost seems to have escaped without her realising it.
She sits.
Hamish now in his own flat, sits on the bed.

Barbara (*in a small voice*)
Come join with me, girls,
Lag not behind.
Pure in your body,
Healthy of mind.

St Gert's! St Gert's! St G— (*She breaks off*)

Hamish Oh, shit . . .

Suddenly and in unison, both jump up.
She runs to her flat door. He runs to his door and rushes down the stairs. He is outside by the time she opens her door. They stare at each other for a moment.

Hamish I'm sorry. Could I just ask you one more thing?

Barbara What?

Hamish Who the hell is Barry Coote?

Barbara smiles. Hamish smiles back. She backs away, allowing him into the flat.

He closes the door and looks at her.
He waits. She moves to him.
Rather tentatively they reach for each other. They
slowly embrace. As they clasp each other tighter they
are reminded of former injuries.

Barbara (*wincing*) Ow!

Hamish I'm sorry.

Barbara It's all right.

Hamish (*as she finds a tender spot*) Ah!

Barbara Oh, dear . . .

Hamish No, it's all right, keep going. Oooo . . .

Barbara Ah!

Hamish Wooo . . .

Barbara Ow . . . No, don't stop . . . Ow . . .

As they kiss, still fondling and wincing, a loving
mixture of pain and pleasure, the lights fade to:

Blackout.

HOUSE & GARDEN

House *and* **Garden** were first performed simultaneously at the Stephen Joseph Theatre, Scarborough, on 17 June 1999. The cast was as follows:

Teddy Platt Robert Blythe
Trish Platt Eileen Battye
Sally Platt Charlie Hayes
Giles Mace Barry McCarthy
Joanna Mace Janie Dee
Jake Mace Danny Nutt
Gavin Ryng-Mayne Terence Booth
Barry Love Simon Green
Lindy Love Alison Senior
Lucille Cadeau Sabine Azema
Fran Briggs Alexandra Mathie
Warn Coucher Peter Laird
Izzie Truce Antonia Pemberton
Pearl Truce Jennifer Luckraft

Maypole Dancers and Bandsmen

Director Alan Ayckbourn
Designer Roger Glossop
Lighting Designer Mick Hughes
Costume Designer Christine Wall
Music John Pattison

A new production was subsequently presented at the Royal National Theatre, London, on 9 August 2000. The cast was as follows:

Teddy Platt David Haig
Trish Platt Jane Asher
Sally Platt Charlie Hayes
Giles Mace Michael Siberry
Joanna Mace Sian Thomas
Jake Mace James Bradshaw
Gavin Ryng-Mayne Malcolm Sinclair
Barry Love Adrian McLoughlin
Lindy Love Suzy Aitchison
Lucille Cadeau Zabou Breitman
Fran Briggs Alexandra Mathie
Warn Coucher Peter Laird
Izzie Truce Antonia Pemberton
Pearl Truce Nina Sosanya

Maypole Dancers and Bandsmen

Director Alan Ayckbourn
Set Designer Roger Glossop
Lighting Designer Mick Hughes
Costume Designer Christine Wall
Music John Pattison

Author's Note

House and *Garden* are two plays
intended to be performed simultaneously
by the same cast in two adjacent auditoria.
They can be seen singly and in no particular order.

House

Characters

Teddy Platt
a businessman

Trish Platt
his wife

Sally Platt
their daughter

Giles Mace
a doctor

Joanna Mace
his wife, a teacher

Jake Mace
their son, a student reporter

Gavin Ryng-Mayne
a novelist

Barry Love
a shopkeeper

Lindy Love
his wife, a shopkeeper

Lucille Cadeau
an actress

Fran Briggs
her driver

Warn Coucher
a gardener

Izzie Truce
a housekeeper

Pearl Truce
an occasional cleaner

Several children of about seven or eight years old

Scene
The summer sitting room at the house.

Time
A Saturday in August between eight o'clock in the
morning and six in the evening.

Act One

Saturday, August 14th, 8.00 a.m.
 The summer sitting room at the house.
 It is an impressive ground-floor room at the back of a Georgian building which overlooks the terrace and small formal garden. Beyond this is a flight of stone steps leading down to the less formal Lower Meadow beyond.
 The room itself has a number of floor to ceiling windows, two of them French windows which lead on to the terrace. It is comfortably furnished in the tastefully shabby, cluttered, casual English country house tradition.
 Two other doors lead off, one to the hall and rest of the house; and double doors into the dining room. These latter are normally closed but, when open, the end of what appears to be a long dining table can be seen.
 In a moment, Trish, a woman in her forties whose soft English beauty has only very faintly faded, enters from the hall. She surveys the room and its clutter, sighs, sniffs the air with mild distaste, goes to the French windows and opens them.
 She makes for the hall door again, then pauses to pick something up, straighten a cushion. A token gesture towards tidying the untidyable.
 As she does this Teddy, a rather red-faced man also in his forties, appears outside the French windows. He is wearing old clothes and boots.

Teddy I'm just taking Spoof for a run in the meadow. All right?

 Trish continues her tidying, appearing neither to hear nor see Teddy at all.

445

So, if anyone phones, can you take a message? Tell 'em I'll ring 'em back in a minute. OK?

No response.

Trish?

Trish finishes what she is doing and goes into the dining room.

(*As she goes*) It's just possible Ryng-Mayne may call to give me an update when he'll – (*As it becomes apparent that she is not hearing him*) Oh, for God's sake, Trish! We can't keep on like this, woman! Trish!

She has gone.

(*Yelling after her*) This is a very important day for me, you know. If you cock it up for me, I'll never forgive you. Do you hear me, Trish?

Outside somewhere Spoof, a large dog, barks with pleasure at the sound of his master's voice.

All right, Spoof, that'll do! Spoof! Stop that at once!

Spoof barks happily on.

Spoof! (*Giving up, muttering*) Oh, give me strength! I don't know. I'm the bloody invisible man round here. Nobody takes a blind bit of notice. Might as well not be here at all. Just a hole in the ether these days.

He starts to go. So does Spoof.

(*As he goes*) SPOOF! Will you just simmer down, you stupid dog.

They have gone. Silence in the empty room for a second. Then Sally enters from the hall. She is Trish and Teddy's only child. Seventeen and still at school, she is a serious, sometimes rather intense girl who has recently grown very concerned with Life and

The World. She is wearing her school uniform and carries a briefcase. She comes into the room and stops, listening. She frowns.

She sits on the sofa and opens her briefcase. She pulls out a sheet of paper and studies it.

Sally (*reading, softly and dramatically*)
'How can I ever hear a heart
My head denies with such insistence?
How do I ever trust a heart,
Which doubt drowns out with such persistence?
How will I ever feel my heart,
Whilst caution proffers such resistance?
How could I ever give my heart
When I deny its whole existence?'

Trish returns. Sally hastily returns her poem to the briefcase.

Trish Oh, good morning, Sally . . . Were you talking to me?

Sally No. What was all that about just now?

Trish When?

Sally Was that Dad . . .?

Trish . . . What are you doing, up and dressed?

Sally . . . I heard him shouting . . .

Trish . . . It's not even midday.

Sally . . . Yelling his head off.

Trish . . . What are you up to? It's Saturday, had you forgotten?

Sally I've got a meeting at nine. Don't say you didn't hear him?

Trish No. I heard Spoof.

Sally Yes. And Dad.

Trish No, I only heard Spoof.

Sally gives up with a sigh.

I think we'll have to use the big table. We always have this problem, don't we? The small table's too small and the large table's too large. We either have to have three people to lunch or forty-six. What meeting's this, then?

Sally Up at the school.

Trish Oh, is that why you're all dressed up?

Sally I'm dressed up because we have enlightened teachers who encourage all sorts of activities outside normal school hours but a reactionary head teacher who won't allow any pupil on the premises unless they're in school uniform . . .

Trish What's the meeting? Anything important?

Sally Senior Political Group.

Trish Oh. We'll never get seven of us round the small table. We'd all be eating off each other's plates. (*Trish starts to move around in the dining room as she tries out various table layouts using table mats as markers. Occasionally she vanishes from sight, sometimes stopping in the doorway to speak to Sally directly*)

Sally Have I got to be here? For lunch?

Trish You certainly have.

Sally I could eat in the kitchen . . .

Trish You'll eat with us . . .

Sally . . . if it would help. I could eat with Izzie.

Trish Sally, you're eating with us, please.

Sally Thought it might help, that's all.

Trish Well, it wouldn't . . . I need you to . . . converse and . . . pass things . . . (*Lingering in the dining-room doorway, surveying the table*) No, I'll put us all up this end. If we're spread out, we'll be yelling our heads off.

Sally French film stars are not exactly my strong point, you know . . .

Trish Nor mine. That's beside the point. You speak French, anyway . . .

Sally . . . I mean, I haven't even seen her film . . .

Trish I don't think anyone's seen her film. Not round these parts . . .

Sally . . . Jake probably has . . .

Trish . . . By the time they get round to showing a film here most of the stars are dead . . .

Sally . . . Jake's bound to have seen it. What's it called, anyway?

Trish The – hang on, I did know – *The Un— The Un—* something or other.

Sally Is it French?

Trish No, English, I think. Well, American.

Sally And how come she's in this neck of the woods?

Trish I'm not quite sure. She was suggested by her agent. Our committee originally wanted the other one – that very famous one who was also in the film. But she was unexpectedly unavailable – *The Unexpected*, that's it! – so they suggested this one instead. Lucille – thingy. Who isn't really famous at all but is apparently very, very good. According to her agent.

Sally Just nobody's ever heard of her.

Trish Don't ask me, I've never heard of anybody. Anyway, she's agreed to open our fête which was more than the other one was, which makes her OK in my book. Can you man the tombola as usual, please?

Sally Oh, you're not going to make me stand out there all afternoon in the pouring rain like last year, are you?

Trish It's not going to rain . . .

Sally Of course it's going to rain . . .

Trish Nonsense. The forecast says –

Sally . . . It always rains. Last year that tombola drum was full of water. All the tickets were floating . . .

Trish Come on, Sally, for goodness sake. Lighten up, darling. Everything's such an effort, isn't it? You're young. Enjoy that while it lasts.

Sally Standing in the rain?

Trish That's all part of it . . .

Sally Selling soggy tickets for prizes people won last year and have put back this year, praying they won't win them again?

Trish Absolutely. All part of the fun.

Sally (*softly mocking*) When I was your age . . .

Trish Yes, all right.

Sally (*continuing*) . . . we used to dance all day. On the lawn. In our nightdresses. (*After a pause*) I'm amazed you still bother, really.

Trish How do you mean?

Sally With all – this . . . going on?

450

Trish What?

Sally All this – that we're not supposed to talk about but we all know about anyway.

Trish I don't know what you mean.

Sally I've noticed.

Trish What time's this meeting of yours?

Sally You two want to get yourselves sorted out, you know. Instead of giving me lectures on lightening up.

Trish If it's at nine o'clock you'd better get moving . . .

Sally You hear what I'm saying, Mum? I'm serious.

Trish . . . You know what the buses are like on Saturdays.

Sally Jake's collecting me. Listen, if you –

Trish You take advantage of him far too much, as well.

Sally What?

Trish Jake. He trails round after you like a lost puppy. You just use him when it suits you.

Sally (*indignantly*) I do not.

Trish Yes, you do.

Sally I don't ask him to follow me around, do I?

Trish You don't send him away either, do you?

Sally It's what makes him happy.

Trish It's called using people, Sally. They – care about you, you care nothing for them but you use them because it suits you.

Sally That's terrible. What a terrible thing to say!

451

Trish It's all right. I'm not blaming you especially. Lots of us have done it. All I'm saying is, try not to. For one reason, it'll rebound on you later. It always does.

Sally What are you talking about?

Trish I'm saying that – in my experience – life pays you back. Sooner or later. Believe me, I know. You behave badly . . . thoughtlessly towards someone . . . as if their feelings weren't important . . . then one day . . .

Sally They behave like that to you? Well, I'm not letting that happen to me, I can tell you that. Never lose control. That's the secret, keep control.

Trish Of other people?

Sally No, of myself. Don't let yourself get used, get manipulated, taken advantage of. And of course, no, don't do it to others either. Which I don't, as it happens. I don't use them, not at all.

Trish Even more alarming if you don't even realise you're doing it. (*Back at her table*) Yes, we'll lay it up like that.

Sally It's another get Sally morning, isn't it? And don't you dare put me next to that man, either.

Trish What's that?

Sally Gavin whosit-whatsit. I'm not sitting next to him.

Trish Why on earth not? I seem to remember he was very charming.

Sally Oh, yes?

Trish Novelist, political wheeler-dealer. Right up your street, I'd have thought.

Sally Sorry. Hardly my kind of politics, Mother.

Trish Oh, well. Karl Marx wasn't free for lunch, unfortunately.

Sally Really . . . I'd love to know what he's doing here.

Trish He's coming for lunch.

Sally What, travelling two hundred miles from London just to have lunch? All this I'm-an-old-friend-of-Dad's. Highly suspicious.

Trish (*drily*) Being a contradiction in terms, you mean?

Sally Listen. Seriously, if you want to talk about things, about what's happening . . . It affects all of us. Not just you, Dad and Joanna. But there's Jake's father as well, isn't there? There's Giles. And then there's Jake. (*Slight pause*) I am thinking about other people, you see. (*Pause*) And me. There's me. You see? So we have to talk, don't we?

Trish I don't know whether to use the cloth or the plain wood with mats. This surface is totally wrecked. We should never have used it as a ping-pong table . . .

> *At this moment Jake, about nineteen or twenty years old, appears on the terrace. He is shy, slightly nervous and clearly besotted with Sally.*
> *Sally sees him. Jake waves through the window to indicate that he's there.*

Sally (*seeing Jake*) Oh, hallo . . .

Jake (*tentatively entering the room*) Hi!

Trish Who's that? Oh, Jake. Good morning.

Jake Good morning.

Trish I'll shut the door. Leave you in peace. Sally's got something to say to you.

Jake Has she?

Trish closes the dining-room doors. Sally has opened her briefcase and is sorting through some papers.

I parked the car down by the gate. Walked up through the garden.

Sally Why d'you do that?

Jake Well, I just thought . . . it might be nice . . . for us to . . . walk through the garden. (*Looking out*) Seeing as it's such a . . . it's a . . . as it's not raining.

Pause.

What did you want to tell me, then?

Sally What?

Jake Your mother said you had something to say to me.

Sally Did she?

Jake What is it, then?

Sally I've no idea. Ask her. (*She studies her papers*)

Jake What's that?

Sally It's my speech.

Jake Ah.

Sally For the meeting. I was up half the night with it. Some of them are so stupid, if you don't spell things out in words of one syllable . . .

Jake (*sympathetically*) Yes. I know, our features editor always says –

Sally What I'm trying to get across, is that in politics, any sort of politics, local or national – these days it's tactics. It isn't always simply a question of voting for what you want . . .

Jake No.

Sally Sometimes you have to vote for what you positively don't want in order to achieve the longer term aim of getting something you do want. You see?

Jake Tactical voting?

Sally (*waving a sheet of paper*) Fact. Colin Theaker is the most unpopular MP this constituency has had since records were started. He wasn't that popular when he was elected and in four and a half years he's managed to halve that support. Pretty remarkable even for Colin Theaker . . .

Jake I know. We ran that article recently . . .

Sally Mind you, he's a crook, which doesn't help.

Jake Well, we don't know that for certain . . .

Sally He is. He's a crooked little shit.

Jake You're not going to say that in your speech, are you?

Sally Of course I'm not. But even his own party which is made up almost entirely of crooks is a little nervous about him. They'd replace him tomorrow only if they did it would amount to a tacit admission they knew he was a crook. The point is if Theaker remains their candidate at the General Election there could be a complete turn-round. They could find themselves out on their ear. The whole lot of them. We'd be in. For the first time. Ever. Think of that.

Jake Lot of ifs.

Sally Dave Bales could be our next MP. Think of that.

Jake Yes, I met him once. He's OK, he's quite –

Sally But you see if that's to happen, it's vital they're not panicked into replacing Theaker. With someone with a bit more – someone new who might just swing it for them.

Jake They might replace him anyway.

Sally They might. I think it's unlikely. That would be a virtual admission that some of the rumours about him are true. No, they'll stick with him if they possibly can. So. QED. I'm going to propose we cool our campaign. Which isn't going to be very popular with some of our lot. But you see my point?

Jake Theaker must stay?

Sally For the time being. Still. Sixth Form Senior Political Society. What are we going to change?

Jake Voters of the future.

Sally Sure. We've been given a voice, use it.

Jake I feel a bit sorry for Theaker, actually.

Sally What? Come on . . .

Jake Well, he had a tough act to follow. Two tough acts. Your grandfather, your great-grandfather . . .

Sally Things were different in those days . . .

Jake Still, you can't help wondering. If, say, your father had decided to stand, for instance . . .

Sally Well, they asked him originally. Dad's not interested, though. Never has been. He told me once he thinks all politics are boring.

Jake You take after your grandfather . . .

Sally He had a passion, yes. I share the passion, if not the same views.

Jake Would you ever want to stand? As an MP?

Sally Maybe. One day. Who knows? If I thought I could be useful. I'd be a very good one. Change things for the better.

Jake (*adoringly*) You'd be fantastic.

Sally Come on, I'm going to be late. (*She starts to pack up her things*)

Jake I saw them again just now, by the way. My mother and your father.

Sally Oh, God. Where?

Jake In the garden. As usual.

Sally Where did you see them . . .? They weren't – you know – ?

Jake Oh, no. They were just standing about. Pretending to talk about bushes, you know.

Sally I don't know what we do, Jake. I really don't. I've tried talking to my mother but she won't even acknowledge it's happening.

Jake How about your father?

Sally I gave up talking to him years ago. After what he's done to my mother, I never want to speak to him again. Have you managed to talk to your mother, yet?

Jake No, she's . . . She's – quite an emotional sort of person, you know . . .

Sally Yes, I have noticed. If you don't mind my saying so, I think she's seriously unstable, actually . . .

Jake Well. Maybe a bit. And my father – I'm sure he still doesn't know.

Sally That's incredible. Where does he live? In a plastic bag?

Jake No, he's . . . well, he trusts her, you see. He trusts most people. Actually, he trusts everyone, that's the trouble. The thing about my father is – well, it sounds a bit boring but I think he's just a very, very nice man.

Sally He's a bloody sight nicer man than my father, anyway. Oh, what's the point of talking about it? They'll have to sort it out between them. There's nothing we can do.

Jake I wish there was, though. I was wondering if . . . Are you going to be at the fête this afternoon . . .?

Sally Unfortunately. Or risk the wrath of my mother . . .

Jake I was just wondering – because I'm going to have to be there – I've got to interview this film actress, you see – and I just wondered, you know – if afterwards – if you – if you – we could drive out to this place I –

Sally Probably not this evening, Jake.

Jake Right.

Sally I have – lots to do. Revision and so on.

Jake Yes.

Sally Shall we go?

Jake Sure, I cleaned the car out, by the way. You'll be relieved to hear. I know last time you said it smelt a bit odd . . .

Sally It did. Disgusting.

Jake I think it was some old pizza. I found it under the passenger seat . . .

They are just going out of the French windows when they meet Teddy coming back in.

Teddy (*to Sally*) Oh, hallo. What are you doing up this early? Been a fire drill, has there?

458

Sally walks past him, totally ignoring him.

Jake She's just going to a meeting.

Teddy Is she? What's that? WI's?

Jake Political, I think.

Teddy (*yelling after her*) Waste of time! Complete waste of time!

Jake (*as he goes*) I'm driving her there.

Teddy Jolly good.

Sally and Jake are gone. Teddy is alone in the room for a second. The dining-room doors open abruptly and Trish sticks her head out.

Trish Would you both like a cup of – (*She looks round the room and appears to see no one*) – Oh, nobody here.

Trish closes the doors again before Teddy can speak.

Teddy (*angrily*) Oh, for God's sake! (*He marches to the dining-room doors and flings them open. Trish is not in view. Shouting into the apparently empty room*) I'm not putting up with this much longer, you know. I've had just about enough!

Their housekeeper, Izzie, comes in from the hall. She is a woman, probably in her late fifties, stern-faced and unsmiling. Somebody who feels their lot to be less than a happy one.

Izzie You calling me, were you?

Teddy No, no, Izzie. I was just – talking to my wife. In the dining room.

Izzie (*looking into the dining room*) She's not in here.

Teddy Isn't she? Well, fancy that.

459

Izzie I'll shut these doors.

Teddy Fine.

Izzie So Pearl can get on hoovering in there.

Teddy Right.

Izzie (*closing the dining-room doors*) If she ever turns up.

Teddy Oh, dear. Gone AWOL again, has she?

Izzie Don't know where she's gone. Needs her feet nailing to the ground, that one. That or a father.

Teddy Bit late to find one of those for her, isn't it?

Izzie (*darkly, as she goes*) I'm working on it.

Teddy Listen, Izzie, I'm expecting Giles – Dr Mace to join me in a minute.

Izzie Oh, yes?

Teddy Could you make us some coffee when he comes?

Izzie Give me a call.

> *Izzie goes out. Teddy goes to the hall door. Opens it swiftly, listens, then closes it. He moves to the dining-room doors and is about to do the same with them when they burst open and Trish comes out, now with gardening gloves and secateurs.*
>
> *Simultaneously, Giles appears on the terrace. He is a pleasant, affable, if somewhat ineffectual man in his late thirties.*

Teddy (*to Trish*) Oh, there you are. Will you kindly not walk away from me every time I –

> *But Teddy is seemingly invisible to Trish. She sweeps past him with no acknowledgement and straight out through the French windows.*

Trish Good morning, Giles. Bit early for lunch, aren't you?

Giles Good morning, Trish. No, I was looking for Teddy, actually. Is he – ?

Trish No idea, Giles. I haven't seen hide nor hair of him this morning, I'm afraid . . .

Giles Oh.

Trish has gone off towards the garden. Giles looks cautiously into the room and sees Teddy.

(*A trifle surprised*) Ah!

Teddy (*grimly*) Did you witness that?

Giles What?

Teddy You see what I mean?

Giles Say again?

Teddy Clear evidence. With your own eyes. She comes in. I see her. I speak to her. She fails to reply, utterly ignores me. She goes out. Meets you. Greets you. You ask where I am. She says she hasn't seen me when less than five seconds earlier, she'd just walked straight past me. Tell me. Is that normal behaviour? Is that the decorum of a sane woman?

Giles See what you mean. Yes.

Teddy What's your opinion?

Giles Well, I'd have to examine her, of course. At least talk to her, but even then . . . It seems to me more of a . . . In the mind. As it were.

Teddy A basket case?

Giles No, no, no . . . I don't think that. I don't really know, really. Not having . . . talked to her, Teddy. But . . .

Teddy I appreciate as a professional you want to hedge your bets but at least you'll agree it's not usual?

Giles No. Not altogether usual . . .

Teddy For a wife to declare her husband invisible? That is abnormal behaviour. Surely? In anyone's book?

Giles It does happen but –

Teddy Does it?

Giles Occasionally.

Teddy Can you ever recall it happening?

Giles No, not off-hand . . .

Teddy Has it ever happened to you? With Joanna?

Giles Well, over brief periods. I mean that's marriage, isn't it? Over the years there are always sticky patches where you tend to ignore each other for a short while. Jo's gone a bit quiet on me now and then for a couple of hours sometimes but . . . How long's it been like this for you?

Teddy Three weeks.

Giles Yes, that is a long time, isn't it?

Teddy I mean, there's got to be something radically wrong, Giles, hasn't there? I mean, three weeks. I'm not a medical man, I don't know all the technical terms, but it doesn't take a brain surgeon to see she's out of her tree. She's bloody good at it, mind you. Very hard to catch her out. I made her blink once or twice but that doesn't mean anything. Apart from stamping on her foot I can't think of any way to catch her attention.

Giles What about – in bed?

Teddy Bed?

Giles Does she ignore you then?

Teddy I've no idea. We sleep in separate rooms.

Giles Ah. Sorry.

Teddy It was her idea. She claimed I was – disruptive in the night.

Giles I see. Teddy, I hate to suggest this, but do you think that that might be at the bottom of it?

Teddy Bottom of what?

Giles Well, bluntly, sex?

Teddy Well. Anything's possible where sex is concerned, I suppose.

Giles Frankly, and I don't want to sound too fiercely Freudian about all this, but I think I'd look to the sex, first and foremost.

Teddy You would?

Giles I would.

Teddy You think I ought to try and – get back into bed with her. Re-establish the territorial claim?

Giles I think you ought to – re-open negotiations, perhaps.

Teddy Right. She's in the garden at the moment, I don't think I should . . .

Giles Heavens, I wasn't talking about now.

Teddy Weren't you?

Giles I was thinking – tonight, perhaps.

Teddy Tonight? I can't wait till then.

Giles You can't?

Teddy No, listen, Giles. I'll have to tell you. This is absolutely hush-hush. Not a word to anyone.

Giles Right.

Teddy The point is, I've got someone rather important coming to lunch today . . .

Giles Oh yes, I know. Lucille Cadeau, the French film star. She's frightfully good. I saw her film when I was in London. *The Uninvited – Unprotected* – something like that. It's really excellent. Unfortunately she gets blown up quite early on . . .

Teddy No, Giles, Giles, I'm not talking about that woman. I'm talking about Gavin Ryng-Mayne.

Giles Ryng-Mayne?

Teddy The novelist.

Giles Oh, yes. I've vaguely heard of him. He's coming as well, is he? Splendid. What a lunch! Thank you for inviting us.

Teddy He's here for a purpose, you see. You probably know he's – no, you probably don't, why should you? – well, he's very thick within Cabinet circles. And especially thick with the Prime Minister. You see?

Giles Is he? I didn't know that . . .

Teddy Apparently writes the odd thing for them. Speeches and so on. He advises, all that. Very much behind the scenes. Occasional low-profile intermediary, you know. Which is why he's coming here, actually.

Giles I see. With what purpose?

Teddy Well, they're – (*Modestly*) The fact is they're intent on dragging me in, Giles. To put it bluntly, they're trying to persuade me to stand as their candidate here in the forthcoming election.

Giles Heavens. How exciting. Instead of Colin Theaker?

Teddy Yes. Well, Colin's been a bit of a wash-out, let's face it.

Giles Yes. Total disaster, poor man.

Teddy Nice enough chap . . .

Giles Oh, lovely man. Sweet man. Still, to be fair, Teddy, your father was a tough act to follow.

Teddy And still is. Even today. That's what's holding me back really. You know sometimes, Giles, I look back on my family, the last two generations anyway – my father, grandfather . . . I mean old Sir Ted who started it all, tough old bastard, absolute dyed-in-the-wool fascist but say what you will about him he was a remarkable old boy. Not only started the business from scratch, built it up and ran it with a rod of iron for nearly forty years, but he was also the sitting MP for nearly twenty. I mean, that's pretty remarkable in anyone's book.

Giles Indeed. I remember he –

Teddy Then my father, Tommy Platt, he carried it all on. Turned the business international, till at one time it was the ninth biggest printers in Europe. Even today, it's the twenty-sixth biggest. Bloody amazing. And then after my grandfather had chucked it in, he also became MP for fifteen years. His is another extraordinary story.

Giles Yes, indeed. I mean, there were –

Teddy And then along comes me. If you see what I mean.

A brief silence.

(*Rising*) Want a sherry or something? I was going to ask for some coffee but I feel rather like something stronger, don't you? (*Teddy goes into the dining room*)

Giles Well, it is only quarter to nine. I'm not sure about sherry.

Teddy No, you're quite right. Hang about . . .

Giles You've done pretty well too, you know, Teddy. Don't sell yourself short.

Teddy (*from the dining room*) Think so?

Giles You've kept the business going . . .

Teddy That's about it, you see. Kept it going. Nothing new, nothing exciting. Just kept it ticking over. Now that I'm heading towards fifty, Giles, I think to myself, what have I done? Halfway, well, over halfway probably, and what the hell have I done with my life? (*Teddy returns with two tumblers of whisky. He hands one to Giles*) Here you are.

Giles (*looking at it doubtfully*) Thank you.

Teddy No, when they lay me out in the family vault next to those two old monsters what are they going to write on my tombstone? 'Here lies Teddy Platt who more or less kept things going . . .'

Giles Oh, come on . . .

Teddy Depressing thought, you know. Cheers!

Giles Cheers!

Teddy But now suddenly here's my chance. I am about to get the call.

Giles Then respond. Why not? Is this sherry?

Teddy No, it's whisky, you're quite right, far too early for sherry. No, the point is, can I do it, Giles, that's the point. Am I up to it? Will I meet the challenge? Take this country forward into the boring old millennium? Or will I just keep things going, ticking over till the right man does come along? Or woman. Sally, who knows? No, not Sally. She supports the other lot, we can't have her. But you see my dilemma?

Giles I don't think you should see it as a dilemma but as a golden opportunity which you should grasp with both hands.

Teddy You think so?

Giles I do. Indeed, I do.

Teddy Even so, you see my problem. Ryng-Mayne's here to give me the once over. Obviously he is. See if I'm up to the job. Old school friend he may be, but I haven't seen him for fifteen years. How's it going to look if my wife ignores me all through lunch? Pretends I'm not even there?

Giles (*laughing*) Well, I'm sure there are plenty of MPs' wives do that.

Teddy Yes, but not before they're elected. Most of them manage to put up some sort of a show till afterwards.

Giles Couldn't you reason with Trish? Plead with her? After all it's her future, too.

Teddy You can hardly reason with a woman who refuses to acknowledge your existence, can you?

Giles Then we'll all rally round, Teddy, don't worry. Me, Joanna . . .

Teddy Joanna?

Giles Yes, of course Joanna. She'll be happy to help. She's very fond of you both, you know that. And Sally? I know she will. And – well, as for the others, maybe they won't even notice with any luck. We can pull it off, Teddy. With a team effort we can pull it off, don't worry. Our next MP. God, this is so exciting, Teddy! Congratulations.

Teddy Now, not a word, Giles. Not yet. Top secret.

Giles Yes, of course. But so exciting.

Slight pause.

Teddy (*casually*) How is – er . . . how is old Joanna these days?

Giles Jo? (*Unconvincingly*) Oh, she's . . . she's fine.

Slight pause.

No, she's not fine at all, really. I wish to God she was.

Slight pause.

The point is, I don't know quite what to do for the best, Teddy.

Teddy How do you mean?

Giles Well, you know Jo, she's – quite highly strung and – lately she's . . . she's just so up and down. Crying for no obvious reason. Getting drunk. Going for long walks on her own. I mean, we always used to walk – to walk together, but now . . . I sometimes feel she doesn't want me near her, you see . . . and I know it's me. I . . . I don't – I don't seem to – seem to – seem to be able to give her what she wants. Frankly. In any department, if you know what I mean.

Teddy Ah.

Giles I mean, if you want to know, the sex was always a bit iffy. She's not a – she's not a – she's not – God, I feel so disloyal saying this even to you – she's not a – she's not a – particularly highly sexed woman, you know.

Teddy (*a trifle surprised*) Really?

Giles Not as women – as women – go. No. Frankly, she's never really cared for it at all. Always making excuses not to – not to – or just lying there grinning and

468

bearing it, if you know what I mean. Probably me, as I say.

Teddy Well. At least she was grinning. (*He laughs rather feebly*)

Giles With some other man she'd probably . . . It might possibly . . . Who can tell? All I know is that somewhere along the way, I feel I've let her down. Been less than the man she wanted. Whom she expected when she married. Had every right to expect. (*A fraction tearful*) She's such a terrific woman, Teddy, you've no idea. I absolutely adore her. Even after all these years.

Teddy Yes, yes . . .

Giles She's not always the easiest person, I know. But I wouldn't swap the difficulty, Teddy. I wake up some mornings, you know. She's already gone. Got up, up, up, dressed and gone out for one of her walks and I think, what would happen if one day she didn't come back to me? And you know I can't face that at all. It's like a nightmare. It's just too terrible to contemplate. I mean, you know what I mean, don't you? Don't you feel like that sometimes with Trish?

Teddy Yes, it – as I say, we're in separate rooms, I've no idea what time she gets up . . .

Giles But you know what I mean?

Teddy Yes, I know what you mean. And it's not going to happen, Giles, it certainly isn't.

Giles No?

Teddy No, old boy. Knowing you, knowing Joanna. No way.

Giles (*moved*) Thank you, Teddy, thank you for that. (*Looking at him with grateful affection*) God, you'll make a wonderful MP.

Teddy (*rather moved*) Thank you.

A silence between them born of a deep male friendship. Trish chooses this moment to return via the terrace. She is still wearing her gardening gloves and now carries a bunch of roses as well as her secateurs. As always, she ignores Teddy, talking directly to Giles as if he was the only other person in the room.

Trish Oh, Giles. Good. I'm glad I've caught you on your own.

Giles Sorry?

Teddy (*rising angrily*) Oh, God. Talk to her, Giles. For goodness sake talk to the woman. (*Snatching the glass from Giles' hand*) I'll get us another drink. I can't stand much more of this. Sit down, both of you. (*Teddy disappears into the dining room*)

Giles Trish . . . This is getting – well, slightly out of hand, isn't it?

Trish Giles, before you say another word, Joanna has something she needs to tell you urgently. She's in the garden.

Giles But I –

Trish Quickly. It's terribly urgent. Quickly.

Giles Yes. Of course. (*He hurries off*)

Trish (*pleased with herself*) Good. That should clear the air. (*She goes out into the hall and closes the door*)

Teddy (*off, from the dining room*) I don't want any more of this nonsense, Trish. I've been talking to Giles there and he's of the opinion and I'm totally in agreement with him that this is all in your mind. There's nothing medically wrong with you at all. Would you say that was a fair summary, Giles? Yes, he would. No, as far as I'm concerned, this is D-Day, Trish. D for don't bugger me about any more, just come out with whatever's on your mind and give it to me straight. I've far too much at stake here to pussyfoot. I've poured you a sherry, we're all going to sit down and talk about this like rational, civilised human beings and nobody's leaving this room, I warn you, until we've got to the bott— (*Teddy returns with two refilled glasses. Surveying the room, frustratedly*) Where the hell's everybody gone *now*? Give me strength . . .

> *He raises one of the glasses to his lips. As he does so, from the garden a long drawn-out distant cry from Giles.*

Giles (*off, distant*) Tedddddddyyyyyy!

Teddy What in the name of heaven is that?

> *As he stands puzzled, the lights fade to:*
>   Blackout.

SCENE TWO

Saturday, August 14th, 11.00 a.m.
  The same. Trish is in the dining room, now attempting the full table layout. Giles, rather irritatingly for her, follows her round like a small child. Trish sort of half listens, busying herself as they talk.

Giles (*in full flow*) . . . I mean, you can imagine the shock.

Trish (*vaguely, surveying her table*) Yes . . . yes . . .

Giles You must understand I had no inkling, Trish. None at all.

Trish No . . .

Giles At least you say you knew . . . Though how you could let it happen and say not a word to me, I can't imagine.

Trish Do you think it would have been helpful if I had?

Giles I think it was only proper.

Trish But the whole thing could have been over in two days, Giles, and then you'd have been none the wiser. It could have been one of those affairs, you know. The sort that if you don't know about them, you're better off not knowing . . .

Giles Has this happened to you before, Trish?

Trish Oh God, yes, masses of times. Is this her first, then? Joanna?

Giles Of course it is. (*He reflects*) As far as I know.

Trish Exactly.

Giles So Teddy has . . . before?

Trish Oh, yes. I rather imagined he'd told you . . .

Giles Well, he made the occasional joke, but I thought they were jokes . . .

Trish I thought, you know, best friends . . .

Giles Ex-best friends, you mean.

Trish Oh, really? What a shame.

Giles What?

Trish Well, you get on so well, don't you? I think you're probably the only real friend Teddy has. I mean, nobody likes him very much, let's face it. Except that half-witted dog. Isn't there some way you could forgive and forget?

472

Giles After what's happened?

Trish I thought that was all part of the man thing. You know, sharing your whisky, sharing your women. Guess who I had the other night, old boy.

Giles You don't like him any more, do you? Teddy?

Trish No, not very much. Not any more. Nothing to do with this, not at all. I mean, saving your presence, I'd hardly let my marriage break up because of someone like Joanna. No, it's been a continuing thing over years, really. Like it usually is.

Giles I know you've . . . I know you've got separate – you know . . .

Trish Separate what?

Giles Bedrooms.

Trish Oh, rather. He told you that much, then? That all went very early on. I think the minute I was expecting Sally, Teddy lost complete interest. (*Slight pause*) Well, so did I, to be perfectly honest. Whenever we made love, he always seemed in a terrible hurry to get somewhere. As if he had a train to catch. Maybe some women like it urgent. I like it to feel more like I'm on a – world cruise.

Giles What kept you together, then?

Trish Oh, God, Giles, I don't know. What keeps any marriage together? Inertia? Lack of viable alternatives? The children? I suppose sometimes if you're lucky, mutual support, deep friendship and someone you can rely on when the going gets tough. I was quite prepared to give way on the sex bit. If he needed other women, so be it – provided they weren't close friends of mine and he didn't bring them home like a cat and leave them on the doormat, I didn't mind. But it was the other bit really. That's when I stopped loving him. When

I realised that I could no longer trust him as a friend;
no longer rely on him to stand by me – when things got
difficult . . . You see?

Giles No chance of – bridge building?

Trish It's not a river between us any more, Giles. It's an
ocean.

Giles Oh, dear. How sad. How very sad. Sometimes, you
know, Trish, just sitting down and talking it out between
you, it can really –

Trish Giles. Thanks awfully for the advice. I'm really
most touched and grateful, but don't you think that you
should be sorting out your own marriage . . .?

Giles Oh. I am – I am so – so sorry.

Trish No, don't take that the wrong way, I just –

Giles No, no, you're quite right, I have no – I've no – it's
just that other people's problems always appear
somehow simpler, don't they?

Trish They seem simpler, anyway. Though, in the case of
Joanna, maybe . . .

Giles She's a – rather unusual person.

Trish Yes?

Giles I – I still love her enormously, you know.

Trish Good.

Giles I can't help thinking that – having done what
she's – she's – she's – done – I should – I should –
I should look a bit to myself. I mean, the guilt's never
just one – one – one-sided, is it?

Trish Usually not. In my case it is. But usually not.

Giles Cast out the – beam in thine own eye, eh? I won't disturb you any more, Trish. Thank you for – thank you for –

Trish Why don't you go home and talk to her, Giles?

Giles I'll try. It's not – she's a bit – funny thing, guilt.

Trish (*unconvinced*) Yes. See you both for lunch, then.

Giles Oh. You'd still welcome us here, would you? At your table?

Trish I certainly would. I've just worked out these bloody place settings. Don't you dare let me down, either of you. Too late to ask anyone else.

Giles I don't know what I'm going to say to Teddy, I'm sure.

Trish If you can't think of anything, do what I do. Ignore him.

Giles It may come to that. I'll be off, then. Start the peace process.

Trish Giles . . .

Giles Mmmm?

Trish I know it's shared responsibility and all that but – do remember it was Joanna who had the affair, not you . . .

Giles Yes, of course . . . Have to talk to Jake as well, I suppose. I don't know how he's going to take it, poor lad. He's so – trusting.

Giles goes out through the French windows. Izzie comes in with some plates of cocktail nibbles on a tray.

Izzie I'm laying out the nibbles in here then, Patricia.

Trish Right-o, Izzie.

Izzie That French woman's driver just telephoned. They're running half an hour behind down the motorway.

Trish Oh, dear.

Izzie I'll hold back lunch, shall I?

Trish If you can.

Izzie I won't be responsible, mark you. You should never have ordered beef.

Trish No, you were quite right, Izzie . . .

Izzie You'll rue the day . . .

Trish (*calling*) Has Pearl vacuumed in here yet, Izzie?

Izzie Probably not, knowing her.

Trish Doesn't look as if she has. There's bits all over this floor. She should have done it before we laid the table.

Izzie She needs boiling in oil and then strangling, that girl.

Trish Can you call her and tell her to do it at once, Izzie? Before people start arriving. Leave those for now . . .

Izzie Right.

Izzie goes out, leaving the tray half unloaded on the sofa. Teddy comes in from the hall. He has now dressed for lunch. He stops in the doorway, hears Trish in the dining room and moves to the double doors.

Teddy Ah, there you are. Good. Right. Trish, it's time for straight talk.

Trish ignores him as usual, continuing to lay her dining table.

Yes, all right, carry on doing that if you have to. You don't even have to speak, if you prefer, but I do want you to listen, Trish. Because what I have to say is vitally important. OK?

No response. During the next, as he warms to his address, Teddy moves away from the doorway and paces the sitting room. At some stage, Trish leaves the dining room by the offstage door. Teddy remains unaware of this and continues to address the empty dining room.

Well, I'll have to take it on trust that you're listening, I suppose. Look, Trish, this cannot go on, this silence between us – this one-sided silence, that is. I'm not silent. I'm not the silent one, am I? I'm happy to talk. I'll talk all day. It's you and this ridiculous . . . I mean, if you'd only explain to me what the problem is, we could sort it out. But you're not giving me the chance, are you? That's the point, old thing. I mean, it can't be this Joanna business surely? I mean, that was . . . well, you know what that was. Of course you do. Bit of mutual nooky, that's all that was. Nothing on either side. But as soon as I – suspected that was affecting you – the minute I did – well, I jacked it in. I said to her, it can't go on, sorry. It's upsetting Trish. The last thing I ever want is for you to be upset. I mean, you're number one, Trish. You're the first officer. I mean, Joanna was just a – midshipman. AB two. Whatever they call them.

Trish has gone. Unseen by Teddy, Pearl comes into the dining room also via the far door. She carries the vacuum cleaner. She plugs it in but stands just inside the doors, poised to start, waiting for Teddy to stop speaking.

The point is today is crunch day, Trish. I can't say too much – not just at present because it's all very hush-hush. Nobody must know about this, not a soul. But. The reason Gavin Ryng-Mayne is here is to make me an offer. I can't be any more precise but let's just say we might be looking very shortly for a little pied-à-terre in Westminster. OK? 'Nough said? Now it's vital we impress this chap. He's an old school friend so he's on our side. Just pull out all the stops, there's a good girl. Laugh at the jokes, I know you've heard them a million times but – tell him I'm sliced Hovis – you know, all the usual rubbish. I don't have to tell you, I – Listen, the – our sleeping arrangements, Trish. I was having a chat with – I was having a think – and I wondered if we should try it on the same mattress for a bit. Just to see if we could – I mean, it's been some time, I know – it's been, well, about seventeen years, hasn't it – so we may be a bit – you may be feeling a bit rusty, you know. But I'm prepared to give it a whirl. Crack open a bottle of bubbly. Root out the frilly night wear, you know . . . all that rubbish . . . How do you feel?

He comes face to face with Pearl.

Pearl Fine by me . . .

Teddy (*furiously*) Oh, for the love of – where's my bloody wife?

Pearl I dunno. Upstairs I think.

Teddy How much of that were you listening to? How much of that did you hear?

Pearl All of it.

Teddy Well, get on with your work. You've no business eavesdropping at doors. That was a private conversation between my wife and myself.

478

Pearl She's not here.

Teddy That is entirely beside the point. Whether she is here or not has nothing at all to do with it. Get on with your work at once, do you hear?

Pearl (*unaffected by this*) Right.

Pearl closes the double doors. Teddy stamps about furiously.

Teddy The whole of my future at stake and the woman isn't even prepared to listen. Well, to hell with her. I'll manage on my own.

He sits on the tray of canapés on the sofa. Izzie comes in with a tray of sherry.

Oh, shit! For crying out loud. Who put these on there? These are new trousers. Now look at them. Did you put these on there?

Izzie I was called away.

Teddy Bloody stupid thing to do. Have you got a damp cloth?

Izzie Not on me.

Teddy Well, where?

Izzie In the kitchen. I didn't know you were going to sit on 'em, did I? Ruined now, those are.

Teddy I have a very important meeting this morning, I hope you appreciate that. With a very, very important man.

Izzie Hope he doesn't like rare beef.

Teddy A top secret meeting. So I want everything done properly, do you hear?

Izzie I can't keep taking it in and out, you know . . .

Teddy You just behave yourself. In a few months you could find yourself having to vote for me . . .

Izzie goes out through the hall door, taking the tray and the spoiled canapés with her. Teddy stamps about looking for a cloth. He finally goes into the dining room, takes one of Trish's carefully folded napkins off the table and, unfolding it, starts to try to clean the seat of his trousers with that. He is performing this somewhat convoluted dance when Gavin is shown in through the French windows by Sally. Gavin is in his late forties, urbane, charming and attractive, the ideal diplomat.

Sally If you'd like to wait in here, I'll see if I can find anyone.

Gavin (*smiling at her warmly*) Thank you, Sally. See you later.

Sally goes off along the terrace. Gavin enters the apparently empty room and, hearing Teddy's efforts from the dining room, cautiously investigates.

(*Seeing Teddy*) Ah! There he is!

Teddy (*hastily stopping his current activity*) Aha!

Gavin Teddy! Dear, dear fellow.

Teddy (*waving the napkin in greeting*) Gavin! Dear chap!

They embrace.

How good to see you, Sparky. Haven't changed a scrap.

Gavin Nor you, nor you . . . And you know, seeing Sally again just now, it made me realise how long it's been. I mean, she was tiny – six months, something like that – when I last saw her . . .

Teddy That long ago, was it . . .?

Gavin If you remember, I was very nearly her godfather.

Teddy Yes, of course – excuse me, got some vol au vent on my trousers – yes, of course you were . . . (*Teddy tosses the napkin back into the dining room and closes the doors*)

Gavin I was trying to remember on the way here. I only met Trish the once, I think. That was at that old school do.

Teddy Oh God, yes. Years ago. At the Savoy. Old Boys' dance. Fund raising.

Gavin You got it. (*Taking in the room*) Oh, just look at this! Look at this! Isn't this wonderful? What a pad, Teddy. What would this place be? Seventeen – what? 1770, 1780?

Teddy 1753.

Gavin Oh, really? That early?

In the dining room, Pearl starts vacuuming noisily.

Teddy Well, the original house was Tudor. Early Tudor – (*registering the noise*) – what is going on in there? – but my great, great, great, great, great whatever – Edward Platt – he succeeded in burning the place to the ground –

Gavin Oh, dear . . .

Teddy Which apparently started as a row with his wife. Only it got a bit out of hand.

Gavin Heavens!

Teddy And his wife –

Next door, the vacuum bumps and bangs.

– what is she doing? – his wife unfortunately died in the fire, poor woman, along with about nine of their

481

children and subsequently he built the present house in their memory –

Gavin Nice gesture . . .

Teddy Which, as you say, was a nice gesture. And he was subsequently killed in a hunting accident and the estate passed to the second son –

Gavin Second *surviving* son, presumably . . .

Teddy Quite. The first son, Thomas Platt, was put away because he was completely barking. And the second son, Edward . . .

The vacuum cleaner now starts banging against the double doors.

And the second son, also called Edward – Oh, for God's sake, this is just too much, excuse me –

Teddy goes to the double doors and flings them open. Pearl is revealed in mid-vacuum.

(*Angrily*) What are you doing?

Pearl What?

Teddy Switch it off.

Pearl strains to hear him.

SWITCH IT OFF!

Pearl switches off.

Pearl I was told to vacuum.

Teddy Not now.

Pearl Mrs Platt told me to vacuum.

Teddy Well, I'm telling you not to. Go and vacuum somewhere else.

Pearl (*affably*) Righty-o. (*To Gavin*) Morning.

Gavin (*charmingly*) Good morning.

Pearl It's staying fine at the moment, anyway. Any luck, it'll stay this way for the fête this aftern—

Teddy shuts the doors on her in mid-sentence.

Teddy And the second son, Edward Platt – they're all called Edward or Thomas, it's very confusing . . . He was apparently quite a bright chap who finished the place off by building the West Wing – what we still call the new wing, although these days it's actually the oldest bit of the building –

Gavin What part are we in now?

Teddy This? This is the old library. Actually built in 1850. But although it's called the old library, it actually replaced the previous library which was much, much older and eventually fell down. But although this was called the old library, curiously enough it was never used as a library. It was built by Thomas Platt for his new young bride as a wedding gift. But on their honeymoon cruise the poor girl fell overboard and as a result this room was never finished. In fact he had it boarded up. And consequently it wasn't used for thirty years and there's hardly been a book in here since.

Gavin What a waste.

Teddy In fact, it was eventually opened up again by my great-grandfather, Tom Platt. Old Tom Platt. His wife Catherine sadly died of food poisoning and he opened it up as a memorial to her. That's her picture up there, you see. That's old Cat Platt as she's generally known.

Gavin Oh, yes.

Teddy She's no oil painting, I'm afraid. But I think he's caught the dog rather well.

Gavin Yes, indeed.

Teddy And that's about it. We had the bomb, of course. German. During the war. That took care of the East Wing. Don't know what the hell they were trying to hit . . . Anyway, I'm afraid they did hit my grandmother, who'd taken up residence there after my grandfather, Ted Platt, died which was very sad for everybody, of course, because she was a deeply wonderful rich character.

Gavin Yes. On the whole they've not had a lot of luck, have they? The women in your family?

Teddy No, it's perfectly true. What was it my father used to say? Marry a Platt and that's that. (*He laughs*)

Gavin (*laughing*) No, it's wonderful to have such a family history, though. Must give you a great sense of permanence.

Teddy Yes, I suppose it does.

Gavin I do envy that.

Teddy You don't go back then?

Gavin Well, yes, we do go back. But in assorted directions.

Teddy Ah.

Gavin Welsh.

Teddy Really.

Gavin Turkish.

Teddy Good Lord.

Gavin I understand Portuguese Jewish . . .

Teddy Grief. I never knew this, Sparky.

Gavin And just a dash of Irish on my mother's side. Quite a mongrel.

Teddy (*laughing*) Gets a bit crowded at Christmas, I imagine.

Gavin No. (*Rather sadly*) No, no.

Teddy Well, I never knew that about you. All these years.

Gavin I think at our particular school, at that time it was prudent to keep a fairly low profile about mixed parentage . . .

Teddy Yes.

Gavin All changed now, of course.

Teddy Oh, yes. Girls as well now.

Gavin Yes. They'd have been a bonus in our day, wouldn't they? Still, we managed, didn't we?

Teddy Yes. (*Changing the subject*) God, it's good to see you again, Sparky.

As they reflect on this, Trish enters.
Gavin springs to his feet. Teddy tardily follows suit.
As always, Trish ignores Teddy.

Trish (*extending her hand to Gavin*) Hallo, there. I'm so sorry I wasn't here to greet you.

Gavin How do you do?

Trish I don't know if you'll remember me. I'm Patricia . . .

Gavin Trish. Yes, of course, how could I forget? Gavin Ryng-Mayne with a Y. Gavin, please. I was just hearing about your –

Trish I'm so sorry, you've been left all on your own, that's terrible. I'll see if I can find my husband, he's around somewhere. Would you excuse me, I won't be one second, then we can have a sherry.

485

Gavin I – er . . .

A crash of a plate breaking in the dining room.

Trish (*hearing this*) Excuse me. (*She opens the dining-room doors*) Pearl, what are you doing?

Pearl (*off*) I was just dusting . . .

Trish Well, don't dust the dining table, girl. We're just about to eat off it. (*To Gavin*) Do excuse me.

Trish closes the doors behind her.
   Gavin, totally bemused, looks at Teddy.
   Teddy, after a second, decides the best course is to laugh it off. He does.

Teddy (*laughing*) Trish! She's legendary. Absolutely legendary.

Gavin Is she?

Teddy Absolutely. Well known.

Gavin I don't quite follow.

Teddy Trish's sense of humour . . . famous throughout the county . . .

Gavin Indeed?

Teddy It's – it takes a bit of getting used to. It's a bit of an acquired taste . . . but once you're on her wavelength . . .

Gavin Yes?

Teddy Great practical joker, too . . .

Gavin Is she?

Teddy Thank your lucky stars you're not staying the night.

Gavin Yes?

486

Teddy Wake up with a hedgehog in your bed. (*He laughs*)

Gavin laughs, too, but still looks a little uncertain.

Anyway. To business. À nos moutons, as our French guest would probably put it. Incidentally, we've got a French film actress coming for lunch, by the way. She's coming to open our annual fête down in the garden there.

Gavin Yes, I saw some activity when I was . . .

Teddy I don't know what films she's been in. Apparently, in her recent one she gets blown up early on.

Gavin Sounds like one of your family . . .

Teddy (*laughing heartily*) Yes. But everyone says she's very good indeed. I'm afraid I haven't seen it. Still, she should liven it up. Hope she speaks English because she's not going to get much out of us otherwise. Now.

Gavin Yes. Well, you know why I'm here. I'm sure you do. We need you, Teddy. It's as simple as that. As you know, I'm fairly close to the PM and we had a private dinner party the other night – just three or four of us – Chris Baxendale . . .

Teddy Yes . . .

Gavin . . . Simon Wickstead . . . Charlie Havers . . .

Teddy . . . yes, yes . . .

Gavin . . . Rowena Todd-Martin . . .

Teddy No, I don't know her . . .

Gavin Rowena? Well, in that rarefied circle, let's just say she's big. She's very, very big. And she's going to get bigger.

Teddy Really?

Gavin There are plans for her. Believe me. Anyway. What we've got with this constituency, Teddy, is a seat that's rapidly slipping from under us. At the next election, it could well turn. I'm sure you're aware of that. I mean Theaker's not the right stuff, he really isn't. Nice enough man . . .

Teddy Oh, yes, very very nice man . . .

Gavin But he's not cutting it and we can't afford to pay his keep. Cruel facts. But these days, politics is a cut-throat business, Teddy. And we're turning to you, cap in hand. Third generation of Platts. Your family made the seat practically a family business, you could easily have taken it on after your father stood down. But you chose, perhaps wisely at the time, not to.

Teddy Well, there was the business, of course.

Gavin Of course, there was the business, we all appreciated that. But as I understand it, these days you're involved slightly less . . .

Teddy Slightly less, yes . . .

Gavin So we're appealing to you. I'm, of course, just the intermediary. But I do speak for the PM. He wants you to know – and I quote his exact words on this – he wants you to know he would be for ever in your debt.

Teddy I see. I see.

Gavin (*slowly*) For – ever – in – your – debt.

Teddy nods.

Yes? Need I say more?

Teddy He'd like me to stand?

Gavin He would.

Teddy At the next election?

Gavin Yes.

Teddy Well, they'd have to pick me first – select me – whatever they do, wouldn't they?

Gavin That's all taken care of. Don't worry.

Teddy Really? What about Colin Theaker? Where does he stand?

Gavin He doesn't. Let's say he's – seen the axe and bowed his head to the inevitable.

Teddy (*filled with regret*) He's such a nice man.

Gavin Charming man. Charming. (*Laughing*) Too nice for politics. Well?

Teddy The thing is, I want to say yes to you, Sparky. I hear what you're saying and I can see where you're coming from and I want more than anything else to say yes. The question, you see, I keep asking myself is – do I need it?

Gavin Teddy, let me put it this way. You can do perfectly well without this government but ask yourself this, can this government do without you?

Teddy Yes. I see. Put like that . . .

Gavin I think the PM's gratitude is not to be dismissed lightly. There are one or two little perks that could quite easily come your way . . .

Teddy You mean, ministerial office . . .?

Gavin (*who wasn't meaning this at all*) Yes . . . eventually . . . that as well. But I think he's pretty happy with the team at present. I mean, there might be some temporary very, very minor post, Arts Minister, something like that – but, no, there are a lot of select committees and commissions, Teddy. POI's as we call them . . .

Teddy POI's?

Gavin Putting Off the Inevitables. Quite high profile, some of them. For instance, he gave me permission to mention the forthcoming Enquiry into the Moral Conduct of Members, which is quite a hot potato, you can imagine. They are looking for someone to chair that, someone who's absolutely squeaky clean. That's vital, as you appreciate.

Teddy Absolutely.

Gavin The trouble is finding anyone who'll stand up to that sort of scrutiny. The sort of scrutiny that those bastards are going to put them under.

Teddy The committee?

Gavin No, the press. I mean, whoever serves on that committee better wear their rubber pants. Because they'll be swarming all over them.

Teddy (*a little worried*) I see.

Gavin But then which one of us is blameless? (*In a slightly dodgy Scots accent*)
'Morality, thou deadly bane,
Thy tens o' thousands thou hast slain!'

Teddy Very, very true.

Gavin Rabbie Burns . . .

Teddy (*nodding gravely*) Especially these days.

Gavin Anyway. What do you say, matey?

Teddy Well, I think I'm bound to say yes, aren't I?

Gavin Then it's yes?

Teddy Looks like it.

Gavin I can tell the PM you've accepted?

Teddy Yes, you can.

Gavin He'll be overjoyed. I'll phone him after lunch.
I have his private number.

Teddy Where is he? Chequers?

Gavin Eastbourne.

Teddy (*laughing*) What's he doing there? Dirty weekend?

Gavin Conference.

Teddy Oh yes, of course. Sorry. Listen, can I offer you a
sherry? While we're waiting for the others? Whisky,
perhaps?

Gavin Sherry, thank you. That would be very nice.

Teddy (*as he pours two glasses*) Incidentally, talking of
morals, I was upset to read all that rubbish about you a
year or so back.

Gavin Oh, that. We soon settled that, don't worry. Cost
them a packet, too.

Teddy Good for you. Under-age, wasn't she? Something
of the sort?

Gavin Yes, she was under age. She was fifteen and a
half. I found the girl on my doorstep distributing
Christian literature, she was absolutely soaked, she'd got
caught in the rain, I invited her inside and gave her some
dry clothes. End of story. Someone gets hold of it. Blows
it up out of all proportion. (*Taking the glass*) Cheers.

Teddy Bastards, aren't they? Bastards. I don't know why
they publish that sort of filth. I mean, who the hell's
interested?

Gavin God knows. Just be warned, Teddy. If you're coming into this line, keep your shirt tucked in. Here's to you.

Teddy Cheers, Sparky!

Gavin Incidentally, I'm not known all that often as Sparky. Not these days.

Teddy Oh, fair enough.

Gavin But then I don't suppose many people call you Penelope, do they?

Teddy No, no. Thank God.

Gavin Incidentally, we must keep all this quiet for a day or two. At least till all the right people have been notified.

Teddy Such as Colin Theaker?

Gavin Yes, Colin Theaker, obviously. I think the Prime Minister will probably want a personal word with him.

Teddy Poor chap.

Gavin Yes.

Trish enters.

Trish No, I'm sorry, Gavin, I can't find Teddy anywhere. Don't know where he's gone.

Teddy laughs. Gavin laughs a little forcedly.

He'll roll up eventually, I expect. Oh, you've helped yourself to sherry. Jolly sensible. I think I'll join you. (*As she pours herself a glass*) Now, we've just heard that their car's turned into the village, so Madame Cadeau plus her driver should be with us any minute. Lucille Cadeau. I don't know if you've heard of her. She's a French film star.

Teddy Yes, I've just told him, Trish . . .

Trish Have you heard of her, at all?

Gavin I hadn't, but –

Teddy I've told him, she's coming to open our fête . . .

Trish She's here to open our garden fête this afternoon.

Gavin Really?

Teddy I've told him that already, Trish . . .

Trish Now, who else have we got coming? Oh, two very special friends of ours, Giles and Joanna Mace. Well, they're our closest neighbours actually. They live just at the bottom of our garden.

Teddy Giles is our local doctor . . .

Trish Giles is the village doctor . . .

Gavin Oh, yes . . .?

Teddy And Joanna's a teacher . . .

Trish And Joanna teaches . . .

Gavin Locally?

Trish What?

Teddy What?

Gavin Locally? Does she teach locally?

Trish Oh, yes . . .

Teddy Yes. Up at Sally's school, actually . . .

Trish Up at our daughter Sally's school. Only Joanna teaches the juniors.

Teddy The juniors.

Gavin Yes.

Silence.
    Teddy laughs, unconvincingly.
    Silence.

Do you – ?

Teddy (*together*) Sorry?

Trish (*together*) Sorry?

Gavin Nothing.

   Giles and Joanna appear on the terrace. They both,
   too, have chosen to ignore Teddy.

Teddy (*seeing them, with some relief*) Ah, here they
are . . .

Trish (*seeing them*) Oh, talk of the devil . . .

Teddy Come in, come in . . .

Joanna (*very tense*) May we come in?

Trish Yes, do. Come and meet Gavin. Gavin, this is Jo,
Joanna Mace, a very old friend of ours. And this is Giles.

Gavin How do you do? Gavin Ryng-Mayne. With a Y.

Joanna With a what?

Gavin With a Y.

Joanna Why what?

Gavin That's how it's spelt. With a Y.

Joanna Oh, I see. With a Y.

Giles Hallo. Giles Mace, how do you do?

Teddy Would you both care for a sherry?

Joanna (*to Gavin*) Did you drive down this morning?

Gavin Yes, I did. I started quite early . . .

494

Teddy Sherry, both of you?

Giles How long did that take you?

Gavin I think almost exactly three hours.

Teddy Do either of you want a bloody sherry, yes or no?

Trish That's terribly good going.

Giles You must have been travelling.

Gavin I think I was just a wee bit the far side of the speed limit.

Trish Now, would you both like a glass of sherry?

Joanna Lovely.

Giles Thank you.

Teddy The fastest I ever did it from London, you know –

Giles What do you drive?

Gavin A little Porsche.

Joanna Golly.

Gavin Just a small one.

Teddy You know, the fastest I ever did it from London . . .

Trish (*handing out the sherry glasses*) Here we are. Jo?

Joanna Oh, thank you.

Teddy The fastest –

Trish Giles?

Giles Thank you so much.

Teddy The fastest time I ever did it –

Giles I'm looking forward to meeting our film star . . .

Teddy – in the middle of the day –

495

Trish Oh, yes. Exciting, isn't it?

Teddy – was two hours –

Trish That reminds me. I must keep an eye out for them. We don't want them going round to the back like you did, Gavin.

Teddy – two hours – and forty-six minutes –

Trish Our gardener's removed all the signs for some reason.

Teddy – door to fucking door.

Gavin Why did he do that?

Trish Don't ask me, he's a law unto himself . . .

Teddy What about that then, you stupid bastards? (*To Gavin*) Sorry.

Sally comes in from the hall. She has changed for lunch out of her school clothes.

Trish Oh, Sally, you haven't seen your father, have you?

Sally No. Mum, they're here. They've arrived. Pearl's just seen their car.

Trish Oh, heavens. Why don't we all go and meet her? Wouldn't that be fun? We can all cheer. She'll think she's at Cannes. You all coming? (*She starts for the hall*)

Joanna (*following her*) Oh, yes. Let's go and meet her.

Giles (*following them*) Why not?

Gavin (*following them*) Good idea.

Sally (*going with them*) She's somewhere round the front . . .

They have all gone, apart from Teddy.
He glares after them.

From the dining room, a crash. Teddy crosses and opens the door. Pearl is standing there.

Teddy What are you doing?

Pearl I dropped one of them fish pasties.

Teddy Well, then scrape it up.

Pearl I'm going to.

Teddy shuts the door on her. He decides this is the moment to rehearse his acceptance speech.

Teddy (*clearing his throat*) Ladies and gentlemen . . . er – fellow party members . . . Prime Minister . . . er – no, minister . . . junior minister . . . whoever you are . . . this is a very, very great . . . this is an extremely . . . huge honour . . . to be your new MP . . . and I can promise you right here and now that I intend fully to carry this fight to the opposition and I shall not cease until I personally see the whites of their eyes as they turn tail and run . . . the seats of their pants as they turn tail and run! I stand before you today – this evening – your sitting member . . . (*He thinks about this*) . . . I sit here your standing mem— no, no, no . . . your fully erected member – oh, bloody hell – your elected representative . . . and I can promise you that your vote for me has meant a vote for sanity, a vote for humanity, a vote for . . . (*He runs through a few rhyming options*) . . . banity, canity . . . danity, hanity, inanity? . . . no . . . vanity . . . yanity . . . zanity . . . and a vote for good old-fashioned common sense. So, as my great uncle Eddie, huntsman and bon viveur, was wont to say, get off your ass, spread your legs, get mounted and get at 'em! Tally-ho and God speed!

As he finishes, Lucille appears at the French windows. She is everything expected of a French film star, attractive, vivacious and charming.

Teddy turns and sees her. He gawps. If there is such a thing as love at first sight, this is it.

Teddy Ah.

Lucille Ah. Pardon. Sorry . . . we have come . . . wrong . . .

Teddy (*who believes the best way to converse with foreigners is to shout at them*) Ah. Tu es . . . vous êtes . . . Madame Cadeau?

Lucille I am Lucille. You . . . are . . . Mr Plate?

Teddy Platt. Teddy. I am Teddy. I am named Teddy.

Lucille Ah. So. Teddy.

Fran, Lucille's driver, appears on the terrace behind her. She seems fairly formidable.

Oh. This . . . my driver. Fran.

Teddy Fran? Ah. Welcome also . . . here. I am welcoming you . . .

Fran (*in a flat London voice*) It's all right. I speak English.

Teddy Oh, splendid. Please, do come in. Entrez! I'm afraid you'll find . . . here . . . very few of us . . . speaking the French. Je regrette. Rien de français.

* **Lucille** (*shrugging*) Oh, c'est pas grave. J'ai l'habitude. Quand on travaille souvent en Angleterre ou en Amérique on s'aperçoit que très peu de gens parlent français. Bien sûr, je devrais apprendre l'anglais, mais j'ai si peu de temps. Et je suis aussi très paresseuse . . .

Teddy Yes. Jolly good. We find that, too. Especially during the summer.

---

* Oh, it doesn't matter. I'm used to that. If you work a lot in England or America you find very few people speak French. I should learn English, of course, but I have so little time. I'm also very lazy . . .

*At this moment, through the hall doors the others
return, led by Trish.*

Trish Oh, you're here. Hallo.

All Hallo!

Teddy Ah, everybody. This is Lucille. I'm afraid she
doesn't speak much English so we'll have to be . . .

Lucille Hallo. I – come in the wrong door. I speak not
good English, so . . . I'm afraid.

* **Trish** Alors nous allons parler français. (*To the others*)
We'll all have to speak French, won't we? (*Plunging into
fluent French*) Bienvenue, Madame Cadeau, c'est gentil
de votre part de nous consacrer un peu de votre temps si
précieux . . .

Lucille Oh, mais tout le plaisir est pour moi. C'est
tellement plus agréable d'être dans la campagne anglaise
plutôt qu'enfermée dans des chambres d'hotel . . . C'est
si beau . . .

Giles Vous avez fait bon voyage? On m'a dit que vous
avez été retardée sur l'autoroute . . .

Lucille C'était épouvantable, la circulation était
épouvantable . . .

Fran Il y avait une foire agricole. La route était pleine de
tracteurs . . .

---

* **Trish** Then we'll speak French. (*To the others*) We'll all have to speak
French, won't we? (*Plunging into fluent French*) Welcome, Madame
Cadeau, it's so good of you to give up your valuable time . . .

Lucille Oh, it's a pleasure. It's so good to see the English countryside
instead of hotel rooms . . . It's so beautiful . . .

Giles How was your journey? I hear you were held up on the motorway . . .

Lucille It was bad, the traffic was very bad . . .

Fran There was some agricultural show on. The road was full of tractors . . .

* **Giles** Oh, vous n'auriez pas dû prendre cette route. Pas aujourd'hui. C'est le jour du 'County Show'.

Fran J'ai utilisé la carte qu'on m'a donnée au studio. Ils n'ont pas parlé d'une foire.

Joanna (*simultaneously with the last*) C'est la première fois que vous voyagez en dehors de Londres?

Lucille Oui, la première fois, j'ai honte de le dire . . .

Sally Eh bien alors, vous n'avez pas encore vu ce qu'il y a de mieux à voir.

Trish Je suppose que c'est ça le problème quand on fait des films, hein? On est toujours cloîtré à l'intérieur, n'est-ce-pas?

Sally Oh, maman, écoute, on n'est pas toujours enfermé. Maintenant la plupart des films sont faits en extérieur . . .

Gavin (*simultaneously over this last, to Lucille*) Dites-moi, est-ce-que vous trouvez qu'il y a une grosse différence entre faire des films en Angleterre et faire des films en France?

---

* **Giles** Oh, you shouldn't have come that way. Not today. It's the day of the County Show.

Fran I used the map the studio gave me. They said nothing about a show.

Joanna (*simultaneously with the last*) Is this the first time you've travelled out of London?

Lucille Yes, it is, I'm ashamed to say . . .

Sally Oh, well, you've not seen the best of the place, then.

Trish I suppose that's the trouble with making movies, isn't it? You're always cooped up indoors, aren't you?

Sally Oh, Mum, honestly, they're not always indoors. Most of the films these days are made on location . . .

Gavin (*simultaneously over this last, to Lucille*) Tell me, do you find it very different making movies in England as opposed to making movies in France?

* **Lucille** Eh! Un film est un film est un film. Non, mais c'est vrai il y a des différences. Surtout en ce qui concerne les studios. Les studios d'Hollywood sont énormes, en gros bien plus grands que nos studios en Europe . . .

> *They all crowd together and chatter happily in a babble of French. Teddy finds himself on the edge of the group, isolated and alone.*

Teddy (*frustratedly*) Oh, for God's sake. Doesn't anybody here speak English?

> *The chatter continues as the lights fade to:*
> *Blackout.*

---

* Well, a film is a film is a film. But yes, there are differences. Mainly in the set-up of the studios themselves. Hollywood studios are very big, of course, far bigger than we have in Europe, on the whole . . .

Act Two

SCENE ONE

Saturday, August 14th, 2.00 p.m.
The same.
Lunch is just about over. In the sitting room are Trish,
Sally and Gavin, finishing their coffee. Sally also has a
glass of red wine. In the dining room, through the half-
open door, the sound and the occasional glimpse of
Teddy and Lucille, who've obviously hit it off despite
the language difficulty. The two alternate between a low
murmur and sudden bellows of laughter. Teddy has
clearly had several drinks over lunch. Joanna and Giles
have left.

Gavin What a simply delicious lunch. Thank you so
much.

Trish Yes. Izzie usually gets her beef rather rarer than
that, I'm so sorry.

A roar of laughter from the dining room. Trish frowns
slightly.

Gavin No, no, actually I prefer it on the – well-done
side.

Sally (*lightly drunk*) It was as tough as old wellingtons . . .

Trish I mean, it was very silly of me to choose sirloin
but I thought it would be rather nice for our French
guest. You know, roast beef of old England.

Sally Roast boot of old England, you mean . . .

Gavin I'm sure Lucille appreciated it.

Trish Are your trousers quite dry now?

Gavin Yes, absolutely fine. Nothing serious.

Trish She's such a clumsy girl. When she's not breaking crockery she's pouring water over people.

Another laugh from the dining room.

I must ask her to do up more buttons in future as well.

Gavin Well. I'd certainly no objection to that. (*He laughs*)

Trish No, but – all the same. It's – I'm sure it's unhygienic. I mean, Giles practically had his nose wedged in there at one point. Incidentally, I must apologise for our friends rushing off in the middle of the meal like that. Joanna had this important overseas phone call, apparently. And Giles had to . . . had to . . .

Gavin Had to go and hold the receiver for her. (*He laughs*) Still, more wine for us, eh?

Trish Helped to wash down the beef, anyway.

Sally The fillet of beef Wellington . . .

Trish Yes, don't keep on, darling. How many glasses of that have you had?

Sally Two. This is my second, that's all . . .

Trish You've certainly –

More laughter from the dining room.

(*Getting up*) Excuse me . . . (*She closes the dining-room doors*)

Sally (*to Gavin*) Two glasses of wine, I'm some sort of alcoholic.

Trish You've had more than two.

Sally How do you know?

Trish Because I've been counting.

Sally You've been sitting there counting the number of glasses I've had? (*To Gavin*) Wouldn't you consider that slightly over-protective? I mean, wouldn't you?

Gavin (*reluctant to be drawn*) Well . . .

Sally Anyway, red wine's good for you. There's been fresh research recently –

Trish I don't care, it's still not good for you to drink too much.

Gavin I don't blame you. It's a stunning claret. Absolutely clock-stopping.

Trish I don't care, she shouldn't drink too much of it. Apart from anything else, by the time you're forty you'll be a red-faced, fat, boring drunk.

Pearl has entered from the hall.

Yes, Pearl?

Pearl I done the dishes. I'll be off now.

Trish Yes, all right, Pearl.

Pearl Got to get ready for my fortune-telling down in my little tent. (*Winking at Gavin*) Your trousers all right, are they?

Gavin Yes, thank you.

Pearl Sorry about that. Hope nothing's shrunk . . .

Trish You've put everything away as well, have you, Pearl?

Pearl Oh, yes.

Trish No more breakages, I hope?

Pearl Oh, no. (*As she goes*) Not so's you'd notice. (*Pearl goes*)

Trish (*sighing*) Excuse me, I'd better go and see what damage she's done. (*Trish opens the dining-room doors*)
* Je voulais seulement vous rappeler que c'est presque l'heure de la cérémomie d'ouverture, Lucille . . .

Lucille Ah, oui, merci.

Teddy I've been introducing Lucille to the joys of single malt whi—

> *Trish closes the doors on Teddy in mid-sentence. She goes out of the hall door.*

Sally You're a – what do you call it – you're a wine buff then, are you?

Gavin Lord, no. I have a working knowledge of one or two favourites. I can tell a good one from el plonko.

Sally Is this a good one?

Gavin Very good. Can't you tell?

Sally Wine's wine to me . . .

Gavin (*smiling*) I don't believe that for a moment.

Sally What is it then? Tell me about it. It's a claret, is it?

Gavin Yes, it's a Bordeaux.

Sally Is that good?

Gavin Not of itself. That's just the generic name. It's a St-Julien from the district of Haut-Médoc. Which is one of the most famous of the French wine growing regions. Which includes Margaux, Pauillac, St-Julien . . . What

---

* Just to remind you, it's nearly time for the opening ceremony, Lucille . . .
Lucille Ah, yes. Thank you.

you're drinking there is a Château Léoville-Barton which is certainly one of the best. It's a second growth, what they term a deuxième cru which is pretty high up the league table – there are some who think it ought to be ranked higher – but what makes that particularly special is that it's a '71 and you can't do much better than that.

Sally 1971. Before I was born.

Gavin Long before.

Sally How old would you have been? In 1971?

Gavin Considerably younger than I am now.

Sally You're not going to tell me?

Gavin No.

Sally I told you my age.

Gavin That's different. It's very good to be your age.

Sally I don't think it is.

Gavin No?

Sally When you're my age you still tend to get treated like a child.

Gavin Only by your parents, surely? And they can't help that, can they, poor things?

Sally You don't look on me as a child, then?

Gavin No. I don't look on you as a child, not at all.

A silence as they stare at each other.

Sally (*holding out her glass, a little coquettish*) Want a sip?

Gavin No, thank you. I'm afraid I can't take it these days. Not at my age.

Sally I don't believe that for a moment.

Jake has appeared on the terrace.

(*Half to herself*) Oh, no . . .

Jake Hi!

Sally (*coolly*) Hallo. What do you want?

Jake I was just wondering if Madame – er . . . Miss –

Sally She's finishing her lunch.

Jake Ah. You haven't seen my dad, have you? Looking for him.

Sally Not since he chased out after your mother. (*To Gavin*) This is Jake.

Jake Hi.

Gavin Hallo, Jake. Gavin Ryng-Mayne. With a Y. How do you do?

Jake Hallo. (*Slight pause*) Is that your car? The Porsche?

Gavin You got it.

Jake The yellow one.

Gavin That's the one.

Jake Cool. (*He stands there*)

Sally What were we talking about? Wine, weren't we? So, how can you tell if they're any good?

Gavin Well, there are several ways. First, you look at the colour. Look, hold up the glass to the light and then tip it ever so slightly. That's it.

Sally (*doing this*) What am I looking for?

Gavin Well, you'll see that's a reddish brown which is a good colour for a fine wine. That means it's fully mature.

Wine can vary from purplish – which indicates a very young wine – to a sort of cherry red in a much lighter wine. Check it isn't cloudy which that certainly isn't – it's good and dark but not cloudy, that's important. Now. Next, you use your nose – hold the glass still . . . sniff the wine – deeply, that's it – now, swill it gently in the glass – good. Now, inhale again – Can you pick up all those varied flavours? Almost meaty, isn't it? What we call gamey . . .

Sally Yes, yes . . . musky . . . animal . . .

Jake Do you ever get around to drinking it, then?

Gavin Whooaa! Whooaa! Not so fast. Don't be so impatient. Make it last. Now the ultimate test. You need to taste it. Take a tiny sip – very, very little – and hold it in your mouth – right? – now, suck in a little air so that it circulates round your entire buccal cavity. Good. You should feel even more aromas at the back of your nose now, as the wine warms up – close your eyes, just enjoy the sensation on your tongue, let it invade all the passages. Yes? Now, savour it . . . enjoy it . . . allow it to linger . . .

Sally (*her mouth full of wine*) Yes . . . yes . . .

Gavin Now, if you must, you can swallow.

Sally (*doing so*) Wow.

A silence.

Jake Well, I'll . . . I'll be out here. When she's ready. (*He goes*)

Gavin Friend of yours?

Sally Well. Vaguely.

Gavin Boyfriend?

Sally God, no. Well, I think he'd like to think he is. But he isn't. Not at all.

Gavin You don't have boyfriends?

Sally Sometimes. But not just at present. I'm too busy with other things.

Gavin Such as?

Sally Well, without wanting to sound selfish, my own future, really.

Gavin Anything particular in mind?

Sally I don't know yet. I might possibly go into politics. I'm quite keen to do that at present.

Gavin Politics? Oh, do beware!

Sally That's one possibility. National politics, of course, not local. I'm not interested in stray dogs or one-way traffic schemes. But then I write. So I might do that.

Gavin You write? How fascinating. Novels?

Sally Poetry, mainly. I find that more satisfying. I've written quite a lot, actually. Some of it's pretty good.

Gavin (*deadpan*) I'm sure it is. Who's your publisher?

Sally Oh, I haven't bothered to publish. Not yet. You need to have enough for a full anthology before you publish.

Gavin Oh, how very sensible. I remember Ted Hughes saying to me very much the same thing . . .

Sally (*oblivious*) Then I design a bit, as well. So there's always that, of course.

Gavin Good gracious . . .

Sally Hard to choose at the moment.

Gavin Spoilt for choice.

Sally (*in full spate*) Just a bit. And then I want to read a lot more. And – learn about things. All sorts of things. That my limited, curriculum-led education hasn't prepared me for. Wine. Life. Life outside this place. I want to travel. I want to go abroad. I want to see things and meet lots of people. So I'm not really too interested in starting relationships with men whose lives seem to begin and end here. Does that sound callous?

Gavin No. It sounds perfectly normal.

Sally Have you travelled a lot?

Gavin Quite a bit.

Sally To research your books, was it?

Gavin Sometimes.

Sally I'm afraid I haven't read any of them. Sorry.

Gavin Ah, well. Never mind. Fortunately a lot of people have.

Sally I'm afraid I'm not really into reading thrillers.

Gavin Good, because I'm not into writing thrillers, either . . .

Sally Oh. I thought they were –

Gavin I regard them simply as novels. But I agree, I think that's how I've been categorised. It's an appalling habit these days, isn't it, wanting to put everything into neat pigeon-holes. It's what I call the Internet Culture. Everything has to be cross-referenced for easy access. Instantly down-loadable knowledge. The thriller writers' website. The best hundred comic writers' website. Britain's tallest female dramatists' website . . .

Sally The world's most distinguished totally bald composers' . . .

Gavin (*smiling*) Right.

Sally smiles at him. Fran enters from the front door.

Fran 'Llo. Back again.

Sally Hallo.

Gavin Hallo, there.

Fran You all finished your lunch, have you?

Sally I think Lucille's still in the dining room.

Fran Nearly time for the opening, isn't it?

Trish hurries on from the hall, dressed and ready.

Trish It certainly is. Come on, we're going to be dreadfully late.

Fran I'd better fetch her then, hadn't I? In here, you say?

Trish (*at the French windows*) We might just miss the rain. It's going to bucket down in a minute.

Fran opens the dining-room doors. A burst of merriment from Teddy and Lucille as she does so. They are doing silly French and English noises to each other, which in their current condition, they both find hilarious.

Teddy (*in French gibberish*) Long-dong-dong-yong – yeeuurr-yeurr-yeuurr . . .

Lucille (*in English gibberish*) Yarrk-yaarrk-yarrah-ho-ho-ho-harr . . .

* **Fran** Voyons, Lucille, le moment est venu d'ouvrir la fête et de partir d'ici.

---

* Come on, Lucille, it's time to open the fête and get you away from here.

* **Lucille** Oh, vous! Quel rabat joie. Chaque fois que je m'amuse vous êtes toujours là pour tout gâcher . . .

Fran Mon Dieu, vous n'avez pas bu, dites-moi? Has she been drinking?

Teddy She's been initiated into the joys of single malt . . .

Fran Vous savez bien que vous ne devriez pas boire. Vous m'avez promis de ne pas boire.

Trish She had the odd glass of wine at lunch and then –

Lucille and Teddy remain in the dining room. They are both unnaturally merry rather than drunk.

† **Lucille** Oh, mais qu'est-ce-que vous racontez? Un petit verre, pauvre pétasse. Qu'est-ce-que ça va changer? Si j'ai envie de boire, je boirai. Si je vous écoutais, je ne m'amuserais jamais. Je resterais dans mon coin, muette comme une bonne soeur.

Fran (*over this*) Why did you let her drink, for God's sake?

Trish What do you mean, let her drink?

Fran She shouldn't be drinking.

Sally Why not?

---

* **Lucille** Oh, it's you! Trust you to break up a good party. Whenever I'm enjoying myself you always manage to ruin it . . .

Fran My God, you haven't been drinking, have you? Has she been drinking?

Teddy She's been initiated into the joys of single malt . . .

Fran You know you shouldn't be drinking. You promised me you wouldn't drink.

† Oh, what are you going on about? One little drink, you miserable bitch. What difference is that going to make? If I want a drink I'll have a drink. If you had your way, I'd never get any fun at all. Just sit in silence like a nun.

Fran Because – because she has a problem with it. You should never have let her near a bloody drink . . .

Trish Well, we didn't know that.

Fran She's like Jekyll and Hyde. After three drinks, she's a liability . . .

Teddy (*from the dining room*) Lucille and I have worked out a perfect way of communication. We have entirely solved the entente koolibar . . . Naysapar?

Lucille (*likewise*) York-york-wobble-wobble-old bean . . .

Teddy Nyooon-onson-ponson-lanson-deeverrr . . . See, perfect understanding?

Trish Well, if you'd told us, we would never have offered her a drink in the first place . . . (*To Sally*) Let this be a lesson to you. (*To Fran*) Why didn't you warn us?

Fran Because I was sent off to the pub for lunch on my own, wasn't I?

Teddy See what I mean? She understands me perfectly. Yakkerdoo-bien – arrrbeurrrr . . .

Trish Yes . . . But I thought . . . That's what you'd prefer to do. As her chauffeur. The chauffeurs usually prefer to do that.

Lucille Hugh-hugh-hugh-bla-bla-bla . . .

Fran I'm not her chauffeur. I work in her agent's office.

Trish Oh, I see. I do beg your pardon. You should have said. I assumed you were the chauffeur.

Teddy She's been getting a bit uppity about inferior French market produce. I was forced to remind her of Agincourt . . .

Lucille (*attacking him*) Pah, Agincourt . . . Agincourt . . .

Teddy (*retreating round the table*) Oui, Agincourt . . .

Fran (*pursuing him*) Not everyone who drives a car's a chauffeur, you know.

Teddy Enri le sank. Waterloo!

Trish No, I'm sorry I . . .

Lucille Oui, Waterloo. Napoléon.

Fran Not everyone who opens doors is a doorman . . .

Teddy (*counter-attacking Lucille*) Wellington!

Trish No, there's been some dreadful confusion, I've said I'm terribly sorry. Did you have a pleasant lunch, anyway?

Lucille (*retreating into the sitting room*) Napoléon!

Fran Yes I did, thank you. Very nice rare roast beef . . .

Teddy (*pursuing her*) Wellington!

Sally Lucky you.

Lucille Napoléon! (*She loses her footing and sits on the floor*)

Trish Oh dear, this is terrible. She doesn't even look as if she can stand up . . .

Teddy She'll be fine, she's fine . . .

> *Barry, a lively man in his thirties and undoubtedly the organising energy behind the garden fête, appears at the French windows.*

Barry (*to Gavin*) Good afternoon. Good afternoon, Sally. Good afternoon, Patricia. I –

* **Lucille** Oh, chouette! Encore ce drôle de petit bonhomme! Celui qu'on a recontré tout à l'heure!

---

* Oh, good! Here's that funny little man again! The one we met earlier!

Fran I don't think she's up to it. I think you'd better find someone else.

* **Lucille** L'idiot du village! I – declare this – fête – open . . .

> *Fran takes a grip on Lucille.*

(*Resenting this*) Ne me touchez pas! Je peux marcher, je peux marcher très bien, toute seule, merci . . .

Fran Pourquoi est-ce-que vous faites ça? Regardez de quoi vous avez l'air, vous pouvez à peine tenir debout.

Lucille Je tiens très bien debout, ne vous inquiétez pas. Vous roulerez sous la table bien avant moi . . .

Fran Ça, j'en suis sûre . . .

Barry Is there a problem?

Trish No, no problem, Barry, she's just . . .

Sally Shouldn't she go and lie down?

Lucille Teddy . . .!

Teddy Wah-wu-war-war-war-mon-brave . . .

Trish I'm sure she'll be fine, once she's in the fresh air. All she has to do is open the thing . . . she doesn't have to hang around . . .

† **Lucille** Teddy. Teddy, prenez mon bras . . .

---

* **Lucille** The village idiot! I – declare this – fête – open . . .

> *Fran takes a grip on Lucille.*

(*Resenting this*) Don't manhandle me! I can walk, I can walk perfectly well on my own, thank you . . .

Fran Why do you do it? Look at you, you can hardly stand up.

Lucille I can stand up, don't worry. I can drink you under the table . . .

Fran I'm sure of that . . .

† Teddy. Teddy, hold my arm . . .

Fran (*to Teddy*) Can you take her arm? She wants you to take her arm.

Teddy (*doing so*) Most certainly. Yuwoo-deezurs . . .

* **Lucille** Ah, Teddy, mon ami Teddy! York-york-york.

Trish Are we going to miss the rain, Barry?

Barry We might. We might be lucky, Patricia, if we hurry . . .

Barry, Lucille, Fran and Teddy go out on to the terrace. As they are going, Fran's mobile rings. Under the next, she locates it and answers it in the dining room. Gavin and Sally seem in no hurry to follow them. Trish also lingers.

Trish Come on, Sally, we need you down there, too.

Sally I think I might come down a bit later . . .

Trish No, now. Come on.

Sally I don't happen to –

Trish (*firmly, sotto*) Sally, please. Do as I ask. Please.

Sally For God's sake! (*Sally stamps off through the door to the hall, embarrassed in front of Gavin. Angrily, over her shoulder as she goes*) See what I mean?

A rumble of thunder.

Trish Now where are you going?

Sally (*off*) To get a coat, of course.

Trish (*to Gavin*) Oh, dear. It's so easy to offend them, isn't it? At that age?

Fran (*during this, on the terrace*) . . . Yes . . . yes . . . yes . . . No, that's the point, she's back on it . . . yes . . .

---

* Ah, Teddy! My friend, Teddy! York-york-york.

Quite a bit by the look of it . . . Well, I wasn't invited
to lunch, was I? Otherwise, I . . . Yes, I will. She's just
going to open it, yes . . . No, that's all right, I don't think
there are . . . Not even a photographer. I don't think they
have newspapers in this part of the world . . . Yes, I will.
Soon as I've delivered her. Yes . . . yes . . . OK. (*She
disconnects*) Shit. (*To Trish*) Where'd they all go?

Trish Down on the lower meadow there. Down the
steps.

Gavin Where are you delivering her? Hollyhurst?

Fran Who told you that?

Gavin Just two and two put together, really.

Fran Well, do me a favour and don't make that four, all
right? We don't want it public. No press here today, are
there? I didn't see any.

Trish Just our local paper. I think Jake is trying to get a
word with her, if he –

Fran Shit. (*She moves rapidly through the French
windows and runs off*)

　More thunder.

Trish What on earth is Hollyhurst?

Gavin It's a very smart, very expensive, very exclusive
clinic. Used by the rich and famous to help quell their
foolish habits . . .

Trish Oh, it's a clinic! I've never heard of it, I'm afraid.

Gavin Just as it should be.

Trish Well. You have children these days, you hold your
breath and pray. Do you have children?

Gavin No.

Trish You're married, though?

Gavin No.

Trish Oh. I somehow thought you were. Don't know where I got that idea. You were married though, weren't you?

Gavin No.

Trish Oh.

A pause.

(*Laughing*) Well, now we know all about you then, don't we?

Gavin And I'm not gay either. Before you ask . . .

Trish No, no, I didn't. Gosh, no. I never thought you were. Heavens, no. Not that I'm – I mean, fine. If you were. But. Super.

Gavin I was, mind you.

Trish Gay?

Gavin Yes. At one stage of my life. But I gave it up.

Trish Really. Why was that?

Gavin I don't know. I think it all just got rather – tedious.

Trish Ah.

Gavin There was an awful lot of hard work to it, you know.

Trish Yes. I can imagine.

Gavin Emotional hard work.

Trish Yes, yes . . .

Gavin Men tend to take it out on each other, rather.

Trish Yes, I can see they might, yes.

Gavin So I – changed shirts, as they say.

Trish Yes, that's very interesting. And are you – happier now?

Gavin Oh, yes.

Trish Good. Good. (*Slight pause*) That's the main thing, isn't it? I don't know why she's taking so long to get a coat, for heaven's sake. Perhaps she's changing her shirt. (*She laughs. A slight pause*) She's seventeen, that's all I'm saying. Just seventeen.

> *Pause.*

Why don't I trust you for some reason? I ought to be able to trust you, I'm sure. But it's rather like finding a fox in one's chicken run.

> *She laughs. Gavin smiles.*
> *Another silence.*

I think you must have gathered that things between Teddy and me have reached a rather peculiar state, just at present.

Gavin Yes, I had noticed.

Trish It's very hard, you see, for someone like me. I'm originally from a navy background, I don't know if you knew?

Gavin I did read that somewhere.

Trish My father was pretty high ranking. He was a rear admiral, actually.

Gavin Yes, I did know that.

Trish And my mother was really of the old school – fiercely loyal. I mean *fiercely* loyal. It was my father first and foremost, all the time, absolutely, without question. And we were all girls, four of us – he desperately wanted a boy but he never got one, poor man – and the four of us, we were unquestionably background. You put your man first. Have a career, by all means, if you really have to – but when the chips were down, the man came first.

Gavin But you did have a career?

Trish Oh, yes I – messed around – designing bits and pieces . . .

Gavin Come on, it was very successful design practice . . .

Trish Yes, it was . . .

Gavin In which you were offered a partnership, weren't you?

Trish Yes, but they were desperately short of people. They were taking on anyone, really, at that time . . .

Gavin A partnership before you were thirty? I don't know much about these things but I'd have thought that was fairly impressive.

Trish Well, it wasn't bad, but – You know an awful lot about me. How do you know all this?

Gavin Oh. I'm always listening out. I hear things.

Trish Anyway. I got the job to do up this place. Of course, I met Teddy. His father was still alive then. And one thing led to – another.

Gavin And then you gave it all up?

Trish Well, I was expecting Sally and – we're a long way from London. You get a bit out of the swing, you know. But lately, things have been a bit tricky. You mustn't think they're always like this.

Gavin No.

Trish Actually, they're usually worse. (*She laughs*) Oh
God, I'm sorry I shouldn't say that. You see, I saw my
mother standing by this man – by my father – making
sure we all stood by him – and it was only about ten
years after he died that I realised, bloody rear admiral
or not, he wasn't worth tuppence. Not compared to my
mother. He was a humourless, insensitive, self-righteous,
self-opinionated, callous bully. And when he died,
shortly afterwards, she died. Because he'd allowed her
no reason of her own to carry on living. That's what it
amounted to. Everybody said she died of grief which was
absolute bollocks. She died because her life was totally
pointless. All the same, it's very difficult to break the
tradition, you see. My sisters all find it the same with
their marriages – well, Joan isn't married, but she might
as well be, she's shacked up with this fearful creature –
but we're all, at heart, little rear admiral's wives . . . It's
very hard to break out of that. My way of coping is to
blot things out completely. I've started editing my life.
Like a stencil, you know. You hold it over the paper and
you just allow the bit you want to bleed through. It
works reasonably well. Most people are coming to the
conclusion that I'm going completely batty – but since
I'm obviously harmless, they're happy to humour me.

Gavin It can't go on, though, can it?

Trish No. It can't, of course it can't.

Gavin I take it a rapprochement is not on the cards?

Trish Oh, golly, no. Long past that, I'm afraid. I think
I should get out, really, shouldn't I? But I don't know.
Where do I go? What do I do? Nice comfy life here, in
many ways. Plenty of money. Daughter doing her A-levels.
All sorts of things to consider. And then I feel – no! In any
case, that's not fitting conduct for an admiral's daughter.
In my family, the women go down with the ship.

Gavin Be careful. I was hearing earlier about the women in the Platt family . . .

Trish Yes, dreadful, isn't it? Do you think we're all cursed? I sometimes sit here in the evening and there's old Cat Platt looking at me saying, you're next! (*Pause*) I suppose telling you all this isn't doing Teddy's chances a lot of good, is it? I mean, I don't really know why you're here but it's obviously something quite important. I don't want to be told, don't worry. It's just, whatever there is between us, I wouldn't want to spoil his chances – despite everything he's done.

Gavin Well, spouses aren't supposed to be part of the equation these days. They still are, of course, very often. But we're not supposed to notice any more if the Foreign Secretary's partner is chewing up the family rug.

Sally returns. She has changed completely into a new outfit. She has also applied additional, quite subtle make-up. The others stop and look at her.

Sally Hallo. (*Looking at them*) What's the matter?

Trish What?

Sally Why are you staring?

Trish You went to get a coat. You've changed completely.

Sally I thought I'd dress up for this fête, that's all. What's wrong?

Trish I don't know why you've got all that lot on to stand in a drizzle selling tombola tickets . . .

Sally All right, I'll go and change again . . .

Trish No, no . . .

Sally If you think I look ridiculous . . .

Trish I didn't say you looked ridiculous. For heaven's sake, Sally, what's got into you? All I said was – you look a bit – overdressed. For a garden fête. That's all.

Pause.

Sally So you do want me to change?

Trish (*snapping*) No, I don't want you to change. I don't care if you come dressed as a scuba diver. I'm going on down there. Are you coming?

Sally I'm coming.

Trish hesitates.

Trish You are coming? Promise me.

Sally *Yes.*

Gavin We'll be down. Promise.

Trish looks at them both anxiously. She can think of no further reason to stay.

Trish (*anxiously*) Right.

Trish goes. A big clap of thunder.

Gavin That doesn't sound so good . . .

Sally What were you both talking about just then? Me, I bet.

Gavin No.

Sally Bet you were.

Gavin Actually, we were talking about your mother. Chiefly.

Sally Oh. I see. I go upstairs for five minutes and you start chatting her up as well.

Gavin Is that what I've been doing? Chatting you up?

Sally Yes. Weren't you?

Before he can reply, the terrace becomes filled with people. Trish, Barry, Izzie, Jake and a group of children. Also Lindy, Barry's wife, dogsbody and occasional scapegoat.

Trish Well, that was short and sweet. It's absolutely bucketing down. Come in everyone. Come along in . . .

Lindy I think the children had better stay out here, Patricia, under the awning. They're all drenched. They'd wreck your lovely room.

Trish OK. Just as you like. I'll organise some tea and juice and things – Izzie, could you mastermind that?

Jake walks into the room but stops when he sees Gavin and Sally.

Jake (*coolly*) Hallo.

Sally (*likewise*) Hallo.

Gavin Hi, Jake.

In a second, Jake wanders back on to the terrace, where Barry seems to be entertaining the children with a game of I-spy, then a sing-song.

Izzie (*looking around, suspiciously*) Where is she? Where's she got to?

Trish Who's that?

Izzie Pearl. The Jezebel's still out there with him. I warned 'em, I warned 'em! (*Izzie goes out through the French windows, and off into the garden, pushing through the others*)

Trish Izzie, you'll get soak— Oh, for goodness sake . . .

Pearl comes in from the hall with her camera.

Pearl What's happened? Rained off, is it?

Trish Oh, Pearl, there you are. What are you doing?

Pearl Just fetching my camera . . . Not much use now, is it?

Trish Izzie just went out looking for you. She seemed rather agitated.

Pearl (*in sudden alarm*) Oh, my God. He better be all right. If she lays a finger on him, I'll murder her . . . (*Pearl rushes out on to the terrace and follows Izzie off*)

Trish Lord . . .

Gavin A crisis?

Trish Heaven knows.

Sally There's always a crisis with those three . . .

Lindy comes into the room cautiously.

Lindy Can I be of any help at all, Patricia? If you're making tea?

Trish Thank you, Lindy. Since the entire domestic staff seem to be having some sort of drama in the rain, that would be much appreciated.

Lindy Always happy to do something . . . (*She sniffs*)

Trish You OK?

Lindy Yes. Just one of those days, you know. You get them, don't you? When you just can't seem to do anything right?

Trish Oh, dear. Yes, I get those frequently. Come and tell me about it.

Fran (*through the doorway, to Trish*) Any idea where your husband and Lucille went?

525

Trish (*sweetly*) None at all, I'm afraid. Haven't seen him all day.

Fran (*muttering*) Oh, bloody film stars . . .

Lindy and Trish go off to the kitchen. Fran goes off into the garden, braving the rain.

Barry (*from the terrace*) I think there'll be a rainbow in a minute, children . . .

Sally Do you mind if I close these doors? It's a bit draughty.

Sally does so. The next is played quite lightly. Two people playing games on the edge of a cliff. Softly, led by Barry, the children sing 'Jesus bids us shine' under the next.

So you deny you were chatting me up, do you?

Gavin I didn't deny it.

Sally (*self-consciously casual*) So what are you going to do about it?

Gavin What do you suggest I do?

Sally I don't know. We could go upstairs, I suppose.

Gavin (*smiling*) Risky. Your mother only downstairs. What would she think?

Sally She wouldn't care.

Gavin Don't you believe it.

Sally We could go out somewhere. For a drive. In your lovely smart car.

Gavin You'd like that?

Sally Love it. I love fast cars. And perhaps – we could stop somewhere . . .

Gavin . . . for dinner . . .

Sally . . . at some smart hotel . . .

Gavin . . . five star . . .

Sally . . . and we could sniff some more wine together . . .

Gavin . . . just a little . . .

Sally . . . and then – who knows?

Gavin We could go upstairs to our huge double room . . .

Sally . . . four poster bed . . .

Gavin . . . at least . . .

Sally . . . and then we'd . . .

Gavin . . . undress each other . . .

Sally . . . if you like . . .

Gavin . . . and we'd indulge in sheer shameless hedonistic pleasure . . .

Sally Sheer shameless hedonistic pleasure, I like that. And what would that be for you? What's your idea of shameless hedonistic pleasure? What would I have to do to please you?

Gavin Me? Oh, I've very simple tastes.

Sally What? Tell me. Come on. You're not going to shock me, you know. Go on. You're not, you know.

Gavin All right. Well, we'd go into the bathroom where I'd run you a deep, piping hot bath, scented with an exotic bath essence, courtesy of Crabtree and Evelyn.

Sally Sounds nice.

Gavin And you'd lie in that bath until you were pink and glowing all over. Then you'd get out and I'd ever so gently pat you dry with a big soft, pure white towel. With me so far?

527

Sally Sure.

Gavin And then you'd get dressed again.

Sally I would?

Gavin Only this time in your school uniform. The one you were wearing today when I first saw you . . .

Sally (*startled*) My school uniform . . .?

Gavin (*leaning in close to her*) And then you'd get under the shower and turn it to the coldest setting until you were soaked to the skin and shivering . . .

Sally (*somewhat bemused*) What?

Gavin And then I'd hand you the Gideon Bible and you'd go outside, still wet through, into the hall, closing the door behind you; you'd count to ten and then ring the bell. And when I opened it, you'd say, good evening sir, I bring good news of mankind's salvation, are you by any chance a sinner? And I'd say, yes my dear, I fear that I am, but I am certain I can be saved. Please come inside and allow me to offer you dry clothes for I see you are drenched through. And I'd lead you into the bedroom, remove your nasty wet uniform, put you over my knee and spank you soundly with your own Bible for being a bumptious, flirtatious, precocious, conceited, smug little prick-teaser.

Sally (*completely shattered*) Oh. (*Suddenly feeling a bit sick*) I – Oh.

> *Sally rushes off through the hall door. She nearly collides with first Trish, then Lindy. Trish is carrying a plate of biscuits, Lindy has a tray of orange juice and mugs of tea.*
> *Simultaneously, Jake who has been watching the exchange between Sally and Gavin through the terrace*

windows, comes through the French doors, closing them behind him, and glares at Gavin. Gavin shrugs and smiles.

Trish (*as Sally goes off*) Sally . . .?

Lindy Whoops!

Trish (*to Gavin*) What's going on? Why did she rush off like that?

Gavin I've no idea. At that age . . . you know. Over-excitement perhaps?

Jake crosses swiftly and goes off into the hall after Sally. The rain has now stopped and people are leaving the shelter of the terrace.

Trish Jake? What's got into everyone suddenly?

Gavin (*seeing the biscuits*) Oh, may I? These look delicious.

Trish They're meant for the kids. (*Going back into the hall, calling*) Sally . . . Sally . . .

Trish goes out. Lindy meanwhile has reached the French windows with the tray, in time to see everyone leaving. She calls to Barry, the last to leave.

Lindy Would you open the door, please, dear?

Barry (*without opening the doors*) What's that?

Lindy Brought the tea and the orange juice for you all . . .

Barry Too late now.

Lindy Oh.

Barry Need you back there. Come on. Hurry up! Hurry up!

Barry hurries off to the garden.

Lindy (*sadly*) Take them back, I suppose. (*She starts on her way back*)

Gavin (*as she passes, taking an orange juice*) Thank you.

Lindy That's for the children.

Gavin (*taking a sip*) Delicious.

> *Lindy goes out by the hall door.*
> *Gavin drains his glass.*
> *He moves to the French windows as if to go out.*
> *Jake returns from the hall.*

Jake (*in quiet anger*) Excuse me.

Gavin (*pleasantly*) Jake?

Jake I'd like a – like a – like a word, please.

Gavin It is Jake, isn't it? I used to have a dog called Jake, you know.

Jake What did you say to Sally just now? What did you say to her?

Gavin Cocker spaniel. Had to have him put down. Broke my heart.

Jake Just now. When you were in here together. I was watching through the – through the window. She was extremely upset. She's just run out of the front door.

Gavin Oh dear, has she? Well, I've no idea what can have upset her.

> *Lindy re-enters from the hall.*

Jake You know bloody well . . .

> *He stops as he sees Lindy. Lindy, realising she has interrupted something rather tense, tiptoes past them self-consciously.*

Lindy (*quietly*) Excuse me.

Lindy goes out through the French windows. Gavin makes as if to follow. Jake crosses to him and makes to block Gavin's path.

Jake Just a minute! I want to know what – know what – know what – upset Sally.

Gavin Perhaps you should ask her, old boy.

Jake I just tried. She was so up— so up— so upset she wouldn't even speak to me.

Gavin I'm afraid that's your problem . . .

Jake Oh, no . . .

Gavin . . . if she won't even speak to you . . .

Jake This is our problem. Yours and – yours and – yours and mine.

Gavin Oh, come now. Stop behaving like a schoolboy.

Jake stands confronting him.

Out of my way.

Jake Not till we've talked about it. I want to know what happened.

Gavin Out of my way, please. (*He tries to move past Jake but his path is blocked*) Come along, now. Don't let it get silly . . . (*He tries to get past again*) I'll only ask you once more, Jake.

He tries to move past rather more forcefully. Jake pushes him back.

Now, you're starting to annoy me . . .

Jake Good.

Gavin Get out of my way, please.

He tries again. Jake repeats the push. Gavin moves with great speed, flooring Jake with a sharp punch in the face. Jake sits heavily on the floor, startled rather than badly hurt.

Now I did ask you nicely. I wouldn't get up again, if I were you. Next time I really will hurt you, old boy.

Gavin strolls out and goes off into the garden. Jake sits on the floor examining his face gingerly.

Jake Ow.

Trish returns.

Trish Well, I don't know what's got into her, she's nowhere in the house, she's not in her room – Jake, what on earth are you doing now?

Jake (*lamely*) I – er – I fell – I fell – I fell – slipped –

Trish Oh, dear. You all right?

Jake Yes, I – Yes. (*Indicating he should leave*) I'll –

Trish Sit down for a minute, Jake.

Jake I really ought to – ought to –

Trish Please. Just for a minute.

Jake does so. Trish follows suit.

What really happened?

Jake He – he ups— upset Sally.

Trish Gavin? Yes, I saw he had.

Jake I – tackled him about it. That's all.

Trish Well, that was brave of you, Jake, but actually extremely foolhardy. People like Gavin are quite dangerous. I was trying to think what it was about him, earlier. I couldn't put my finger on it at first. What it is

532

about him, of course, is that he's completely – devoid of real feeling. No genuine emotion, not even sexual. He's not a fox, I was wrong. He's more a lizard. So nothing really can reach him. Which is what makes him dangerous because people like that can so easily manipulate the rest of us, who do feel, who do care. You see?

Jake What was he doing with Sally, then? If he wasn't –

Trish He was playing a nasty little game with her that's all, Jake. Nothing to worry about. Hopefully all that's been hurt is her pride. You'll need to be specially nice to her for a day or two, that's all.

Jake If I can get close enough.

Trish Oh, don't worry . . .

Jake She seems to want to push me away half the time. Just ignores me. Then other times . . .

Trish Oh, well, that's all part of it, isn't it? This ridiculous dance we all do – if we're not born Gavin Ryng-Maynes, that is. You know, the other evening I was out there in the garden watching the village children with Joanna – with your mother – rehearsing their Maypole dance. There they were, all clinging to their coloured ribbons as if their lives depended on it. Well, judging from Joanna's tone of voice they probably did. And I thought, that's how it is for all of us, really. When we're young we're each given a ribbon – we're desperate for a ribbon – any ribbon – to cling on to – and once we have our ribbon we're taught the dance. And from then on, for the rest of our lives, we obediently move round and round our Maypole, observing respective little set patterns, weaving in and out, keeping our distances, careful never to step on each other's toes . . . Clinging on to our ribbon, terrified of deviating in case we get hurt or lost or rejected. But the older we get, despite all our efforts, the more we get entangled with other people. Yet never for a minute do most of us ever dream of doing the obvious and just letting go. We're terrified. The hardest thing believe me sometimes, Jake, is never to take hold of a ribbon, never to join the bloody dance in the first place; but actually stand still and say to someone, I love you. And mean it. You'd think it would be so simple, wouldn't you?

Jake Do you think she loves me?

Trish I'd have thought so, wouldn't you? You don't go to all that trouble for someone you don't like. You don't bother to dance at all.

Jake If only she'd say . . .

Trish Well, to be fair. Have you ever said it to her?

Jake What, 'I love you'?

Trish Have you? In so many words?

Jake Well, I've – I think I've – shown it – in the way I've –

Trish Takes two, Jake. Go on. Give it a try sometime. What's the worst she can she say? Too bad, buster.

Jake That's what I'm afraid of . . .

Trish (*getting up, smiling*) Garn! Plenty more girls, aren't there? Gorgeous bloke like you . . .

She turns to go back through the hall door. Pearl is suddenly standing there, breathing hard and somewhat déshabillé in her fortune-teller's outfit.

Pearl . . .

Pearl Sssshhh! She's after me.

Trish Oh, God. Now what? Who's after you, Pearl?

Pearl Her. She said she'd get us and now she's out to get me . . .

Trish Pearl, for goodness sake. Who is out to get you? If you'd only –

Izzie appears in the front windows. She is holding a very large carving knife. Pearl screams.

(*Seeing her*) – Oh, dear God!

Pearl (*with a scream*) No!!! (*She rushes into the dining room and closes the doors behind her*)

Trish Pearl! Izzie, what are you doing?

Izzie I just want to talk to her, that's all, Patricia. I just want to talk –

Trish Well, why have you got the knife, Izzie? Do you need the knife to talk to Pearl?

Izzie I cut 'em. I cut 'em, you see.

Trish You cut them. Who did you cut?

Izzie I cut the guys. I cut right through the guys.

Jake Which guys?

Trish Which guys, Izzie? Who are we talking about?

Izzie I didn't mean to cut their guys. I thought it were them two. That's why I cut the guys. I thought it were them there.

Trish Izzie, just give me the knife, please.

Trish moves forward and holds out her hand. Izzie draws back and waves the blade threateningly.

Izzie No!

Trish Izzie! (*To Jake*) Warn. We need Warn, Jake. Can you fetch him here? He may be able to sort this out . . .

Jake Will you be all right?

Trish Just find Warn . . .

Jake Unless she's killed him . . .

Trish Oh, God, I hadn't thought of that. Izzie, you haven't killed Warn, have you? You haven't hurt Warn? God, we'd never find another gardener.

Izzie I didn't mean to hurt no one. I just cut the guys.

Jake Who's she talking about?

Trish I don't know who she's talking about. Off you go. Quick as you can . . .

Jake dashes out of the French windows.

Izzie would you please put down the knife. Then we can talk properly. I'm going to bring Pearl out here, then we can talk about it sensibly. There's no need for knives. There's never any need for knives. (*Knocking on the dining-room doors*) Pearl . . . Pearl . . .

Pearl (*muffled, from within*) Don't let her in here . . .

Trish Pearl, stand away from this door. I'm coming in.

Pearl (*within*) She's not coming in here, she's not –

Trish It's only me. I'm coming in.

Trish opens the door. A plate is hurled and smashes against the dining-room wall – some distance from Trish but still close enough to cause her to close the door sharply.

Dear God! It's getting like a war zone.

Muffled muttering from Pearl.

Pearl, please don't do that. That is not helping.

More muffled muttering from Pearl.

If you do that again, I shall dock it from your money.
Now, I'm coming in, Pearl . . .

*Trish opens the door a fraction. Another plate
smashes.*

Oh, Lord. Izzie, can't you do something?

Further muffled muttering from Pearl.

Pearl, if you want to throw plates, can you throw the
service with the gold rim. You've already broken so
many of those it doesn't matter. But not the Crown
Derby, please.

Pearl mutters some more.

(*In despair*) I don't know what to do. I really don't
know what to do. I think I'm just going to go to bed.

Pearl continues to mutter.

(*Angrily*) Pearl! I am fast losing patience. Pearl! (*She
thumps on the door*)

Another smash.

That was. That was the Crown Derby. I recognised it.

*Warn, the gardener, appears at the French windows
with Jake following. He is probably in his late fifties
or early sixties but he is not a man whose age it is
easy to assess.*

Trish Oh, Warn, thank heavens . . .

Jake He was already on his way . . .

Trish Warn, can you possibly sort this out?

Warn (*walking briskly into the room, to Izzie*) Give that
to me. Cut yourself.

Izzie hands the knife over without a murmur.

(*Indicating the dining room*) In there?

Trish Yes.

Warn (*shouting through the door*) Pearl! (*Silence*) Pearl! (*Silence*) Pearl!

Pearl (*at last, from within*) Who is it?

Warn Who d'you think? It's Warn.

Silence from within.

Pearl! D'you hear me? Come on out, now. It's Warn.

Silence.

Come on then, girl! Come on. It's . . . It's . . .

He looks at Izzie. She nods encouragingly.

(*With great difficulty*) It's . . . Dad. It's your dad.

Izzie (*softly*) Oh, Warn!

A slight pause. The dining-room door slowly opens. Pearl appears.

Pearl (*tentatively*) Dad? Dad?

Warn Come on. Go home now.

He puts an arm round her. They move towards the French windows. Izzie rushes to join them.

Izzie (*letting it all spill out*) He never would before, you see, he never would. I said to him when I moved in, I said, now it's got to be different, you see, with me being her mum, that would make you like her dad. It don't matter what he was before, he has to be her dad, now her mum's moved in, don't he? 'Sides, Pearl needed a dad more than anything, 'cause she didn't have one not originally, 'cause he pissed off, the bugger, and I never saw him not after that one night and a girl needs a dad, she needs someone to clip her round the ear, but Warn never would, you see, 'cause he thought it were wrong but it can't never be wrong for a girl to have a dad, can it? But now it's going to be all right, you see? It's all worked out now and we're all proper and circumcised at last.

Izzie, Pearl and Warn go out into the garden.

Trish I can't pretend to understand what that was about.

Jake shrugs.

As I was saying. Love is essentially a very simple business. But in the hands of human beings it often becomes monstrously complicated.

Teddy and Lucille arrive at the French windows. They are both extremely bedraggled and wet and muddy. She has no shoes. He has no shoes, socks or trousers. Trish and Jake stare at them.

Teddy 'Fraid we both got caught in the rain . . .

Trish goes out through the hall door slamming it behind her.

Still not bloody talking to me, is she?

*The lights fade to:
Blackout.*

SCENE TWO

Saturday, August 14th, 5.00 p.m.
Gavin is standing by the windows. Teddy comes in from the hall. He has now changed and smartened up a bit.

Teddy Ah, here you are . . .

Gavin Teddy, I'm just off – I've said goodbye to Trish – I just wanted to thank you for a fabulous day. Thoroughly enjoyable.

Teddy Yes? Oh, good . . .

Gavin I do envy you all this. I mean, stuck in the smoke there, you really forget what real life's about, don't you? I do hope you'll ask me down again some time . . .

Teddy Yes, of course. Always welcome.

Gavin Will you say goodbye to Sally for me? I'm afraid I've managed to miss her . . .

Teddy Yes, I'll say –

Gavin Lovely girl, Teddy. You must be very proud. Bright as a button, isn't she? Good brain on her.

Teddy Yes, well, I don't know where that comes from, I'm sure . . . (*He laughs*)

Gavin No, seriously, Teddy. Credit to you both. It says a great deal for the future of this country if we've got young people like that in the pipeline.

Teddy Yes. Yes. True.

    A brief silence.

Gavin (*making to leave*) Well . . .

Teddy Er . . . I'm taking it the – offer of – of political candidacy is not currently still on the cards . . .

Gavin Well . . .

Teddy No, no, no. Just wanted to clear it up . . .

Gavin You know, Teddy, seeing you here – amongst all this – the social life, the family – the commitment you have to the local people – the irons in the fire – so many fish to fry – I just don't think you'd have time for it all, Teddy. With the best will in the world. I mean, these days an MP's job – nose to the grindstone, Teddy – and, let's face it, desperately single-track stuff . . .

Teddy Yes, yes, yes . . .

Gavin I mean, if I was to sum you up – which I shall be doing, incidentally, to the PM when I see him – I'd be tempted to describe you as a good old-fashioned Renaissance man, Teddy . . .

Teddy Would you? Would you?

Gavin And, God bless you, I wish there were more of you. Bloody specialisation, be the death of us all . . .

Teddy That's always been my view . . .

Gavin So. Short answer. Don't expect the call but not to worry. I'll explain to the PM your reasons for turning it down and as you know, he's nothing if not reasonable. I know he'll be absolutely flat-batted, but I'm certain he'll understand. OK? Must dash. Don't see me off, please. I know you have masses to do. Take care, old boy, wonderful to see you. I'll be in touch very soon. Bye.

Teddy Bye.

Gavin (*as he goes*) Incidentally, terrific wine, too. (*He goes off into the garden*)

Teddy Ah, well. Can't win 'em all, I suppose . . .

He is about to go into the dining room when Fran comes in from the hall.

Fran She's just about ready now. I'm going to fetch the car. I'll bring it round to the front, all right?

Teddy No, don't bother, I'll walk Lucille down – I'll walk down with her through the garden.

Fran Sure?

Teddy Say goodbye properly.

Fran Well, don't take any more detours, will you? I have to deliver her to that place and then get back to London tonight.

Teddy How long is she likely to be there, do you know?

Fran No idea. A week or so. Why?

Teddy I just thought I might visit her. Must get a bit dull in those places.

Fran Suit yourself. Do us a favour, just take her a bunch of flowers if you do.

Fran goes off into the garden.
Teddy goes into the dining room. Trish comes in from the hall. She looks for Teddy, sees he is in the dining room and goes and sits in a chair in the sitting room and waits. Teddy comes out of the dining room. He has a large whisky. He sees Trish but, accustomed to her silence, chooses to ignore her. He sits in another chair and sips his whisky. Silence.

Trish (*quite suddenly*) Teddy . . .

Teddy (*whisky slopping all over him*) Oh, my God! Would you kindly not do that?

Trish Sorry. I have something to say to you, Teddy.

Teddy Oh well, super. Three weeks of total silence and suddenly we're going to get a speech, are we?

Trish Teddy . . .

Teddy Whoopee! I can't wait.

Trish Teddy . . .

Teddy Hang on a tick, I'll get the cassette recorder, just in case it's the last words you ever say to me. Like a permanent record, you know. Just for the family archives. These are the wife's last words. Thought you'd like to hear them.

Trish Teddy! These may well be my last words. To you.
They might well.

Teddy (*a little startled*) What? You haven't – er . . . You
haven't done anything stupid, have you?

Trish Like what?

Teddy I don't know. You haven't taken poison or
something?

Trish No, of course I haven't. If I was going to poison
anyone, it would be you.

Teddy (*laughs, then*) You haven't, have you?

Trish Teddy. The point is, I'm leaving. I've tried to avoid
this. It's against everything I stand for. Desertion. Walking
off a sink – But I can feel it, Teddy. The curse of the Platt
women. It's there, breathing heavily. Just behind me. I
have to go. I'm sorry. I've discussed this with Sally, don't
worry, and she fully understands. She said if it wasn't for
her A-levels she'd come with me. So you won't be
entirely abandoned. You'll also have Izzie and you'll
have Pearl, God help you . . . You'll have masses of
people to look after you, so don't worry . . .

Teddy Just no wife . . .?

Trish You haven't had a wife for ages, Teddy, what are
you talking about? More important, with me out of the
way, you can get a clear run of the field. You can have
the entire village. Droit de seigneur. Whatever you fancy,
be my guest.

Teddy I see.

Trish That's all I wanted to say. So – cheerio, really. I
wish I could say it's been fun but these last few years
have been utter hell. I don't know how I've put up with
it for as long as I have, actually. (*She rises*)

543

Teddy Come on, we've had a few laughs.

Trish Teddy, we haven't even *smiled*. Not for years. Still, no hard feelings –

Trish kisses Teddy lightly on the head.

God, you reek of whisky – I'll leave this evening. I'll take the little car. I can never park the Jag . . .

Teddy Where are you going?

Trish What's it matter?

Lucille comes in from the hall. She has also tidied up a bit since we last saw her and has changed her dress for one of Trish's.

* **Lucille** Eh voilà . . . C'est pas mal? (*She twirls*)

Trish Oh, ça vous va bien. Ça vous va mieux qu'à moi.

Lucille Je vous la renverrai par la poste.

Trish Ce n'ai pas la peine. Je n'en aurai plus besoin où je vais . . .

Lucille Vous allez où?

Trish Je quitte mon mari. Je vais habiter à Londres.

Teddy (*muttering*) Nyong, nyong, nyong, nyong, nyong . . .

Lucille À Londres? Vous avez un amant là-bas?

---

* **Lucille** Here I am at last . . . Does it look all right? (*She twirls*)

Trish Oh, that suits you. Looks better than it does on me.

Lucille I'll post it back to you.

Trish Oh, there's no need. I shan't need it again where I'm going . . .

Lucille Where are you going?

Trish I'm leaving my husband. I'm going to live in London.

Teddy (*muttering*) Nyong, nyong, nyong, nyong, nyong . . .

Lucille London? You've got a lover there?

* **Trish** Non, seulement une soeur.

Lucille Oh, pauvre Teddy . . .

Trish Oui, pauvre Teddy. Vous pourriez peut-être passer un jour pour lui remonter le moral.

Lucille D'accord, à mon retour de la clinique. Dites-lui que je m'arrêterai pour prendre un verre avec lui . . .

Teddy Is anyone allowed in on this bloody conversation or have I got to wait for the subtitles . . .?

Trish Lucille says, poor old you and she'll look in on her way back from her clinic and have a drink with you.

Teddy Jolly good.

† **Lucille** (*kissing Trish extravagantly*) Au revoir, Trish. Et bonne chance dans votre nouvelle vie . . .

Trish Merci . . . Teddy va vous accompagner à votre voiture . . .

Lucille Ah, Teddy . . .

Teddy I'll see you to your car. I'm seeing her to her car. You'll be here when I get back?

Trish Possibly.

Teddy No, hang on. We need to talk about this some more, Trish . . .

---

* **Trish** No, no. Just a sister.

Lucille Oh, poor Teddy . . .

Trish Yes, poor Teddy. Maybe you can look in and cheer him up.

Lucille I will. On my way back from the clinic. Tell him I'll stop by and have a drink with him . . .

† **Lucille** (*kissing Trish extravagantly*) Goodbye, Trish. Good luck in your new life . . .

Trish Thank you . . . Teddy will see you to your car . . .

Trish Not really, we don't.

Teddy I also need to know where everything's kept. No, don't go. For God's sake, don't go till I come back . . .

Lucille (*on the terrace*) Au revoir . . .

Trish Au revoir . . .

Teddy and Lucille go off to the garden.

(*To the picture*) No, sorry, Cat, this one's breaking with tradition, I'm afraid. She's getting out while she can still walk.

She goes to leave and nearly collides with Sally, who is in her dressing gown and looking very mournful.

Oh. Nice bath?

Sally nods.

Aren't you getting dressed again?

Sally shakes her head.

Bit early for bed, isn't it? Not even six o'clock.

Sally sits, gloomily.

Don't you want me to go, now? An hour ago you told me I should.

Sally (*muttering*) I don't care.

Trish Well, thank you. It doesn't matter one way or the other, I take it?

Sally Nothing I say's going to make any difference anyway, is it?

Trish Yes, it is. Of course it is. Do you want me to go or not?

Sally Yes. I don't want you to go but I think you should go. For your sake.

Trish You can come and see me in London. At Kirsty's. You're always looking for excuses to come to London, aren't you? You are. Oh, don't make this more difficult for me than it is already, Sally. Please.

Sally I don't think I want to go to London any more.

Trish Why not?

Sally I don't belong in London. I belong down here. I'm an ignorant, bumptious, stupid country lump. Like everyone else.

Trish Oh, for God's sake. What are you talking about, stupid? At school you're streets ahead of anyone, you're captain of this and head of that –

Sally I'm a tiny little fish in a minuscule puddle, that's all –

Trish Oh, I'm not talking to you when you're like this. Everything I say is wrong.

Sally Well, it's true, isn't it?

Trish (*angrily*) It is not true. And what's more, if you listened to yourself, you'd realise what an arrogant thing that is to say. Because it implies that everyone other than you is *incredibly* stupid. And if that is genuinely what you believe, Sally, then I promise you, you are in for a very rough ride indeed. Because although you are extremely bright and I'm terribly proud of you, as you go on you are going to meet lots and lots of people who are equally as bright as you and some, dare I say it, who are even brighter. And if you continue to look down your nose at the rest of the human race and don't show it a little more respect then all I can say is you're in for one hell of a life, darling. Now, please excuse me, I'm going to pack a suitcase.

Trish stamps out. Sally sits unhappily. In a moment she starts to cry. Jake comes on to the terrace with his briefcase. He stops when he sees Sally, considers what to do, then goes off again and comes back whistling noisily. Sally hastily pulls herself together.

Jake Hi.

Sally Hallo. You're very cheerful.

Jake Yes. Sorry.

A silence.

You're very gloomy.

Sally What do you want?

Jake I – er – I came to apologise, really.

Sally What for?

Jake This morning. In the garden. I read your private poem and I shouldn't have done, I'm just very sorry. You had every right to be angry with me.

Sally I was angry because you'd obviously been through my briefcase, that's all.

Jake Well, actually, I hadn't, but I can understand that you might think I had. So – anyway – here to make amends – (*He hold out his briefcase*)

Sally What's this?

Jake My briefcase. I brought it so you could go through my briefcase.

Sally (*smiling, despite herself*) Really . . .

Jake Go on.

Sally No, I don't want to. Don't be silly.

Jake No, take it. Please. Please.

Sally takes the briefcase reluctantly.

Now open it. Go on. Snoop through everything, I don't mind . . .

Sally I'm really not –

Jake Please. Please.

Sally sighs and opens the briefcase. She stares at the contents, then lifts out a single red rose.

Sally What's this?

Jake It's for you.

Sally Thank you.

Jake I got it from the flower stall. At the fête.

Sally Yes. Thanks very much.

Jake Secondly . . .

Sally What?

Jake I think we should – we should – both go out somewhere tonight . . .

Sally No, Jake, honestly . . .

Jake . . . I don't care what we do, but I think we should go somewhere, the pub, the disco, a drive, a walk, it doesn't matter . . .

Sally . . . I don't think I could face . . .

Jake . . . because it's now half past five and, after all that's happened to us today, if you sit around here on your own till bedtime you're going to be suicidal. We both are. Let's face it.

Sally (*after a slight pause*) Yes, you're quite right.

Jake (*slightly surprised*) Good.

Sally (*getting up*) I'll get dressed. Come back in an hour for me.

Jake Right. Great.

Sally moves to the door. She has forgotten her rose.

Er – thirdly . . .

Sally What?

Jake Thirdly, I have something else to tell you.

Sally Yes?

Jake I – I – (*Giving up*) – I'll tell you later on.

Sally (*smiling*) All right. (*She goes out through the hall door*)

Jake (*furious with himself*) Why can't you say it, you pillock? I love you. That's all it is. I love you. I love you. I love you. I love –

Sally has come back. Jake breaks off embarrassed.

Sally Forgot my rose. (*She picks up the rose and makes to go out again*)

Jake I love you.

Sally What?

Jake I love you. I love you.

Sally I – I – (*Sally looks at him. She looks at her rose. She looks at Jake again. Today, it is all too much for her. She starts to cry and runs out through the door*)

Jake (*despairingly*) Now what did I do? I'll never understand women. I know I won't. I'll never understand them . . . never . . .

Jake goes out. Trish comes in through the dining-room doors with her suitcase.

Trish (*as she enters*) And another thing you – (*Seeing the empty room*) Oh. (*She stands for a moment, holding her case, looks around her. As if making her final decision. Decisively*) Yes. Yes. (*To the room, the portrait, the house in general, resignedly*) Ah, well. That's life, I suppose.

> *Trish goes out into the hall. In a moment the front door slams.*
> *The lights fade to:*
> *Blackout.*

GARDEN

Characters

Teddy Platt
a businessman

Trish Platt
his wife

Sally Platt
their daughter

Giles Mace
a doctor

Joanna Mace
his wife, a teacher

Jake Mace
their son, a student reporter

Gavin Ryng-Mayne
a novelist

Barry Love
a shopkeeper

Lindy Love
his wife, a shopkeeper

Lucille Cadeau
an actress

Fran Briggs
her driver

Warn Coucher
a gardener

Izzie Truce
a housekeeper

Pearl Truce
an occasional cleaner

Several children of about seven or eight years old

Scene
The lower meadow area of the garden.

Time
A Saturday in August between eight o'clock in the
morning and six in the evening.

Act One

Saturday, August 14th, 8.00 a.m.

Part of the garden of the house, known as the Lower Meadow. It is reached from the terrace at the back of the house via a more formal garden and then down a flight of stone steps.

The area is not quite as informal as perhaps its name suggests but merely the lower part of a much larger garden which has been allowed to grow wild. As a reminder of this, in the middle there is a murky-looking, overgrown stone pond with a central fountain which long ago ceased to function.

The remaining area is rather flat and uneventful, surrounded by bushes with the odd gap for a pathway. However, shortly, this is the place where the full paraphernalia of an English garden fête will be assembled and erected: trestle tables, tents, stalls, side-shows and roped-off areas intended for special displays including, in this case, children's Maypole and adult morris dancing.

It is long past dawn but the place still has an air of peace, not yet shattered by human intrusion. Birds are in full song. The sky is unsettled. Later, it could well rain.

In a moment, Joanna, a woman in her late thirties, tense and anxious and behaving decidedly suspiciously, enters. She looks nervously towards the house, hesitates and then, hearing someone coming, hurriedly hides in the bushes.

Joanna (*obviously finding this rather painful*) Aaah! Ooooh!

Warn, the gardener, enters along one of the paths with a barrow. He is probably in his late fifties or early

sixties but he is not a man whose age is easy to assess.
He stops, rests the barrow and stares at the sky.

(*Softly, from the depths of the bushes, in some discomfort*)
Ah! Ah!

Warn hears this and glances incuriously in Joanna's
direction. He is evidently well used to hearing strange
noises from bushes. He is about to set off again when
Izzie enters. She is a woman of about Warn's age
(*whatever that is*), *stern-faced and unsmiling.*
Someone who feels her lot to be less than a happy
one.

Izzie There you are, then.

Warn grunts.

(*Handing him a small Tupperware box*) Brought your
'levenses. You got 'em early. I'm busy today. Going to
rain, you reckon?

Warn looks at the sky and sucks his teeth.

Wash out the garden fête then, won't it? Shame that.
Rained last year, didn't it? Rains every year.

Warn reflects on this.

One thing. Keep her out of trouble anyway. I'm not
having it again this year, Warn. I'm not having it. She
monkeys about again in that little tent of hers, I warned
her. I won't be questionable . . . Fortune tellin' she calls
it. Fortune tellin'! Bloody Gypsy Rose with half her arse
showing.

Warn looks at the sky again.

Fortune's not in her face, wherever else. No, I won't have
it this year. I won't have it . . . She's a pyromaniac, that
girl. She needs a father, Warn, before she runs out of

control completely . . . Thirty years old next February.
Time she had a father.

Warn stares at the grass.

We got to do it right by her, Warn. What's past is past,
I'm telling you. No use crying over spilt milk, it's all
flowed under the bridge, now. You think about it.

Another little squeak from Joanna.

What's that, then? That them? Them, innit? What they
up to in there? Grown people in bushes. Patricia I feel
sorry for. She wouldn't be found dead in no bushes.
Trying to smile like it ain't happening. Whole village
knows, doesn't it? Not right for her. Admiral's daughter
she were. She were bred for better.

They think about this.

No, they're shameless, those two. Like rhinos in rut.
Teacher? She's more like a prostitute. Wouldn't have no
child of mine taught by her. Not that Pearl needs much
teaching. Well, I told her, she misbehaves today, she'll
feel my restitution, I'm warning her. I'll bring your lunch
down later, all right?

Izzie goes off. Warn looks after her for a second.

Warn (*tossing the sandwich box into his barrow,
muttering*) Bloody women.

*Warn goes off with his barrow. As he goes, the sound
of a large dog barking in the distance and the sound
of a man's voice.*

Teddy (*off*) SPOOF! Will you stop that racket at once!
Now, come on! Come on! Good boy! Come here, Spoof!
Fetch, Spoof! Fetch the stick, boy! Gooooood boy,
Spoof.

Renewed barking from Spoof.

Spoof, will you come back here at once, you bloody stupid animal. Right! That's it. I'm putting you down this time. That's your lot. This time I'm having you put down.

Teddy finally enters, a rather red-faced man in his forties. He is wearing old clothes and boots.

Spoof meantime, from his barking, appears to have made his way to the far side of Joanna's hiding place in the bushes.

Some low growling.

Spoof! Come on, boy. What you found, boy? You found a rabbit, boy?

More growling and a squeal from Joanna.

What the hell have you got in there?

Joanna comes out of the bushes, hurriedly.

Joanna (*to the dog in the bushes*) Get off! Get off me! (*Recovering*) My God, that bloody dog! Look what it's done to my trousers. Can't you control it at all, Teddy?

Teddy Your own fault, you shouldn't hide in bushes. He mistook you for wild life. He's a hunter. Those dogs were originally bred for hunting. Basic instinct. He scents something in a bush, he'll flush it out.

Joanna Lethal.

Teddy What were you doing in there, anyway?

Joanna Hiding.

Teddy Hiding?

Joanna From your gardener.

Teddy Warn? He wouldn't say anything.

Joanna He was with that housekeeper of yours.

Teddy Izzie. Ah, yes. You'd do well to avoid her. The other one's all right.

Joanna Pearl? Is he still living with both of them?

Teddy Apparently.

Joanna I can't believe it. Even in this village. Do they all . . . you know? In the same bed?

Teddy Don't ask me, I just pay him to dig. I don't enquire. I pay him to dig, her to housekeep and the daughter to meander round the house breaking things, as far as I can gather . . . (*Seeing someone approaching along one of the paths, softly*) Look out. (*Loudly*) No, these are *gregarius maximosa* with the bigger flowers but with the much smaller leaves . . .

Joanna (*loudly*) Oh, how interesting . . .

Jake, about nineteen years old, has entered. He is shy and slightly nervous. Seeing Teddy and Joanna, he smiles awkwardly.

Teddy (*to Jake*) Morning.

Joanna Hallo, Jake.

Jake (*embarrassed*) Hi, Mum.

Joanna I thought you were having a lie-in this morning?

Jake No, I have to – I have some things . . . You know.

Joanna Right. Mr – Teddy was just showing me these interesting shrubs.

Jake Oh, yes. Great. Right. Well. See you later.

Joanna Yes.

Teddy Cheerio, Jake.

Jake Dad's just . . . in the kitchen. Having breakfast.

Joanna Oh, good.

Jake goes off. They watch him go.

(*Quieter*) He definitely knows.

Teddy Well . . .

Joanna He does, he definitely does. Which means Sally must know.

Teddy Not necessarily.

Joanna Obviously. They're . . . good friends. Jake will have told Sally – assuming she doesn't already know anyway. And then Sally will have told her mother. She'll have told Trish . . .

Teddy Not necessarily . . .

Joanna Daughters always tell their mothers everything . . .

Teddy No, they don't . . .

Joanna I always tell my mother everything.

Teddy Have you told her about us?

Joanna No, don't be silly, of course I haven't.

Teddy There you are then.

Joanna The thought of Trish ever finding out . . . I couldn't face it. Giles doesn't know. I'm certain. But then he and Jake – all they ever talk about is football . . .

Teddy I'm glad about that. I mean, Giles and I, we go back a long – way. I think I'm practically his best friend, poor bloke . . .

Joanna (*keen to change the subject*) Well?

Teddy What?

Joanna You wanted to see me. Urgently, you said.

Teddy Yes. (*A sudden yell*) Spoof, you come off that! Off! Off! At once! You keep right away from there! Bad boy!

Joanna Shhh! Shhh!

Teddy Did you see that? He was trying to dig up that sapling. Most dogs are just content to pee on them. He has to dig the bloody things up first. (*To Spoof*) That's better. You sit there. Good boy. Yes, you eat that. (*To himself*) Whatever it is. Looks like someone's head.

Joanna I don't know how we can ever have secret meetings if you insist on bringing that dog along.

Teddy He's my alibi. Why else would I be wandering about at the crack of dawn? Anyway, he needs the exercise, poor bastard.

Joanna Wouldn't it be wonderful? Just once. To meet indoors. I just suddenly long for the great indoors for once. I mean, flat on my back in all these summerhouses and potting sheds and gazebos and ditches. God, how could I ever face Giles if he found out? You know I've loved every minute of it, of course I have, but wouldn't it be lovely, Teddy, just for once, to lie together in clean sheets? We're getting a bit old, aren't we? Well, I am. I'm beginning to feel the wear and tear a bit, that's all . . . My back's playing up again – and then, the other day, when that bloody dog jumped on us . . . I mean, let's face it – we're not teenagers any more, are we?

Teddy Well, that was what I was . . . Listen. I'm glad, in a way, that you've said all that because . . . Erm. This will probably come as a relief, in that case. Erm. I had it all worked out. Erm. I think it's got to stop.

Joanna Stop?

Teddy 'Fraid so.

Joanna What has?

Teddy Us.

Pause.

Joanna You're joking.

Teddy No, I'm –

Joanna You're ditching me?

Teddy Not really. I'm –

Joanna Just like that? I can't believe it. You're joking? Teddy, please tell me you're joking.

Teddy I'm sorry, from what you were just saying just now, I thought perhaps it might have been a relief . . .

Joanna What have I done? Is it me? Tell me what I've done.

Teddy You haven't done anything, Jo. It's not you. Not at all, it's not you. It's just – things are getting a bit out of hand.

Joanna With Trish? You mean with Trish?

Teddy Partly, but –

Joanna Sally has told her, I knew it. Trish does know.

Teddy No, she doesn't. I swear she doesn't. At least I don't think she does.

She is on the verge of breaking up.

Jo . . .

Joanna Listen, Teddy, I didn't mean all those things. I'm perfectly happy with sheds, I really am. I was only just saying that . . .

Teddy Jo, I – (*Yelling*) Spoof, will you put that down at once! (*Softly again, to her*) It's just that circumstances have altered, you see, Jo.

But Joanna is now a limp rag of misery.

Joanna Tell me what I have to do, Teddy. What I can do to get you back. I'll do anything. I'll change. Whatever you want . . .

Teddy No, no. Really, you don't want to do that. Don't change a hair. It's me. I'm just a bastard who's walking away. I'm not worthy of you, Jo. I'm a worthless womaniser. (*Getting quite angry with himself*) A selfish, egotistic, self-centred, licentious, egocentric bastard. God! Sometimes I get so filled with self-loathing . . .

Joanna Ssshhh. You're none of those things. You're a wonderful lover. I couldn't bear it if you stopped making love to me. You've brought me alive again, Teddy. I was dead. You've brought me back to life . . .

Teddy (*a trifle alarmed*) Don't talk like that, Jo. You make me sound like some bloody faith-healer. Forget all about me. Put me out of your mind, Jo, out of your life.

Joanna How can I?

Teddy It's the only way . . .

Joanna We're all supposed to be having lunch together today, anyway.

Teddy Oh God, are we?

Joanna It's the garden fête.

Teddy Oh, yes. Of course.

Joanna Maybe we could live like your gardener does? All together in the same house? You, me and Trish, all together . . .?

Teddy No, I don't honestly think that's a frightfully good idea, Jo.

Joanna I wouldn't mind. I've no pride.

Teddy No, but I don't think that sort of thing would be Trish's bag. Not at all. Listen, I've got to get back, Jo. I'm sorry.

Joanna (*in a tiny voice*) Will I see you tonight? Can we meet tonight?

Teddy (*gently*) Best not, Jo. Really. (*He takes her hand*) Really and truly.

Joanna removes her hand from his and gives a little whimper.

OK? Listen, I'm afraid I've got this meeting with . . . someone important. In a minute.

Joanna (*as small as can be*) Go. Go on, then.

Teddy See you . . . see you around. At lunchtime, I suppose. We'll both just have to put on a – brave face, won't we? Yes.

They stand for a second. She frozen in her misery; he with nothing more to say.

I really hate to leave you like this. (*Another pause*) Must get Warn to fix that fountain, you know. There's a blockage somewhere. That's all it is, I'm certain. I remember as a kid, it used to look quite spectacular . . . Yes. (*Suddenly yelling*) Spoof! Come on then, boy. Come on!

Barking from Spoof.

Biscuit! Let's go and get a biscuit! That's a good boy! Away you go!

Spoof's barking recedes rapidly.

And keep off that, you stupid dog. How many more times?

*Teddy goes off after Spoof, back towards the house.
Joanna left alone can contain it no longer. She lets out
a terrible wail of grief and sinks to her knees. In time,
Warn returns with his barrow, now empty. He passes
Joanna without appearing to notice her and goes off
again. She continues to cry. In a moment, Pearl enters.
She is as different from her mother, Izzie, as it is
possible to be. In her late twenties, lithe and attractive.
She carries a small container with another snack for
Warn.*

   *She stops when she sees Joanna, hesitates and then
comes and sits down near her. She says nothing for a
moment. Joanna notices her and then chooses to
ignore her.*

Pearl (*at length*) Be a feller then, will it?

Joanna looks at her.

Yes. It'll be a feller. The only bugger make you cry like
that'll be a feller.

   Pause. Pearl reflects.
   Joanna stares at her, rather startled.

No offence? Don't mind me saying, do you?

Joanna (*faintly*) No. Thank you.

Pearl Got a good bloke there. That one. Mind my
saying? (*Indicating towards Teddy and the house*) Not
him. T'other one. Your husband. You ought to try and
hang on to him. Good bloke, he is.

Joanna (*beginning to have heard enough*) Yes, thank
you.

Pearl Good doctor an' all. Some of 'em don't give a
stuff. But my friend's kid, he sat up all night with her.
Terrible fever. All night. Not many do that. Not on the
National bloody Health, they don't.

Warn enters. He has an oily rag and a dipstick in his hands.

Hallo, here he comes. Better give the bugger his elevenses, then. All else fails, feed 'em, eh? (*She laughs*) Eh? Eh?

Joanna smiles faintly.

There you are. Looking for you.

Warn (*to Joanna*) Be there long, are you?

Joanna Sorry? Oh. Do you want me to move? I'll move. Sorry.

Pearl Warn'll be wantin' to mow.

Joanna Yes, of course. Mow. You'll be wanting to mow, won't you? For this afternoon for the fête. I'll move, don't worry. I'll move . . .

Pearl 'Less you want to get mowed.

Joanna (*laughing feebly*) Yes.

Pearl Cheaper than waxing 'em. (*She laughs*) You all right, then?

Joanna Yes. Thank you. I'm fine. Yes. I know precisely what I have to do now. Precisely. Thank you. (*She starts to move off down one of the paths*)

As Joanna goes out, Giles, her husband, comes from that same direction in something of a hurry. He is a pleasant, affable if somewhat ineffectual man in his thirties.

Giles Hallo, darling. What are you doing here?

Joanna Nothing, I was just . . .

Giles You all right?

Joanna Fine.

Giles You look a bit . . .

Joanna No. (*She goes off*)

Giles (*to the others*) She gets this terrible hay-fever. My colleague prescribed these drops but she never takes them. (*He laughs*) Typical.

> *Warn and Pearl stare at him impassively.*
> *Giles gets a little embarrassed.*

Think it might hold off. The rain. Don't you? Hope so. (*He feels the ground*) Pretty firm. Pretty firm. Take a bit of spin. (*He laughs*) No, I was thinking underfoot. We've got the morris dancing team today. We're doing a little display. Usually quite popular. I think people enjoy it. I think they do. All part of our common cultural and social heritage. Unites us all in a funny way. Rich and poor, young and old. Great leveller, the dance. Don't you think?

Pearl Bit of a laugh.

Giles (*loath to argue*) Well . . . possibly, yes. Got the Maypole too, this year. Really branching out. That's my wife's project. Joanna's been rehearsing them for weeks. Some of her class, that is. I saw a rehearsal the other night. I think they've really got into the swing of it. Try and catch it, if you can. See what you think. I think you'll be impressed.

> *Pearl and Warn don't look greatly enthused.*

Well, must get on. (*As he goes*) Excuse me.

> *Giles has gone off towards the house. Warn belches.*

Pearl He's all right. Poor bloke. She don't know when she's well off. I'd have him. She don't want him, I'd take him off her hands. Bit borin' but not a bad looker. Being a doctor, could be useful, too. Like being married to a plumber. If you spring a leak, he'll fix it for you.

Warn is feeling the grass and looking at the sky again.

Here. Brought you your 'levenses. Busy today. Got all
them people coming to lunch. Doing me silver service.
I nearly got it off. 'Less we have sprouts. I'm all over the
place with bloody sprouts. I can do carrots. If they're cut
long, you know. And beans. I'm all right with beans now.
I've mastered beans. Runner beans. Not them broad
buggers, they're right bastards. I had 'em everywhere last
time. We were pickin' them up for months. I don't know
why they don't bung it all on the plate and have done
with it. Like normal people.

Warn is studying the fountain now.

Mum's on the warpath. Been on at me all day. We better
not do nothing this year, Warn. She'll be watching us.
She can get right barmy, you know that. Like when she
went at us with that hot iron, you remember. Bloody
lucky it were still plugged in, it could have killed us.
Remember? First time she caught us in bed together.
Remember? (*She laughs*) That was a laugh. Still, that
were before. It's different now. Circumstances have
changed. That's all I'm saying. Know what I mean?

Warn appears not to know or care.

I mean, I don't care. Don't matter to me. I never ask
anything of anyone. Liberty Hall, I am. But my mum,
she . . . Well, anyway. You suit yourself. Be nice to get it
settled though, wouldn't it? Get a bit of peace then. You
suit yourself, though. It's between you and Mum.
Nothing to do with me. I'm easy. I don't care. (*A silence.
She reckons she's pursued this tricky topic as much as
she can*) Bloody garden fetes, eh? Bet you're looking
forward to it, in't yer? In't yer? You love 'em, don't you?
Eh? Make your bloody year, don't they? All your lawns
churned up. People parking all over your verges. Bloody
pig got loose last year, remember? Dug up half the

bloody veg. I hope we have that army again, they're all right. Big lads shooting each other every which way. Nuclear war they'd be off like bloody rabbits, wouldn't they?

Warn sniffs noisily.

Got a film star today. French one. She were in a film. *The Unex— Unin— Uninspiring* . . . I don't know. I never seen it. She gets blown up early on. Deirdre told me. But she's good while she lasts. You ought to clean this pond out. It's disgustin'. Breeding ground for things is this. You want to get a stick and clean it out.

Sally and Jake appear, coming from the house. Sally is Trish and Teddy's only child. Seventeen and still at school, she is a serious, sometimes rather intense girl who has recently grown very concerned with Life and The World. She is wearing her school uniform and carries a briefcase.

Sally (*calling as they enter*) Pearl, Izzie's looking for you.

Pearl Oh, right, Sally. Thank you.

Sally It seems there's something you haven't yet done that you're supposed to have done . . .

Pearl Yes, I'll go and do it. Be my hooverin', I expect.

Pearl hurries back to the house.

Sally All right, Warn?

Warn grunts.

Ready for the invasion this afternoon? Don't blame me. Blame my mother.

Warn nods and goes off.

I always say there's nothing can set you up more for the day than a good conversation with Warn.

Jake They were standing just over there.

Sally I see.

Jake Quite close together. Pretending to look at the shrubbery. Your father was pretending to show my mother the shrubbery.

Sally Oh.

Jake He hadn't even bothered to learn the right names.

Sally Well. At least they were both standing up.

Jake (*gloomily*) Just.

Sally There's nothing we can do, Jake. I've said. If they don't want to talk about it, what can we do? I know what I'd like to do. Get them all together in one room, sit them down and say come on, you stupid lot, now sort yourselves out. But somehow I don't think that's going to happen because that's not the way they do things.

Jake I just hope my dad never finds out. He's such a – he's a really decent guy, you know, he really is. He's devoted to Mum, it would just – destroy him . . .

Sally Perhaps he's tougher than you think, Jake. People can surprise you sometimes.

Jake I still don't understand why Mum . . . I mean, no disrespect to your father, but . . .

Sally Say what you like about him, I don't care . . .

Jake My dad's so . . . he's got this incredible faith in people. He trusts. He's always determined to find the good side. You hear him reading the paper in the morning. (*In a fair impersonation of Giles*) 'Oh, I don't think this man really meant to cut his wife's throat, you know. He was probably showing her his new razor, that's all.' It's amazing in someone of his age, really.

Most people by then are – eaten up with mistrust and cynicism, aren't they? He's somehow survived all that.

Sally Must be nice to love your parents . . .

Jake Don't you love your mother?

Sally Sometimes. Sometimes she drives me up the wall. Like now. Why won't she talk about it? She knows. We all know she knows. Yet she behaves as if it isn't happening.

Jake Her way of coping.

Sally Well, maybe. But it's very tough on the rest of us. On me. (*After a slight pause*) Tell me, do you think I'm . . .?

Jake What?

Sally Nothing. Just something someone said.

Jake You're what?

Sally Selfish. Do you think I'm a selfish person?

Jake No.

Sally You don't think I take advantage of people? Use them?

Jake No, I don't think so. Not at all.

Sally No, I don't, either. It's rubbish, isn't it? Parents talk utter rubbish sometimes, don't they? They give birth to you and as you grow up they immediately start reading themselves into you – whether they're there or not. It starts innocently enough with innocuous physical features – oh, look, she's got my nose, isn't that sweet? – but it finishes up, oh, look, she's got all your megalomania, isn't that terrible? It's guilt, that's all. I am selfish therefore surely you must be selfish as well.

Jake Possibly.

Sally You got a lot on this morning?

Jake (*eagerly*) No, why?

Sally Good. Then you can wait for me at the school and bring me back if you like.

Jake (*unfazed*) Sure. I've got nothing till this afternoon. Till my interview with Madame Lucille Cadeau.

Sally Oh yes, of course. Ace Mace, Boy Reporter. Big deal.

Jake She's the best bit in the movie actually. It's a pity she gets blown up so early on . . .

Sally (*as they start to go*) Been dreaming about her, have you?

Jake No, of course not . . .

* **Sally** Je suis à vous pour toujours, mam'selle. Je vous aime. Prenez-moi, je suis à vous.

Jake Oh, Sally, knock it off . . .

Sally Embrassez-moi, mon amour. Prenez mon corps et faites-en ce que vous désirez. Je suis votre esclave pour toujours, ma chère Lucille, mon amour . . .

Jake Oh, Sally . . .

Sally Got your notebook?

Jake Yes.

Sally Inside your Ace Mace briefcase . . .?

---

* **Sally** I am yours for ever, mam'selle. I love you. Take me I am yours.

Jake Oh, Sally, knock it off . . .

Sally Kiss me, my love. Take my body and use it as you desire. I am your slave for ever, my dearest Lucille, my love . . .

Jake Give it a break. It's just till I go to college, that's all . . .

They have both gone. Their voices continue into the distance. Silence.
Somewhere nearby, a motor mower starts up, splutters briefly and dies.

Warn (*off*) Ah, you bugger!

Trish, a woman in her forties whose soft English beauty has only very faintly faded, comes on from the direction of the house. She is wearing her gardening gloves and carries some roses she has just cut with her secateurs.

Trish (*calling*) Warn, I've just taken some of these for the table, all right? (*She listens. To herself*) Yes? I think that sounds like a yes. Jolly good.

A guttural mumbling from Warn.
Another failed attempt to start the mower. Another muffled oath.

(*To herself*) Dear God. He'll rupture himself. We must get a new mower. Or a new gardener.

Joanna appears. She has changed her clothes, pulled herself together and now looks pale and determined. She stops as she sees Trish. She takes a deep breath.

Joanna Oh. Trish . . .

Trish turns and sees her for the first time.

Trish Jo. Hallo . . .

Joanna Trish . . .

Trish How are you today? Feeling any better?

Joanna Better?

Trish Yes, haven't you had terribly bad hay-fever? Someone was saying. Giles, probably.

Joanna Trish . . .

Trish I think it'll stay fine . . .

Joanna Trish.

Trish The forecast says rain . . .

Joanna I have something to say to you.

Trish . . . but then they're always getting it wrong, aren't they?

Joanna Patricia, please.

Trish Mmm?

Joanna I have something to say to you. To tell you. It is something I would give anything in the world not to have to tell you, I would cut off both my arms rather than tell you, but you need to be told. I can't live with myself for another minute unless I do tell you.

Trish Oh, dear.

Joanna Sit down.

They sit.

Yet now I've decided to tell you, I don't know quite how to put it into words . . .

Trish You and Teddy are fucking each other.

Joanna (*on the brink of tears*) Yes.

Trish There. That wasn't so difficult, was it?

The sound of the mower starting, spluttering, stopping again and Warn's muffled oath.

Joanna How did you know?

576

Trish (*impatiently*) Oh, come *on* . . . Credit me with some intelligence, Jo, for God's sake. Between you, you've flattened every bloody bush in the garden cavorting around . . .

Joanna (*starting to cry again*) That's not true . . .

Trish Every flower bed's imprinted with your wretched rear end. I don't mind, Jo, I really don't – not that it would make a blind bit of difference if I did mind – but, no, I don't give a tinsel fairy's fart what you do – but just don't come snivelling to me when Teddy decides to dump you, as he obviously has done. You want a shoulder to cry on, find someone else's. All right?

Joanna (*after a slight pause*) Do you really hate me, Trish?

Trish No. I don't hate you. Frankly, I think you're a very, very stupid woman, Jo, but then I've always thought that, even before all this.

Joanna I am, I am . . .

Trish God knows how you manage to teach anyone . . .

Joanna They're only five-year-olds . . .

Trish They've still got to be brighter than you. Oh, do blow your nose . . .

Joanna (*fumbling for her tissues*) What's going to happen?

Trish Well, you've had your romp. Now you have to face up to it all, don't you? That's how it works. You've told me. Now you'd better go and tell your husband.

Joanna (*horrified*) Giles? I couldn't tell Giles.

Trish Of course you must.

Joanna I couldn't, Trish, I just couldn't . . .

Trish Oh, Jo, for heaven's sake, woman . . .

Joanna You don't know him. It would kill him if he knew. He's the dearest, most trusting man in the world. He'd trust me with his life.

Trish Then he's an idiot as well, isn't he? All right, if you won't tell him, I will.

Joanna No! No!

Trish Someone's got to tell him, Joanna. Otherwise it's only going to be left for him to find out for himself. Accidentally. Probably in the village pub. And that is definitely not the way. That is no way to treat anyone. Giles is up at our house now. I'll send him down to you. Wait here.

Joanna (*drawing back*) I can't. I just can't. I'm sorry.

Trish You have to. It's the price you pay. Don't go away. See you at lunchtime. And I expect you there, Jo. You can wreck my marriage but I'll never forgive you if you ruin my luncheon party.

Trish marches off towards the house in determined fashion, still carrying her roses and secateurs. Joanna stares after her, dismayed.

Joanna (*feebly to Trish's retreating back*) Trish . . . Trish . . . Oh God!

The sound of the mower bursting into life again. Once again, it rapidly dies with a splutter.

Warn (*off, in a fury*) Bloody bastard bollocking bitch bugger . . .

Joanna stares, startled for a moment, then plunges back into her own welter of self-pity.

Joanna Giles . . . there's something you have to know . . . I've had this meaningless fling . . . it meant nothing . . . it was just . . . animal lust . . .

Warn has come stamping across.
Joanna attempts to cover the fact that she has been caught talking to herself by singing.

(*Lamely, for Warn's benefit*) Diddly-diddly-dee . . .

Warn ignores her, involved as he is in his own private battle, man and machine. He goes off.

(*Trying again*) It was just an affair. For God's sake, Giles. A silly old affair. What's so special about it . . .? (*Frustratedly*) Oh . . . (*She stares up at an overhanging tree branch. She takes off her scarf wondering if it's long enough to hang herself. It isn't. Trying again*) Giles, I've reached that stage in life when I'm at a crossroads . . . Teddy just happened to be the one who was standing by the signpost . . . it could have been anyone, Giles . . . it could have . . .

She breaks off again as Warn returns with an oil can. She smiles weakly at him. He ignores her.

(*Trying again when he's gone*) He swept me off my feet, Giles, I was particularly vulnerable. Unsure. A woman needs constant reassurance, Giles, you must understand that . . . She has to be told occasionally that she's still – desirable . . .

Warn's mower roars into life once more. This time, instead of dying, the engine catches and roars some more.

Warn (*off, in triumph*) Whey-hey! There you goes, you bugger!

Joanna is only dimly aware of this. She is now at the fountain. She steps on to the rim and gazes into the depths.

Joanna (*trying again*) I've been a complete and utter fool. Forgive me, my darling. If you want to hit me,

I'll quite understand . . . but what I need more than anything in the world is for you to take me in your arms and try and forgive . . . try and forgive your stupid, foolish wife . . . (*She is about to jump. She loses her balance and slips, one foot going into the water, then the other. She stands in about eight inches of water. Feeling somewhat foolish*) Oh.

Warn returns, punching the air briefly in triumph, and crosses the garden. He sees Joanna and looks at her sourly. Joanna, aware of him, laughs feebly. Warn goes.

(*Trying again, still standing in the water, in a baby voice*) Gilesy . . . Jo-Jo's been a silly girl . . . (*Joanna steps out of the pond in her sopping shoes, squelching slightly. She cries softly. She, too, starts up the terrace steps. As she does so, trying again*) Jake, I wonder if you could possibly pass on a message to your father . . .

She reaches the terrace and gazes over the upstage parapet, contemplating the drop. Below her, the unseen mower chugs merrily on.

(*Turning sharply away from the prospect and trying again*) Dear Giles, by the time you read this letter, I shall be far away. Don't try to find me, my darling . . . Oh, God.

She takes courage and climbs on to the parapet.
   Warn re-enters with a signpost reading TO THE HOME FARM. *He climbs the steps staring down at the lawn, inspecting it, and failing to notice Joanna. As he draws level with her, Joanna gives another little cry.*

Oh . . .

Warn turns slightly at the sound, inadvertently clipping Joanna with the end of the signpost and knocking her off the parapet.

(*As she falls*) Aaaaah!

A crash as she lands on the mower. The engine roars
briefly and dies with a final splutter.
   Silence. A plume of smoke rises above the parapet.
   Warn, incredulous and speechless, walks to the
parapet edge and looks over.
   From below, a moan from Joanna.
   Giles enters from the house.

Giles What is it? What's happening? Warn? What's
going on?

   Giles joins Warn and looks over the parapet.

(*Very alarmed*) Jo? Jo?

   Another groan from Joanna.

Are you all right? Warn, what happened to her?

Warn Bloody women! (*He sets off again with his*
signpost, furious)

Giles (*hurrying down the steps*) Wait there, darling!
Don't try and move! Don't try and move!

   Giles hurries down the steps.
   As he reaches the bottom, Joanna stumbles on,
battered, a little dazed and slightly oily.

(*Stopping and looking at her, incredulously*) Jo . . . Jo . . .?

Joanna (*faintly*) Giles . . .

Giles (*moving to her*) What happened, darling? What is
it? (*He makes to touch her*)

Joanna (*drawing back*) Nooo.

Giles What?

Joanna Don't touch me . . . don't touch me . . .

Giles What?

Joanna . . . you mustn't touch me!

Giles What is it?

Joanna Giles, I . . . Giles, I . . . I've . . . I've been hoping . . . I've been trying . . . I've been wanting . . . I've been so . . . I've been . . . I've been . . .

Giles (*gently*) You've been what? You've been what, darling?

Joanna (*after a deep breath*) I've been having an affair with Teddy.

Giles (*taking this in by degrees*) You've been . . .? You've been . . .? You've been . . . Teddy?

Joanna (*tiny*) Yes.

Giles quite suddenly lets out the most terrible drawn-out cry of despair and rushes off.

Giles (*as he goes*) Teddddddddyyyyyy!

Giles has gone.
Joanna walks a few paces as if to follow him. She stops. She is still in shock.

Joanna Oh.

Warn has entered with his sandwich box in one hand and the flattened grass bin from the mower in the other. He tosses the latter on to the ground disgustedly. He gives Joanna another glare. He then sits and starts to eat.
After a second, Joanna starts to totter off after Giles, whimpering softly as she does so, half in unhappiness, half in pain. Warn watches her till she goes.

Warn (*looking upwards at the sky*) Reckon we're in for a storm . . . the bugger.

As he sits there, chewing contentedly, the lights fade to:
Blackout.

SCENE TWO

Saturday, August 14th, 11.00 a.m.
The same. The grass, unsurprisingly, remains unmown.
It is still overcast. Pearl enters from the house. She has
another, slightly larger, sandwich box. She stops and
looks around.

Pearl (*calling*) Warn! Warn! Lunch! Where you hiding,
then?

Pearl goes off in search of Warn. As she does so, from
a different direction, Barry and Lindy Love enter.
They are in their thirties. He is undoubtedly the
driving force behind the fête. Lindy loyally serves as
his dogsbody and scapegoat. They stagger on, the first
of many journeys they will make, carrying equipment
for the forthcoming event – tents, bunting, ropes and
poles to form enclosures, produce, etc.

Barry (*as they enter*) . . . Right, that's it . . . come on,
come on . . . with me, with me, with me!

Lindy Yes, yes, yes . . .

Barry . . . and just here . . . one – two . . . huuup!

Lindy (*with him*) . . . huuup!

They set down their burden together, a well-rehearsed
team. They stand, catching their breath.

Whew! She's loaded down today, isn't she? She's loaded
down today is our Winnie . . .

Barry Certainly is. Right down on her axles. That's why I was driving so slowly . . .

Lindy Yes.

Barry Ready for the next?

Lindy So far so good with the weather.

Barry Thus far.

Lindy (*wagging her finger at the sky*) Don't you dare rain, do you hear me? Don't you dare!

> *Barry and Lindy go off.*
> *As they go, Warn has entered with a sign in one hand, inscribed* TO THE MAIN HOUSE.
> *He watches them with distaste.*
> *He glares at the small pile of gear on his grass.*
> *Pearl enters, still in search of him with her sandwich box.*

Pearl (*calling*) Oy!

> *Warn turns.*

There y'are. Brought your lunch.

> *Warn takes the box with a grunt.*

Is it you took down all them signs, then? It were, weren't it? It were you. You old bugger, you do it every year, don't you? Soon as the fête's here down come all the signs. Nobody can find their way in or out of the place. If I didn't know you better, Warn Coucher, I'd say you done that deliberate.

> *She examines the pile of stuff so far accumulated by Barry and Lindy.*

There's my little tent there. Look. You goin' to put it up for me? Well, long as someone does. I'll be laughing if it rains. Only one sittin' in the dry, won't I? I'll have queues round the block.

Warn is staring at the pile of stuff.

She's in a fury, my mum. Their dinner's spoilin' 'cause
half of them are late. Probably 'cause you uprooted all
the signs. They're all drivin' round the country looking
for the main gates, I bet. Anyway, her dinner's spoilin'.
She said by the time they arrive the beef will be indelible.
(*Laughing*) Indelible. Good one that. You get it?
Indelible. Piss ignorant old bag, isn't she? See you later.

> *Pearl goes back to the house.*
> *Warn glares after her.*
> *Sally enters along one of the paths. She is in a fury.*
> *She hurls her briefcase on to the ground ahead of her.*
> *Jake trails unhappily along behind.*
> *Sally stops. Jake stops, too. They stand in silence.*
> *Warn stares at them and then goes off.*

Sally (*at length*) No, I'm sorry. I just cannot believe it.

Jake Right.

Sally How people can be so *thick*, so *dim*, so *stupid*, so
short-sighted. It's unbelievable.

Jake Well . . .

Sally *Unbelievable.*

Jake I wasn't at the meeting, of course, but it certainly
sounds as if –

Sally Those are supposedly mature, intelligent sixth-
formers. The so-called cream of the school. God help
us all! If they're incapable of listening to a rational
proposal without screaming and banging tables –

Jake Some of them agreed with you, surely – ?

Sally How could they? I was never allowed to finish.
I was just shouted down and then told to sit. As if I was
a child of three. God, I'm so bloody angry. I'm going to
resign. This time I'm going to resign, I really am.

Jake I wouldn't do that . . .

Sally See how they get on without me. See how far they get with Catriona Braithwaite . . . Good luck to them, I say. God, she's so *stupid*. (*Mimicking, savagely, in a high whining voice*) 'I don't think we can possibly do that, Sally. It's against everything we stand for . . .'

> *Silence.*
> *Barry and Lindy return, this time with separate loads.*

Barry Good morning, Sally. Good morning, Jake.

Jake Morning.

Lindy Good morning.

Sally (*tersely*) 'Llo.

Barry (*to Lindy*) No, no, no, no, no, Lindy. Over there, dear. Over there.

Lindy Oh, I'm sorry.

Barry (*as he goes off again*) Do try and listen to me. Do try and listen, dear . . .

Lindy I was listening, dear, I was just . . .

Barry Saves a lot of time later if you listen, doesn't it?

Lindy (*cheerily, back to Sally*) Is it going to rain, that's the question?

Sally (*sourly*) Haven't a clue.

> *Barry and Lindy go off.*

Jake Well. Maybe you should resign, then.

Sally (*sharply*) What?

Jake I said, maybe you should resign . . .

Sally We can't just walk away from everything, Jake. Every time we feel –

Jake (*anxious not to incur her wrath*) No, no. Right.

A silence between them.

What about this evening, then?

Sally Maybe I should resign. I don't know. Maybe you're right.

Jake Are we going out somewhere? Do you fancy going out?

Sally Not tonight.

Jake (*sadly*) OK. If you change your mind . . .

Sally Take someone else out, Jake.

Jake I don't want to take anyone else out.

Barry comes on with Gavin. Gavin is in his late forties, urbane, charming, the ideal diplomat.

Barry I say, Sally, sorry could you possibly help, please? This gentleman's driven to the back gate by mistake. Could you possibly show him up to the house, do you think?

Gavin I'm so sorry. I got completely lost. There don't appear to be any signs.

Sally Aren't there? There's usually masses of them.

Barry I think Warn may have taken them down. He's cutting back the vegetation . . . I'll leave you, then.

Gavin (*to Barry*) Thank you, so much. You're very kind.

Barry goes off.

Sally. Right?

Sally Yes, how did you . . .?

Gavin Gavin Ryng-Mayne with a Y. Gavin. Hallo. I think when we last met you were about six months old. I'm an old friend of your father's.

Sally Oh, right. Well, let me . . . How do you do? Follow me.

Gavin (*as they go*) Thank you. What a glorious place. I'd no idea . . .

Jake (*calling after them, rather slighted*) Hallo. I'm Jake, incidentally . . .

Gavin (*almost off*) Hallo, Jake! See you later, I hope.

Gavin and Sally have gone off towards the house. Jake, rather put out by this interruption, stands undecided.
Barry and Lindy return carrying something between them. They are in the midst of one of their minor differences.

Barry . . . I never said that . . .

Lindy . . . I think you did, dear . . .

Barry . . . I would never have said that . . .

Lindy Well, you said something like that . . .

Barry . . . I'm sorry, I would never have said anything remotely like that . . .

Lindy . . . Well, I wouldn't have made it up, would I?

They set down their load with the other things.

Barry I don't know, do I? Frankly, Lindy, most of the time, I don't know what goes on in that head of yours . . .

Lindy You definitely said . . .

Barry I beg your pardon, I did not say that. I said *possibly*, that's all . . .

Lindy I don't remember any possibly . . .

They have gone off again. Jake sees Sally's briefcase which she has left. He picks it up. He holds it. It is unfastened. He goes to fasten it. Curiosity gets the better of him. He looks inside rather guiltily. He spies a sheet of paper. He pulls it out. It is a hand-written rough draft of a verse.

Jake (*reading*)
'How can I ever hear a heart
My head denies with such insistence?
How do I ever trust a heart,
Which doubt drowns out with such persistence?
How will I ever feel my heart,
Whilst caution proffers such resistance?
How could I ever give my heart,
When I deny its whole existence?'

Giles enters from the house. He is deep in his own thoughts. Jake hurriedly replaces the paper and closes the briefcase.

Dad . . .

Giles Oh. Hallo, Jake. There you are. I was . . . Glad I caught you. I wanted to . . . Seen your mother this morning?

Jake Briefly.

Giles Right.

Pause.

How's things, then?

Jake Oh. You know.

Giles That your briefcase?

Jake No.

Giles No, I didn't think it was. Hadn't seen it before.

Jake It's Sally's.

Giles Uh-huh. How is she?

Jake Pretty well.

Giles Are things between you – moving along?

Jake No. Not really. Well, they're sort of moving but not going anywhere. If you know what I mean.

Giles Oh. I'm sorry to hear that.

Jake It's difficult, isn't it? Sometimes. To know if someone is telling you it's OK or to go away. You know. Women especially. They seem to . . . seem to . . . seem to . . . I don't know.

Giles This is Sally we're talking about?

Jake Yes. She gives you – she gives me different signals, you know. I think she likes me . . . sometimes she's really glad to see me . . . and it's really good between us. And then another time, it's like she puts the shutters up, you know. Doesn't want to know. I don't quite know what to do. I mean, half of me wants to say well, to hell with this, I'm off. But the other half of me . . . You know.

Giles Yes.

Jake I couldn't bear not to see her again.

Giles Ah. I know the problem.

Jake So. It's not a very happy time for me. At the moment. Pretty pathetic, just hanging around. Like a dog. I don't know – I don't – I don't know what to do for the best.

Giles Yes. It's never . . . never easy, Jake. I have to say. Well, for some people it seems to be but . . . People like you and me, I think we're probably rather the – rather the – rather the –

Jake The – the – same.

Giles Yes. I mean, with your mother, for instance . . . I wanted to talk about her actually, Jake. Talk about. Her.

Jake Yes?

Giles I have to tell you, Jake, I wish I could keep this from you but – you'll have to know sooner or later – Joanna's been having an affair.

Jake Yes.

Giles You knew?

Jake Yes. With Mr Platt.

Giles Ah.

Jake I'm sorry.

Giles I seem to be the only one who didn't know. You should have told me.

Jake I didn't know how to.

Giles I was very . . . I'm going to have to be very careful how I talk to her – we both are, Jake.

Jake Sure.

Giles She'll obviously be feeling terrible about it. Guilt, probably, and insecurity and rejection . . .

Jake Rejection?

Giles Well, I understand it was Teddy who broke it off . . .

Jake Yes, sure, but . . .

Giles All I'm saying is, Jake, your mother's a very special person and we'll have to nurse her back to emotional health. That's all. She needs us.

Jake What about you? Don't you feel a bit rejected, a bit hurt . . .?

Giles Well, yes. Naturally. But when something like this happens with someone like Jo . . . It's yourself you rather tend to question. What went wrong? What drove her to do it? Do you see?

Jake Well, I'd have thought it was fairly obvious what –

Giles She's complex. I met her, you know, when I was still a medical student . . .

Jake Yes, I know . . .

Giles She was a drama student at that time, you know. But she never went on with that, which was a pity, she could have been really good. I saw her once in one of her end of term shows, you know – but then she decided she wanted to teach instead – so – anyway, we met at this dance. She came with another student – she was – she was quite the most beautiful person in the room actually – and I started staring at her, you know – the way you do. You're not supposed to but you do. You don't expect anything to come of it, it's just I couldn't take my eyes off her – she was just so – incredibly beautiful. And she was dancing away with all these nine-foot-tall Adonises and I was thinking, oh well, home for cocoa – or whatever – and suddenly she was standing there at my table – looking down at me. And you can imagine, I jumped about a foot. And she said, are you going to ask me for a dance or are you just going to sit there staring all evening. And I said, sorry, I'm not an awfully good dancer actually. And she said, well, that's too bad because I'm going to have to spend the rest of the

evening teaching you, aren't I? And I said, fair enough.
That's fine by me. And then for the rest of the – rest of
the – evening I danced with this . . . with this . . . with
this . . . beautiful . . .

*Giles is suddenly crying. Jake watches rather
helplessly.*

I'm sorry, Jake. I don't think I want to talk about this
just at the moment if you don't mind . . .

Jake No, no. Fine . . .

Giles Poor you. The last thing you need is a crying
father, isn't it? Got problems of your own, haven't you?

Jake Go right ahead.

Giles No, no. Sorry for myself, that's all. Pathetic.
(*Fiercely to himself*) Come on! Come on! Come on!

Barry and Lindy have re-entered.

Barry That's it, you tell him, Giles. That's telling him.

Giles What? Oh, yes . . . (*He smiles weakly*)

Lindy You listen to your father, eh?

Barry Father knows best, eh?

They set down their latest load.

Right. On we go . . . By the way, if either of you are
suddenly moved to lend a hand, we won't object. (*He
laughs*)

Giles I'm so sorry, I would normally. It's just I'm
expected up at the house in a minute, otherwise . . .

Barry All right for some, eh? It's a sandwich in the back
of the Transit for us . . .

Jake You're going up to the house for lunch?

Lindy Think about the workers.

Giles Yes, Trish is expecting us.

Jake (*to Barry*) Sorry. I'm afraid I'm doing an interview.

Giles The last thing we should do is let her down.

Barry All offers gratefully received . . .

Barry and Lindy go off.

Giles I have to say, I'd prefer to be anywhere else but – sitting down at the same table as – I could do without this wretched fête this afternoon too, actually.

Jake Do you have to be here? Can't you – ?

Giles No, no. Not possibly. My whole troop's turning up. I couldn't let them down. They're relying on me.

Jake Your troop?

Giles Yes.

Jake You're going to be morris dancing as well?

Giles Yes, of course. I know you think it's all very silly and quaint, Jake –

Jake No. It just seems sort of inappropriate today, that's all. How can you possibly morris dance at a time like this?

Giles It's enormous fun. Great camaraderie. I wouldn't miss it for the world. I won't have my heart fully in it today of course, but . . . No, I couldn't possibly let them down. Anyway, take me out of myself, won't it? I must go and have a word with your mother. Collect her for lunch. I hope she's remembered . . . See you in a minute.

Jake Yes.

Giles We ought to talk more often.

Jake Yes.

Giles Any time you need a . . . I'm here for you, you know that, Jake.

Jake Thanks very much, Dad.

Giles gives him a thumbs-up sign and goes off.
As he does so, Barry and Lindy return with more gear.

Barry . . . Right . . .?

Lindy . . . right . . .

Barry . . . putting it down then . . .

Lindy . . . putting it down . . .

Both . . . Hooof!

They set this bundle down with the other things.

Lindy Whew! Just trying to remember. The fortune tent went there, didn't it? That I do remember.

Barry No. Over there. I've written it all down. I have the plan.

Lindy I'm sure it was over there.

Barry I have the plan!

A silent moment between them.

Don't let's argue and spoil the day, Lindy. Come along. Winnie awaits. Plenty more to unload.

Barry and Lindy go off. Sally returns from the house. She has changed out of her uniform.

Sally (*indicating her briefcase*) Oh, there it is. Thought I'd left it up at the school. Major panic over.

Jake I was going to bring it up to you . . .

Sally Thank God. Got my whole life in here . . . I saw you talking to your dad.

Jake Yes.

Sally How was he?

Jake Bit shaken up, really. He had such total trust in Mum, you see, it's come as a terrible shock. I don't think he can quite believe it. He keeps blaming himself.

Sally Himself? Why?

Jake God knows. Because he's – because he's my father. Who blames himself for everything. If it rains this afternoon, he'll blame himself for that. How's your mum?

Sally Well, not blaming herself, certainly. I don't think she's ever blamed herself for anything. She usually finds somebody else to blame. Me, for instance. My father, of course, is sailing on as usual as if it was nothing to do with him. Having long talks to the slightly sinister Gavin Ryng-Mayne. With a Y.

Jake Sinister?

Sally Yes, I find him a bit creepy. He was being awfully, awfully charming to me all the way up to the house. Which is always a bit suspicious with someone you've only just met. What's he doing here, I wonder?

Jake Come for lunch, hasn't he?

Sally Ha, ha. All the way from London? Not a chance. No, there's something brewing. He's not just a writer, he's quite politically involved, too. You know, personal adviser, writing speeches and so on . . .

Jake How do you know?

Sally I have my sources.

Jake (*smiling*) Really?

Sally (*smiling*) Yes.

Jake And you find him creepy?

Sally Well, that's not the right word. Just a bit underhand. A tiny bit – I don't know. Unscrupulous. Actually rather attractive.

Jake Oh, I see. Here we go . . .

Sally No, not in that way. For God's sake, he's my father's age. They were at school together. What do you think I am? You just sit there and wait for your elderly film star . . .

Jake She's not elderly . . .

Sally Aha . . . aha . . . Have you got your notebook?

Jake Yes. And my recorder. Which I hope she'll let me use.

Sally Cheat.

Jake No. I'll use both. Shorthand and a recorder. Most people do these days. Make doubly sure.

Sally What are you going to ask her?

Jake I don't know. How she likes this country . . .

Sally Boring!

Jake I've been told to ask that. Has she ever been to a garden fête before?

Sally Predictable!

Jake Did she enjoy working on a film in England?

Sally Does she find English men attractive?

Jake No. As it happens I'm not asking her that . . .
I'll talk about her working methods, whether they're
different, continental methods . . .

Sally Ask her what she's doing here.

Jake How do you mean?

Sally Well, why is she here?

Jake Well, she's publicising the film presumably.

Sally I beg your pardon. At a fête? At a garden *fête*? Big
budget movie, is it?

Jake See what you mean. I hadn't thought of that.

Sally Maybe she's having a secret affair.

Jake Who with?

Slight pause.

Both (*laughing*) Gavin Ryng-Mayne!

Jake With a Y.

Sally Do you think he has a brother with an X? Gavin
Rynx-Manx?

They laugh.

Interview me, then.

Jake What?

Sally Come on. Interview me. Practice for you.

Jake Serious?

Sally Yes. Serious.

Jake (*producing his notebook and recorder*) All right.
Hang about. Ready?

Sally (*preening herself*) Just a minute, yes.

Jake Serious. You've got to take it seriously.

Sally I will. Go on, then.

Jake Sally Platt, you come from a family with a long tradition of politicians – grandfather, great-grandfather. Do you intend to follow in their footsteps?

Sally Well, it's a bit early for me to decide just at the moment. I am considering it.

Jake But you are excited by politics.

Sally Yes, I am. I've always been very practical, in that I've never enjoyed being just an onlooker. Ever since I was a child I've always wanted to be in control. I consider politics to be the most practical way to take control of my life.

Jake And presumably to some extent other people's?

Sally Possibly. To some extent.

Jake You think you're qualified to do that? To control the lives of others?

Sally You're making it sound as if I'd be standing as dictator. I'd merely be pursuing their best interests. Nothing to do with controlling them.

Jake Nonetheless, you feel you're the person to do it?

Sally Well, presumably if they'd elected me, they would too.

Jake What if I didn't vote for you? And I didn't feel your choices were in my best interests?

Sally Too bad. That's called democracy.

Jake OK. How about other interests? Do you have any hobbies?

Sally Well, I make a lot of jam. And I do embroidery at weekends . . .

Jake Come on! Come on!

Sally Well, honestly! Hobbies. I'm also waiting for the right man to come along, before you ask . . .

Jake Are you?

Sally What?

Jake Waiting for the right man?

Sally Certainly not.

Jake Truthfully?

Sally Not at the moment. I'm too busy with A-levels, anyway.

Jake By that, I take it you're not in love with anyone at the moment?

Sally (*uneasy now*) No. None of your business, anyway.

Jake But you do have feelings for people?

Sally Of course I do. What is this?

Jake Feelings you prefer to hide? Keep hidden? Because perhaps they frighten you? Maybe you're a bit afraid of them? Strong emotions?

Sally I'm stopping this now, this is getting stupid.

Jake Sometimes you write them down, don't you?

Sally (*flippantly*) Yes, in my diary. Every night. How did you guess?

Jake I was thinking more about poetry.

   A silence.

Sally (*quietly*) What?

Jake I said, you write poetry.

Sally (*taking this in*) Have you been in my briefcase? You've been in my bloody briefcase, haven't you?

Jake Just this one poem. It fell out, I couldn't help –

Sally No, it didn't. It didn't fall out at all. You rifled through my briefcase and you read it. How dare you? You bastard!

Jake Look, all I did was –

Sally (*livid*) How dare you go through my private belongings! How dare you!

Jake Listen, Sally, I didn't . . .

Sally (*grabbing up her case and leaving*) Well, that's it. That's it, as far as I'm concerned! Don't ever speak to me again!

Jake Sally . . .

Sally Fuck you!

Sally goes off. Jake sits appalled.

Jake (*in despair*) Oh, my God! What have I done? What have I done?

Joanna and Giles have entered in time to hear this last. They are walking in silence, well apart from each other. Joanna now crosses to Jake and hugs him to her, somewhat melodramatically.

Joanna (*in a low voice*) Jake, my darling. You mustn't blame yourself. It's all us. It's not your fault. It's all us.

She releases him and starts again, walking towards the house. As he passes, Giles pats Jake affectionately on the shoulder.
Joanna and Giles go off. Jake continues to sit miserably on the grass.
Barry and Lindy return with yet more stuff.

Barry . . . OK . . .?

Lindy . . . OK . . .

Barry . . . nearly the lot . . .

Lindy . . . nearly the lot . . .

Barry . . . one – two . . . huuup!

Lindy (*with him*) . . . Huuup!

They set this down with the rest.

Barry Whew!

Lindy Whew!

Barry (*to Jake*) We've got Winnie loaded to the gunwales, today . . .

Jake Oh, yes.

Lindy That's our van. The Transit. We call her Winnie.

Warn enters, looking particularly out of sorts.
Jake, under the next, wanders away down one of the paths.

Warn Two rear wheels on the verge back there . . .

Lindy Oh, dear . . .

Barry Now who was supposed to be seeing me back? Make sure that precise thing didn't happen? Whose job was that?

Lindy Sorry.

Barry Don't apologise to me. It's Warn you should be apologising to.

Lindy Sorry.

Barry Sorry, Warn, I'm afraid we have my wife to blame for that . . .

Lindy So sorry.

Barry (*hurrying off*) Don't worry, Warn, I'll move her straight away. Don't worry, Lindy, stay there. I'll see myself forward, it'll be safer. (*Barry goes off*)

Warn (*muttering*) Too late now. Buggered, in' they?

Lindy (*after Barry, vainly*) Shall I start unpacking some of this . . .? (*To Warn*) So, so, sorry.

Lindy starts to unpack the upright poles that will form the enclosure.
    Izzie enters from the house. She has a sandwich box with Warn's lunch.

Izzie Here, your lunch, then. You're lucky to get it at all. It's chaos up there. Total hymen. All arriving at the wrong time through the wrong gates. Why'd you move all the signs today, then, eh?

Warn does not reply.

God, you're a cantabulous old bastard, aren't you? (*She pauses for breath*) Well, I don't know. The carrots are par-boiled, the beans are waitin', my puddin's are poised, the roast potatoes are shot and that beef's been in and out so many times, it's like a candle in a spinster's bedroom. I'm not answerable. I told her, I can't be answerable. She should have had pork. You can muck about with pork; you can't do that with beef.

Warn watches Lindy impassively.

Well . . . (*Seeing something in the direction of the house*) Oh, no. Is that them? Yes, there's a car. Must be them. I'd better get back. You behave yourself this afternoon, that's all. I'll be watching both of you.

Izzie hurries off to the house.
    Jake comes on.

Jake Did someone say a car?

Lindy I think there's one just arrived, Jake . . .

Jake At last. (*Jake hurries off after Izzie*)

Lindy Oh! Great excitement, isn't there?

Warn does not deign to reply.
Barry comes back with a few more items.

Barry Car just arriving . . .

Lindy Yes, we know. That'll be her, I expect.

Barry It seems to be heading round the back there. Like the other one.

Lindy Oh . . .

Barry No signs, are there?

Warn goes off.

I think I'd better serve as welcoming committee again, hadn't I?

Lindy I'll come with you.

Barry No, Lindy. You carry on with that. That's more important. I can do it.

Fran, Lucille's driver, appears down the path. She seems fairly formidable.

Fran (*in a flat London voice*) Excuse me. Do you know how we get to the house from here?

Barry Ah, good morning. Are you Madame Cadeau? Lucille Cadeau?

Fran No, I'm not. I'm the driver.

Barry Oh, right. Sorry for the confusion. Barry Love, how do you do?

Lindy (*unnoticed*) Hallo.

Barry Now then. You can either get in your car, make a U-turn, return down the back drive and once you come to the fork, take the right one not the left one, otherwise you'll finish up at the home farm, over the cattle grid and then, when you get to the bottom, you're on the road again. Turn right, it's a bit of a blind corner so be careful, up to the crossroads, very much the way you came, then right again – don't go straight on because that just takes you the back way to the village –

Lindy Past our house . . .

Barry Yes, thank you, Lindy, I don't think that's particularly relevant – right at the crossroads and then go very slowly up the hill till you'll see on your right, clearly signposted – well, it isn't clearly signposted at present because it's been temporarily removed – normally clearly signposted a notice to the house. And you take that right and you'll find yourself at the front door. Is that clear enough?

Fran (*drily*) Beautiful.

Barry Want me to repeat it for you?

Fran No, thank you.

Barry Or else you can walk straight up that path there. Probably be quicker.

At this moment, Lucille appears along one of the paths. She is everything expected of a French film star, attractive, vivacious and charming.

* **Lucille** Que c'est beau ici . . .

Barry Ah! Here she is!

Lindy Hallo. This must be her.

---

* It's so beautiful here . . .

* **Lucille** C'est sublime non! Je n'aurais jamais imaginé que ce serait aussi beau.

Barry (*moving forward to greet her*) How do you do? Lucille? I'm Barry. Welcome. May I call you Lucille?

Lucille Hallo. (*To Fran*) C'est le propriétaire, c'est Monsieur Plate?

Lindy (*unnoticed*) Hallo.

Fran Non, je ne sais pas qui c'est, l'idiot du village, je crois . . .

Barry How – finding – you – our – countryside?

Fran Nous sommes arrivées par la porte arrière, parait-il.

Lucille Il y avait aucun panneau.

Fran Quelqu'un les a arrachés. Cet idiot peut-être. Ce serait sans doute plus rapide d'y aller à pied. Ça ne vous ennuie pas de marcher?

Lucille Non. Après quatre heures enfermée dans cette voiture . . .

---

* **Lucille** Isn't this the most glorious place? I had no idea it was going to be this beautiful.

Barry (*moving forward to greet her*) How do you do? Lucille? I'm Barry. Welcome. May I call you Lucille?

Lucille Hallo. (*To Fran*) Is this the owner, is this Mr Plate?

Lindy (*unnoticed*) Hallo.

Fran No, I don't know who he is, the local village idiot, I think . . .

Barry How – finding – you – our – countryside?

Fran We've come to the back gate, apparently.

Lucille There weren't any signposts.

Fran Somebody's pulled them all up. Perhaps this lunatic. It's maybe quicker to walk. Do you mind walking?

Lucille No. After four hours in that car . . .

Barry Have – you – much – been – out – of – London – before?

Fran We'll walk. It's OK.

Barry Oh, yes. Permit me to show you . . .

Fran (*sharply*) It's all right, honestly. Thanks very much.

Barry Well . . .

* **Fran** Vite, on ne va jamais se débarrasser de lui. La maison est par ici.

Lucille (*as they go*) Quel petit bonhomme extraordinaire. Ils sont tous comme ça par ici?

Fran Très probablement. Je vous l'ai dit, nous avons abandonné la civilisation après Hammersmith . . .

Lucille and Fran go off towards the house.

Barry Well. What a beautiful woman. Absolutely stunning, wasn't she? Took your breath away.

Lindy You might have introduced me.

Barry Now that's what I call an attractive woman. Only the French, eh? Only the French. Frenchwomen, they have that – je ne sais quoi – that little extra, don't they?

Lindy Another leg, you mean?

Barry (*unamused*) Don't be silly, Lindy. Don't be silly now.

Jake enters breathlessly from one of the paths.

Jake Where've they gone?

---

* **Fran** Quick, we'll never get rid of him. The house is this way.

Lucille (*as they go*) What an extraordinary little man. Are they all like that round here?

Fran Very likely. I told you, we left civilisation after Hammersmith . . .

Barry Sorry?

Jake I got to the front gate, they drove right past. I've just chased them round to the back gate.

Lindy They're walking up to the house.

Jake Oh, grief . . .

Jake runs off after them.

Barry He's not going to catch them, is he? Never make a paparazzi.

Lindy Poor boy. I feel so sorry for him.

Barry Jake? Let's get started on these poles, shall we? Why should you feel sorry for Jake?

They start to sort out the poles that Lindy has unpacked, during the next.

Lindy Well . . . all this business with his parents.

Barry Oh, you mean the carryings on?

Lindy Shh! Yes. Can't be nice for him, can it?

Barry Don't imagine it would be. I think we've got time to lay these out you know, Lindy. Then we'll sit in Winnie and have an early sandwich and wait for the rest of the mob. Now, let's see . . .

Lindy Do you think that could ever happen to us?

Barry What?

Lindy You know. One of us going off with someone?

Barry Certainly not. What are you saying?

Lindy Don't you ever think about it?

Barry No.

Lindy Not even now and then?

Barry I've got better things to do with my time, Lindy. And so have you. Now hold that. (*He hands her a pole*)

Lindy I think about it now and then.

Barry What? Us having love affairs?

Lindy Well, you having love affairs, mostly.

Barry Me? That's not very likely, I must say.

Lindy Why not?

Barry Because I've got you, haven't I? More than a handful.

Lindy Don't you ever get bored with me?

Barry You're exciting enough for me, Lindy.

Lindy I get bored with me. Sometimes I get so bored with me. I don't know how you stand it sometimes. I wouldn't. If I were you, I'd go off. I would.

Barry (*sitting on the grass*) Sit down for a moment, Lindy.

Lindy sits beside him.

You see that yellow car out there, Lindy? The one that man was driving? That's a Porsche, Lindy.

Lindy I know. Beautiful.

Barry Now. Could you ever in a million years, even given all the lottery money we could spend, could you ever imagine me behind the wheel of that?

Lindy No, not really.

Barry Conversely, could you ever imagine yourself behind the wheel of that?

Lindy I can't even drive . . .

Barry Now, what's parked next to that vehicle, next to the Porsche?

Lindy Our old Transit.

Barry Exactly. Good old faithful Winnie. Winnie, the Transit. And how do we both feel about Winnie?

Lindy We're very fond of her.

Barry (*patting her leg*) What more can I say than that? (*He bounds up*) Now hold that pole upright for a minute and I'll walk back a bit and line it up, all right? Just hold it there.

> *Barry goes off along the path. Lindy stands unhappily, holding the pole.*
> *Jake returns from the house, even more out of breath. He flops on the grass.*

Jake Missed them! After all that.

Lindy (*in her own thoughts*) Oh, dear.

Barry (*off, distant*) That's it, Lindy. Keep it upright! Keep it upright!

Jake What are you doing?

Lindy Holding this pole.

Jake Oh, yes. Have you seen that car out there? The Porsche. Beautiful. I wouldn't mind driving that.

Lindy What about the one next to it?

Jake What, the old bashed up Transit, you mean?

Lindy That's ours.

Jake Oh, no offence.

Lindy Fancy driving that, do you?

Jake Well, frankly, not a lot, no.

Lindy No, I didn't think you would somehow.

Lindy suddenly throws down the pole and hurries off, weeping. Jake is rather startled.

Jake (*puzzled*) Sorry? (*To himself*) What did I say?

Barry (*off, distant*) Lindy! Don't let go of it! Lindy? What are you doing? Lindy?

Warn comes on with his sandwiches. He sits and starts to eat. Jake lies out.

Jake I don't think this is my day somehow.

A distant rumble of thunder.

Warn (*looking at the sky, with satisfaction*) Here it comes.

He continues to sit there as the lights fade to: Blackout.

Act Two

SCENE ONE

Saturday, August 14th, 2.00 p.m.
    The same.
    It is overcast and, to everyone but the most optimistic, clearly about to rain.
    Some things have been set up including the Maypole. Several of the stalls, including the hoop-la, are also complete.
    Jake comes on anxiously as though looking for someone. There are sounds of activity all around and occasionally people come in and out of sight.

Jake (*calling vaguely in all directions*) Mum . . . Mum!

    Barry passes busily.

Barry (*unconcerned*) No sign of her?

Jake No . . .

Barry She'll turn up. (*As he goes*) She's got her Maypole dance, hasn't she? She won't miss that. We'll be opening the gates in just a minute . . . (*Barry goes*)

Jake (*calling*) Mum . . .

    The bushes rustle and Joanna's voice is heard.

Joanna (*hissing*) Jake . . . Jake . . . Jake . . .

Jake (*trying to locate her*) Mum?

Joanna Jake . . .

Jake Where are you?

Joanna Over here. In the bushes . . .

Jake (*seeing her*) Oh, there you are. What are you –

Joanna (*fiercely*) No! Don't look in my direction!

Jake What?

Joanna You mustn't give away my position, whatever you do. He mustn't know I'm here. It's vital he doesn't know I'm here . . .

Jake Who? Who mustn't know? Who are we talking about, Mum?

Joanna Ssssh! Keep your voice down . . .

Jake Sorry. Mum, I don't know what's going on. Why are you in the bushes?

Joanna I'm hiding from him.

Jake Him?

Joanna Harold.

Jake Harold?

Joanna Jake, I have something terrible to tell you.

Jake Who's Harold?

Joanna You have to know. You have a right to know. You're my son, you have a right to know these things . . .

Jake Mum, I wish you'd come out of the bushes, it's very hard trying to talk to you –

Joanna I'm trying to tell you, Jake, it's –

Barry and Lindy come on carrying more stuff.

Shhh! Later! Walk away! Walk away! You haven't seen me. Please!

Jake walks away.

Jake My God, what's happening?

Lindy All right, Jake?

Jake Yes, yes. Sure. I just need to find my dad. (*Jake goes off towards the house somewhat dazed*)

Barry (*laughing*) Lost his dad as well. This is unforgivable, you know. There should be thirty volunteer helpers here. And how many are there? Four. Including you and me. And old Mr Eldridge whose foot's so bad he can't lift anything anyway. We're way behind. Way behind.

Lindy I know, dear, you keep saying . . .

Barry We've never been so behind. In eleven years of organising this – even during the floods – we were never this far behind . . . Have you checked the tent? Lindy?

Lindy (*who has become aware of Joanna in the bushes*) What?

Barry Do listen, Lindy, for heaven's sake . . . I said have you checked the tent?

Lindy Yes, I've already said. I put it up personally and checked it . . .

Barry That tent is your responsibility, you know . . .

Lindy (*distracted by something*) Yes . . . yes . . .

Barry I deliberately delegated that to you – What are you doing?

Lindy There's someone – (*Confidentially*) . . . I think there's someone in the bushes over there . . .

Barry The bushes?

Lindy I saw the branches move.

Barry Are you sure?

Lindy Yes. There! Can you see?

Barry Good gracious!

Lindy Who is it?

Barry I've no idea.

Lindy It could be a lurker.

Barry I don't like the look of that. In another five minutes this place will be swarming with old people and youngsters . . .

Lindy It will. Toddlers.

Barry Just keep talking a minute . . .

Lindy What about?

Barry What does it matter? Just keep talking. I'm going to try and take them by surprise . . . Keep talking, go on.

Lindy (*after a second's thought*) I can't think of anything to say . . .

Barry Lindy, for goodness sake . . .!

As Lindy starts her recitation, Barry gives her a despairing look, then wanders casually close to the bushes to investigate.

Lindy
'We've got a nasty ickle baby come to live with us,
I fink it really isn't fair, the way they make a fuss
About a fing that's got no sense and hardly any hair,
And isn't half so pretty as my ickle Teddy Bear.
What is the use of baby? Well, I cannot really –'

Barry pounces into the bushes with a cry. There is a great deal of commotion.

Barry Haaaarrrrrr!! (*He emerges*)

Lindy You all right, dear . . .?

Barry They – ran off.

Lindy Did you see who it was?

Barry Yes. It was Joanna Mace. Mrs Mace.

Lindy Oh.

Barry She looked – quite wild. I would almost say dishevelled.

Lindy She's usually very smart.

Barry Exactly. Something wrong. Something very, very wrong. What was I saying earlier, Lindy? Precisely that. You indulge in extra-marital activities and look where you end up.

Lindy In the bushes.

Barry My point precisely. We'll have to keep an eye on her, she looked a trifle unbalanced. Certainly casts a shadow over the Maypole dance, doesn't it?

Lindy Oh, we can't cancel that!

Barry I hope it won't come to that.

Lindy They'd be so disappointed. They've all got their little costumes specially made and everything . . . We couldn't cancel it. It would break their hearts after all their rehearsing . . .

Barry I can assure you that will be a last resort. Since the dog handler's cancelled, I was relying on it as the high spot of the afternoon.

Warn and Izzie enter with some books for the stall.

(*To them*) Well done, well done. I think we're nearly there. Come on, Lindy. Follow me . . .

Giles comes on. He is dressed in his morris dancer's outfit. He is also looking for Joanna.

Lindy (*seeing him, excitedly*) Oh, Giles . . . We've just seen Jo—

Barry (*quietening her, sharply*) All right, Lindy! That'll do! That'll do!

Lindy What?

Barry Not in front of the world, if you don't mind. Discretion please.

Lindy Oh.

Giles What's going on?

Barry Off you go, Lindy. I'm sure you've got plenty to be getting on with . . .

Lindy Yes. I must be – getting on . . . Excuse me. (*To Giles*) I'm so sorry.

Lindy goes off.

Giles What's going on?

Barry I just wanted a quiet word if I could.

Giles Really?

Barry Man to man. In your ear.

Under the next, Warn and Izzie go off again.

Giles Look, if it's about John Whittle I'm sorry. I'm sorry, I have tried his mobile but I'm not getting any reply. He's certainly left home anyway, I ascertained that.

Barry Pardon?

Giles John Whittle, our morris dance co-ordinator. I don't know where on earth they can all be. I hope nothing's happened to them.

Barry I'm sure they'll turn up, I'm sure they will. Listen, Giles, this is a bit embarrassing, a bit awkward but – frankly – the wife.

617

Giles Lindy? Is something wrong? She does look a little –

Barry No, no, not Lindy, I'm not talking about Lindy. Joanna.

Giles Ah.

Barry Nothing the matter with Lindy. Lindy's perfectly fine. It's all in her head. No, Joanna. Look, Giles, I have no wish to pry into your private affairs. As we know full well, women, bless them, are creatures of whim . . .

Giles That's perfectly all right, Barry. None of my affairs are any longer private. Feel free to discuss them along with the rest of the village . . .

Barry I'm sorry, it must be very –

Giles (*quite sharply, for him*) Yes, it is, actually. If you want to know. It is. Very. Now, what is it you want to tell me?

Barry (*secretively*) The bottom line. She's in the bushes. She's been sighted. Lurking in the bushes.

Giles What's she doing in the bushes?

Barry I rather hoped you could tell me.

Giles I've no idea. She rushed away in the middle of lunch. Threw down her cutlery and fled –

Barry Don't get me wrong. It's a free country. I'm as broad-minded as the next man. I'm just a little worried she might alarm people. Once we let the general public in. I was thinking particularly of old folk, you know, they can get a trifle apprehensive if they feel they're being observed from the shrubbery . . .

Giles Well, all right, I'll see if I can – I can locate her. Where's Jake, I wonder? I rather need Jake.

Barry (*starting up towards the house*) He was here a minute ago. He may have gone up to the house, looking for you. I'll tell you what I'll do. When I come back, I'll get Lindy to muster the little Maypole dancers. If we can group them round their pole, that might just serve to lure Joanna out of hiding.

Giles (*doubtfully*) Yes, I suppose that's possible.

Barry I'm just popping up to the house, to inform the official party we're ready to start. (*Loudly*) Everyone to your posts, please. We'll be opening the gates in a few minutes.

Barry goes off towards the house.
  Giles, somewhat aimlessly, starts to look into the shrubbery in the hope of locating Joanna.
  Warn and Izzie enter with some more books.

Izzie I been made a mockery today. I been held up and humidified. I never cooked a meal like it. Never. There were this Frenchwoman there. Expecting her Gordon Blue. And what's she get? Had to throw the rest of that beef away. Spoof wouldn't touch it neither.

They set down their load.

I left her washing up. Little madam. Kitchen'll be full of debrage when I get back. She wants electrocuting and hanging up by her hair, that girl. Pouring wine with half her chest hanging out. That doctor, he was practically down inside her vest. I don't care what you say, she needs a dad. She needs a man's firm hand, Warn.

Warn clears his throat in a sort of growl.

And I don't want to hear no more arguments, neither. She were always too young for you, even when you were younger, she were still too young for you but that were all right then, what you two did in your own home were your own business. But now I'm moved in that's all changed. Because she's my daughter and now you're sleepin' with me that makes you her father whether you like it or not. And it ain't right to sleep with your own daughter. Because now you're committin' incense and that's a seven deadly sin, I know that 'cause it's in the Bible, right?

Warn moves off.

(*Calling*) You can walk away. Don't make no difference.

Warn is about to exit in the direction of the house but he nearly collides with Pearl. She is now dressed in her fortune-telling outfit.

Warn (*moving away*) Bloody women.

Warn goes off.

Pearl What you done to him?

Izzie You behave like a daughter, you hear? Or you'll feel my wrath.

Izzie goes off.

Pearl (*despairingly, to herself*) How can I behave like a daughter when he don't even want to be a father? He don't want a daughter. He don't want me as a daughter. He only wanted me for lust. That's all he wanted me for. What's he want a daughter for? (*Glaring after Izzie*) This'd never have happened if you hadn't pinched him off me in the first place.

Giles emerges from the bushes. Pearl watches him.

Giles Oh, I give up . . . I really do . . . (*Calling*) Joanna . . .! Jo!

He sees Pearl. She smiles at him.

Pearl Still looking for her, then?

Giles Er, yes . . . Just . . .

Pearl What makes you think she'll be in the bushes, then?

Giles Er – just a – wild hunch.

Pearl No reason for her to be in the bushes, is there?

Giles Probably not.

Pearl (*significantly*) Not today, anyway.

Giles droops a little.

(*Instantly regretting this*) Sorry. No call for that. Sorry.

Pause.

Shame you had to rush away from your dinner, though.

Giles Yes. As I explained, my wife suddenly remembered she had a very important phone call from overseas that she simply had to take. And then I remembered that stupidly I'd not given her the number. In case they wanted her to call them back.

Pearl Missed your treacle tart, didn't you? (*Twirling for his approval*) Like my new fortune-telling dress?

Giles Very nice.

Pearl Coming in my tent this year, are you? Have your fortune told?

Giles Well, I don't – I don't – I don't think so. I already have a fairly clear idea of my fortune. I don't think I want to know much more about it.

Pearl Fortunes can change.

Giles Sometimes.

Pearl (*smiling at him again*) Be surprised.

Giles I think at your age that's possible, Pearl. But at my age . . .

Jake appears from the house during the next.

Pearl Your age? Get on with you. I'm acquainted with older men than you, I can tell you. Prefer a bit of vintage, me.

Giles Yes, I . . . did realise. Well, I'm certainly vintage. Practically oxidised, I'm afraid. (*He laughs a little*)

Pearl (*shrugging*) I'm into most things. Try anything once . . .

Giles (*seeing Jake*) Ah, Jake.

Jake (*a little mystified by what he's overheard*) Hallo.

Pearl Oh. Best get my camera. Nearly forgot. Always nice to get a photo, isn't it? See you later.

Pearl smiles at them both and goes off.
Giles and Jake stand awkwardly, each not knowing quite where to start.

Jake Just been – up to the house.

Giles Oh, yes.

Jake Thought you might be up there.

Giles No, I'm – I'm down here.

Jake Yes.

A pause.

Giles Listen, there's no easy way to do this – I'm going to have to plunge straight in. Apparently, Joanna, your mother is – is – is –

Jake In the – in the – bushes.

Giles – bushes. Yes, you knew?

Jake Yes. As a matter of fact, I spoke to her.

Giles You did?

Jake Yes.

Giles How was she?

Jake A bit – strange. The point is, I think I've got some really bad news for you.

Giles Go on.

Jake Well, you know all along we were thinking – well, most of us were thinking that she was just having an affair with Mr Platt. I've got a feeling there was someone else as well.

Giles Someone else? Who? Tell me?

Jake Er – it's er – it's er – Harold.

Giles Harold?

Jake That's what she said.

Giles Who is Harold?

Jake That's what I asked her.

Giles And she said?

Jake She – said she'd tell me later. She wanted to talk to me on my own. She seems to think people are after her. That's why she's hiding.

Giles Yes, yes. Well, I suppose you'd better try to do that. I'll leave you to it. It's obvious she doesn't want me, isn't it? Harold . . .

Jake Dad, I don't think Mum knows at the moment what she wants. I wouldn't take it too personally.

Giles It's bloody hard not to, Jake, it really is. Harold . . . OK, I'll keep out of the way. I'll be over there by the Bat the Rat. Call me if you think I can be of any help.

Jake Right. Assuming I can find her.

Giles I think she's nearby. I – have a feeling she's watching us, don't you?

Jake Yes.

Giles I'll tell Lindy to round up the Maypole dancers. Barry has this theory that if we group them round their pole it might lure Joanna out.

Jake Sort of Judas goat, you mean?

Giles (*smiling weakly*) That sort of thing, yes. (*A wave of depression sweeping over him*) Harold . . . God, what sort of husband, am I? Married to a serial adulteress and I didn't even realise. God . . .

> *Giles leaves. Jake, on his own, moves round the garden, calling gently to various clumps of bushes. Two very small bandsmen pass clutching oversized brass instruments.*

Jake Mum . . . Mum . . . are you in there? Mum . . .

Joanna (*from within a clump of bushes*) Jake?

Jake Yes, it's me.

Joanna Has he gone?

Jake Dad? Yes, he's gone.

Joanna No, Harold. Has Harold gone, Jake?

Jake Mum, I don't really know any Harold – nor does Dad. Do you think you'd like to come out of the bushes now? It's perfectly safe.

Joanna I can't come out, Jake. If Harold catches sight of me talking to you, that'll put you in terrible danger as well . . .

Jake It will?

Joanna You don't know him, Jake. Nobody spotted him. He's been so clever. He's had us all fooled. He's been so diabolically clever . . .

Jake Who has?

Joanna Harold!

Joanna emerges slightly from the bushes in order to draw Jake closer to her. Her clothes are torn and she is covered in leaves and twigs.

Jake, listen very carefully . . .

Jake (*alarmed at her appearance*) Mum . . .

Joanna Listen! Listen! I haven't much time. He may catch up with me at any minute. That man is not your father.

Jake Who's not my father?

Joanna That man you were talking to just now. He is not your father.

Jake Do you mean Dad?

Joanna Yes! Yes!

Jake Dad's not my father?

Joanna No! No! Why are you being so stupid all of a sudden, Jake?

Jake I don't – I don't – I don't – I don't – I don't – know – I . . .

Joanna You're never normally stupid. He's not your father, Jake. He has never been your father. Can you get that through your head?

Jake I see. I see. Let's get this straight. Somebody else is my father, then?

Joanna Yes.

Jake But not that man?

Joanna No.

Jake Then who's my father, Mum?

Joanna Giles. Giles is your real father.

Jake But that was Giles, Mum. The man I was just talking to. That was Giles.

Joanna No, no, it wasn't, it wasn't!

Jake Then who was that?

Joanna That was Harold. They replaced Giles. They replaced your father with Harold.

Jake Who? Who's replaced my father with Harold?

Joanna I don't know, do I? They're doing these things all the time. And the terrifying thing is that I never realised. Harold's been in our home for years. All the time you were growing up, Jake. And I never even realised.

Jake Mum, what makes you think that man isn't Giles?

Joanna Because if you'd known the real Giles you'd have seen through this man, Jake. Like I should have done years ago. God, I've been so blind. Giles, the real Giles, was the gentlest man in the world, Jake. He loved me so much. He used to hold me in the night, you know . . . when I needed him. He gave me so much love. I would never have had to go to anybody else for love if Giles had still been here, Jake. You must believe that. I would never have done something like that. Giles was all I ever needed. He was so tender, so understanding. I wish you'd known him, Jake. I would never have hurt the real Giles like this . . .

Jake And this man – Harold – he doesn't do any of that . . .?

Joanna (*with a shudder*) Harold? Harold doesn't love me. Harold doesn't love anybody. Jake, he's not even human. He's like a machine. A cold, heartless machine. He doesn't love me, he doesn't love you.

Jake Why do you call him Harold?

Joanna Because I finally caught him out, Jake. We were walking up to the house this morning and I called out, Harold! And he turned round, Jake, he turned round and looked straight at me. And I thought, gotcha! He wouldn't have done that if his name wasn't Harold, would he?

Jake Listen, why don't you come with me and we'll find – Harold – and perhaps, you know, we can discuss this. Just the three of us.

Joanna (*drawing back*) With Harold? You want us to talk with Harold? What are you suggesting? He's got at you too, hasn't he? He's got at you? Oh, God, are you Jake? Maybe you're not even Jake . . .

Jake Mum . . .

Joanna (*drawing back deeper into the bushes*) Get away! Get away from me! You're not my son! My son would have understood! Jake would have understood!

Jake Oh, God . . .

He stands, uncertainly, then waves to his father. Giles comes hurrying on.

Giles Well . . .

Jake It's rather complicated, Dad. I don't know quite where to start.

Joanna (*from the bushes, calling*) Gordon!

627

Jake (*turning, startled*) What?

Joanna *(triumphantly)* Gotcha!

Giles Jake, what on earth is –

He is interrupted by the arrival of Teddy and Lucille, both of whom have had rather a lot to drink. They enter from the direction of the house. They are accompanied by Barry. Lindy also returns from another direction, having assembled Joanna's young Maypole dancers. Also Warn and Izzie.

* **Lucille** (*as they enter*) . . . c'est absolument magnifique. J'adore vos merveilleux jardins, ils sont si sauvages, si authentiques . . .

Teddy (*not understanding a word*) All of that, yes. As far as the eye can see. Right, here we are, everyone . . .

Lindy (*over this*) Right, Maypole dancers into your starting positions, please. (*To Barry*) We've opened the gates.

Barry Were there many waiting?

Lindy About eight.

Barry Ah, well. They'll come later. They often come along later.

Barry goes off. Teddy and Lucille make a tour of inspection. Lindy gathers the dancers.

† **Lucille** (*examining the hoop-la*) C'est quoi ça? Ça?

Teddy That? That's hoop-la. (*Demonstrating*) You know, le hoop-la.

---

* . . . this is absolutely magnificent. I love your wonderful gardens, they're so wild and unspoiled . . .

† What is this? This?

* **Lucille** Ah, oui. Les anneaux. Je vois.

Jake (*moving in on them*) Excuse me, I'm from the press.

Lucille Pardon?

Teddy (*shouting*) He's from the press. A journalist.

Lucille Oh, c'est un journaliste.

Jake Excusez-moi. Mon français n'est pas très bon mais j'aimerais vous poser quelques questions.

Lucille (*amused*) Yes. We speak.

Jake Merci. D'abord. Est-ce-que c'est votre première visite dans cette région?

Lucille Oui, c'est ma première visite.

Jake Qu'est-ce-que vous en pensez?

Lucille Je trouve que c'est magnifique.

Jake Et qu'est-ce qui vous amène ici? Vous faites de la publicité pour le film? Vous êtes en vacances?

---

* **Lucille** Oh, yes. Hoop-la. I know it.

Jake (*moving in on them*) Excuse me, I'm from the press.

Lucille Sorry?

Teddy (*shouting*) He's from the press. A journalist.

Lucille Oh, he's a journalist.

Jake Excuse me. My French is not very good but I would like to ask you a few questions.

Lucille (*amused*) Yes. We speak.

Jake Thank you. Firstly. Is this the first time you have been to this part of our country?

Lucille Yes, this is the first time.

Jake How do you like it?

Lucille I find it very beautiful.

Jake And what brings you here? Are you promoting the film? Or on holiday?

* **Lucille** Non, je me rends dans une clinique.

Jake A clinic? Vous allez en clinique?

Lucille Oui. Pour ma santé.

Jake Oh, I see. You mean a health farm. Ici, on appelle ça un centre de remise en forme.

Lucille Non, non, non. Pas un centre de remise en forme. Je connais ça. Je parle d'une clinique. Pour une thérapie.

Jake Thérapie? Quelle sorte de thérapie?

Lucille Pour accoutumance, vous voyez.

Jake Addiction? Vous voulez dire la drogue?

Lucille La drogue aussi, mais seulement un peu. Surtout pour l'alcool.

Fran has entered from the house.

Jake Alcohol . . . Je vois.

---

* **Lucille** No. I am on my way to a clinic.

Jake A clinic? You're on your way to a clinic?

Lucille Yes. For my health.

Jake Oh, I see. You mean a health farm. Over here we call them health farms.

Lucille No, no, no. Not a health farm. I know about health farms. This is a clinic. For therapy.

Jake Therapy? What sort of therapy?

Lucille For addiction, you know.

Jake Addiction? You mean drugs?

Lucille Drugs as well, but only a little. Mainly for alcohol.

Fran has entered from the garden.

Jake Alcohol . . . I see.

* **Fran** Right. That's it. End of interview. Thank you. (*To Lucille*) Ne dites pas un mot de plus. Cet homme est journaliste, nom d'un chien . . .

Lucille shrugs and moves away rather sulkily.

Fran (*to Jake*) Forget anything she said, all right? That was off the record.

Jake I don't think it was, you know. It was very much on the record.

Fran You print one word of that, sunshine, we'll sue you, all right?

Jake Oh, yes? Who's we?

Fran Her agents, IMI. International Murder Incorporated.

Barry has returned with a hand mic.

Barry (*into mic*) Ladies and gentlemen. Thank you, everyone, who's braved –

He is interrupted by an eccentric fanfare from the offstage band. He pauses.

Our junior band, ladies and gentlemen, who this year are gallantly standing in for our senior band who have an unexpected prior engagement. As I was saying, thank you, everybody, who has braved the elements to come here today. Without fur—

An enormous clap of thunder and a torrential downpour. Everyone rushes for cover, pulling sheets of polythene over the uncovered stalls as they go. Barry, Lindy, Fran, Izzie and the children all head for the house. Teddy and Lucille dive into the tent. The garden is empty for a second or two. Then Lucille's head sticks out of the tent.

---

* Right. That's it. End of interview. Thank you. (*To Lucille*) Don't say another word. This man's a journalist, for God's sake . . .

* **Lucille** Quel déluge! Je n'ai jamais vu une pluie pareille. Il pleut toujours comme ça en Angleterre?

Teddy (*his head also appearing*) It's only a shower, I think. Probably all pass over in a – in a year or two . . .

Lucille Les pauvres. Et leur fête champêtre? Tout ce travail. C'est comme ça tous les ans?

The band strikes up again, playing a selection of discordant melodies.

Teddy What the hell is that?

† **Lucille** (*coming out of the tent*) Oh, un orchestre! Avec de tous petits musiciens. Ce sont des nains?

Teddy Be careful! You'll get very wet. You – will – get – wet . . .

Lucille (*shrugging*) Oh, ce n'est pas grave. Mais, ce sont des enfants qui jouent. Des petits enfants, c'est mignon. Les instruments sont plus grands qu'eux. C'est adorable!

Teddy Bloody awful row. Where's the proper band, for God's sake?

Lucille wanders further away.

---

* **Lucille** What a downpour! I've never seen rain like this. Does it always rain like this in England?

Teddy (*his head also appearing*) It's only a shower, I think. Probably all pass over in a – in a year or two . . .

Lucille Poor people. What about their garden fête? All this hard work. Is it like this every year?

† **Lucille** (*coming out of the tent*) Oh, look. It's a band. A band with very tiny players. Are they midgets?

Teddy Be careful! You'll get very wet. You – will – get – wet . . .

Lucille (*shrugging*) Oh, that's not important. Look, they're children playing. Little children, it's so sweet. The instruments are bigger than they are. It's enchanting!

(*Still in the tent*) Lucille, what are you doing?

* **Lucille** Oh! Les anneaux! Je veux jouer aux anneaux!

Teddy Oh, for God's sake! You mad French person. (*Coming out of the tent at last*) You want to play hoop-la, do you?

Lucille Oui, hoop-la!

Teddy All right, we'll play hoop-la. God almighty, I'm getting drenched . . . (*Teddy uncovers the stall*) Now, it says here, three rings for fifty p. Have you got fifty p?

† **Lucille** Fifty p? Non, je n'ai pas fifty p. Je n'ai pas d'argent sur moi.

Teddy You haven't got it? Well you'll have to owe me. You – owe – me. Here you are. (*He hands her three rings*) Now, you've got to get them over these things. You know what to do?

Lucille (*throwing a ring wildly*) Voilà!

Teddy Yes. I think the idea though is to get the ring somewhere in the vicinity of the table.

Lucille (*a similar wild throw*) Voilà!

Teddy Yes, that killed the vicar, jolly good. One more!

Lucille winds up for the big throw.

(*Throwing himself flat*) No!

The ring sails over his head.

‡ **Lucille** (*really enjoying herself*) Oh, j'adore cet orchestre. J'ai envie de danser!

---

* Look! The hoop-la! I want to play hoop-la!

† Fifty p? No, I haven't got fifty p. I have no money on me.

‡ Oh, I love this band. I want to dance!

Teddy Don't for God's sake bowl for the pig, we'll have dead pork everywhere. Hey, hang about. Look what's here. (*He indicates the hoop-la table*) A bottle of scotch. Le scotch – ici.

Lucille Whisky?

Teddy Yes, now watch this – I'll have a go for this one. (*Taking up three more rings*) Watch this! Hup!

He misses.

Damn!

* **Lucille** Ah, c'est nul. Recommencez!

Teddy (*trying again and missing*) Oh, bull nuts!

† **Lucille** Encore une fois! Encore une fois!

Teddy throws again, misses, but Lucille guides the hoop safely over the scotch bottle.

‡ Bravo! Bien joué!

Teddy Oh, excellent stuff. By God, we make a fine team.

He takes the bottle, removes the top and offers it to Lucille. She drinks long and thirstily.

(*Alarmed*) Hang on, hang on! There are two of us, you know.

Lucille Agincourt!

Teddy Agincourt! Yes, indeed. (*He also drinks*)

Lucille (*bounding on to the edge of the fountain*) Teddy! Teddy!

---

* Ah, no. Shame. Try again.

† Once more! Once more!

‡ Bravo! Well played!

Teddy Now what are you doing?

* **Lucille** Je vais nager dans le bassin.

Teddy What?

Lucille Pourquoi ça ne marche pas? La fontaine?

Teddy The fountain? It doesn't work. It hasn't worked for several years. We think it's clogged. Probably leaves, weeds and dead animals. Clogged.

† **Lucille** Clogged? (*Kicking off her shoes*) Clogged. (*She starts to paddle in the fountain*) Ah, c'est bon!

Teddy Aren't you wet enough? You're barking, woman.

Lucille Barking. Clogged. Allez, Teddy, venez faire trempette avec moi. (*She beckons*)

Teddy I'm not getting in there.

Lucille Teddy! Teddy!

Teddy Oh, God. All right. (*He takes off his shoes*) I don't know what you're walking on. All sorts of nasty things. (*He steps into the fountain*) Aaah! It's absolutely perishing. I'm not standing in this!

Teddy steps out again. During the next, he sits on the edge of the fountain, takes off his socks wrings them out, then puts them on again. Lucille also gets out, finds the whisky bottle, sits beside him and drinks.

---

* **Lucille** I'm going to swim in your pond.
Teddy What?
Lucille Why doesn't it work? Your fountain?

† **Lucille** Clogged? (*Kicking off her shoes*) Clogged. (*She starts to paddle in the fountain*) Ah, this is good!
Teddy Aren't you wet enough? You're barking, woman.
Lucille Barking. Clogged. Come on, Teddy, paddle with me. (*She beckons*)

635

Lucille (*ruffling his hair*) Teddy!

Teddy You know, just this short time I've known you . . . it's extraordinary. I'd forgotten what it's like to have a good laugh, you know. Everyone around me's so bloody serious. I've got a serious wife, I've a seriously serious daughter and I've just got shot of a mistress who was serious for Britain. Where's the fun gone, eh? You know what I'm saying? You see, I understood that the whole thing between men and women was somehow meant to be sort of joyous . . . and then you look around at all these miserable bastards. And you think why are you all bothering? If you're that miserable, why don't you just say piss off to each other and then just get on with having a spot of fun? You know what I'm saying? Take sex. It's a bloody brilliant invention, isn't it? It's all made to fit. This bit goes in there and everybody has a good time. But you read the bloody books and you'd think it was the university entrance exam. It's so depressing, it really is. And you feel yourself getting more and more crushed by it all. Guilty. And then someone like you passes through my life. I don't understand a bloody word you're saying, but I realise just for these few seconds how wonderful it all could have been. And could be again. You see?

* **Lucille** (*who has caught his mood*) Moi, qu'est-ce que j'ai fait de ma vie? J'avais de l'ambition. Je rêvais d'être une grande actrice, à la Comédie Française peut-être. Et je me retrouve à jouer une pépée d'Hollywood dans un petit film minable bourré de terroristes. Et même pas la pépée vedette. Ma plus grande scène, c'est celle où je

---

* Me? What's my life been like? I used to have ambitions. I used to want to be this great actress with the Comédie Française, perhaps. And I end up playing Hollywood crumpet in a tacky little film about terrorists. Not even the main crumpet. My biggest scene is where I get blown up. Only it isn't even me that's blown up. It's my stunt double. God, what a mess I've made

reçois une bombe en pleine figure. Et ce n'est même pas moi qui reçoit la bombe. C'est une doublure. Mon Dieu, quel gâchis ma vie. Deux maris, le premier m'a poussée à boire, le second à me droguer. Maintenant, regardez-moi. Dans quelques années, je ne ressemblerai à rien. Personne ne voudra plus de moi. Je ne vaudrai plus que dalle, ni au cinéma, ni même pour recevoir une bombe en pleine figure. Ah, si je vous avais recontré plus tôt, peut-être que les choses auraient été differéntes. Nous aurions peut-être trouvé le bonheur. Au moins, on serait morts en s'étouffant de rire. Mais maintenant, c'est trop tard. Je dois aller dans cette clinique, ça fait partie des conditions de ma liberté surveillée. Sinon j'irai en prison pour trafic de drogue. Et vous, vous allez rejoindre votre anglais collet-monté qui ne vous regarde même pas et refuse d'admettre votre existence. Mon Dieu, quelle tristesse. Vous êtes gentil, Teddy. Idiot mais brave.

Teddy I don't think I've ever talked like this with anyone . . . thank you for listening to me, Lucille. And for saying that. I found it very moving.

† **Lucille** (*getting up and extending her hands*) Vous comprenez, n'est-ce-pas? Je sais que vous comprenez . . .

Teddy What?

---

of my life. Two husbands, one of whom drove me to drink, the other one introduced me to drugs. Now look at me. In a few years, I'll look like nothing. No one will want me. Not in any movies. I won't even be worth blowing up. Oh, if I'd met someone like you at the start, perhaps things might have been different. Perhaps we'd have found happiness. At least we'd have died laughing together. Now it's too late. I have to go to this clinic, because that's the terms of my probation. Otherwise I go to jail for drug trafficking. And you – you go back to your stuffy English wife who won't even look at you and refuses to acknowledge your existence. God, how sad. You're a sweet man, Teddy. A silly man but a good man.

† You understand, don't you? I know you understand . . .

* Lucille Venez, Teddy. Dans ma tente.

She takes his hands and pulls him to his feet. She starts to pull him towards the tent.

Teddy Where are we going?

† Lucille Je suis Cléopâtre. Je vous emmène dans ma tente, Teddy . . .

Teddy Cleopatra? What's she got to do with anything?

‡ Lucille Vous êtes mon Marc-Antoine. Nous allons faire magnifiquement l'amour une dernière fois avant de mourir. Je suis votre Thisbe, vous êtes mon Pyrame. Vous êtes mon Tristan, je suis votre Isolde . . .

Teddy I don't know who any of these people are. Never mind . . .

Lucille (*drawing him into the tent*) Teddy . . .

Teddy Lucille . . .

Lucille Teddy . . .

They go into the tent. The band plays on.
An initial cry from Lucille, then from Teddy.
Suddenly, for the first time, the fountain makes a rusty gurgling sound and spurts into life.
Izzie enters from the house. She stands and stares at the tent, listening to the sounds from within. After a moment, she dives for a box under the home-made cake table and finds a big vicious-looking carving knife. She marches up to the tent. For a minute we

---

* Come on, Teddy. Into my tent.

† I am Cleopatra. I am taking you into my tent, Teddy . . .

‡ You are my Mark Antony. We will make glorious love one last time before we die. I am your Thisbe, you are my Pyramus. You are my Tristan, I am your Isolde . . .

fear carnage, then she contents herself by sawing at the principle guy ropes. The tent collapses on the occupants. A cry of surprise from within. Pearl comes on with her camera. She stops as she sees Izzie.

Izzie (*realising her error*) Oh no, I done the wrong ones. Pearl – (*She moves towards Pearl*)

Pearl (*in terror*) Get away! Get away! You get away from me!

Pearl rushes off. Izzie follows her.

Izzie Pearl, come back here. I didn't mean nothing . . . It was a miscopulation! (*Izzie goes off*)

Teddy (*from under the collapsed tent*) My God, I think the earth moved for me!

* **Lucille** (*likewise*) Oh, mon Dieu! Quel amant! Qui dit que les anglais sont frigides!

Some movement under the canvas.

Teddy Can you get out?

† **Lucille** Non, je crois que je suis coincée. Il faudrait qu'on nous aide.

Teddy No, I don't think I can. (*Struggling*) Har . . . har . . . no!

Warn comes on. He stops when he sees the fountain working. As Teddy and Lucille start to shout, he inspects the fallen tent.

We'll have to get some help. (*Calling*) Help!

Lucille Help!

---

* Oh, my God! What a lover! Who says the English are frigid!

† No, I appear to be stuck. I think we need some help.

They continue to shout. Warn takes up one of the guy ropes and examines the cut end.

Warn Bloody women!

He strides off to the house, ignoring their cries.

Both (*continuing*) Help! . . . Help! . . .

Giles enters along one of the paths.
He hurries over.

Giles (*alarmed*) Hallo! Are you all right? Who's under here?

Teddy Who's that?

Giles I'm a doctor, can I help . . .?

Teddy Giles . . .

Giles Who's that?

Teddy It's me, Teddy.

Giles Teddy! Who's that with you?

* **Lucille** Hallo! Pouvez-vous nous aider? On est coincé là-dessous. Il faudrait qu'on nous délivre . . .

Giles Lucille?

Lucille Hallo.

Giles My God, I don't believe this. You're obscene, Teddy, you're utterly debauched. It's just one woman after another, isn't it, as far as you're concerned?

Teddy Look, spare us the bloody moral lecture, Giles, just get us out of here . . .

Fran enters from the house.

Fran What's happened?

---

* Hallo! Could you possibly help us? We appear to be a bit stuck under here and we need rescuing . . .

Giles The tent appears to have collapsed on them, I'm just –

Fran Who's under there? Lucille?

Giles Yes and Mr –

* **Fran** Lucille! Ça va?

Lucille Oui, ça va. On est juste un peu serrés . . .

Fran Attendez une seconde. Je vais vous sortir de là.

Lucille Merci!

> *Fran reaches under the tent and starts to pull Lucille out. The rain starts to ease off.*

Fran (*to Giles*) Give me a hand here.

Giles Careful! They may have broken limbs . . .

> *Fran ignores this and together they pull Lucille clear.*

† **Lucille** Ça va mieux! Vive la liberté! Où est Teddy?

Fran Comment vous sentez-vous? Vous allez bien?

Lucille Oh oui, je ne me suis jamais si bien sentie. Je n'ai pas fait l'amour comme ça depuis une éternité . . .

Fran On ferait mieux de rentrer à la maison, vous êtes trempée.

---

* **Fran** Lucille! Are you all right?
Lucille Yes, I'm fine. We're just a little squashed . . .
Fran Just a second, I'll pull you out.
Lucille Thank you!

† **Lucille** That's better! Free again! Where's Teddy?
Fran How are you feeling? Are you all right?
Lucille Yes, I've never felt better. I haven't made love like that in ages . . .
Fran We'd better get you back to the house, you're soaking wet.

* Lucille Non, je dois faire l'ouverture de la fête d'abord . . .

Fran Qu'ils aillent se faire voir avec leur fête. Je ne veux pas être responsable devant le bureau si vous attrapez une pneumonie . . .

Teddy I say, are you going to stop all that jabbering and rescue me, or what?

Giles (*reaching under the canvas*) It's all right, Teddy, I've got you. (*To Fran*) Would you mind?

Fran moves to assist him.

All right, Teddy, now gently . . . Heave!

Teddy's head and shoulders appear.

Heave . . .

Teddy (*urgently*) Hold it! Hold it! Hold it a second!

Giles That hurting?

Teddy I think I may have a bit of a problem . . .

Giles All right . . . (*To Fran*) Ease off, ease off . . . Where's the problem located, Teddy? Can you describe it?

Teddy It's just generally my – lower half.

Giles I see. (*Sotto to Fran*) My God, it could be spinal . . . Teddy, lie there perfectly still, till there's more of us here to lift you . . .

† Lucille (*to Fran*) Il y a un problème?

Fran Le médecin pense qu'il a peut-être une blessure à la colonne vertébrale.

---

* **Lucille** No, I have to open their fête first . . .

Fran To hell with their fête, I'm not going to be answerable to the office if you catch pneumonia . . .

† **Lucille** (*to Fran*) What's the problem?

Fran The doctor thinks he may have a spinal injury.

* **Lucille** Oh, mon Dieu! Ce n'est pas possible. (*Kneeling by Teddy*) Teddy, vous êtes blessé?

Teddy Oh, hallo, old thing . . .

Giles Teddy, just lie still, please. It may be serious.

Teddy Right you are. In that case I wonder if I could have a final request?

Giles What?

Teddy Could you tell that bloody band to stop that din?

Giles Yes, of course. (*Calling*) Could you stop playing, please? There's someone here been badly injured. Yes, stop! Thank you!

> *The band tails to a halt. From the house, Barry and the Maypole dancers appear.*

Barry (*alarmed*) What's happened? What on earth has happened?

† **Lucille** (*grasping Teddy's arm*) Le pauvre Teddy, il est blessé. Tout à l'heure il etait si heureux, et voilà que maintenant . . .

Giles Please don't shake him around, he may be injured. Ne le secouez pas.

Barry Injured? How badly injured?

Giles We don't know. He was sheltering in the tent. It fell on him.

---

* Oh, my God! That's not possible. (*Kneeling by Teddy*) Teddy, you're injured?

† **Lucille** (*grasping Teddy's arm*) Poor Teddy is injured. One minute he was so happy, the next . . .

Giles Please don't shake him around, he may be injured. Do not shake him.

Fran The doctor thinks he may have spinal injuries.

Barry Oh, my goodness!

* **Lucille** C'est de ma faute, c'est moi qui l'ai emmené sous la tente . . .

Barry Has someone summoned an ambulance? We need the paramedics.

Teddy No, I don't need a bloody ambulance. Don't call an ambulance whatever you do, for God's sake.

Barry He sounds delirious.

Teddy Do your bloody Maypole dance or something . . .

Giles Hardly the time for a Maypole dance, surely.

Barry Might be a good idea. Take his mind off the pain. If he has major spinal injuries . . .

Giles I never said that . . .

Barry Right. Come along, children. Time for the dance now . . .

Giles Oh, well. I'll see if I can find the cassette player. I put it somewhere.

As the dancers assemble round the Maypole, Lindy enters. Giles finds the cassette machine under a table and checks the tape.

Lindy What's happened?

Barry Ah! There you are. I'll tell you what's happened, Lindy. The tent which you put up and swore you had checked, has just fallen on Mr Platt.

Lindy Oh, no . . .

Barry As a result of which, he has multiple injuries to his lower body and may never walk again . . .

---

* It's my fault for taking him into the tent . . .

Giles Now, I never said . . .

Barry All of which is entirely down to you, Lindy. We could be in for a million-pound lawsuit, do you realise that?

Lindy (*sitting on the grass*) Yes, all right, all right . . .

Barry All because you rush things, you don't concentrate, you're careless and never ever bother to check. Well, now it's home to roost, Lindy, as I said it would be. I'm going to get my mobile and phone an ambulance.

> *Barry goes off. Lindy sits in a miserable heap. Giles starts the cassette machine and the Maypole dance gets under way. The children start their routine, quite well at first, given the incongruous nature of the occasion.*
> *The bushes rustle. Giles is aware of this but can't locate the sound.*

Giles (*to Lindy*) I wouldn't worry too much. He'll be fine, I'm sure.

> *Lindy doesn't reply.*

Grass is quite wet. Be careful . . .

> *Fran watches the dancers. At some stage Gavin enters from the house and also watches. Giles gives them gentle encouragement. Lucille decides to play The Death of Nelson with Teddy's prostrate body.*

* **Lucille** Oh, Teddy. Je veux que vous sachiez, si vous n'en réchappez pas que vous êtes le meilleur amant que j'ai jamais eu . . . je me souviendrai toujours de vous, Teddy . . .

---

* Oh, Teddy. I want you to know, if you don't survive, you were the best lover I have ever had . . . I will remember you for ever, Teddy . . .

Teddy What are you on about now, you batty woman?

* **Lucille** Je ne vous oublierai jamais. Embrassez-moi encore une fois, Teddy. Oh, mon pauvre chéri. S'il vous arrivait quelque chose, je ne me le pardonnerais jamais . . . Je serai votre Brunhilde. Je me jetterai dans les flammes s'il vous arrivait quelque chose . . .

Teddy (*during her last*) I can't think of a more inappropriate way to die, I really can't . . .

As the dance continues, Lucille throws herself across Teddy's body and showers him with kisses.

Oh, I don't know though . . .

Suddenly the bushes part and there is Joanna, eyes blazing, a completely deranged figure. Wet and muddy from the rain, she looks more like the Swamp Creature. Everyone freezes.

Fran What the hell . . .?

Joanna (*focusing on Teddy*) Sebastian?

Teddy (*startled*) What?

Joanna Gotcha! (*Rushing at him in a wild charge*) AAAAArrrrrhhhh!!!

Teddy Oh, my God!

Lindy screams. Lucille screams. The Maypole dancers panic and rush about getting hopelessly entangled. Giles takes a pace forward and kicks over the cassette machine which unaccountably goes into double speed. Gavin watches, the disinterested bystander. Joanna kicks Teddy through the canvas.

---

* I will never forget you. Kiss me one more time, Teddy. Oh, my poor darling. If anything's happened to you, I will never forgive myself . . . I will be your Brunhild. I will hurl myself into the flames if anything happens to you . . .

Joanna (*as she does so*) You bastard! Bastard! Bastard! Bastard!

Teddy Aaaah! What the hell are you doing! Jo! Jo!

Giles Joanna! For goodness sake!

Joanna (*kicking him again*) Bastard! Bastard!

* **Lucille** Ne donnez pas de coups de pieds à mon Teddy, petite salope!

> *Lucille attempts to pull Joanna away. Joanna wheels on her attacker and takes the fight to her. Barry returns during this and watches open-mouthed.*

Fran Hey! Hey! Hey!

Giles Come along, calm down, calm down.

> *Joanna throws herself at Lucille and the two start a hand-to-hand fight which Giles, Barry and Fran try to break up. Lindy attempts to disentangle the dancers. The band starts up again.*

† **Lucille** Ne me touchez pas, espèce de folle! Au secours! Elle est complètement folle!

> *Teddy, alarmed as anyone by this spectacle, gets up from under the tent. He is barefoot, in his underpants, without his trousers, but is otherwise completely unharmed.*

Barry Lindy, get the youngsters to safety. Get them away from here!

> *Lindy goes, shepherding the dancers.*

Teddy Now, break it up, that's quite enough of that. I'm not worth fighting over . . .

---

* Don't you kick my Teddy, you little bitch.

† Get your hands off me, you madwoman! Help me, someone! She's completely mad!

Joanna is finally overpowered.

Giles (*breathless*) It's all right! She's calmer now. I'll get her home. Don't worry. Leave her to me. I'll give her a sedative.

Barry You sure?

* **Fran** (*to Lucille*) Ça va?

Lucille Oui, ça va. Qu'est-ce-qui se passe? Ça fait partie de la fête?

Giles Come on, darling, home now. It's only me. It's Giles. Come on.

Joanna (*exhausted*) Giles? No, you're not Giles. You're Harold. You're Harold, I know you are . . .

Giles Well, maybe just temporarily, darling . . . Giles will be back in a minute, I promise.

Giles and Joanna go off. Everyone is suddenly aware of Teddy's state of undress.

Lucille (*delighted*) Oh, Teddy!

Barry Well, I'm delighted to see that there was no damage done, Teddy. No bones broken . . . (*He too stares, the last to notice Teddy*)

Teddy No. Extraordinary freak accident. You'll hardly believe this. Quite remarkable. We were standing in the tent sheltering from the rain. And the thing suddenly collapsed on us. And as it did so, the central pole, you follow me, the central pole as it fell, caught in the waist band of my trousers and ripped them off like that. Extraordinary.

A silence.

---

* **Fran** (*to Lucille*) Are you all right?

Lucille Yes, I'm all right. What was that about? Was it part of the fête?

Do excuse me. I'm just going to root out another pair.
Excuse me. (*To Lucille*) You coming up to the house to
dry off? Dry off?

Lucille Dry off? Oui.

Teddy Come on then. My little bonbon . . .

Teddy and Lucille go off. Lindy returns.

Lindy They're all safely in the mini-van.

Fran There is an additional feature to all this. Which
I didn't like to mention.

Barry What's that?

Fran Someone's deliberately cut these guy ropes.
(*Holding up a severed rope*) Look at that.

Barry My goodness. Foul play, you think?

Fran Worth considering, eh?

Fran goes. Barry inspects the ropes.

Barry (*to Lindy*) Well. There's a turn up for the book,
eh? Yes. Well. Puts us in the clear, anyway, doesn't it?
That's a relief. Oh, Mr Ryng-Mayne, I didn't see you
there. You staying for a bit of the fun?

Gavin Sadly, I have to be under way pretty soon.

Barry Ah. Busy man. If you have a minute to spare,
before you go, I wonder if you'd mind very much
judging the junior fancy dress?

Gavin Ah, well . . .

Barry It won't take a moment of your time. I was going
to ask Lucille – but she's – rather indisposed at present.
It would be a great thrill for them, if you would . . . I'll
just assemble them – I'll be back in a minute . . .

Barry goes off before Gavin can protest.

Gavin (*to himself*) Oh, God.

Lindy Excuse me . . .

Gavin Hallo, there.

Lindy That is your car, isn't it? The yellow one?

Gavin Yes. Sorry, is it blocking someone, I'll . . .?

Lindy I couldn't help overhearing you saying you'll be leaving soon.

Gavin Yes, I'm afraid I've –

Lindy Would that be back to London, would it?

Gavin That's right.

Lindy Would you . . . I know this sounds very cheeky of me but – would you be able to give me a lift?

Gavin Where to?

Lindy To London.

Gavin Oh, I see. (*Searching for an excuse*) Well . . .

Lindy I wouldn't ask normally, but it is a matter of great urgency . . .

Gavin I see. It's important you go tonight, is it?

Lindy Very important. If I don't go tonight, I may not go at all, you see.

Gavin (*rather mystified*) I see. Well, I hope you don't have a lot of luggage – ?

Lindy Oh, I've got no luggage at all. Not so's you'd mention.

Gavin Right. Well, I'll be setting off in about an hour, so . . .

Lindy (*as she goes*) I'll be waiting. I'll be by the car.

Gavin Right.

Lindy goes off.

(*To himself*) God.

Barry returns.

Barry Here we all are. Parade across, children. Let Mr Ryng-Mayne get a good look at you.

An assortment of small fancy-dress figures parade on and off again. Gavin looks appalled.

There! Hard to choose, eh? Hard to choose?

Gavin Almost impossible. What a magnificent turnout. Well done, chaps.

Barry Come and take a closer look. (*Following them off*) By the way, don't choose the letter-box, he won last year.

Gavin (*as he goes off*) Oh, my God . . .

As they go, the lights fade to:
Blackout.

SCENE TWO

Saturday, August 14th, 5.00 p.m.
The same, though it has been tidied up a bit. The collapsed tent is gone. The band has stopped playing.
Giles and Jake are packing away the Maypole, which is now lying on its side. Giles is still in his morris outfit. Jake's briefcase is nearby.

Giles I didn't think they were going to score at all . . .

Jake Nor did I . . .

Giles The last ten minutes, though . . .

Jake Amazing . . .

Giles Did you see that final cross, the one that eventually went in? I mean he was practically behind the net. I thought he's overshot, he'll never bring it back from there . . . never . . .

Jake Amazing . . .

Giles I don't know, then he managed to just curl it, didn't he? Beautiful cross. I mean, the keeper was way out of position, wasn't he? No way . . . Wish I'd been there.

Jake Amazing . . .

Giles We needed it.

 Silence.

Jake I suppose we ought to talk about Mum, really.

Giles Yes, yes. I suppose we should.

Jake I mean, what's going to happen, Dad?

Giles Well, I think we just – have to see her back to health. I think it might take some time but we can do it. We can do it. She needs patience, she needs understanding, she needs – love. That's all. And I suppose if that means answering to the name of Harold for a month or two, that's what it'll have to be. I wish to God she'd chosen some other name.

Jake I'm not too keen on Gordon, actually.

Giles I keep saying we, Jake. But I want you to understand this is not primarily your problem.

Jake She's my mother, for God's sake . . .

Giles Yes. But what's happened to Jo – it's none of your doing . . .

Jake It's nobody's doing . . .

Giles It's down to me, Jake. It's all down to me.

Jake Look, Mum has an illness, that's all . . . Nobody's to blame. I mean, she needs professional help, surely?

Giles And she'll get professional help, don't worry. I'm making enquiries first thing tomorrow. Well, on Monday. She'll get the best, Jake. Don't worry.

Jake I just don't want you worrying yourself to death. I mean, by taking unnecessary blame. You're a good person. Bloody hell, I'm sure you drove her nuts on occasions, but you're a good person.

Giles (*quite touched*) Thank you. No, what I'm really trying to say, Jake, is that you mustn't get yourself too embroiled in all this. It is my problem. Really it is. And I promise I won't let it all get on top of me more than's absolutely vital. But you've got a life of your own to lead. You've got university in a few weeks, you've got to think about a career – I don't know – you've got Sally perhaps – I don't know . . .

Jake (*drily*) Ha, ha, ha . . .

Giles No, don't give up on that. I think she likes you, you know . . .

Jake Yes. So people keep telling me. Only person who doesn't tell me is her.

Giles Well . . . Ever thus, eh?

Jake I'm going to give it one more go in a minute . . .

Giles Ah. Worked out a strategy?

Jake You bet. I'm going to get down as far as her goal line and then send her a deep swirling cross, right in front of her net. Catch her out of position.

Giles That should do it.

Jake Won't stand a chance. Right. Well. See you later, then . . . (*He picks up his briefcase*)

Barry comes on briefly.

Barry Nobody's seen my wife, have they? Anyone here seen Lindy?

Giles Not for some little while.

Jake No.

Barry Unbelievable. I've had to load that whole van on my own. Lindy's completely vanished. If you do happen to see her, would you tell her I have now driven home where I will be unloading the van single-handed. I will then be back here in forty-five minutes to pick up the second load. And that I would be eternally grateful on that occasion for a modicum of her help. And she might be interested to know that I think my back is playing up again as well. If you could tell her all of that. Thank you.

Barry goes off.

Giles I wonder if I should nip down to the village and get Joanna some herbal bath crystals. I might persuade her to have a bath when she wakes up. Help to ease some of her tension.

Jake Why don't you just go and get pissed, Dad? Go on, treat yourself. (*Jake goes off towards the house*)

Giles Now, what's that ever solved, Jake? What's that ever solved, eh?

Giles picks up the tape recorder. He removes the cassette tape, is about to put it away, then he reads the label on the other side. He replaces the cassette and plays it. Some suitable morris dance music. Giles smiles rather regretfully and is about to switch it off

*when Pearl arrives. She has changed out of her
fortune-teller's gear. Giles switches off the music.*

Pearl Not goin' to get a dance then, aren't we?

Giles (*smiling*) Alas, no. I'm afraid the rest of my troop
are in Peterborough, would you believe? They finally
phoned me at four fifteen. A cross-booking. Nobody let
me know.

Pearl Shame.

Giles Yes. It was.

Pearl Like a dance, do you?

Giles It's – rewarding, yes. Some people think it's rather
quaint. Comical, even. But they're very powerful these
dances. Some of them. Go back a long way. Fourteenth
century. Edward III.

Pearl Whey-hey!

Giles And before that probably from Spain . . .

Pearl Olé . . . Do us a bit, then. Go on.

Giles I can't. There's only me.

Pearl Come on. No one's watching. I'd like to see a bit.
Honest.

Giles (*a little uncertain as to whether she's sending him
up*) Well . . . It'll look a bit silly but . . . Just a little
section. (*He switches on the tape. He begins to dance, a
little self-consciously at first. It does, as he says, look a
bit silly but Pearl is entranced*) You have to imagine
there's about sixteen of us doing this, not just me.

*After a time, Pearl joins in. Although her dancing has
no relation to any known morris step, the result is not
displeasing. Fran comes from the house, crosses and
goes off staring at them curiously. As they dance,*

Gavin appears from the direction of the house. He watches, amused. The dance on the tape finishes.

Pearl Hey! That were great.

Giles Well, I'm rather glad my colleagues weren't here. I might have been drummed out of the United Kingdom Morris Federation . . .

Pearl Don't allow women, then?

Giles Oh yes, indeed. There's a lot of female morris dancers. We're totally liberated these days . . .

Gavin Like the MCC.

Giles Oh, hallo.

Gavin (*clapping them*) Well done. Jolly good.

Pearl Well, I must get on. Thanks for the dance. Going for a drink later. Want to join us?

Giles Us?

Pearl Just a few of us. Me, my mum. And my dad.

Giles Your dad? I didn't know you'd – ?

Pearl Warn. He's my dad.

Giles Is he? Good heavens, I – I think a lot of people thought he was – well –

Pearl Nar. That wouldn't be right, would it? Not with me own dad.

Giles No, certainly not.

Pearl Want to come?

Giles (*torn*) Ah, well . . . probably not. My wife's a bit under the . . . Normally I'd love to –

Pearl We'll be in The Wheatsheaf if you do. Beer's piss down The Plough . . .

Giles Right. Thank you very much. I'll see what I can arrange.

Pearl Cheers, then.

Giles Bye.

Gavin Goodbye.

Pearl goes off.

Sounds a tempting invitation. I think you're in there with a chance.

Giles (*laughing inordinately*) Oh, good heavens. Hardly! Hardly! You're off, are you?

Gavin Afraid so. It's been a marvellous afternoon. Thoroughly enjoyed myself.

Giles The weather was a little disappointing, I'm afraid. I don't think we did financially as well as we'd hoped. Well, have a safe journey. Shouldn't take you long in that thing of yours . . .

Gavin About twenty-five minutes, I should think. Ciao.

Giles Bye.

Giles goes off. Gavin is about to go when Lindy steps out from the bushes into his path. She has a small case.

Lindy Hallo.

Gavin (*rather put out*) Ah –

Lindy Here I am. All ready.

Gavin Yes. Right. Is that – all your luggage? Because I have limited boot space . . .

Lindy No, this all I'm taking.

Gavin Just a short visit, is it?

Lindy No.

Gavin Ah.

Lindy But I'm taking as little as possible.

Gavin (*completely mystified*) I see.

Lindy Then I can't be accused of taking anything, you see.

Gavin I should warn you, when I travel I like to put my foot down.

Lindy I won't be any trouble, I promise.

Gavin No, no, no. I like to travel at speed. You're comfortable with high speeds, are you?

Lindy The faster the better.

Gavin And there'll be a bit of a din. You don't mind loud noise?

Lindy Oh, no. I'm used to that. Our old Transit makes a dreadful racket, I think it's the gearbox . . .

Gavin No, what I meant was, I'll be playing rather loud music. OK?

Lindy Classical?

Gavin No. Late sixties – seventies rock. Is that OK?

Lindy Oh, yes. The Monkees?

Gavin (*wincing*) Along those lines, yes . . . Well, off we go. After you and fasten your seat belt.

He ushers Lindy ahead of him.

(*As they go*) God!

> *As they leave, Fran returns rattling her car keys rather impatiently. From the direction of the house, Teddy's voice is heard.*

Teddy (*off*) It's all right! She's coming, she's coming.

Lucille (*off*) I'm coming!

Teddy (*off*) I was just showing her our gazebo.

Lucille (*off*) Gazebo!

Teddy and Lucille enter.

Teddy Do you know, the poor girl had no idea what a gazebo was. Can you imagine? She's led a completely sheltered life . . .

* **Fran** I said we'd be there by six, we're going to be very late. (*To Lucille*) On va être en retard.

Lucille Oh, ne dites pas de sottises. Comment peut-être en retard pour faire un régime sec? Teddy. Au'voir. On se reverra bientôt.

Teddy Absolutely. And I'll write to you.

Lucille Vous êtes sans aucun doute l'homme le plus bête que j'ai jamais rencontré.

Teddy Thank you. Thank you.

Lucille Vraiment l'anglais le plus bête. Mais je vous aime. Vous êtes normalement une nation si solennelle, si pompeuse. Tellement sérieuse surtout.

---

* **Fran** I said we'd be there by six, we're going to be very late. (*To Lucille*) We're going to be late.

Lucille Oh, nonsense. How can I be late to go on the wagon? Teddy. Au 'voir. We shall meet again, soon.

Teddy Absolutely. And I'll write to you.

Lucille You are without doubt the silliest man I have ever met.

Teddy Thank you. Thank you.

Lucille Certainly the silliest Englishman. But I love you. You are usually such a solemn, pompous nation. So serious about everything.

Teddy Yes, well, it could have been nicer, but that's the English climate for you, I'm afraid . . .

* **Lucille** Mais vous avez prouvé qu'ils avaient tort. Je me souviendrai de vous pendant longtemps. Je reviendrai, Teddy, aussitôt que je serai guérie, et on fera l'amour ensemble dans toutes vos drôles les petites cabanes de jardin. Oui?

Teddy You betcha. (*To Fran*) What's she saying?

Fran I don't think you should know. Not at the moment, we'd never get away from here. (*To Lucille*) Allez, venez s'il vous plaît.

Lucille Ne venez pas plus loin avec moi, Teddy. Restez-là, c'est ça. Laissez-moi vous embrasser – (*She kisses him*) – et puis partir. Nous serons comme Philémon et Baucis, Teddy. Nous nous aimerons dans ce jardin et puis, quand nous serons morts, nous serons transformés par les dieux. Vous deviendrez un chêne, et moi je deviendrai un tilleul, et nos branches s'entrelaceront pour toujours. Alors, mon amour, au revoir.

Teddy Goodbye. I don't know what the hell you're talking about but by God you're beautiful when you say it . . .

---

* **Lucille** But you have proved them wrong. I shall remember you for a long time. I'll be back, Teddy, as soon as I'm cured and we shall make love together in all your funny little garden sheds. Yes?

Teddy You betcha. (*To Fran*) What's she saying?

Fran I don't think you should know. Not at the moment, we'd never get away from here. (*To Lucille*) Come on, please.

Lucille Don't come any further with me, Teddy. Stand just there, that's it. Let me kiss you – (*She kisses him*) – and then walk away. We will be like Philemon and Baucis, Teddy. We will love each other in this garden and then, when we die, we will be transformed by the gods. You will become an oak tree and I will become a linden and our branches will intertwine for ever. Goodbye, my love, goodbye.

Lucille Au revoir.

Fran Cheers.

Lucille goes off with Fran.
Teddy watches them go rather sadly.

Teddy Right then. Right.

He stands, undecided what to do. Barry appears
briefly.

Barry Any sign of her yet?

Teddy Who?

Barry Day of the vanishing wives, isn't it? Unbelievable.
This is unbelievable. We're going to have to have serious
words about this . . .

Barry goes. Teddy sits on the edge of the fountain.
Giles comes across. He has changed into his normal
clothes.

Giles Oh. Don't mind if I cut across, do you?

Teddy Help yourself.

Giles I'm off to the pub. The Wheatsheaf. Beer's piss
down The Plough. I'd invite you along, Teddy, but I'm
sorry I think it will be another day or two before I can
actually sit and drink with you.

Teddy That's all right. I don't fancy drinking with you
either, just at present.

Giles Fair enough. Oh, Trish just passed me in her car.
She told me, if I saw you, to say cheerio. That you'd
know what she meant.

Teddy Oh, yes. I know what she meant.

Giles Well, cheerio, then.

Teddy Cheerie-bye.

He sits and whistles mournfully.
Nearby, the sound of Spoof barking.

Ah, there you are, boy. Somebody let you out, did they?
Good boy! Come on, here we are! Come on! Come to
Daddy, come on! That's it! Come-boy, come-boy, come-
boy . . . Ah.

Spoof's barking recedes as he runs off into the
distance. Teddy droops a little lower.
Silence.
Quite suddenly, there is a gurgling sound and the
fountain behind him splutters and shuts off.

(*Looking at it, resignedly*) Ah, well. That's life, I suppose.

As he continues to sit there, contemplating his lot, the
lights fade to:
Blackout.